PLATO'S LATE ONTOLOGY

PLATO'S LATE ONTOLOGY
A RIDDLE RESOLVED

By Kenneth M. Sayre

PRINCETON UNIVERSITY PRESS
PRINCETON, NEW JERSEY

Published by Princeton University Press, 41 William Street,
Princeton, New Jersey 08540
In the United Kingdom: Princeton University Press, Guildford, Surrey

Library of Congress Cataloging in Publication Data will be
found on the last printed page of this book

Publication of this book has been aided by a grant from the Paul
Mellon Fund of Princeton University Press

This book has been composed in Linotron Sabon and Optima

Clothbound editions of Princeton University Press books
are printed on acid-free paper, and binding materials are
chosen for strength and durability

Printed in the United States of America by Princeton
University Press, Princeton, New Jersey

IN MEMORY OF
LUCILLE,
FOR HER GAIETY, LOVE
AND IRREPRESSIBLE HUMANITY

CONTENTS

Contents

PREFACE

For Socrates, as Plato portrayed him, the love of wisdom was nurtured in conversation. Among the consequences of this understanding of philosophy are that philosophic growth is stimulated by teachers who guide rather than instruct, and that philosophic achievement is more a matter of discernment than of argument and counterargument.

Plato retained this understanding of philosophy. Although the theory of recollection upon which at one time it may have been based did not survive the middle dialogues, and although Socrates himself was upstaged in most of the late dialogues by philosophically more powerful protagonists, the major dialogues of the later period (with the exception perhaps of the *Timaeus* and the *Laws*) were constructed to serve as dialectical instruments rather than repositories of doctrine. For the interpreter of these dialogues this means (1) that Plato's own philosophic beliefs cannot be culled directly from the remarks of any single character (major protagonists included), (2) that for the purpose of revealing Plato's thought the dialectical structure of a dialogue is no less important than its individual arguments, and (3) that the dramatic structure for this purpose may be comparably important. Against the regrettable tendency of many contemporary commentators to concentrate their analytic attention on isolated arguments, we can reasonably hope to recover the philosophic contents of such a dialogue only by approaching it as a dialectical whole.

This does not entail the paradoxical consequence that we must study all aspects of such a dialogue to study any. The *Philebus*, like the *Sophist* and the *Parmenides* before it, is too rich to be exhausted by a single commentary in a single volume, or even by a whole school of commentary over several lifetimes. The justification I claim for focusing on a relatively few passages of the *Philebus*, and upon those parts of the *Parmenides* that are directly related, is that the ontological contents of these passages by themselves form a dialectical unity, and that the philosophic thought behind these particular passages is even more revolutionary and exciting than commentators as far back as Aristotle seem to have realized. The reader must form his or her own judgment on the adequacy of this claim; I can only ask that this judgment be deferred until the evidence has been examined.

Although in one sense my only teacher of Plato has been Plato himself, there are literally hundreds of scholars—students and colleagues alike—who in writing and conversation have taught me things about the dialogues I would have missed otherwise. To all these I am grateful. Among those to whom I am particularly indebted are Frederick Crosson, Gatesby Taliaferro, Robert Vacca, Stephen Gersh, Richard McClelland, Frederick Miller, and Robert Turnbull. I have also been strongly influenced by the work, example, and in several cases sage advice, of Harold Cherniss, G.E.L. Owen, Gregory Vlastos, Reginald Allen, and Edward Lee. Needless to say, no person among these is likely to agree with everything said in this volume, and none is in any way responsible for the errors remaining in it. But the latter would have been far more numerous without the former's good influence.

I mention with deepest gratitude and love the support of my late wife, who taught me the kind of affection necessary to hold conversation with Plato through his written dialogues. Although she produced no books during her very productive lifetime, the present volume is her work no less fully than mine.

PLATO'S LATE ONTOLOGY

INTRODUCTION

In *Metaphysics* M, Chapter 4, Aristotle gives a succinct account of the relationship between Socrates and those who first affirmed the existence of the Ideas. While Socrates was "busying himself with moral excellence" (περὶ τὰς ἠθικὰς ἀρετὰς πραγματευομένου: 1078b17-18), they were concerned with questions of knowledge and its ontological requirements. As Aristotle puts it:

> Those who stated the theory of Forms were led to it because, as regards truth, they were persuaded by the Heraclitean argument that all sensible things are always in flux [συνέβη δ' ἡ περὶ τῶν εἰδῶν δόξα τοῖς εἰποῦσι διὰ τὸ πεισθῆναι περὶ τῆς ἀληθείας τοῖς Ἡρακλειτείοις λόγοις ὡς πάντων τῶν αἰσθητῶν ἀεὶ ῥεόντων: 1078b12-15]; so that if there is to be knowledge of anything, or practical wisdom, there must be other objects that are permanent besides those that are sensible [ὥστ' εἴπερ ἐπιστήμη τινὸς ἔσται καὶ φρόνησις, ἑτέρας δεῖν τινὰς φύσεις εἶναι παρὰ τὰς αἰσθητὰς μενούσας: 1078b15-16]. For there is no knowledge of things in flux [οὐ γὰρ εἶναι τῶν ῥεόντων ἐπιστήμην: 1078b16-17].

Although Socrates was concerned with universals, Aristotle then observes, "he did not make the universals separate" (τὰ καθόλου οὐ χωριστὰ ἐποίει: 1078b30). But the others "made them separate, and called these entities Ideas" (οἱ δ' ἐχώρισαν, καὶ τὰ τοιαῦτα τῶν ὄντων ἰδέας προσηγόρευσαν: 1078b31-32). Such at least was the way those who first affirmed the theory of the Ideas "understood it originally" (ὑπέλαβον ἐξ ἀρχῆς: 1078b11).

The implied distinction between an original and a subsequent understanding of the theory is made explicit in an earlier passage

3

presenting essentially the same information, but adding some remarks about participation:

Having first become familiar in his youth with Cratylus and the Heraclitean doctrines, that all sensible things are always in flux and that there is no knowledge of them, he held the same in later years [ἐκ νέου τε γὰρ συνήθης γενόμενος πρῶτον Κρατύλῳ καὶ ταῖς Ἡρακλειτείοις δόξαις, ὡς ἁπάντων τῶν αἰσθητῶν ἀεὶ ῥεόντων καὶ ἐπιστήμης περὶ αὐτῶν οὐκ οὔσης, ταῦτα μὲν καὶ ὕστερον οὕτως ὑπέλαβεν: 987a32-b1].

While Socrates was busying himself with ethics, Aristotle continues, and with definitions in that domain—utterly neglecting nature as a whole—Plato followed his lead, but held that definitions must apply to things other than sensible things which are always changing. These other things are what Plato called Ideas:

and all sensible things are both dependent upon them and named after them (τὰ δ᾽ αἰσθητὰ παρὰ ταῦτα καὶ κατὰ ταῦτα λέγεσθαι πάντα: 987b8-9); for the many exist by participation in the Forms that share names with them [κατὰ μέθεξιν γὰρ εἶναι τὰ πολλὰ τῶν συνωνύμων (τοῖς εἴδεσιν):[1] 987b9-10].

The comparison of Plato with Socrates concludes a few lines later with Aristotle's laconic remark that what participation in the Ideas might amount to was left unexplained.[2]

These two passages (1078b11-32 and 987a32-b10) contain what appears to be a basically accurate summary of both the motivation and the content of the theory of Ideas through the middle dialogues at least. At 987b10 Aristotle then resumes his comparison of Plato with the Pythagoreans begun several lines earlier. Before contending with the considerably more obscure contents of these subsequent passages, let us fill in some details of what may be called the "middle theory."

Knowledge, it was assumed (*Theaetetus* 152C5), is unerring, and takes only what exists as its proper object. On both counts, a consequence is that knowledge is possible only of objects not subject to change. If knowledge is to be unerring, it must provide an awareness of its object that is wholly reliable without respect to time or circumstance. But if its object were to change, then the knowledge state itself would have to change to remain reliable (*Cratylus* 440A-B), and thus would be a different knowledge state. Hence the object of a given knowledge state is not subject to change, and is itself independent of time and place. In like fashion, since the object of a given knowledge state must exist, it must be free from becoming. For an object in process of change is in part both the thing it has been and the thing it is becoming, and hence cannot be a single object of a single state of knowledge. So once again, knowledge is possible only of changeless objects.

Inasmuch as the domain of sensible things is constantly in flux (as Heraclitus allegedly taught), it lacks existence in the sense required by knowledge. And inasmuch as sense perception is our access to this domain, the processes of perception are extraneous to our grasp of existence. To the extent that the objects of sense perception enjoy intelligible existence at all, this is due to their participation in the unchanging Ideas. As Aristotle puts it in the passage cited above, sensible things exist "by participation in the Ideas," and "all are named in relation to these." In whatever sense of 'cause' relevant,[3] it is participation in the Ideas that causes sensible things to share in existence, and to be called by one name instead of another.

These several facets of Plato's theory in the middle dialogues can be characterized under five standard headings. Let us consider in more detail, and with reference to the dialogues, the various senses in which the Ideas are (1) real, (2) absolute, (3) directly knowable, and both (4) causes of and (5) criteria for naming (hence identifying) sensible things.

1. Ideas or Forms are real in the sense of being wholly what they are, and hence entirely free from being otherwise. Far from being tautological, this means that such an entity in no sense admits its opposite. Although a particular instance of holiness, for example, might also be unholy—inasmuch as a man may be holy in one respect but not in another—the Form Holiness itself can in no way be unholy.[4] The reason is that if Holiness were both holy (as at *Protagoras* 330E1) and unholy, then it would be divided in itself and hence admit parts. But Forms are incom-

posite (ἀξύνθετα: *Phaedo* 78C6) and simple (μονοειδεῖ: *Phaedo* 80B1). As Socrates[5] says in the *Republic*, although bodily things present a multiplicity of aspects, "each [Form] is one in itself" (αὐτὸ μὲν ἓν ἕκαστον εἶναι: 476A6-7; see also 479E7-8). A consequence is that "these unified entities do not admit their opposites" (μόνον ἐκεῖνα τὰ ἐναντία ἄλληλα οὐ δεχόμενα: *Phaedo* 104B6-7; a similar remark appears at *Hippias Major* 291D1-3), and hence are indissoluble (ἀδιαλύτῳ: *Phaedo* 80B1)[6] and not subject to change. As put with utmost emphasis at *Phaedo* 78D6-7, "no one of them, in any way, at any time, ever admits any kind of alteration" (οὐδέποτε οὐδαμῇ οὐδαμῶς ἀλλοίωσιν οὐδεμίαν ἐνδέχεται).

2. Forms are absolute in the sense of being autonomous. Not only are the Forms often referred to as "themselves so-and-so" (αὐτὸ τὸ . . . : e.g., *Euthyphro* 6D10-11; *Phaedo* 78C9, D3, 5, E5), but moreover there are central passages in which their autonomy is emphasized as the focus of their self-identity (e.g., ἀεὶ . . . κατὰ ταὐτὰ ἔχοντι ἑαυτῷ: *Phaedo* 80B1-2). The point of this emphasis upon self-identity is that the Forms in no way depend upon other things for being what they are. In particular, they do not depend upon sensible things.[7] Although there is a basic respect in which sensible things depend upon the Forms for being, this dependency is not reciprocal. To take the example of *Euthyphro* 6D, although it is by the Form of the Holy that all holy things are such, the Form itself would exist even though there were no other things called 'holy' at all. Because the Form Holy is self-identical in this sense, and because it is invariable, it has the character we label 'absolute'.

3. The theme that the Forms are directly knowable appears in several dialogues roughly midway in Plato's career, notably the *Meno*, the *Phaedo*, and the *Republic*. In each case, its appearance is in connection with a discussion of how knowledge is attained. In the *Meno*, recollection is identified as "the spontaneous regaining of knowledge in the subject" (Τὸ δὲ ἀναλαμβάνειν αὐτὸν ἐν αὑτῷ ἐπιστήμην: 85D6). The distractions of sensation are emphasized in the *Phaedo*, when Socrates says that the eyes and the ears, and indeed the whole body, "disorder and hinder the mind from obtaining truth and wisdom" (παράττον-

τος καὶ . . . ἐῶντος τὴν ψυχὴν κτήσασθαι ἀλήθειαν τε καὶ φρόνησιν: 66A5-6). The only means to this end is arguing dialectically (ἐπιχειροῖ: 66A2) through "unmixed thinking in and by itself" (αὐτῇ καθ' αὑτὴν εἰλικρινεῖ τῇ διανοίᾳ: 66A1). This theme is repeated in the climactic moments of Book VII of the *Republic*, where Socrates proclaims that it is by dialectic and reason, "entirely apart from sensation" (ἄνευ πασῶν αἰσθήσεων: 532A6), that one can arrive at the Good itself.

This is not to say that sense perception, properly managed, might not provide an occasion for the exercise of intellect. In an earlier part of Book VII, Socrates speaks of how conflicting sensations can excite the mind to thought and reason, considering whether a pair of similar objects, for example, are one or two. In this manner, sensation can "stimulate thought" (παρακλητικὰ τῆς διανοίας: 524D3), and lead the mind to "the contemplation of being" (τὴν τοῦ ὄντος θέαν: 525A1-2). Basically the same message is communicated at *Phaedo* 74B where, in the course of a discussion of recollection, Socrates remarks that the apparent equality of sticks and stones can serve as "that whence we grasp" (Πόθεν λαβόντες: 74B3) knowledge of equality itself.

The sense in which the Forms are directly knowable, accordingly, does not rule out perception as totally irrelevant. Nor, as *Republic* 511B-C and 532A make clear, does it rule out the exercise of discursive reason. Indeed, the middle dialogues contain several quite distinct descriptions of the discursive processes by which knowledge of the Forms is to be achieved. The point upon which all these descriptions agree is that the apprehension of the Forms, once achieved, involves no admixture of sense perception.

4. Forms are causes of sensible things in a sense intimately connected with the notion of definition. A definition of the type that the historical Socrates is said by Aristotle to have pioneered is a formula (λόγος) that expresses of a thing what it is (τί ἐστιν: *Theaetetus* 147B3; also *Meno* 81E2, 100B6-7). This formula applies to all instances of things exhibiting the character in question (*Theaetetus* 148D6-7), and also tells what it is that imparts that character to all such instances (*Euthyphro* 6D11; *Meno* 72C6-7). Applying to all instances so characterized, the

definition must express necessary conditions for being of that type. Telling what imparts that character to all its instances, conversely, the definition also shows what is sufficient for being so characterized. In brief, an adequate definition gives conditions that are both necessary and sufficient for having the character in question.

As Aristotle says at Metaphysics 987b31-32, Plato's introduction of the Forms was due to his inquiry into formulae (λό-γοις) of this sort. The connection between Forms and definitions is that participation in the Form constitutes what the formula defines: necessary and sufficient conditions for having the associated character. Forms are causes in the (rather basic, but non-Aristotelian) sense that participation in them is both necessary and sufficient for being a thing of a given type.

This is made explicit in the remarkable passage in the Phaedo (100B-101C) where Socrates describes his theory of causation in contrast to that of Anaxagoras. Rejecting shape or color as the source of beauty, on the one hand, and difference in height as the cause of tallness on the other, Socrates asserts that the only causes he recognizes in these cases are the Forms Beauty and Tallness themselves. A certain shape or color is inadequate as a cause of beauty because there may be beautiful things with other shapes and colors—that is, because no particular color or shape is necessary for being beautiful. Difference in height is not the cause of tallness, by contrast, because the same difference accompanies the shortness of the other object compared—that is, because difference in height is not sufficient for being taller. What makes participation in Beauty the cause of beauty is that all and only beautiful objects so participate. Participation in Beauty is both necessary and sufficient for being so characterized.[8] And so forth and so on for Tallness, Shortness, Unity, and all the others. As Socrates suggests waggishly to an amused Cebes, he should loudly announce that he knows of no way in which an object can come to be, other than by "participation in its essential Idea" (μετασχὸν τῆς ἰδίας οὐσίας: 101C3). The same view of causation is expressed at Euthyphro 6D10-E1, where Socrates refers to "the Form [Holiness] itself that makes all holy things holy" (αὐτὸ τὸ εἶδος ᾧ πάντα τὰ ὅσια ὅσιά ἐστιν) and says there is one Idea only (μιᾷ ἰδέᾳ) that has that effect.

5. It is because of its relationship to a given Form that an object is called by a given name. As Socrates asks rhetorically in posing the problem of their joint enquiry to Theaetetus, how can a person understand the name of a thing if he does not know its nature (what it is, τί ἐστιν, *Theaetetus* 147B3)? And to know a thing's nature is to know its Form. A rather less believable connection between names and natures is featured at the beginning of the *Cratylus*,[9] where names are said to "distinguish among natures" (διακριτικὸν τῆς οὐσίας: 388B13-C1) and to be in the order of things natural (φύσει πεφυκὸς: 389D4) to what they designate. Perhaps the most explicit statement in this regard, however, occurs in the *Phaedo*, where in applying his account of causation in the final proof of immortality Socrates observes that "the proper name of a Form belongs not only to the Form itself" (αὐτὸ τὸ εἶδος ἀξιοῦσθαι τοῦ αὐτοῦ ὀνόματος: 103E2-3) but also to the other things that have its configuration (μορφὴν: E5).

What is important about this basic theme in the development of Plato's thought through the middle period, however, is not a question merely of nomenclature or etymology. The point is that by knowing the Form in which a thing participates one can identify that thing for what it is. Thus does Socrates implore Euthyphro to tell him what the Form Holiness is, in order that he may be in a position to call (πράττῃ φῶ: *Euthyphro* 6E7) the latter's or some other action holy, and yet another unholy. In this role, Forms are taken to provide standards or criteria by which sensible things (actions or objects) can be identified and distinguished from each other. As put at *Phaedo* 75B, for instance, it is to the Form itself that we refer in saying of sensible equals that they fall short of pure Equality. The one term that most frequently expresses this role of standard or criterion is παράδειγμα.[10] It is with reference to the Idea of Holiness as παράδειγμα, according to *Euthyphro* 6E6, that one is to judge the holiness of a particular act; and the *Republic* contains several mentions of the παράδειγμα of the state (472C5, D11; 500E3; 592B3).

These five themes (or their equivalents) are characteristic of Plato's thinking about knowledge and its ontology in the middle dialogues. There are several indications, however, that his views in this respect had changed in the later period. By the time of the *Sophist,* for instance, Ideas are portrayed as admitting their opposites (contrary to [1] above); and in the *Timaeus* (47A-B) vision plays a distinctive role in moving the intellect to knowledge (an apparent retrenchment of [3]). These and other departures from the middle theory prepare the reader for Aristotle's reference at 987a34-b1 to the tenets of Plato's "later years." Yet the particular tenets Aristotle is attributing to Plato in the immediately following passages appear entirely foreign to any of the later dialogues.

For one thing, Aristotle uses the terms εἶδος and ἀριθμός as if in Plato's thought they were interchangeable. After noting at 987b9-10 that the many (sensible things) exist by participation in the Forms that share names with them, for example, Aristotle proceeds with the baffling comment that:

the name 'participation' was the only new thing; for the Pythagoreans say that things exist by imitation of numbers, while Plato says it is by participation, thus changing the name [τὴν δὲ μέθεξιν τοὔνομα μόνον μετέβαλεν· οἱ μὲν γὰρ Πυθαγόρειοι μιμήσει τὰ ὄντα φασὶν εἶναι τῶν ἀριθμῶν, Πλάτων δὲ μεθέξει, τοὔνομα μεταβαλών: 987b10-13].

Again, after remarking that for Plato "the Forms were causes of other things" (αἴτια τὰ εἴδη τοῖς ἄλλοις: 987b18-19), he says without further explanation that Plato agreed with the Pythagoreans in saying that "numbers are the causes of the existence of the other things" (ἀριθμοὺς αἰτίους εἶναι τοῖς ἄλλοις τῆς οὐσίας: 987b24-25).

Another baffling but quite prominent feature of Aristotle's account is the notion of the "Indefinite Dyad," or the "Great and Small." A respect in which Plato differed from the Pythagoreans, he says at 987b26, is in making the indefinite two instead of one—that is, in making "the indefinite from the Great and Small" (τὸ δ' ἄπειρον ἐκ μεγάλου καὶ μικροῦ). It is this dyad of the Great and the Small, he says a few lines on, that Plato made "the underlying matter of which the Forms are predicated in the case of sensible things, and Unity in the case of the Forms" (τίς ἡ ὕλη ἡ ὑποκειμένη καθ' ἧς τὰ εἴδη μὲν ἐπὶ τῶν αἰσθητῶν τὸ δ' ἓν ἐν τοῖς εἴδεσι λέγεται: 988a11-13). The ultimate assault upon any standard conception of Plato's philosophy, however, comes at the end of this section of the *Metaphysics* with Aristotle's announcement that Plato "assigned the causation of Good and Evil to these elements" (τὴν τοῦ εὖ καὶ τοῦ κακῶς αἰτίαν τοῖς στοιχείοις ἀπέδωκεν: 988a14-15)—the obvious implication being that Unity and the Great and Small are causes of Good and Evil, respectively.

Generations of Plato scholars have agreed that these doctrines cannot be found in the written dialogues, but opinions diverge widely on the significance of their absence. One time-honored option is (A) to associate these doctrines with the contents of the comparably mysterious "lecture on the Good" reported by Aristoxenus and others, and then to speculate (with the help of the problematic Seventh Letter) on reasons Plato might have had for withholding this material from his written corpus.[11] An awkward consequence of this approach is that Plato's final philosophy was contained in some "unwritten teachings," to which the dialogues themselves provide no access. The only way of recapturing Plato's late thought is to study Aristotle instead. A directly opposed alternative is (B) to argue that the account in the *Metaphysics* is largely a misrepresentation, deriving from Aristotle's misunderstanding of the same written sources that we have today.[12] In effect, this option treats Aristotle as the first of a long line of commentators bewildered by the contents of the later dialogues, who regrettably failed to take advantage of his opportunity to check his interpretations with Plato personally. Whereas (A) makes Aristotle our main resource in coming to understand Plato's late philosophy, option (B) rejects Aristotle's testimony as unreliable. Although it is not part of my purpose to become involved in the controversy between these two viewpoints, Chapter 2 provides occasion to examine it more thoroughly.

Another possible attitude toward Aristotle's testimony in the

Metaphysics is (C) to rule it out as ultimately irrelevant to our understanding of the later dialogues—in effect, to ignore it.[13] Among scholars who adopt this expedient, the standard view is roughly the following: In the first part of the *Parmenides* (hereafter, *Parmenides I*), written relatively early among the late dialogues, Plato mounted a surprisingly vigorous attack on the central tenets of his middle theory. He then moved on in subsequent dialogues (at least in part) to repair the damage. In the *Sophist*, for example, he realigned certain features of the account in the *Phaedo* which seemed to imply that the human mind (being changeable) is excluded from Being, while in the *Timaeus* he finally achieved a coherent theory of participation. Although other late dialogues are occupied with other matters, the ontology of the *Timaeus* remains in force to the end of his career.

A commonly acknowledged problem for this approach (apart from Aristotle's testimony itself) lies in the fact that Plato never explicitly responded to the difficulties raised in *Parmenides I*, which seems peculiar given the intensity of that attack. A more severe problem arises with the fact that both the second part of the *Parmenides* (hereafter, *Parmenides II*) and the *Philebus* contain lengthy passages on ontological issues that appear quite out of harmony with the *Timaeus* in particular. Although these passages are generally recognized as the most difficult in the entire corpus, no adequate account of Plato's late thought can be lightly excused for overlooking them.

A more promising alternative in the face of these difficulties, I believe, has been (D) to construe the attack in *Parmenides I* on the middle theory as seriously intended,[14] and to approach the *Philebus* unencumbered by this earlier theory.[15] One burden to be accommodated by this approach is the rather considerable mass of stylometric data that seems to place the *Timaeus* after the *Parmenides* and near the *Philebus* (a topic reconsidered in Appendix B). If Plato indeed intended to disqualify the theory of the *Phaedo* and the *Republic* by the arguments of *Parmenides I*, we would not expect a theory similar to it in essential respects to play a prominent role in a later *Timaeus*. The most serious obstacle, however, remains that of arriving at an intelligible interpretation of the *Philebus* and of *Parmenides II*. It is of little

immediate interest to the Plato scholar to be told that the notoriously difficult passages in these dialogues contain an ontology
basically different from that of the middle period, as long as their
contents remain inaccessible.

The approach of my book is indebted to the precedent of (D),
while agreeing with (A) in accepting a good deal of Aristotle's
testimony and with (B) in rejecting the notion of an "unwritten
teaching." The basic interpretative premise in which it departs
from all four approaches above, however, is that the main tenets
attributed to Plato in the first book of the *Metaphysics* in fact
are present in the *Philebus*. The reason they so long have escaped
detection is that the terminology in which Plato expressed them
is different from Aristotle's.

A general preview of the picture this approach reveals will
help explain the ordering of the following material. Plato's thinking on ontological matters changed in several respects during the
period of his late dialogues. Nonetheless, I shall maintain, the
changes did not at first involve rejection of the five theses identified above. Although these theses posed a number of serious
problems that the theory of the *Phaedo* and the *Republic* was
unable to handle, Plato seemed bent in early dialogues of the
late period (the "early late" or intermediate dialogues) upon
preserving this theory in basic outline. One central problem was
to become clear about the notion of participation, which remained little more than a metaphor in the middle dialogues. At
the heart of this problem is the question how Forms and sensible
objects can be related at all, given their radically different natures.
An allied problem upon which Plato seems to have reached an
impasse in the middle dialogues is that of providing a discursive
(nonfigurative) account of knowledge, adding substance to the
images of Books VI and VII of the *Republic*. Even more basic
ontologically, however, was the problem of elucidating the status
of sensible objects—which, lacking the features to make them
objects of knowledge, become intelligible by partaking in the
eternal Forms.

What changed as Plato moved into his later period was, not
at first his commitment to the middle theory, but rather his
approach to the problems inherent in it. In the domain of on-

tology specifically, the main contribution of the *Theaetetus* was an account of the nature of sensible objects. Building upon a newly elaborated theory of relationships among Forms, in turn, he developed in the *Sophist* a remarkably sophisticated account of philosophic knowledge. The accounts of both the *Theaetetus* and the *Sophist*, like those of the *Phaedo* and the *Republic* before them, remained essentially dependent upon a "two world" ontology.

After turning in the *Timaeus* to the critical task of making sense of the notion of participation, however, Plato seems finally to have realized that this ontology—based as it was upon a radical separation of Forms and sensible objects—simply could not provide an intelligible account of their interrelationship. For not only is the *Timaeus* the last dialogue to say anything constructive about the notion of participation at all, but moreover its discussion is confined to the level of images. Even worse, the several different images employed in this discussion appear ultimately incompatible amongst themselves. The basic problem emerging from the ontological exercise of the *Timaeus* (distinct from its cosmology) is that entities which themselves are eternal and changeless—the Forms and the Receptacle—cannot account for the becoming of temporal objects. Plato's abrupt termination of Socrates' conversation with Timaeus and his companions only a few pages into the *Critias*, in fact, might possibly signal his ultimate disaffection with the "two world" ontology upon which these dialogues are explicitly based.

The ontology of the *Philebus* is entirely different. One fundamental departure from the earlier theory regards the ontological status of the Forms themselves. Whereas in the middle period Forms differed from sensible objects both in being noncomposite and in not depending upon other things for what they are, in the *Philebus* the Forms are ontologically derivative. Like sensible objects, Forms now are constituted from more basic principles. The main difference between Forms and sensible objects with respect to their constitution is that the composition of the former is prior to that of the latter. For whereas sensible objects are composed of Forms and the Unlimited, Forms themselves are composed from the same Unlimited in combination with the principle of Limit. The fact that both Forms and sensible objects are constituted from the Unlimited, moreover, marks a second major innovation of the later theory. In contrast with the thesis of radical separation that prevailed from the *Phaedo* to the *Timaeus*, Forms and objects in the *Philebus* are ontologically homogenous. Nonetheless, Plato is able in this later context to provide a clear sense in which Forms are directly intelligible. Paradoxical as it may at first appear, as a consequence of relinquishing the "two world" ontology of the earlier theory (intimated at *Metaphysics* 1078b11, 31-32), Plato finally achieves a precise conception of how Forms can be known independently of sensible objects. The *Philebus* thus fulfills his primary quest (as indicated at *Metaphysics* 1078b15-16) of providing an ontology that makes knowledge possible.

Extracting these results from the *Philebus* understandably requires preparation. For one thing, the *Parmenides* must be factored into the story. Commentators almost universally read *Parmenides I* as presenting a series of arguments against the theory of the middle dialogues. Hence it is natural for someone who believes Plato has in fact relinquished this theory by the time of the *Philebus* to assume that these arguments explain why. A difficulty with this assumption is the fact that the arguments as they stand are neither carefully wrought nor compelling (unlike key arguments in the roughly contemporaneous *Sophist*), posing the question of why Plato could be swayed by such inconclusive reasons. Contrary to the current scholarly trend of trying to tighten these arguments into intellectually respectable form and thereupon to speculate whether Plato would have accepted them, I think the arguments should be viewed instead as a rhetorical exercise. In particular, I suggest in the initial section of the following chapter that *Parmenides I* is basically a forensic display of those features of the middle theory that Plato had already rejected on other grounds, functioning primarily to set the stage for his entry into the historical controversy between the Pythagoreans and the Eleatics. Since I believe, moreover, that the failure of the *Timaeus* to resolve the problem of participation was Plato's main reason for giving up the earlier theory, I am attracted to the opinion that *Parmenides I* was written after the *Timaeus*.

Although this ordering is not essential for my argument, I have included in an appendix my particular reasons for rejecting stylometric arguments to the opposite effect.

Be this as it may, I am convinced that *Parmenides II* was written after the *Timaeus* and close in time to the *Philebus*. My reasons for this conviction are (i) that *Parmenides II* contains a massive and formally conclusive refutation of the Eleatic conception of Being which stood behind the *Timaeus*, and (ii) that it provides a number of important links in the conceptual development leading to the ontology of the *Philebus*. According to the viewpoint of the present study, in brief, the *Parmenides* as a whole is a transitional link between the old theory of the middle period, inadequately repaired in the intermediate dialogues, and the radically new theory of the *Philebus*—Plato's final discussion of ontological topics. The primary task of Chapter 1 is to establish the *Parmenides* in this transition role.

Chapter 2 undertakes the burdensome task of marshaling evidence from early sources bearing on the nature of Plato's late ontology. Paramount among these sources are (i) various fragments from Plato's contemporaries recording reactions to his Lecture on the Good, (ii) Aristotle's characterization of Plato's ontology, including passages from the *Metaphysics* cited above, (iii) later commentators on the *Metaphysics* and other works of Aristotle, some actually linking his characterization to the *Philebus*, and (iv) the history of Greek mathematics around the time of the later dialogues. Most of the relevant data from sources (i)-(iii), of course, have been examined before, albeit with varying degrees of thoroughness. The often polemical circumstances in which these earlier examinations have taken place, however, have tended to reflect uncertainty upon the data themselves—notably regarding their bearing on the controversial "unwritten teachings." The approach of the present study has been to circumvent controversies of this sort whenever possible, and to concentrate instead upon what the data tell about the contents of the *Philebus*. Evidence from source (iv), on the other hand, has too frequently been ignored in discussions of the ontology of the later Platonic dialogues. If indeed Chapter 2 does succeed in shedding new light upon the *Philebus*, the reasons are (a) that data from sources (i)-(iii) are applied directly to deciphering this dialogue, and (b) that these data are analyzed in the light of then-current mathematics.

With the groundwork laid in Chapters 1 and 2, I turn finally in Chapter 3 to the task of showing that the main tenets of Aristotle's testimony in the *Metaphysics* are point by point in correspondence with the ontology of the *Philebus*. Each document, accordingly, enhances the intelligibility of the other. My claim for the interpretation resulting is that it makes better sense of the ontological passages of the *Philebus*—word by word and line by line—than previous interpretations. An accounting of this interpretation according to the recently published criteria of Gosling (1975) is included as a final appendix.

Since the argument of Chapter 3 involves a number of crucial terminological variations, and since its cogency depends largely upon its success in elucidating individual passages of the dialogue, I have adopted the practice (followed elsewhere in the book as well) of presenting both the Greek and the English translation of all passages discussed. In each case, the translation is aimed at literalness rather than literary merit.

An additional criterion of success is the extent to which a given interpretation is able to offer intelligible accounts of other traditional riddles of Platonic scholarship. Along with (1) the perplexing ontological passages of the *Philebus*, and (2) the difficulties associated with Aristotle's testimony in the *Metaphysics*, the perennially most troublesome problems affecting the late philosophy of Plato have been (3) what to make of Plato's lecture on the Good (which even its listeners termed 'enigmatic'), and (4) how *Parmenides II* relates to the rest of the corpus. An additional advantage of the present approach, accordingly, is that it shows how all four problems can be resolved simultaneously.

CHAPTER ONE

PLATO'S BREAK WITH THE MIDDLE PERIOD

1. A BATTERY OF PROBLEMS IN *Parmenides I*

Plato's *Parmenides* probably has been subject to a wider variety of interpretations than any other major text of ancient philosophy. One obvious reason is the extreme difficulty of the second part of the dialogue. Another reason is the apparent discontinuity between the two parts, encouraging commentators to fix upon one while ignoring the other. Against this, we may adopt the interpretive principle that an adequate account of any significant portion should make clear its relationship to the rest of the dialogue.

A third contributing factor is more controversial, pertaining to an error some commentators would not be prepared to acknowledge. Simply stated, the error is that of taking Plato's arguments at surface value when the context indicates they should be taken otherwise. This error can occur in several forms, none confined to the *Parmenides* alone. One pervasive form is to assume that Plato endorses the conclusion of every argument he puts in the mouths of his main protagonists—akin to the mistake of assuming that every thesis affirmed by Socrates is espoused by Plato himself. Upon reflection this assumption appears so implausible that merely pointing it out should be enough to render it pointless. Another form is to assume that Plato intends all arguments articulated by his protagonists to be logically tight and philosophically sound. This assumption rules out construing any argument by a major protagonist as having primarily an elenctic[1] or rhetorical[2] role, either of which would make it inappropriate to take Plato to task for producing a "bad" argu-

18

ment. To help counteract a common tendency toward this mistake, it will be helpful to allow Plato the benefit of the doubt—in effect, to assume that for the most part when he puts an unsound argument in the mouth of one of his characters (Socrates and Parmenides included) Plato himself is aware of its logical deficiency.[3] A logically unsound argument, after all, might be a rhetorical masterpiece, and when we encounter good rhetoric we should be prepared to recognize it.

The most deceptive form of this error, however, is a combination of the two above. This is to assume that whenever a major protagonist[4] develops an extended argument for (or against) a philosophic thesis, Plato himself accepts (or rejects) that thesis *on the basis* of that specific argument. Our tendency to fall prey to this mistake is even more insidious when we have evidence on some other basis that Plato did in fact accept (or reject) the thesis in question.

A prime example of this mistake is afforded by the series of arguments with which the fully mature and experienced Parmenides browbeats the very young Socrates in *Parmenides I*. The proper interpretive stance for these arguments, I suggest, should accommodate the fact that the arguments are not at all conclusive, while remaining open to the strong likelihoods (a) that Plato knew they are not conclusive and did not intend them to be, but nonetheless (b) that he had rejected or was prepared to reject, on independent grounds, certain aspects of the theory they are directed against. The independent grounds include both his failure to make coherent sense of the notion of participation as it figures in the middle dialogues (see Appendix A) and his disaffection from the doctrine of radical distinction between Forms and sensible things so forcefully argued in *Parmenides II* (see below). A consequence of taking this interpretive stance is that it appears misguided either (i) to concern oneself with subtle deficiencies in the arguments of which Plato allegedly was not aware, but which need repairing if the arguments are to have the effect Plato allegedly thought they should have,[5] or (ii) to attempt an explanation of how Plato could continue to maintain the theory in question, after offering arguments against it which he never counters.[6]

The present section develops my reasons for thinking that Parmenides' arguments against the early theory represented by Socrates were not intended by Plato to be conclusive at all, but that they were intended to serve a rhetorical function instead. To this end, I argue that the main purpose of *Parmenides I* is to highlight those aspects of the theory of Forms in the middle dialogues which Plato thinks must be reexamined if an adequate theory is to be forthcoming. The following section shows how *Parmenides II* explores the conditions of the required alterations, thereby establishing continuity between the two parts of the dialogue.

The main participants in the dialogue are a *very* young (σφόδρα νέον: 127C5-6) Socrates, the master dialectician Zeno (in his prime, about forty: 127B5), a Parmenides to whom Zeno defers and whom Socrates later recalls as awesome and fearful (*Theaetetus* 183E6), and a colorless Aristotle even younger than Socrates (137C2). Young as he is, Socrates shows considerable confidence and insight in posing to Zeno certain questions regarding the treatise that the latter had just finished reading when the dialogue proper begins. Socrates has the audacity, in fact, to confront Zeno with what we must understand as his own theory of Forms—the theory, that is, of which Socrates is the main expositor in the middle dialogues. When Parmenides enters the conversation at 130A9, however, Socrates quickly becomes subdued, and is unable to take a firm stand on the question of which sensible objects have Forms and which do not. Passing this indecision off as a result of youth, Parmenides reiterates the main features of the theory that Socrates is supposed to hold. First, "the Forms (some at least) exist" (εἴδη εἶναι ἄττα: 130E5). "Other things, participating in them, are called by their names" (ὧν τάδε τὰ ἄλλα μεταλαμβάνοντα τὰς ἐπωνυμίας αὐτῶν ἴσχειν: 130E5-7). And by participating in Likeness, Largeness, Beauty or Justice, these things become (γίγνεσθαι: 131A3) like and large and beautiful and just.

What Parmenides stresses first, last, and foremost, however, is that these Forms are supposed to exist in complete separation from things that come to be by participating in them. In his initial speech at 130B, after complimenting Socrates on his eagerness for debate, Parmenides asks whether Socrates himself has drawn the distinction just mentioned, with "separate Forms themselves on the one side" (χωρὶς μὲν εἴδη αὐτά: 130B2) and "on the other the separate things that participate in them" (χωρὶς δὲ τὰ τούτων αὖ μετέχοντα: 130B3). In particular, Parmenides asks, does Socrates believe "there exists a Likeness in itself separate from the likeness we have" (εἶναι αὐτὴ ὁμοιότης χωρὶς ἧς ἡμεῖς ὁμοιότητος ἔχομεν: 130B3-4), and so on for the other characters in Zeno's argument which he has been criticizing? Is there a "Form in and by itself of Rightness" (δικαίου τι εἶδος αὐτὸ καθ' αὐτὸ: 130B7-8), Beauty, Goodness, and such things? Further, Parmenides asks (as Socrates becomes increasingly less confident), is there a "Form of man separate from us" (ἀνθρώπου εἶδος χωρὶς ἡμῶν: 130C1) and all others like us—"a Form of Man just by itself" (αὐτό τι εἶδος ἀνθρώπου: 130C2)—or a Form of Fire or a Form of Water? And what about such very undignified and paltry objects as hair and mud and dirt? "Are there Forms of each of these, separate" (τούτων ἑκάστου εἶδος εἶναι χωρίς: 130C9-D1) from things like these we can touch? In the course of a few brief questions, Parmenides uses the term χωρίς five different times,[7] and reiterates that what he meant by 'separate' is "existing in and by itself" (αὐτὸ καθ' αὐτὸ).

It is just by "distinguishing such things as Forms existing in and by themselves" (εἴδη ὄντα αὐτὰ καθ' αὐτὰ διορίζηται: 133A9), says Parmenides, that Socrates finds himself in the difficulties pointed out between 131A and 133A. But the worst difficulty is that the Forms, if such as Socrates has been saying they must be, cannot even be known. The argument to this effect begins with the assumption that each of these Forms exists "in and by itself" (αὐτήν . . . καθ' αὐτήν: 133C5), and ends with the threat that even more difficulties are involved in "distinguishing each of these Forms as something just by itself" (ὁριεῖταί τις αὐτό τι ἕκαστον εἶδος: 135A2-3).

The cross-examination ends with a surprising reversal of positions. Having convinced Socrates that his theory of Forms is in serious difficulty (135B4-5), Parmenides cautions that intolerable consequences follow if the theory is given up entirely. If someone persists in not accepting the existence of these Forms of things, on the basis of arguments like those Parmenides has been giving, and "does not distinguish a single Form in each case" (μηδέ τι ὁριεῖται εἶδος ἑνὸς ἑκάστου: 135B8-9) such that "each thing has its own character that is always the same" (ἑῶν ἰδέαν τῶν ὄντων ἑκάστου τὴν αὐτὴν ἀεὶ εἶναι: 135C1), then "he will have nothing upon which to fix his thought" (οὐδὲ ὅποι τρέψει τὴν διάνοιαν ἕξει: 135B9) and "the power of dialectic will be totally destroyed" (τὴν τοῦ διαλέγεσθαι δύναμιν παντάπασι διαφθερεῖ: 135C2). What Parmenides obviously has omitted from this last-minute defense of the theory is any mention of the Forms as entirely separate entities.

All of this is in the text, and is scarcely problematic. Its effect, however, is far from trivial. What Plato has Parmenides saying is that certain aspects of this theory Socrates has been maintaining, here and in earlier dialogues, indeed are essential for intelligible discourse—namely those aspects providing Forms that are definite and always the same—but that the notion that these Forms exist in total separation from the things that participate in them not only is inessential but leads to endless difficulties. Development of an adequate theory of Forms that avoids these problems requires a discipline which Socrates does not possess, but which Parmenides proceeds to describe between 135D and 137B. In the remainder of the dialogue we find Parmenides (by this time bearing little resemblance to his historical counterpart) is not only illustrating the discipline he has in mind but also taking broad strides toward the development of the required new theory.

Given this schema of the dialogic structure of *Parmenides I*, what are we to make of the role of the several arguments between 131A and 134E? At very least we should expect them to reveal something of Plato's dissatisfaction with the theory of the middle dialogues, which Socrates has represented in the passages preceding. But given the arguments as we find them, it would be quite unreasonable to expect these arguments themselves to constitute Plato's reasons for wanting to replace this particular theory. For one thing, the arguments are highly schematic and far from conclusive—not at all the kind of consideration that would induce Plato to make a major theoretical revision so late in his career. For another, they involve a number of rhetorical tricks that Parmenides pulls on an overawed Socrates, of a sort more characteristic of the eristic dialogues of the middle period than of the sober later dialogues. Most importantly, however, the arguments are put forward and passed by without dialectical examination of the sort we have learned to associate with the solid philosophic results of the *Theaetetus* and the *Sophist*. Socrates in *Parmenides I* does not have the acuity of Theaetetus, nor Parmenides the candor of the Eleatic Stranger. All in all, the interchange between the aged master and the youthful novice is a display more of eristic than of philosophic argument.

An examination of the first argument illustrates the extent to which this is so. Parmenides begins by posing a dilemma in the form of a question: does each thing that participates participate in the "whole of a Form or in part" (ὅλου τοῦ εἴδους ἢ μέρους: 131A5)? Or, he asks rhetorically, might a way of participating arise apart from these? whereupon Socrates agrees that there is no other way. This dilemma represents a misdirection from the beginning. A whole presumably is a unified aggregate of parts,[8] in which case the Form is not a whole at all and is not available for participation either as a whole or in part. What is questionable is not whether there is another way of participating, the only line of possible disagreement Parmenides leaves open to Socrates, but rather whether Forms should be represented either as wholes or as having parts in the first place. After having been accused of being "too young for philosophy yet to take hold of" at 130E1-2, however, Socrates, not surprisingly, is not eager to argue with Parmenides on fine distinctions. The next question Socrates faces is whether "the Form is in each of the many participants as a whole, a single thing, or in some other way" (ὅλον τὸ εἶδος ἐν ἑκάστῳ εἶναι τῶν πολλῶν ἓν ὄν, ἢ πῶς: 131A9-10). Sensing that he is about to be caught in an absurdity already, with the argument scarcely begun, Socrates stalls for time and asks defensively "Why not?" (Τί . . . κωλύει: 131A11). Parmenides gives the obvious answer: because that way, while one and the same, the Form as a whole will be in

23

many separate things, and thus be separate from itself (131B1-2).

Meanwhile Socrates has thought of a good response, in the form of an analogy. Could not a Form be present in all the separate things in the way that "one and the same day is in many places at the same time" (ἡμέρα . . . μία καὶ ἡ αὐτὴ οὖσα πολλαχοῦ ἅμα: 131B3-4) and still is not separate from itself? Not only is a day present in the same way in many different places without thereby in any sense being apart from itself, but moreover the analogy shows what is wrong with approaching the problem of participation with reference to the distinction between whole and part in the first place. For the manner in which a day is present in many different places has nothing to do with whether it is divided into parts—hours and minutes are multipresent in just the same manner. If Socrates had been allowed to pursue this insight, a really constructive discussion might have ensued.[9] But Parmenides instead counters with a subtle change of analogy, after first intimidating the boy with a condescending remark:

> I enjoy the way you make one and the same thing be in many places at once, Socrates. You might as well cover many people with a sail and then say that one sail as a whole is over many ['Ηδέως γε, φάναι, ὦ Σώκρατες, ἐν ταὐτὸν ἅμα πολλαχοῦ ποιεῖς, οἷον εἰ ἱστίῳ καταπετάσας πολλοὺς ἀνθρώπους φαίης ἓν ἐπὶ πολλοῖς εἶναι ὅλον: 131B7-9]. Doesn't what you're saying amount to that? [ἢ οὐ τὸ τοιοῦτον ἡγῇ λέγειν: 131B9-10].

But it is obvious that the two analogies do not amount to the same thing at all. Covering is a spatial relationship, and there is no way in which one object in space can cover several different objects without different spatial parts of the former being involved with each of the latter. Hence the analogy proposed by Parmenides requires that the sail cover the several men part by part rather than in its entirety. All that follows from this is that the sail is a poor analogy for the Forms, to which spatial dimensionality is totally foreign. Instead of returning to his original analogy, however, Socrates has been so demoralized that he prac-

tically retires from the discussion, confining himself for the remainder of the argument to very terse answers.

Doesn't what you're saying amount to that?
Perhaps ['Ἴσως: 131C1].
Would the sail as a whole be over each man, or only a part
    of it?
A part [Μέρος: 131C4].
In that case, the Forms themselves must be divisible, and
    only a part will be in each thing that participates in them.
So it seems [φαίνεται οὕτω γε: 131C3].
Then will a Form that is divided still be one?
Not at all [Οὐδαμῶς: 131C11].

With dispirited responses like these occasionally interspersed,
Parmenides proceeds to draw a series of absurd conclusions from
the notion of a Form's being partitioned, and then asks Socrates
point-blank how he is going to make sense of participation in
his Forms (τῶν εἰδῶν σοι: 131E4) if things can partake of neither part nor whole. Expressing his frustration with an oath (Οὐ
μὰ τὸν Δία 131E7), Socrates can only say that defining participation strikes him as being not at all easy (131E7-8).

If Plato in this passage were offering serious arguments against
the theory of Forms in question, he would not have arranged
such a mismatch of dialectical talent, he would not have imparted
such a heavily rhetorical (indeed, emotion-laden) cast to the discussion, and he would not have passed up several opportunities
to have one of his characters say something genuinely constructive about the problem. But if serious argument is not the purpose
of the passage, what is? The answer, I believe, is that Plato, in
this conversation between master and novice, is drawing attention to certain difficulties involved in the theory—but doing so
dramatically rather than dialectically. And the reason Plato chooses
this modality of presentation is that the difficulties have to do
with aspects of the theory which had remained unintelligible in
earlier dialogues, and hence could not even be articulated in the
clear manner required for dialectical discussion.

In the Introduction above, the theory of Forms as it appeared
in the middle dialogues was characterized with reference to five

theses, following Aristotle's account in the *Metaphysics*. These theses may be summarized as follows: (1) The Forms are real, in that they are wholly what they are without any tinge of being other. Although a particular man might be holy in one respect but unholy in another, for instance, the Form Holiness itself is in no respect unholy.[10] This is because the Form otherwise would be divided in itself and hence admit parts; but Forms are incomposite (*Phaedo* 78C6) and each one in itself (*Republic* 476A6-9). (2) The Forms are absolute, in the sense of being self-identical and "in and by themselves." They are what they are without any dependence upon sensible things. (3) The Forms are directly knowable by mind, independently of sense experience. (4) Participation in Forms is the cause by which sensible things come to have this or that characteristic, where 'cause' has the sense of "necessary and sufficient conditions." And (5) Forms provide standards or criteria by which sensible things are identified and given names.

Although the *Theaetetus* and the *Sophist* (and, as argued in Appendix A, the *Timaeus* as well) are concerned in considerable part with making various aspects of these five theses intelligible, the theses themselves being subjected to various reinterpretations in the process, all five appear to remain part of Plato's ontology in the early part of his final period. The first major break appears in the very passages of the *Parmenides* examined here. In reviewing the main features of the theory attributed to the youthful Socrates, as I have noted, Parmenides mentions (1) that the Forms exist (130E5), (4) that participation in Forms is the cause of sensible things coming to have certain characteristics (130E6-131A3), and (5) that it is by participation that sensible things are called by the same names as the Forms (130E6-7). In summing up his list of complaints, further, Parmenides emphasizes that the reason it is important to maintain the existence of these Forms is that otherwise there will be nothing "to anchor thought" (τρέψει τὴν διάνοιαν: 135B9)—that is, (3) that Forms are knowable in a manner providing our "capacity for discourse" (τὴν τοῦ διαλέγεσθαι δύναμιν: 135C2). The one thesis Parmenides omits from the list, and against which he raises specific complaints in these passages, is (2) that the Forms are "in and by themselves," completely separate from sensible things.

The passages from 131A to 134E are commonly recognized to contain five distinct arguments. Not coincidentally, each argument corresponds in content to one of the five components of the original theory of Forms—the theory attributed to the youthful Socrates in this particular dialogue. The first argument, which was considered above, focuses upon problems associated with the incomposite nature of the Forms. According to (1), the Forms are real, which means in the context of the *Phaedo* that they are wholly what they are (i.e., cannot admit features opposite to themselves), and hence not subject to decomposition. Further reasons for stressing their incomposite nature in this early context appear with the objections Parmenides fabricates out of the part/whole distinction at 131A-E, and his vigorous pursuit of the sail analogy. For what is not distinguishable as part or whole is as such incomposite. But if Socrates cannot with impunity admit that the Forms are subject to participation either in parts or as wholes, how can anyone explain the manner in which many different things, at different times and different places, can participate in one and the same Form? The youthful Socrates has no clear answer to the problem (131E7-8); nor has the sympathetic interpreter of the Socratic theory of Forms. The early theory of Forms remains incoherent in the face of this version of the one-many problem, the version identified as philosophically "serious" at *Philebus* 15B-C. A new departure is needed if the problem is to be resolved.

At 132B-C Parmenides sketches another argument, the first of two that have dominated most recent discussions of *Parmenides I*. These are the so-called[11] "third man" arguments, the second of which appears at 132D-133A. A careful examination of these arguments from the present viewpoint will show them considerably more diverse than most commentators assume. The content of the first relates to the topic ([4] above) of Forms as causes.

A tenet which is central to the early theory of Forms, and which Plato continues to maintain as late as the *Philebus*, is that things come to have the characters they have by participation in Forms which uniquely exemplify these characters. One of the earliest statements of this tenet occurs at *Euthyphro* 6D10-E1, where Socrates reminds Euthyphro that he should be concerned with "the Form in itself which makes all holy things holy" (αὐτὸ τὸ εἶδος ᾧ πάντα τὰ ὅσια ὅσιά ἐστιν), the "single Idea" (μιᾷ ἰδέᾳ) by which unholy things are unholy and holy things holy. A single Form imparts its character to many particular things. Basically the same formula is repeated at *Parmenides* 132A, where Parmenides rehearses the standard reason given in the early dialogues for positing the Forms. In the case of largeness, he says, "whenever several things seem to you to be large" (ὅταν πόλλ᾽ ἄττα μεγάλα δόξῃ σοι εἶναι: 132A2), "there seems to be a certain single character which is the same when you look at them all" (μία τις ἴσως δοκεῖ ἰδέα ἡ αὐτὴ εἶναι ἐπὶ πάντα ἰδόντι: 132A2-3), and "hence you suppose Largeness to be a single thing" (ὅθεν ἓν τὸ μέγα ἡγῇ εἶναι: 132A3).

But the notion of the Form Largeness imparting to other things a character which it somehow shares poses a problem of intelligibility, as Parmenides proceeds to show. Consider "Largeness itself and the other large things" (αὐτὸ τὸ μέγα καὶ τἆλλα τὰ μεγάλα: 132A5), and "look at them all in your mind with the former consideration in view" (ἐὰν ὡσαύτως τῇ ψυχῇ ἐπὶ πάντα ἴδῃς: 132A5-6). "Does not another single Largeness appear by which these all necessarily appear[12] large" (οὐχὶ ἕν τι αὖ μέγα φανεῖται, ᾧ ταῦτα πάντα ἀνάγκη μεγάλα φαίνεσθαι: 132A6-7)? What Parmenides is saying amounts to this: If the presence of a shared character in several similar things is to be accounted for by positing a Form (a) which is singular, (b) which causes that character in these several things by participation, and (c) which in some manner exemplifies that character itself, although not a member of the original group, then the account introduces a new group with a shared character to be accounted for in turn. For if there were *n* similar things in the original case, the single Form (by [a]) exemplifying the property they share (by [c]) would make it *n* + 1. And "straightway another Form of Largeness is shown forth" (Ἄλλο ἄρα εἶδος μεγέθους ἀναφανήσεται: 132A9), "besides the original Largeness itself and the things participating in it" (παρ᾽ αὐτό τε τὸ μέγεθος γεγονὸς καὶ τὰ μετέχοντα αὐτοῦ: 132A9-10). And again, since there now would be $n + 2$ large things, "over all these yet another [appears] by which they all are large" (ἐπὶ τούτοις αὖ πᾶσιν ἕτερον, ᾧ ταῦτα πάντα μεγάλα ἔσται: 132Α10-Β1).

The alleged upshot is that the Form posited to account for the common character among several similar things, instead of being singular as (a) requires, appears to mushroom in an ever progressing fashion. As Parmenides puts it, "each of your Forms is no longer single but indefinitely multitudinous" (οὐκέτι δὴ ἓν ἕκαστόν σοι τῶν εἰδῶν ἔσται, ἀλλὰ ἄπειρα τὸ πλῆθος: 132Β2-3). Particular attention should be given the wording of this conclusion. Plato does not have Parmenides say, as commentators from Aristotle onward seem to have assumed,[13] that an infinite regress of Forms results. This indeed is claimed explicitly to be the result of the second version of the "third man" argument at 133Α1-2. The result claimed here, however, is that the Forms turn out not to be ἕν after all, but rather ἄπειρα πλῆθος. Although the significance of this opposition between unity and the indefinitely multitudinous cannot be fully appreciated until we have proceeded to the second part of the dialogue and beyond (into the *Philebus*), it is a nontrivial oversight to have neglected the fact that both ἕν and ἄπειρον πλῆθος are key expressions in *Parmenides II*. One prominent meaning assigned to ἄπειρον πλῆθος there is that roughly of "unlimited manyness," with 'unlimited' understood in the sense of "without definite limits or boundaries"—hence "indefinite multitude." And one of the roles prominently assigned to τὸ ἕν (Unity) in that context is to provide a limit enabling "manyness" to be differentiated into identifiable parts. The most straightforward way of reading 132Β2-3 is that, as a result of the argument, Forms turn out not to provide limits after all, but rather themselves are indefinite factors.

In positing Forms as causes of characteristics in sensible things, one problem Plato is trying to solve is that of explaining how things presented in sense experience, while constantly changing, nonetheless exhibit characters enabling them to be identified. Left to themselves, objects of sensation admit "no words that bring them to a standstill" (οὐδὲν ὄνομα ὅτι ἂν ἱστῇ: *The-*

29

aetetus 157B4-5)—that is, which would assign to them definite characteristics. Left to themselves, in fact, sensible things are only motions that are indefinitely multitudinous (πλήθει . . . ἄπειρα: *Theaetetus* 156B1, A6). For sensible things to be identifiable is for them to possess features which persist from moment to moment, and which distinguish them each from other things. In the theory of the middle period, participation in the changeless Forms is supposed to provide the requisite features. Forms are causes in the sense of providing fixed characteristics with reference to which sensible things retain identity from moment to moment. In this sense, participation in the Forms was thought to be both necessary and sufficient for having distinguishing features. One major deficiency of the theory that becomes apparent in the *Timaeus* (see Appendix A) is that no clear conception was ever reached of how exactly changeless Forms were supposed to impart definite characteristics to changing things.

Another indication that Plato was aware of this problem, and concerned with the consequences of not being able to solve it, comes with the impasse reached in the "third man" argument we have been considering. To be identifiable requires being characterized by repeatable features, and features are patently repeatable when exhibited in similar objects. For this reason, the appearance of a common feature in several different objects was alleged to be sufficient (if not necessary[14]) for the existence of a Form corresponding to that feature. Thus Parmenides recounts one major motivation for the theory of Forms when he observes at 132A2-3 that the appearance of several large things makes us think of a single Form of Largeness. In being singular and hence determinate in this manner, Largeness is supposed to provide the defining or limiting characteristic that imparts identity to otherwise indefinite sense presentations. But if the Form itself turns out to be indefinite—turns out, in fact, to be ἄπειρα τὸ πλῆθος (132B2-3) like the motions of sensation themselves—then Forms cannot play the causal role for which they were intended.

There are, of course, various ways in which Socrates could have responded to this objection.[15] The response Plato actually puts in his mouth is noteworthy in two respects. For one, it does not appear to be a particularly strong response. It certainly is not the best Plato could have mustered if his main concern at this point were to find a viable way of avoiding the "third man" argument. Second, the response given by Socrates relates directly to Plato's primary motivation for developing the theory of Forms in the first place, to provide an ontology that will show how knowledge is possible.[16] The basic requirement in this regard is that thought must have access to immutable objects, so that knowledge can be fixed and not subject to error. Perhaps this essential provision of the theory can be protected, Socrates appears to be reasoning, if we make the Forms out to be, not objects independent of thought, with the attendant problem of how separately existing entities can impart their characteristics to sensible things, but rather thoughts themselves, without concern for their relationship to objects of sensation. Forget about the mind-independent ontology of the theory and the problems that go with it, Socrates seems to be saying in effect, and let the mental objects of thinking themselves be immutable; that is, let Forms be thoughts.

Socrates' remarks at 132B thus appear to relate to the central tenet of the theory of Forms identified above, namely (topic [3]) that the Forms are directly knowable by mind. As he puts it there, "might not each of these Forms just be a thought, properly occurring nowhere save in our minds" (μὴ τῶν εἰδῶν ἕκαστον ᾖ τούτων νόημα, καὶ οὐδαμοῦ αὐτῷ προσήκῃ ἐγγίγνεσθαι ἄλλοθι ἢ ἐν ψυχαῖς: 132B4-6)? In this way, "each [of the Forms] can be *unique*, yet not suffer the difficulties of which we have just been speaking" (ἂν ἕν γε ἕκαστον εἴη καὶ οὐκ ἂν ἔτι πάσχοι ἃ νῦν δὴ ἐλέγετο: 132B6-7).

In his brief response to this proposal, Parmenides directs the discussion back to the issues at hand. Thought, he says, must be of something that exists; and (in the case of a Form) must be of "some one thing" (ἑνός τινος: 132C3) which is thought present "in a whole range of cases" (ἐπὶ πᾶσιν ἐκεῖνο: ibid.), "constituting a certain unique character" (μίαν τινὰ οὖσαν ἰδέαν: 132C4). But is not this thing that is one and always the same in all cases a Form (132C6-7)? And given, according to the theory, that "the other things participate in Forms" (τἆλλα . . . τῶν εἰδῶν μετέχειν: 132C9-10), does not what you propose "make

31

each thing consist of thoughts, so that all [the other] things think" (ἐκ νοημάτων ἕκαστον εἶναι καὶ πάντα νοεῖν: 132C10-11); "or else there are thoughts deprived of thinking" (ἢ νοήματα ὄντα ἀνόητα εἶναι: 132C11)?

At this point Plato allows Socrates one final attempt to rescue this aspect of the theory. The way "it appears most manifest to me" (μάλιστα ἔμοιγε καταφαίνεται: 132D1), Socrates says, is that "these Forms, as it were, are patterns established in the nature of things" (τὰ μὲν εἴδη ταῦτα ὥσπερ παραδείγματα ἑστάναι ἐν τῇ φύσει: 132D1-2)—that "the other things are like them and resemble them" (τὰ δὲ ἄλλα τούτοις ἐοικέναι καὶ εἶναι ὁμοιώματα: 132D3), and that "the participation other things come to have in the Forms is nothing other than being an image of them" (καὶ ἡ μέθεξις αὕτη τοῖς ἄλλοις γίγνεσθαι τῶν εἰδῶν οὐκ ἄλλη τις ἢ εἰκασθῆναι αὐτοῖς: 132D3-5). In brief, the final attempt Socrates can muster is a reiteration of the mirror-image model of the *Timaeus* (examined and found wanting in Appendix A).

The issue Parmenides now turns to address is that of how the Forms can possibly share properties with sensible things, and how as a consequence the latter can share names with the former (topic [5]). The mode of approach here is to construct another so-called "third man" argument, superficially resembling the one at 132B-C. That the two arguments are not the same should be evident from the fact that they respond to different issues, and from the fact that they result in different conclusions.[17] The upshot of the second argument is not that Forms come to lose their determinate character, and hence fail to serve a delimiting function. It is rather that the notion of Forms as paradigms imaged in sensible objects leads to an endless multiplication of paradigms.

"If something is like a Form" (Εἰ οὖν τι . . . ἔοικεν τῷ εἴδει: 132D6), asks Parmenides, "is it possible that this thing not resemble the Form, insofar as the thing is made in its likeness" (οἷον τε ἐκεῖνο τὸ εἶδος μὴ ὅμοιον εἶναι τῷ εἰκασθέντι: 132D6-7)? And "is it not wholly necessary that the resemblance and what it resembles share one and the same character" (Τὸ δὲ ὅμοιον τῷ ὁμοίῳ ἆρ᾽ οὐ μεγάλη ἀνάγκη ἑνὸς τοῦ αὐτοῦ [εἴδους] μετέχειν: 132D10-E1)? "And will not that in which resemblances share, to be resemblances, be just the Form itself" (Οὗ δ' ἂν τὰ ὅμοια μετέχοντα ὅμοια ᾖ, οὐκ ἐκεῖνο ἔσται αὐτὸ τὸ εἶδος: 132E3-4)? But if so, Parmenides claims, nothing can resemble a Form, nor can a Form resemble other things. "For otherwise another Form will always make its appearance besides the first Form, and if that other is like the first, yet another" (εἰ δὲ μή, παρὰ τὸ εἶδος ἀεὶ ἄλλο ἀναφανήσεται εἶδος. καὶ ἂν ἐκεῖνό τῳ ὅμοιον ᾖ, ἕτερον αὖ: 132E7-133A1). "And this emergence of Forms will have no end for ever and aye, if the Form resembles what comes to participate in it" (καὶ οὐδέποτε παύσεται ἀεὶ καινὸν εἶδος γιγνόμενον, ἐὰν τὸ εἶδος τῷ ἑαυτοῦ μετέχοντι ὅμοιον γίγνηται: 133A1-3).

The problem is this. One thesis integral to the theory of Forms in the middle dialogues is that things come to share the names of Forms by participating in them.[18] Whatever the nature of this participation, it must be such as to explain the likenesses among sensible things by virtue of which several come to be called by the same name. The explanation Socrates offers here—the last explanation he can offer (and the one offered in the *Timaeus*)— is that sensible things resemble each other, and can be called by the same names, simply because they resemble the Forms themselves. Conceived in this light, participation is a matter merely of sharing likenesses. But if this is the way Socrates is going to explain likeness among several things, then he cannot escape the consequence that in each case a new likeness emerges to be explained—namely, the likeness which the Form shares with things that participate in it. And given this manner of explaining likenesses, the new likeness has to be explained with reference to a new Form; and so on indefinitely. The upshot is that likeness is not explained at all, for the explanation assumes the very thing it is intended to explain. As a consequence, Parmenides points out, "participation of other things in Forms is not a matter of likeness" (Οὐκ ἄρα ὁμοιότητι τἆλλα τῶν εἰδῶν μεταλαμβάνει: 133A5).

Parmenides thus far has raised four different objections to the theory of Forms represented by the youthful Socrates in the first part of the dialogue. None of these objections constitutes a challenge to any unambiguous thesis that Plato has maintained in earlier dialogues. Hence no pertinent question arises about specific logical moves Plato might have made to counter the objections. To the contrary, the objections draw attention to aspects of the "Socratic" theory which in one way or another have been featured in earlier dialogues, but which have never been articulated well enough to permit definitive arguments either for or against. Plato's posture at thus juncture, as he pits the formidable Parmenides against the ineffectual Socrates, is not one of raising (for some unaccountable[19] reason) objections he cannot answer against a well-formulated theory to which he considers himself committed, nor one of posing specious difficulties (for the reader to expose[20]) against a theory to which he remains committed to the end of his days. His posture rather is that of a philosopher in his prime who realizes that an embryonic theory which showed considerable promise as deployed in his earlier writing in fact has never developed much beyond the promissory stage. The role of Parmenides in the first part of the dialogue is to locate the areas in which the theory is weakest. In the second part, his role is to lay the groundwork for a radically new theory. Before passing on to this more constructive task, however, Parmenides fabricates one final argument to expose the basic difficulty of the earlier theory, and to exhibit the hopelessness of trying to repair it.

These difficulties already examined, Parmenides points out, stem from "defining as Forms things existing in and by themselves" (ὡς εἴδη ὄντα αὐτὰ καθ᾽ αὐτὰ διορίζηται: 133A9). But the greatest difficulty is this. "If the Forms are as we say they have to be [existing separately, in and by themselves], then they cannot properly even be known" (μηδὲ προσήκειν αὐτὰ γιγνώσκεσθαι ὄντα τοιαῦτα οἷά φαμεν δεῖν εἶναι τὰ εἴδη: 133B5-6). This consequence is so obvious, Parmenides says, that to maintain the contrary would require a long, laborious argument and a patient listener.

The difficulty stems from "positing each of these realities as existing in and by itself" (αὐτήν τινα καθ᾽ αὐτὴν αὐτοῦ ἑκάστου οὐσίαν τίθεται εἶναι: 133C5-6). "You would admit first off," along with anyone else taking this position (133C4), he says to Socrates, "that these beings cannot exist in our world" (ὁμολογῆσαι ἂν πρῶτον μὲν μηδεμίαν αὐτῶν εἶναι ἐν ἡμῖν: 133C6-7). The response Plato gives Socrates at this point leaves no doubt about what aspect of the theory generates the problem that is about to be exposed: "how else," he says, "could they be in and by themselves" (Πῶς γὰρ ἂν αὐτὴ καθ' αὑτὴν ἔτι εἴη: 133C8)? This final and most formidable difficulty is nothing less than an exposé of the intolerable consequences of that very feature of the theory (topic [2]) that Parmenides had stressed so heavily at the beginning of his questioning. If the Forms are entirely separate from things of sense, then we cannot know them as they are in themselves.

Parmenides begins by distinguishing "those Forms that are what they are relative to one another" (τῶν ἰδεῶν πρὸς ἀλλήλας εἰσὶν αἵ εἰσιν: 133C9-10. "These [Forms] have their being in such correlation" (αὐταὶ πρὸς αὑτὰς τὴν οὐσίαν ἔχουσιν: 133C10-D1), and are indeed what Aristotle calls "correlatives."[21] When Socrates professes not to understand, in fact, the example chosen for illustration is one of Aristotle's favorite examples—that of master and slave. In Aristotle's words, it is of a master that a slave is said to be a slave (ὁ γὰρ δοῦλος δεσπότου δοῦλος λέγεται: Categories 7a39-b1), and of course vice versa. An additional proviso upon which Parmenides insists (and which Aristotle of course would not accept) is that only Forms are correlative with Forms and only sensibles with sensibles. It is the Form Master with which the Form Slave is correlative, and not a particular slave among men, whereas a particular slave must be correlative to a particular master. As he puts it generally, "it is with things in that domain [of the Forms] that things in themselves are correlative, and in the same fashion things in our domain are correlative with themselves" (αὐτὰ αὐτῶν καὶ πρὸς αὑτὰ ἐκεῖνά τέ ἐστι, καὶ τὰ παρ' ἡμῖν ὡσαύτως πρὸς αὑτά: 133E6-134A1).

Having set up this framework of correlative terms, Parmenides moves to his conclusion in a few easy steps. "Knowledge itself is of the truly real itself" (αὐτὴ μὲν ὃ ἔστι ἐπιστήμη τῆς ὃ ἔστιν ἀλήθεια αὐτῆς: 134A4-5), "while knowledge of our world is of that which is true of our world" ('Η δὲ παρ' ἡμῖν

ἐπιστήμη . . . τῆς παρ' ἡμῖν ἂν ἀληθείας εἴη: 134A10-11).
And the same is the case with branches of knowledge in each
domain.²² "But we do not have possession of the Forms themselves, nor can they possibly exist in our world" ('Ἀλλὰ μήν
αὐτά γε τὰ εἴδη . . . οὔτε ἔχομεν οὔτε παρ' ἡμῖν οἷόν τε
εἶναι: 134B3-4). "And is not the discerning of Kinds, each as
it is itself, due to a Form itself—that of Knowledge" (Γιγνώσκεται δέ γέ . . . ὑπ' αὐτοῦ τοῦ εἴδους τοῦ τῆς ἐπιστήμης
αὐτὰ τὰ γένη ἃ ἔστιν ἔκαστα: 134B6-7)? As Socrates expresses agreement, step by step, the conclusion is immediate.
Since that Form of Knowledge "is not possessed by us" (ἡμεῖς
οὐκ ἔχομεν: 134B9), "none of the Forms at all is discerned by
us" (Οὐκ ἄρα ὑπό γε ἡμῶν γιγνώσκεται τῶν εἰδῶν οὐδέν:
134B11), "since we have no part of Knowledge itself" (ἐπειδή
αὐτῆς ἐπιστήμης οὐ μετέχομεν: 134B12). A further untoward consequence is that the perfect knowledge of the gods
cannot be concerned with human affairs.

One of the primary motives behind the theory of Forms in the
first place, as we have had several occasions to observe, was to
develop an ontology that assured the possibility of human knowledge. One of the basic tenets of this theory was that the Forms
are absolute, in the sense of existing in and by themselves. Since
sensible things, by contrast, possess only a dependent existence,
this means that the Forms and sensible things are radically separated in mode of existence. What Parmenides has shown in this
final argument is that if this thesis of radical separation is taken
strictly, a result is that human knowledge of the Forms is not
possible after all. Since it was by grasping the Forms that the
human mind was supposed by the theory to attain the certainty
typical of knowledge, the tenet of radical separation renders the
theory self-defeating.

This final consequence indicated by Parmenides is not a challenge merely to an incidental conceptual commitment that Plato
might try to dodge by one expedient or another. It is instead a
challenge to an entire ontology.²³ But at the same time it is a
challenge to a position Plato no longer considers worth defending. Like the character Socrates who presents it for dismember-
ment, this version of the theory is a thing of the past. A new

version must be constructed if Plato is going to be able to develop intelligible responses to the problems Parmenides has dramatized.

A new departure is needed. In the *Philebus*, an older and philosophically much more mature Socrates reveals the direction along which the new approach is headed, and responds to most of the problems raised in *Parmenides I*. This approach bears no sign of the separation thesis.[24] Before Socrates is ready for this assignment, however, he must undertake a rigorous course of training—far more demanding than the methods of the early dialogues. Under the guise of demonstrating this exacting exercise, Parmenides marks off the boundaries of a new ontology. For nothing less than this is the burden of *Parmenides II*.

2. The Architectonic of *Parmenides II*

The flaw in his approach that exposed Socrates to the difficulties we have been examining is that he "has set about to define Beauty, Rightness, Good, and each other Form one by one" (ὁρίζεσθαι ἐπιχειρεῖς καλόν τέ τι καὶ δίκαιον καὶ ἀγαθὸν καὶ ἓν ἕκαστον τῶν εἰδῶν: 135C9-D1) without the necessary "preliminary training" (πρὶν γυμνασθῆναι: 135C8).[25] Without this training, Parmenides warns Socrates, "the truth will escape you" (σὲ διαφεύξεται ἡ ἀλήθεια: 135D6; also 135C5-6). Submitting to the urging of the company, Parmenides reluctantly agrees to provide a demonstration. The demonstration consists of an examination of the consequences of eight hypotheses regarding the existence of Unity.

This second part of the dialogue from 137C to the end has proven itself the single most difficult and variously interpreted sustained argument in the entire Platonic corpus. Yet what Parmenides does on these pages is just what he prescribes between 135C and 136C, and this methodological prescription itself is relatively straightforward.

"If you wish to be more thoroughly disciplined" (εἰ βούλει μᾶλλον γυμνασθῆναι: 136A2), he says to Socrates, "you will not merely hypothesize that such a thing exists[26] and consider the consequences of that hypothesis" (μὴ μόνον εἰ ἔστιν ἕ-καστον ὑποτιθέμενον σκοπεῖν τὰ συμβαίνοντα ἐκ τῆς ὑπο-θέσεως: 135E9-136A1), "but also hypothesize that the same thing does not exist" (ἀλλὰ καὶ εἰ μὴ ἔστι τὸ αὐτὸ τοῦτο ὑποτίθεσθαι: 136A1-2).

Although the text does not make this certain, the contrast intended is probably with the method of hypothesis variously described at *Phaedo* 100A-101E and *Republic* 510B-511D.[27] In the former passage the philosopher is advised to hypothesize in each case the thesis he judges to be soundest (*Phaedo* 100A3-4), testing its consequences for consistency, and then to test the hypothesis itself by deriving it from a more ultimate hypothesis, and so on until he reached a hypothesis that is satisfactory (101D7-E1)—that is a hypothesis well enough established as to require no further accounting. In the latter passage the advice is similar, save that the dialectician now is characterized as someone who is not content merely to hypothesize his objects and to pursue the consequences, as the mathematician does with the odd and even (510C3-D2), but who rather treats his hypotheses as temporary starting points from which to mount toward nonhypothetical principles (511B5-7; also 510B7). In both cases the method of reasoning to be employed is a matter of deriving consequences. By drawing conclusions from his initial hypothesis and testing them for consistency (*Phaedo* 100A5, 101D5-6; *Republic* 510D1), the dialectician determines conditions necessary for the truth of the hypothesis. The major weakness of the method (see Appendix A) is that sufficient conditions are supposed to be determined in essentially the same way—by reaching an independently established starting point (a "satisfactory hypothesis" in the *Phaedo*, a "nonhypothetical beginning" in the *Republic*) from which the initial hypothesis could be derived in turn. In neither of these earlier discussions of philosophic method did Plato have more than a vague and metaphorical description of how these sufficient conditions are to be established. One notable improvement of the procedure recommended at *Parmenides* 136A is that now the philosopher has a perspicuous technique for determining sufficient conditions for the truth of his hypothesis.[28] By assuming that the thing in question does not exist, and considering the consequences of this assumption, he arrives at sufficient conditions for the thing's existence (let H be the hypothesis that a thing exists; if the denial of H entails C, then the denial of C entails H—i.e., the denial of C is sufficient for the truth of H).

Another important part of the method advocated by Parmenides is that the philosopher considers consequences not only for the thing hypothesized, but also for other things. For example, in the case of Zeno's hypothesis ("if there is a plurality") consequences must be considered for Unity as well as for plurality. Again, if it is hypothesized that likeness exists, or does not exist, the consequences must be considered under either hypothesis "both for what was hypothesized and for other things" (καὶ αὐτοῖς τοῖς ὑποτεθεῖσιν καὶ τοῖς ἄλλοις: 136B3-4). How exactly the other things are to relate to what was hypothesized, however, is not generally specified, and in fact is left to the philosopher's discretion (136C2). In particular, no requirements are made that "the others" be limited to Forms or to sensible things. That Forms would be acceptable in this role is evident both from the specification at 135E3-4 that the method applies to Forms, and is not to be confined to sensible things, and from the contrast above of (presumably) the Form Unity with the plurality of Zeno's hypothesis. That sensible things also are acceptable, on the other hand, is evident both from the things Parmenides mentions as possible subjects for hypothesis (motion, generation, and perishing, 136B5-6), and from the others chosen to contrast with Unity in the demonstration following. A consequence of Hypothesis VII, for example, is that the others must be indefinitely multitudinous (ἄπειρος . . . πλήθει: 164D1; also 165C1-2); and a Form could never answer to that description.

Thus far we have identified four different considerations to be pursued in application of the method to a given topic. Given a thing or character A (e.g., plurality, likeness, generation), and what is other than that thing or character ("other-than-A") we must consider the consequences both for A and for other-than-A of the two hypotheses, "if A exists," and "if A does not exist." One further provision makes the method complete. In considering the consequences for A of a given hypothesis, A could figure in these considerations either with reference just to itself or with reference to other-than-*A*, and other-than-A could enter in turn with reference either to itself or to *A*. As we see with even a preliminary reading of the demonstration following, whether consequences for a thing are considered with reference to the thing itself or with reference to other things makes a radical difference in the outcome of the reasoning. This in fact is what we should expect on the basis of the criticism of the doctrine of separation between Forms and sensible things in *Parmenides I*. The hallmark of the theory of Forms during the middle period was that Forms have their being in and by themselves, and that the philosopher should treat them as such in his dialectical investigations. The final argument of Parmenides in the first part of the dialogue showed that this doctrine, strictly construed, makes the Forms unknowable, a result soon to be reinforced under the first hypothesis. To save the theory of Forms as an intelligible account of how knowledge is possible, it is necessary to consider the Forms in relation to other things—not just in and by themselves.

With this final distinction between things considered with reference to themselves alone and things considered with reference to other things, dialectical examination of a given thing or character *A* is expanded to include eight steps in all: under the hypothesis that A exists, we consider the consequences for *A* (1) with reference to itself and (2) with reference to other-than-*A*, and the consequences for other-than-*A* with reference (3) to itself (themselves) and (4) to *A*; and under the hypothesis that *A* does not exist, we consider the consequences for *A* and other-than-*A* respectively with reference (5) and (6) to the former, as well as (7) and (8) to the latter. As Parmenides puts it by way of summing up, whenever you hypothesize that something exists, or does not exist, or "has any other character" (ὁτιοῦν ἄλλο πάθος πάσχοντος: 136B8), you ought to consider the consequences "with reference to itself and with reference (a) to any one of the others you may select or (b) to several, or (c) to all in that manner" (πρὸς αὐτὸ καὶ πρὸς ἓν ἕκαστον τῶν ἄλλων, ὅτι ἂν προέλῃ, καὶ πρὸς πλείω καὶ πρὸς σύμπαντα ὡσαύτως: 136C1-3); "and the others with reference to themselves and to whatever other you may have selected, whether you have hypothesized the thing to exist or not to exist" (καὶ τἆλλα αὖ πρὸς αὐτά τε καὶ πρὸς ἄλλο ὅτι ἂν ἀεὶ προαιρῇ, ἐάντε ὡς ὂν ὑποθῇ ὃ ὑπετίθεσο, ἐάντε ὡς μὴ ὄν: 136C3-5).

Eight steps are included in the technique which Parmenides cautions is the only way to gain "ability to discern the truth" (κυρίως διόψεσθαι τὸ ἀληθές: 136C5-6). And eight hypotheses follow in his demonstrations. A reasonable first step in our approach to these hypotheses is to correlate them with the steps specified in the description of the method. To do this, we must determine for each hypothesis (i) whether the Unity in question is affirmed or denied to exist, (ii) whether consequences are drawn from the hypothesis for Unity itself or for things other than Unity, and (iii) whether the consequences are for that factor (Unity or others) with reference to itself or to the other factor.

Determination of (i) and (ii) can be made immediately on the basis of a simple list of hypotheses and conclusions. Since each conclusion either attributes or denies basically the same set of characters either to Unity or to the others, and since many of these characters are mutually opposed, we may refer to them summarily (with Parmenides at 159A7-8) as "all the contrary characters," or "these characters" for short. The eight hypotheses, with their associated conclusions in summary form, are as follows:

I. If Unity exists (137C), it has none of these characters (142A).

II. If Unity exists (142B), it has all these characters (155E).

III. If Unity exists (157B), the others have all these characters (159A).

IV. If Unity exists (159B), the others have none of these characters (164A-B).

V. If Unity does not exist (160B), it appears to have all these characters (163B).

VI. If Unity does not exist (163B), it has none of these characters (164B).

41

VII. If Unity does not exist (164B), the others appear to have all these characters (165D).

VIII. If Unity does not exist (165E), the others neither have nor appear to have these characters (166B).

From this list, it is clear that Hypotheses I through IV affirm the existence of Unity, while V through VIII deny it, and that I, II, V, and VI yield conclusions about Unity, while the remaining conclusions are about the others.

To determine which of these conclusions are about Unity with reference to itself, however, or about Unity with reference to the others, and so forth, requires a somewhat more penetrating examination of the text. A clue is provided by the way Unity is characterized at the initial statement of each hypothesis—a characterization that is by no means uniform across all eight hypotheses.[29]

In the remarks immediately following the introduction of the first hypothesis (εἰ ἕν ἐστιν: 137C4), Unity is denied either to have parts or to be a whole on the grounds that it "is not many but one itself" (μὴ πολλὰ ἀλλ᾽ ἓν αὐτὸ εἶναι: 137D2-3). If the expression ἓν αὐτὸ εἶναι is understood to mean that this Unity exists in and by itself, it is entirely predictable that in the consequences drawn over the next several pages this Unity has neither limit, shape, nor place, is neither at rest nor in motion, is neither similar nor dissimilar, and so on. In brief, the subject of Hypothesis I is a Unity that admits no relationships to other things. Necessarily, the conclusions following from hypothesizing such a Unity must be drawn for that Unity with reference to itself alone.

Hypothesis II, on the other hand, posits a Unity that is immediately identified as "having being" (οὐσίας . . . μετέχειν: 142B6)—a "being that is not the same as Unity" (οὐ ταὐτὸν οὖσα τῷ ἑνί: 142B7-8). Thus from the beginning we realize that the argument drawing consequences from this hypothesis is about a Unity admitting relationships to other things.[30] The summary statement of these consequences, to the effect that "whatever characters happen to apply to the others apply to Unity as well" (καὶ ὅσαπερ καὶ περὶ τἆλλα τῶν τοιούτων τυγχάνει ὄντα,

42

καὶ περὶ τὸ ἓν ἔστιν: 155E1-2), makes explicit that these consequences pertain to Unity with reference to the others.

The argument based on Hypothesis III,[31] as Parmenides notes (157B5), leads to conclusions about the others; and although different, "these others nonetheless are not wholly lacking in Unity, but somehow participate in it" (Οὐδὲ μὴν στέρεταί γε παντάπασι τοῦ ἑνὸς τἆλλα, ἀλλὰ μετέχει πῃ: 157C1-2). Among these conclusions for things other than Unity is the following: that "from the combination of them with Unity there is generated some other thing in them that makes them determinate toward one another" (ἐκ μὲν τοῦ ἑνὸς καὶ ἐξ ἑαυτῶν κοινωνησάντων . . . ἕτερόν τι γίγνεσθαι ἐν αὐτοῖς, ὃ δὴ πέρας παρέσχε πρὸς ἄλληλα: 158D3-6). Clearly, this conclusion concerns the others with reference to Unity.

By contrast, Hypothesis IV generates an argument regarding the other things, based on the explicit understanding that these "others are separate from Unity" (χωρὶς δὲ τἆλλα τοῦ ἑνός: 159B8). The conclusion of this argument is that these others have no characters at all, "completely lacking [as they are] in Unity" (τοῦ ἑνός γε πάντως στερομένοις: 160B1-2.[32] Hypothesis IV thus produces consequences for the others with reference merely to themselves.

Although Hypotheses V and VI both deny the existence of Unity, the Unities concerned are not the same. Although nonexistent, the Unity of Hypothesis V is identified as something knowable (γνωστόν: 160C7) and distinguishable from the others (διάφορον τῶν ἄλλων: 160D1-2); hence it relates to other things. In tracing out its relationship with all the characters, this argument treats Unity with reference to the others. Hypothesis VI, however, concerns a Unity which "partakes of existence in no way whatever" (οὐδέ μῃ μετέχει οὐσίας: 163C7), such that "nothing can exist in relationship to it" (μηδὲν αὐτῷ δεῖ εἶναι: 164A5). The conclusion at 164B3-4 that this Unity is without characterization thus pertains to Unity with reference to itself.

Hypotheses VII and VIII also deny the existence of Unity, and lead to consequences for other things. Although Unity does not exist, the others under Hypothesis VII at least appear to be one, both individually (164E1-2) and collectively (165B6-C1). Its conclusion concerns the others in apparent reference to Unity. Under Hypothesis VIII, however, the others neither are (165E5) nor appear (166A1) to be one or many, hence are totally removed from Unity. Its consequences treat these others with reference only to themselves.

These textual references provide an unambiguous identification of the subject concerning which conclusions are drawn under each of the eight hypotheses, and hence enable an unproblematic correlation with the eight steps specified as part of the philosophic method Parmenides undertakes to demonstrate. Combining this information with other prominent features of the arguments noted above, we can devise a perspicuous representation showing for each hypothesis (a) whether the existence of Unity is affirmed or denied, (b) the subject of the inferences that the hypothesis generates, and (c) its summary conclusion regarding possession of the characters in question.

	If (a)	then (b)	(c)
I	Unity is	Unity πρὸς Unity	has no characters
II	Unity is	Unity πρὸς others	has all characters
III	Unity is	others πρὸς Unity	have all characters
IV	Unity is	others πρὸς others	have no characters
V	Unity is not	Unity πρὸς others	has all characters (apparently)
VI	Unity is not	Unity πρὸς Unity	has no characters
VII	Unity is not	others πρὸς Unity	have all characters (apparently)
VIII	Unity is not	others πρὸς others	have no characters (even apparently)

This schema not only shows that all steps are accounted for in the demonstration, but also exhibits a striking symmetry between the first and second sets of four hypotheses.[33] The question arises whether the symmetry is incidental, or whether grouping is pertinent to interpretation.

This question of grouping is all the more crucial because modern commentators have assumed, without notable exception, that the hypotheses should be paired for interpretative purposes in order of their appearance within the dialogue (I with II, III with IV, and so forth). This assumption almost certainly is erroneous.[34] The main difficulties with pairing I and II, for instance, are (1) that they posit the existence of different Unities, and (2) that they yield conclusions about Unity considered in different relationships. The two hypotheses yield conclusions about Unity in different relationships in that conclusions of the first are about Unity with reference to itself, while those of the second are about Unity with reference to others. They posit the existence of different Unities, as already noted, in that the Unity of Hypothesis I exists in and by itself, not admitting relationships with other things, while this restriction is explicitly removed under Hypothesis II. Thus the customary pairing of Hypotheses I and II violates the instruction at 135E8-136A2, that the seeker after truth should consider the hypothesis that a certain thing exists, in conjunction with the hypothesis that the *same thing* (τὸ αὐτὸ τοῦτο: 136A1-2) does not exist. A further difficulty with the customary pairing is that the only explicit directive Parmenides provides in this regard is that a hypothesis asserting existence should be paired with one denying it, which clearly requires that if Hypothesis I is to be considered in conjunction with another hypothesis at all this other must be selected from the second group of four.

In view of these considerations, the table above leaves no doubt about the proper pairing for interpretive purposes. Hypothesis I should be paired with a hypothesis denying the existence of a Unity that admits no relationships with other things, and generating conclusions about that Unity with reference to itself—that is, with Hypothesis VI. For parallel reasons, II should be paired with V, III with VII, and IV with VIII.

One erroneous inference many commentators have drawn from the customary pairing is that each hypothesis yields conclusions that are contradicted by those of another. For example, the summary conclusion of Hypothesis I appears on superficial reading to be contradicted by that of Hypothesis II, and so forth for III and IV, V and VI, and VII and VIII. But I and II are not about the same Unity, nor are III and IV, and so forth. Given the proper pairing of I with VI, however, not only is there no contradiction between the two hypotheses (either genuine or apparent), but moreover the two exist in a very interesting logical relationship.

Associated appropriately with its consequence, Hypothesis I reads, "If Unity exists, then this Unity with reference to itself has no characters." In like fashion, Hypothesis VI and its consequence amount to, "If Unity does not exist, then this Unity with reference to itself has no characters." Since the Unity in both cases is the same (a Unity admitting no relationships with other things), and since the consequence in both cases is identical, we have a conjunction of two conditional propositions of the form 'if p then q, and if not-p then q', which resolves into the unconditional proposition q. That is to say, Hypotheses I and VI appropriately associated with their consequences yield the unconditional conclusion that the Unity in question has no characters. The Unity in question is a Unity that is entirely separate from other things, but otherwise unspecified.

This consequence can scarcely be without relevance to the first part of the dialogue, where Parmenides exposes the difficulties of the immature theory of Forms. For in that discussion the Forms several times were referred to as unities (132A1, 132C6, 135B9),[35] and the fact that they were conceived as entirely separate from sensible things (called 'others' at 130E6, 131E5, 132A5, 133A5, passim), as we have seen, was stressed repeatedly. In addition to the other difficulties involved in conceiving the Forms as separate units, which were pointed out in the uneven exchange between Parmenides and Socrates, Plato in the second part of the dialogue has indicated what may well be the most basic difficulty of all. If the Forms are conceived as unities entirely separate from other things, then they must be denied all characteristics whatsoever. The notion of such Forms is not even intelligible—is subject to "neither knowledge, opinion, perception nor discourse" (ἢ ἐπιστήμη ἢ δόξα ἢ αἴσθησις ἢ λόγος: 164B1-2; also 142A3-4). This consequence is directly entailed by the argument of *Parmenides II*. The apparent fact that it has remained hidden to commentators for twenty-five hundred years attests to the importance of the question about how the several hypotheses are related.

46

An equally devastating result follows from combining the consequences of Hypotheses IV and VIII. By the same pattern of inference (by which 'if p then q' in conjunction with 'if not-p then q' entails q unconditionally), it follows in the case of a unique Form entirely separate from other things that these others also have no characters at all. Far from helping explain how sensible things come to exhibit certain properties, the theory of separated Forms here is shown actually to preclude such an explanation.

These difficulties posed by conceiving the Forms as entirely separate unities, moreover, cannot be resolved merely by opening the Forms up to relationships with other things indiscriminately. This is shown by a combined result of Hypotheses II, III, V, and VII. Hypotheses II and III show, in their summary conclusions, that in the case of an existing Unity which admits relationships with other things both the others and Unity itself have all the characters. In like fashion, Hypotheses V and VII show that if such a Unity does not exist, then both Unity itself and the other things appear to have all the characters. Whether this Unity exists or not, accordingly, it is indistinguishable from the other things to which it is related. Other basic differences (than in mode of existence) in the ontological roles assigned "Unity" and "the others" must be brought into account before a solution can be found for the problems of radical separation.

A preliminary examination of the logical relationships among the eight hypotheses of *Parmenides II* has shown that this second part of the dialogue continues the attack begun in the first on the doctrine, typical of Plato's middle dialogues, that the Forms are separate in being from sensible things. Considered on this level of generality, and without regard to the question of the soundness of the often very complex arguments following the several hypotheses themselves, these critical inferences in the second part are logically impeccable. It would be too improbable to surmise that Plato did not put them there for us to discover.

Also lurking within the architectonic of the second part of the dialogue, however, is a devastating critique of the central doctrine of the historical Parmenides. Although Plato's deep respect for Parmenides may have inspired his choice of the character through which the Socratic theory of the separated Forms would be dismantled, it did not prevent Plato from using Parmenides also as a spokesman through whom the basic tenet of the "Way of Truth" would be directly countered.[36] The basic tenet of Parmenides' doctrine was that One Being alone exists, without differentiation of any sort. Essential to this claim are both (a) that this One exists (μόνος δ' ἔτι μῦθος ὁδοῖο λείπεται ὡς ἔστιν, "there is only one way left to be spoken of, that it is": fragment 8, 1-2[37]); and (b) that other things, by contrast, do not exist (οὐ γὰρ μήποτε τοῦτο δαμῇ εἶναι μὴ ἐόντα, "for never shall this be proved, that things that are not are": fragment 7,1). Among the effects of Hypotheses I, IV, VI, and VIII in combination, we find, are direct denials of (a) and (b). As the argument following Hypothesis I purports to demonstrate, the consequence of assuming a strict Unity admitting no relationships to other things is that this Unity has no characters whatever. Exactly the same consequence follows from assuming that such a Unity does not exist, which is the burden of the argument following Hypothesis VI. The combined effect of these arguments thus is that the existence of this Unity is indistinguishable from its nonexistence; in neither case does it possess any thinkable characters. "That it is" is no more thinkable or sayable than "that it is not," which Parmenides prohibited in his "Way of Truth" (οὐ γὰρ φατὸν οὐδὲ νοητὸν ἔστιν ὅπως οὐκ ἔστι, "for it is not to be said or thought that it is not": fragment 8,8-9). Hence to maintain (a) that this Unity exists (and does not "not exist") is an untenable thesis.

Aligned against (b) we find the consequence that, in the case of this exclusive Unity, there is no contrast whatever between it and the others. This consequence follows from I and IV among the affirmative hypotheses, and VI and VIII among the negative. Assuming with I and IV that this Unity exists, Parmenides concludes that neither Unity nor the others have or even appear to have any characters. Whether Unity exists or not, it is indistinguishable from the other with which it allegedly is contrasted.

As in the *Sophist* where Plato, arguing through an Eleatic Stranger, mounted a respectful but firm attack against the two most formative influences of an earlier period—Socrates, the

"Sophist of Noble Lineage," and "the mighty Parmenides"—so here in the *Parmenides* itself he solidifies his case against these two great masters. The stage is set for a new beginning.

3. TAKING SIDES IN AN ANCIENT CONTROVERSY

Whatever his actual motivation, Plato had at least two reasons for repudiating the influence of the historical Parmenides. One was his growing dissatisfaction with the doctrine of the separated Forms, existing in and by themselves entirely apart from sensible objects. Plato's original concern in espousing this doctrine, Aristotle tells us (*Metaphysics* 1078b13-17), was to develop an ontology providing for the possibility of knowledge. Within the confines of the later period, however, not only is the doctrine explicitly criticized in the *Parmenides*, but moreover it plays no role whatever in the two dialogues directly concerned with ontological problems of knowledge—the *Sophist* and the *Philebus*. Although the account of the "blending Forms" and the associated analysis of the conditions of true and false discourse in the *Sophist* are stated in the terminology of eternal objects (Forms, Ideas, Kinds), no sharp opposition appears in that dialogue between sensible things and proper objects of knowledge. If it were otherwise, then the Stranger's choice of illustrations of true and false discourse from the realm of the sensible ("A man understands," 262C8; "Theaetetus sits," 263A2; and "Theaetetus flies," 263A8) would seem singularly inappropriate.[38] Plato's break with the doctrine of radical separation, nonetheless, is made "official" only in the *Philebus*. For in that dialogue, not only are Forms and sensible things both viewed as being constituted from more ultimate principles, but moreover knowledge of becoming (ἐπιστήμης . . . ἐπὶ τὰ γιγνόμενα: 61D1-E1) is given explicit status.

Plato's second reason for taking a stand against Parmenides has to do with a theme that will dominate the discussion from this point onward. Aristotle strikes the keynote with his rather startling remark in the *Metaphysics*, immediately after canvassing the views of the Pythagoreans on relevant topics, that the philosophy of Plato "in most respects conformed with these views" (τὰ μὲν πολλὰ τούτοις ἀκολουθοῦσα: 987a30). This remark is followed by a rather lengthy comparison of Platonic with Pythagorean ontological doctrines, in which the differences between them appear surprisingly minimal. Difficulties in making sense out of these passages, and others like them sprinkled throughout the *Metaphysics*, have caused endless controversy among the commentators. One thing upon which they generally have agreed, however, is that Aristotle is referring in these passages to views typical of Plato's later period. This topic will be explored in the following chapter. For the moment it is enough to observe that, according to long tradition, Plato's views at some point took a Pythagorean shift.

The presence of such a shift is evident in *Parmenides II*. For whatever immediate personal reasons, from this point onward Plato is a partisan of the Pythagorean viewpoint.[39]

Although it is not without precedent to detect Pythagorean sympathies in the second part of the *Parmenides* (e.g., Cornford [1939]), the extent of Plato's involvement in the disagreement between the Eleatic and the Pythagorean viewpoints has not generally been noted.[40] I have already indicated how the overall structure of argument in *Parmenides II* yields consequences directly opposed to basic Eleatic doctrines. It remains to be shown how the individual arguments join the controversy on a more particular level. In this section it will be seen (1) that the several arguments following Hypothesis I are directed one by one against specific claims in Parmenides' "Way of Truth," and (2) that the several arguments following Hypothesis II are aimed in sequence to establish the possibility of a Pythagorean derivation of sensible things from numbers.

The topics treated under Hypothesis I are the following, in order of appearance:[41]

(1) limit and the unlimited (137D)
(2) shape (137E)
(3) place (138A-B)
(4) motion and rest (138B-139B)
(5) same and other (139B-E)

50

(6) similar and dissimilar (139E-140B)
(7) equal and unequal (140B-D)
(8) temporal order (140D-141D)

The conclusions of the several arguments pertaining to these topics, in effect, are that all descriptions under each heading are to be denied the Unity that admits no relationships with other things: in sum, that such a Unity in no sense is, has no properties or relations, has no name or description, and cannot be the subject of opinion, knowledge, or perception (141E9-142A4).

Item by item, the eight topics treated under the first hypothesis correspond to prominent features attributed by Parmenides to the single being in the "Way of Truth." There is no more direct way to show this than to reproduce several lines from fragment 8,[42] although several topics could be illustrated from other fragments as well. In the passage below, key Greek expressions are noted in parentheses, with numbers indicating corresponding topics from the list above.

> But, motionless [ἀκίνητον (4)] within [ἐν (3)] the limits [πείρασι (1)] of mighty bonds, it is without beginning or end, since coming into being and perishing have been driven [ἐπλάχθησαν (8)][43] far away, cast out by true belief. Abiding the same [ταὐτόν (5)] in the same place [ἐν ταὐτῷ (3) (5)] it rests [κεῖται (4)] by itself, and so abides firm where it is; for strong Necessity holds it firm within [ἐν (3)] the bonds of the limit [πείρατος (1)] that keeps it back on every side, because it is not lawful that what is should be unlimited [ἀτελεύτητον (1)]. . . . But since there is a furthest limit [πεῖρας (1)], it is bounded [τετελεσμένον (1)] on every side, like [ἐναλίγκιον (6)] the bulk of a well-rounded sphere [εὐκύκλου (2)], from the center equally balanced [ἰσοπαλὲς (7)] in every direction . . . for being equal [ἴσον (7)] to itself on every side, it rests uniformly within [ἐν (3)] its limits [πείρασι (1)].

Every character positively attributed to the One Being in this passage from Parmenides is expressly denied in the course of the argument following Hypothesis 1 of the dialogue, and every topic under that hypothesis figures in Parmenides' description of this Being. That this should be entirely coincidental would be too much coincidence to assume. In effect, Plato seems to be responding to the "Way of Truth" by pointing out that every attribute figuring in the characterization there of Parmenides' single existing Unity is ruled out under the assumption that such a Unity exists. Although characters can be denied this Unity without mishap ("it is without beginning or end"), any positive attribution—even of privative features ("motionless")—runs in contradiction of a Unity that exists by itself exclusively.

The ultimate rejection of Parmenides' single existing Unity, of course, is the conclusion at 141E9 that "such a Unity in no sense can participate in being" (Οὐδαμῶς ἄρα τὸ ἓν οὐσίας μετέχει). Strict adherence to the assumption of a Unity that exists in and by itself, and hence admits no relationships with other things, dictates the conclusion that such a Unity cannot even relate to being. The assumption of such a Unity is self-contradictory.[44]

Parmenides II thus contains two distinct frontal attacks on the central thesis of historical Eleaticism. The first is among the conclusions strictly implied by the conjunction of conditional propositions comprised by the several hypotheses and their associated consequences. In their most general form, as we have seen, these conclusions are that the existence of a strictly exclusive Unity is indistinguishable from its nonexistence, and that things other than this Unity are indistinguishable from the Unity itself. The second massive attack on the historical Eleatic position is to show, as the arguments under the first hypothesis purport to do, that nothing Parmenides actually said in description of his exclusively existing Being could consistently be maintained, including the statement that such a Unity exists. The undeniable appearance of two such attacks as these can leave no doubt about Plato's rejection of Eleaticism as he moves into his final period.

Equally undeniable, however, is the appearance under the second hypothesis of a sustained argument in defense of two basic Pythagorean theses. One is that Unity generates number, the other that number is constitutive of sensible things. Against a history of Eleatic attempts to discredit these theses, the argument under Hypothesis II purports to show (1) that if Unity exists, then number exists also, and (2) that if number exists then there might exist things with properties and relations characteristic of spatiotemporal objects.

The logical key to this derivation is the order in which the eight topics are treated, which is the same as the order of treatment under the first hypothesis. Topics (1) through (4) are ordered by the relationship of necessary conditionality. Nothing can have shape, for example, unless it is limited—for the simple reason that shape is the border a thing shares with what surrounds it. Nothing can have place, in turn, unless it has shape. Or, to put it the other way around, having limit (1) is a necessary condition of having shape (2), which in turn is a necessary condition of having place (3). A logical consequence is that having limit (1) is a necessary condition of having place (3).[45] Since motion is change of place, and rest remaining in place, finally, having place (3) is a necessary condition of (4) rest and motion. In brief, (1) is necessary for (2), (2) for (3), and (3) for (4). For purposes of Hypothesis I, this order permits considerable efficiency of argument, since once Parmenides has established that the Unity of that hypothesis does not admit limit, relatively direct proofs can be constructed to show that it admits neither shape, nor place, nor motion and rest in turn.

In the context of Hypothesis II, where Parmenides is driving toward the general conclusion that the Unity which relates to other things (unlike the strictly exclusive Unity of the first hypothesis) admits characterization under all eight headings, no comparable logical tactic appears available. Given that (1) is necessary for (2), (2) for (3), and (3) for (4), it could of course be shown that the relevant Unity admits characterization under (1), (2), and (3) by showing that it admits characterization under heading (4) itself. The problem with this possible approach seems to be that in order to show this for (4), it is necessary first to show it under the other three headings. At any rate, Parmenides' tactic is to show first that the relevant Unity admits characterization under (1), and then to show that the manner in which this is so leaves open the possibility of its being characterized under (2). And so, mutatis mutandis, for (3) and (4). Since the move from affirming characterization under (1) to affirming it under (2), and so forth, requires more logical work than the move from denial of (1) to denial of (2), which was the tactic under the previous hypothesis, treatment of these four headings takes considerably longer under the second (142C-146A) than under the first hypothesis (137C-139B).

Headings (2) through (4) pertain to properties. The next three headings, same and other (5), similar and dissimilar (6), and equal and unequal (7), pertain to relations. A similar order exists among these three headings of relationship. Unless a thing admits being same or other, it cannot admit similarity (sameness in some respect) or dissimilarity, and further it can admit neither equal (sameness in all relevant respects) nor unequal. Hence the argument under Hypothesis I can establish with dispatch (from 139B to 140E) that if the exclusive Unity is neither same nor other, it cannot be either similar or dissimilar, or either equal or unequal. A much longer argument (146A to 151E) is required under Hypothesis II to show that this other Unity does admit characterization under these three headings in sequence.

Plato's Pythagorean intentions begin to surface with the initial argument from 142B to 145A. The aim of this section in the overall scheme is to show that the Unity of Hypothesis II is both limited and unlimited. On the way toward this goal, however, Parmenides produces two independent generative arguments, the combined effect of which is to demonstrate that if this Unity exists, then number must exist also. The first of these two arguments (142B-143A) shows that Unity yields an unlimited multitude.

Starting for the second time with the hypothesis "if unity exists," Parmenides reasons that this existing Unity must "partake of Being" (οὐσίας . . . μετέχειν: 142B6) which is not the same as the Unity itself. Hence this existing thing will have two constituents (μόρια: 142D5), unity and being. As member of a pair, however, each of these constituents itself is one, and as being an aspect of an existing thing each also possesses (literally, neither is wanting in—ἀπολείπεσθον: 142E1) being. Each of the two constituents of the original Unity thus itself has two constituents, namely being and unity, each of which in turn possess being and unity, ad infinitum. The consequence is that any constituent "always necessarily is becoming two, and never is one at any time" (ἀνάγκη δύ ἀεὶ γιγνόμενον μηδέποτε ἓν εἶναι: 142E7-143A1). What is one being thus turns out to be "unlimited in multitude" (ἄπειρον . . . πλῆθος: 143A2).

Positing an existing Unity, Parmenides demonstrates the existence of a numberless multitude. It is important to be clear about the sense in which this multitude is numberless. The ἄπειρον πλῆθος here in question is not the infinite series of positive integers, nor any number series whatever.[46] Rather, the constituents within the ἄπειρον πλῆθος fail to be integral, hence are numberless in the sense of lacking identity. For, as Parmenides has pointed out at 142E7-143A1, any supposedly single constituent necessarily and always is becoming two.

Despite the inherently unlimited character of this multitude, however, it possesses the capacity for being transformed into a number series.[47] Any transformation that would accomplish this would amount to the imposition of a limiting principle within the multitude that would impart the character of unity to its members seriatim. In terms specific to the present context, the ἄπειρον πλῆθος generated from the existing Unity could be made into a number series by participation of its members in πέρας or limit.

From our present vantagepoint various conceptual devices appear available that could achieve this effect. One of the simplest would be to conceive unity and being as states in a binary code (say, unity = 1, being = 0), with successive divisions of constituents ordered by level in an "inverse tree" as follows:

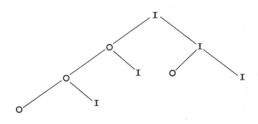

Each element then would be identified uniquely (would acquire limit and hence uniqueness) by its place in the array, and the endless process of "always becoming two" (142E7-143A1) would amount to an endless expansion of the resulting series rather than a loss of identity of previously generated elements. The result would be equivalent to an expression of the natural number series in binary notation:

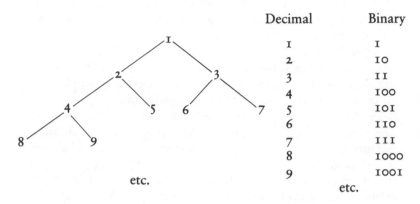

	Decimal	Binary
	I	I
	2	10
	3	11
	4	100
	5	101
	6	110
	7	111
	8	1000
	9	1001
etc.		etc.

This device would not have been available to Plato, however, since he did not have the binary notation.

Another expedient would be to define a successor relationship, to specify a first element, and then to generate an infinitely long series of successors to that element with an appropriately selected set of axioms, including the axiom that all successors of members themselves are members, and an axiom (or assurance in some other form) that additional members are always available. Identification of this series with the series of natural numbers would then be accomplished by defining the first member as the smallest integer,[48] and by defining the basic arithmetical operations (addition, multiplication, etc.) within the series. But since Greek mathematics had not reached a comparable level of formalization, this approach also was not available to Plato.

The technique Plato actually uses, however, is similar to the above in important respects. Instead of generating a series of elements based on the successor relationship, and then defining

56

multiplication and the other operations of arithmetic, Plato assumes the operation of multiplication and then projects the series of positive integers by successive application of this operation. And instead of positing an axiom of infinity to assure the endless availability of additional members, he relies (implicitly)⁴⁹ upon the demonstration of unlimited plurality accomplished by the argument from 142B to 143A. As with the axiomatic approach just summarized, however, Plato begins with what he understands to be the smallest integer (two).

Given a Unity that has being (ἓν οὐσίας μετέσχεν: 143B3), necessarily this Unity and its being are different things. Since it is neither Unity nor being that makes them different, but rather a third thing, difference, there are several pairs of things we might select: being and difference, being and Unity, or Unity and difference (143C1-2). In each case we may speak of a pair, or two; and each member of a given pair is one. Starting with an existing Unity, Parmenides thus establishes the existence of the number two and of the numerical unit. The number three then can be arrived at by adding this unit to a given pair. And with two and three we have the odd and the even. Successive numbers then are specified as products of 2 × 2, 2 × 3, 3 × 3, etc., or in general in terms of odd and even. As Parmenides puts it, there might be "even taken even times, odd taken odd times, even taken odd times, and odd taken even times" (Ἄρτια τε ἄρα ἀρτιάκις ἂν εἴη καὶ περιττὰ περιττάκις καὶ ἄρτια περιττάκις καὶ περιττὰ ἀρτιάκις: 143E7-144A1). And "if that is so," he asks rhetorically, "can any number remain that is not necessarily existent" (Εἰ οὖν ταῦτα οὕτως ἔχει, οἴει τινὰ ἀριθμὸν ὑπολείπεσθαι ὃν οὐκ ἀνάγκη εἶναι: 144A2-3)?

An obvious anomaly of this derivation of number is that it is incapable of establishing a place for the primes within the number series.⁵⁰ To remedy this it would be enough to augment multiplication with addition as generative relations. Then five could be defined as the sum of two and three, and all subsequent primes defined by successive additions of two.⁵¹ Perhaps Plato intended to introduce summation as a generally available operation in the derivation when at 143D three was generated by adding one to a pair.⁵² Whatever the explanation of this apparent oversight,

Parmenides announces that as a result of this derivation the existence of number has been established. Under the assumption of an existing Unity, both an unlimited multitude of elements and a device for introducing serial order among these elements have been constructed. Thus "if Unity exists," he concludes, "there must also be number" (Εἰ ἄρα ἔστιν ἕν, ἀνάγκη καὶ ἀριθμὸν εἶναι: 144A4-5). This is the first mention of number under the second hypothesis. The next step is to show that Unity admits limit.

Yet surely if number exists, Parmenides continues, "there might be indefinitely many things that exist" (ἂν εἴη καὶ πλῆθος ἄπειρον τῶν ὄντων: 144A5-6);[53] for number—indefinitely many as has been shown—also has being. Thus being is distributed over the smallest and the largest, and has an "unlimited number of parts" (μέρη ἀπέραντα: 144C1).[54] Moreover, each of these parts itself is one, so Unity is distributed as widely as being. In this respect Unity and being are equal (ἐξισοῦσθον: 144E2),[55] both having the greatest multitude of parts (πλεῖστα . . . μέρη: 144C1-2, D7). Both in fact are indefinitely numerous (ἄπειρα . . . πλῆθός: 144E5).

A perfunctory final step shows that this Unity which can yield indefinitely many numbers therefore admits limit. The parts of Unity are parts of a whole, and are contained by the whole. But a container is a limit. The conclusion of the first argument at 145A1-3 thus is that this existing Unity is one and many, whole and parts, and both limited (shown at 144E) and an unlimited multitude (shown at 143A).

The question has been raised whether this argument itself in any sense constitutes a generation of number.[56] Clearly it does not in any sense that involves production—as might be suggested by one interpretation of Aristotle's remark at *Metaphysics* 987b33-988a1 that for Plato the numbers could be produced from the dyad as from some plastic material. What has been shown by the argument (questions of soundness aside) is rather that if the Unity of Hypothesis II exists then nothing bars numbers from existing also. The effect of the argument, as noted previously, is to defend a basic Pythagorean thesis against Eleatic attack. According to several ancient authorities,[57] the Pythagoreans had maintained that numbers proceed from the One. According to some commentators, at least, Zeno's argument against plurality was directed toward this Pythagorean doctrine specifically.[58] The form of Zeno's argument was hypothetical:[59] if plurality exists, then such and such consequences follow. Since these consequences presumably were unacceptable to the Pythagoreans, Zeno's argument amounted to a reductio ad absurdum of their view—a view in which plurality was a necessary ingredient. Plato's argument through the character of Parmenides is basically of the same form. Strategically, however, it is even more powerful than that of Zeno. For it not only shows that the hypothesis of Unity, typical of the Eleatic philosophers, leads to the conclusion that many things exist—thus convicting the Eleatic view of inconsistency—but it shows moreover that this hypothesis leads to consequences affirming the existence of "the many" in the very manifestation which the Eleatics found so objectionable—the numbers of the Pythagoreans. This is the sense in which Parmenides' argument (to the ghostly horror of his historical counterpart) "generates" numbers. It shows that *if* Unity is assumed to exist, the Unity of the Eleatics which admits being, then nothing can stand in the way of affirming the existence of numbers also.[60] In a masterful rhetorical turnabout, Plato has his character Parmenides show that the historical Parmenides and his school, while affirming their single being, cannot consistently deny the numerical plurality of the Pythagoreans.

According to traditional Pythagorean doctrine, moreover, not only are numbers generated from Unity, but moreover numbers are the cause in turn of sensible things. As Aristotle says repeatedly in the *Metaphysics*, the Pythagoreans "took the elements of number to be the elements of all things" (τὰ τῶν ἀριθμῶν στοιχεῖα τῶν ὄντων στοιχεῖα πάντων ὑπέλαβον εἶναι: 986a1-2), they said that "numbers are the causes of the existence of the other things" (τὸ τοὺς ἀριθμοὺς αἰτίους εἶναι τοῖς ἄλλοις τῆς οὐσίας: 987b24-25), and they considered that "number is principle both as matter for things and as modifications and permanent states" (τὸν ἀριθμὸν . . . ἀρχὴν εἶναι καὶ ὡς ὕλην τοῖς οὖσι καὶ ὡς πάθη τε καὶ ἕξεις: 986a16-17). Plato's next task on the agenda for his turncoat Parmenides is to show, in stepwise progression, that if the Unity of Hypothesis II exists, and has the numerical characteristics just demonstrated, then it might have the properties and relations characteristic of sensible things. In particular, Parmenides shows that if there is number, and the limit typical of number, then there might be things characterizable by shape, place, motion and rest, and all the other features denied the Unity of the first hypothesis.

We will return to the arguments under several of these headings in later sections. Moreover, the arguments become increasingly complex as the list progresses, and little would be gained for present purposes by dwelling indiscriminately upon their structural details. There is one aspect of the brief argument at 145A-B to the effect that Unity might have shape, however, that is noteworthy with regard to Pythagorean antecedents. Now "since it is limited," the argument begins, "it will have extremes" (ἐπεί-περ πεπερασμένον, καὶ ἔσχατα ἔχον: 145A4-5). And "if a whole," as has been established, "might not it have beginning, middle, and end" (εἰ ὅλον, οὐ καὶ ἀρχὴν ἂν ἔχοι καὶ μέσον καὶ τελευτήν: 145A5-6)? That the limits of this thing include beginning and end follows from a proposition that has already been agreed upon at 137D7-8, namely "the beginning and end of each thing are its limits" (τελευτή . . . καὶ ἀρχὴ πέρας ἑκάστου). That the middle is also included follows from the definition at 145B2-3, identifying "the middle as equally removed from the extremes" (τό γε μέσον ἴσον τῶν ἐσχάτων ἀπέχει). So "the one being of this sort," it turns out, "might partake in some sort of figure" (σχήματος δή τινος . . . τοιοῦτον ὂν μετέχοι ἂν τὸ ἕν: 145B4-5)—whether straight, round or a mixture of these. The upshot is that this Unity might possibly have shape. And on the basis of its admitting spatial properties, Parmenides then proceeds with his argument that it also admits place, motion and rest, and so forth, down through temporal order.

What makes this passage particularly noteworthy for our purposes is that the Pythagoreans also apparently considered the trio "beginning, middle, and end" to be among the basic determinations of the sensible world. As Aristotle records in *De Caelo*, they held that "beginning, middle, and end give the number of everything—the triad—and thus the world and all in it are de-limited by three" (τὸ πᾶν καὶ τὰ πάντα τοῖς τρισὶν ὥρισται, τελευτὴ γὰρ καὶ μέσον καὶ ἀρχὴ τὸν ἀριθμὸν ἔχει τὸν τοῦ παντός . . . τῆς τριάδος: 268a12-14). Similar references to this trio as basic determinants of the universe appear other places in Plato's writings. In the *Laws*, the Athenian alludes to the "old saying" that "god holds the beginning, the middle, and the end of all that is" (θεός . . . ἀρχήν τε καὶ τελευτὴν καὶ μέσα τῶν ὄντων ἁπάντων ἔχων: 715E8-716A1). And in the *Philebus*, Soc-rates berates pleasure by saying it belongs to that class—the unlimited (τὸ ἄπειρον)—"which does not and never will in itself or from itself hold either the beginning, the middle, or the end" (μήτε ἀρχὴν μήτε μέσα μήτε τέλος ἐν αὐτῷ ἀφ' ἑαυτοῦ ἔχοντος μηδὲ ἕξοντός ποτε: 31A9-10). The composite picture derived from these remarks is that, according to an old tradition, "beginning, middle, and end" are fundamental among the de-termining factors of everything in the world, that they pertain to limit rather than the unlimited, and that this old tradition is Pythagorean. Given Plato's intentions of justifying against Eleatic attack the Pythagorean program of generation from number, it presumably is not coincidental that, after number, this trio is the first in his list of derivations.

Our examination of the arguments of *Parmenides II* has shown thus far (1) that these arguments contain a multileveled and massive attack on basic Eleatic doctrines, and (2) that they pur-portedly establish the credibility against Eleatic attack of the Pythagorean theses that number is generated from Unity and sensible things from number. If the arguments are sound, in other words, it has been shown that the Eleatics are necessarily wrong and that the Pythagoreans just might be right. But susceptibility to Eleatic attack was not the only problem besetting the Pythag-orean program. There was in addition the staggering problem of incommensurability, about which much has yet to be said. Moreover, no hints have emerged thus far about how Plato is going to attempt to manage the problems of radical separation that have proved to be the downfall of the Socratic theory of Forms. If Plato is going to give rein to his obvious attraction toward Pythagorean ontology, these are issues he will not choose to ignore—and they are difficult issues indeed.

The full result of Plato's preoccupation with these issues does not appear in the *Parmenides*. It is reserved for the *Philebus* instead. But there are several features of the argument in *Parmenides II* that foreshadow these future developments, and that are interesting in their own light. An examination of these features will prepare us for the later dialogue.

4. Anticipations of the Indefinite Dyad

The expression ἄπειρον πλῆθος appears infrequently throughout the dialogues. Of somewhat more than a dozen occurrences overall, over half are in the *Parmenides*, and five are in the passage 143A-145A pertaining to the derivation of number. As noted previously, the expression carries two quite distinct meanings within this passage. At 143A2 it refers to a multitude that is numberless in the sense of lacking definite constituents. This multitude fails to contain even one distinct element, since every part of it always is becoming two (142E7-143A1). It is not a set with indefinitely (or infinitely) many members, for in fact it has no specific members at all. And the reason it has no specific members is that no part of it is ever unified (143A1). When unity is brought to this limitless multitude in the form of limit imposed by the multiplier operation, however, the result is a set of specific elements that is numerically unlimited in membership. At 144A6 and 144E5, accordingly, the expression ἄπειρον πλῆθος refers to an indefinitely (or infinitely) numerous set of elements, each of which is unique unto itself. This latter is the sense also conveyed at *Theaetetus* 147D8-9, where the young mathematician is referring to an indefinite (or infinite) number of irrational roots. This possibly is the sense also at *Theaetetus* 156A6 and B1, where Socrates is describing the motions (also called δυνάμεις, as are the irrational roots at 147D) that make up the sensible world. The former sense of indefinitely multitudinous, on the other hand, is conveyed by the expression at *Republic* 525A4-5, at *Philebus* 17B4 and E2-3, and in the remainder of its appearances in *Par-*

menides II.[61] These other appearances follow Hypotheses III and VII.

At 157B5, Parmenides once again poses the hypothesis that Unity exists, this time to consider the consequences for the others with reference to Unity itself. To begin with, "that which is other than Unity has parts" (τὰ ἄλλα τοῦ ἑνὸς μόρια ἔχοντα: 157C3), since "should [these others] have no parts they would be entirely one" (εἰ γὰρ μόρια μὴ ἔχοι, παντελῶς ἂν ἓν εἴη: 157C3-4). "But that of which they are parts is a whole" (Μόρια . . . τούτου ἐστὶν ὃ ἂν ὅλον ᾖ: 157C4-5), and "a whole must be one consisting of many" (τό γε ὅλον ἓν ἐκ πολλῶν ἀνάγκη εἶναι: 157C6). It apparently follows that the parts must be part of many. And yet, Parmenides says, "each of the parts cannot be a part of many" (ἕκαστον γὰρ τῶν μορίων οὐ πολλῶν μόριον χρὴ εἶναι: 157C7-8), else each would be part of itself, which is impossible (157D1-2). The way out of this apparent paradox is to distinguish two respects in which the others are ἄπειρον πλῆθος, corresponding to the distinction between part in the sense of member and part in the sense of character.

In one sense, "a part is part not of many or all, but of some single form or unity we call a whole" (Οὐκ ἄρα τῶν πολλῶν οὐδὲ πάντων τὸ μόριον μόριον, ἀλλὰ μιᾶς τινος ἰδέας καὶ ἑνός τινος ὃ καλοῦμεν ὅλον: 157D8-E1). Such a part (μόρια, as distinct from mere μέρος) belongs to the whole, not as member of a collection, but as constituent of an unsegmented unity. An example might be unity itself, which is constituent of any given whole as one of its essential characteristics. The other sense, of course, is that of part as member of a whole collection, each member of which "is a kind of unity, differentiated from the others, and being by itself" (εἶναι ἓν δήπου . . . ἀφωρισμένον μὲν τῶν ἄλλων, καθ' αὑτὸ δὲ ὄν: 158A1-3).

Now in both these senses, Parmenides argues, the others participating in Unity must be unlimited in multitude. Consider first the others which by participating in Unity become a whole. These things are other than the Unity in which they come to participate. Whatever these other constituents might be, as "others than Unity they would be many" (Τὰ δ' ἕτερα τοῦ ἑνὸς πολλά που ἂν εἴη: 158B2-3). Considering next the others as members of a collection, we see that they too are not Unity but are different from Unity and hence many. In both cases, then—"those participating in Unity as part and those participating as whole" (τά τε τοῦ ἑνὸς μορίου καὶ τὰ τοῦ ἑνὸς ὅλου μετέχοντα: 158B6-7)—"those things that come to take on Unity, just by themselves, necessarily are multitudinous without limit" (ἀνάγκη ἤδη πλήθει ἄπειρα εἶναι αὐτά γε ἐκεῖνα τὰ μεταλαμβάνοντα τοῦ ἑνός: 158B7-8). We may see this as follows, says Parmenides. "These things take on Unity. But at the time when they take on Unity, they neither are one nor participate in Unity" (Ἄλλο τι οὐχ ἓν ὄντα οὐδὲ μετέχοντα τοῦ ἑνὸς τότε, ὅτε μεταλαμβάνει αὐτοῦ, μεταλαμβάνει: 158B9-C1). Hence they are multitudes (πλήθη: 158C1) from which Unity is absent.

In these terse and difficult passages, Parmenides is proposing an exercise in abstraction. We are to think of a collection of individual members in such a fashion as to be able to distinguish between the collection as a unified whole and the unity that makes it a whole, on the one hand, and on the other between its parts as unique individuals and the unity that makes each unique. In either case, the result is the same. Without Unity, neither whole nor part is anything other than sheer multitude. The unlimited character of this multitude is stressed by continuing the conceptual exercise in the following manner.

Let us "abstract in thought the portion that seems to us smallest" (ἐθέλοιμεν τῇ διανοίᾳ τῶν τοιούτων ἀθελεῖν ὡς οἷοί τέ ἐσμεν ὅτι ὀλίγιστον: 158C2-4). "That very part itself, since it does not partake of Unity, must be not one but a multitude" (ἀνάγκη . . . τὸ ἀφαιρεθὲν ἐκεῖνο, εἴπερ τοῦ ἑνὸς μὴ μετέχοι, πλῆθος εἶναι καὶ οὐχ ἕν: 158C4-5). "Considering again and ever again the nature other than the Form in this way, just in and by itself, we see that it forever is unlimited in multitude" (ἀεὶ σκοποῦντες αὐτὴν καθ' αὑτὴν τὴν ἑτέραν φύσιν τοῦ εἴδους ὅσον ἂν αὐτῆς ἀεὶ ὁρῶμεν ἄπειρον ἔσται πλήθει: 158C6-8).

The final appearance of the expression ἄπειρον πλῆθος in this dialogue occurs in the context of Hypothesis VII. If Unity is not, Parmenides asks at 164B5, what befalls the others? The conclusion to which this question leads is parallel to the conclusion of the third hypothesis. Whereas the third hypothesis yields the consequence that things other than Unity have all the relevant characters, however, the conclusion of the seventh is merely that the others appear to have these various characters. As with the case of the third hypothesis also, it is the interpretation of "the others" rather than the conclusion itself that is presently of interest.

Without Unity, the "otherness" of the other things must be "according to multitudes" (Κατὰ πλήθη: 164C7), rather than "according to one" (κατὰ ἓν: 164C8), since there is "no single thing" (μὴ ὄντος ἑνός: 164C8). Consider a given mass (ὄγκος: 164D1) of such others, and take from it what seems to be a minimum (σμικρότατον: 164D2). Since comparison is only between multitudes, this minimum must also be a multitude. So "what was previously taken for one suddenly appears many, and the smallest immense, with reference to the cuts within it" (ἐξαίφνης ἀντὶ ἑνὸς δόξαντος εἶναι πολλὰ καὶ ἀντὶ σμικροτάτου παμμέγεθες πρὸς τὰ κερματιζόμενα ἐξ αὐτοῦ: 164D3-5). The result is that any such given mass is multitudinous without limit (ἄπειρός . . . πλήθει: 164D1). As under Hypothesis III, things other than Unity considered in abstraction from Unity are (or in the present case, seem to be) an unlimited multitude—a mass not differentiable into individual parts.

Considered as indeterminately multiple, the ἄπειρον πλῆθος of Hypothesis VII is indistinguishable not only from that of Hypothesis III but also from that of 143A involved in the derivation of numbers. In the latter case, the indefiniteness arises from a partitioning process in which every part is constantly becoming two (δύ' ἀεὶ γιγνόμενον: 142E7-143A1). Under Hypothesis III the indefiniteness arises from abstracting the unifying factor from a whole with individual parts. And under Hypothesis VII it results from contrasting multitude with multitude, in absence of a Unity with which to contrast it. At 143A, again, combining limit with the ἄπειρον πλῆθος yields the integral numbers, and this limit is provided in the form of operations that make each a single number. In brief, it is by participating in Unity that the ἄπειρον πλῆθος yields the number series. Under Hypothesis III, combination of the ἄπειρον πλῆθος with Unity yields a whole with uniquely individual parts. And under Hypothesis VII, the ἄπειρον πλῆθος is of such a nature that only the addition of Unity, should it exist, would remove the indefiniteness of the multitudinous mass. In each case, the limit that makes the difference between sheer unlimited multiplicity and a set of numerically distinct parts is Unity itself—a Unity which, under Hypotheses II, III, and VII, admits relationships with other things. It is clear that, in the context of these hypotheses, the unlimited multitude and Unity constitute a pair of principles of fundamental importance.

This observation finds support in some texts by Aristotle. At *Parmenides* 158C6-7, the ἄπειρον πλῆθος is referred to as "the nature other than the Form" (τὴν ἑτέραν φύσιν τοῦ εἴδους), where the Form in question must be either Unity or the limit brought by Unity.[62] The expression τὴν ἑτέραν φύσιν is sufficiently unusual in Greek philosophy to make it worthy of note that exactly the same words appear at *Metaphysics* 987b33, at the end of a lengthy comparison of Platonic with Pythagorean ontology. The differences Aristotle points out between these two systems are surprisingly few, but one difference he emphasizes concerns this "other nature." Whereas the Pythagoreans thought that "the Unlimited and Unity" (ἄπειρον καὶ τὸ ἕν: *Metaphysics* 987a16; also 18) were principles (ἀρχὰς: 987a14) of things, Plato thought the principles were "the Great and the Small" (τὸ μέγα καὶ τὸ μικρὸν: 987b20) and Unity (τὸ ἕν: 987b21). Moreover, Plato thought that "the numbers come from these [the Great and the Small] by participation in Unity" (ἐξ ἐκείνων γὰρ κατὰ μέθεξιν τοῦ ἑνὸς [τὰ εἴδη] εἶναι τοὺς ἀριθμούς: 987b21-22.[63] The reason Plato made the "other nature" (τὴν ἑτέραν φύσιν: 987b33) a dyad, Aristotle said, is because he thought that "the numbers, other than the primes, could be neatly produced from it as from some plastic material" (τοὺς ἀριθμοὺς ἔξω τῶν πρώτων εὐφυῶς ἐξ αὐτῆς γεννᾶσθαι ὥσπερ ἔκ τινος ἐκμαγείου: 987b33-988a1).

There are some striking parallels between these remarks by Aristotle and the passages we have been considering from *Parmenides II*. If we were to retain the Pythagorean terminology for the two basic principles ("unlimited and Unity," instead of "The

Great and the Small and Unity" attributed to Plato) we would have a close description of what Plato actually tries to accomplish in the passages of the *Parmenides* that we have been examining. The main difference is that the Pythagoreans called their principle other than Unity the ἄπειρον, whereas Plato in the *Parmenides* speaks of the ἄπειρον πλῆθος. The terminological similarity is less immediate if we compare what Plato said in the *Parmenides* with what Aristotle said in his behalf in the *Metaphysics*. In the dialogue, the basic principles are the Unlimited Multitude and Unity; in the Aristotelian account, the Great and the Small and Unity. But the fact remains that what Plato seems to be doing in these passages of the *Parmenides* with the Unlimited Multitude and Unity is just what Aristotle said he did with Unity and the Great and the Small. For one thing, he establishes the existence of numbers on the basis of these two principles. For another, he shows how the spatiotemporal properties of sensible things are possible given the properties of the numbers thus generated. And as Aristotle says at *Metaphysics* 987b24-25, for both Plato and the Pythagoreans "numbers are the causes of the being of other things" (τοὺς ἀριθμοὺς αἰτίους εἶναι τοῖς ἄλλοις τῆς οὐσίας). Another conditional comparison thus is in order. If what Aristotle called the Great and the Small is what Plato referred to as the ἄπειρον πλῆθος, then Aristotle's description of Plato's ontology, in these respects at least, matches what we find in *Parmenides II*.

Tentative as it is, the hint that maybe Aristotle used different terminology in describing Plato's ontological position from what Plato himself ever used in the dialogues is worth pursuing for at least two reasons. One is that the passages quoted above are part of a section of the *Metaphysics* that commentators have found perennially puzzling, largely on the basis of not being able to find a corresponding position in Plato's writings. The other is that coming to understand these passages, if that proves possible, may help us reach a better understanding of the later dialogues. We return for a closer look at these passages in the following chapter.

Even if we were to become convinced of some correspondence between these passages from the *Metaphysics* and what Plato does in *Parmenides II*, however, no especially significant accomplishment on Plato's part would thereby be revealed. What we have observed thus far is an attempt by Plato to vindicate the traditional Pythagorean program by showing (i) that the existence of numbers must be admitted by anyone who accepts an existing Unity, and (ii) that the possibility of sensible things follows from the existence of numbers. This in itself does not constitute an advance in Plato's own ontological thinking. In particular, it does not solve the problems of participation that carry over from the first part of the *Parmenides*, nor, as far as Pythagorean ontology itself is concerned, does it suggest any solution to the fundamental problem of incommensurability.

There are two other developments in *Parmenides II* that foreshadow subsequent approaches to these problems which emerge in the *Philebus*. The first of these is the appearance under both Hypotheses I and II of language and concepts associated with an especially significant section of Euclid's *Elements*. The second is a particular way of introducing limit in the corollary to Hypothesis II (155E-157B), which resembles an important mathematical discovery attributed to Eudoxus, a sometime member of Plato's Academy. We will consider first the association with Euclid's *Elements*.

The seventh topic treated under both Hypotheses I and II, as noted above, is that of the equal and unequal. In the case of this particular topic, not only is the order of treatment identical under the two hypotheses but moreover the language of the respective passages displays striking parallels. At 140B-D, Parmenides undertakes to demonstrate that the Unity not admitting relationships to other things can be neither equal nor unequal to itself or to others. The argument begins with the observation that, if Unity is equal, "it will have the same measures[64] as that to which it is equal" (τῶν αὐτῶν μέτρων ἔσται ἐκείνῳ ᾧ ἂν ἴσον ᾖ: 140B7-8). Apart from its intuitively apt character, this conception of equality appears identical to that operating in Book V of the *Elements*.[65] Although the Unity of *Parmenides* 140B is not identified as a number or even a magnitude specifically, the sense of equality involved in that passage corresponds to the sense of equality first applied by Euclid to magnitudes generally in Definition v of Book v.

Since by Proposition 15, Book v, parts of magnitudes are in the same ratios as their equimultiples, it follows by Proposition 10 that magnitudes sharing a measure are greater or smaller one to another as they admit more or fewer applications of this common measure. This is exactly the sense of the next remark at *Parmenides* 140B9-C2, namely that if Unity is greater or less than other things "with which it is commensurable, it will have more measures than the lesser, fewer than the greater" (οἷς μὲν ἂν σύμμετρον ᾖ, τῶν μὲν ἐλαττόνων πλείω μέτρα ἕξει, τῶν δὲ μειζόνων ἐλάττω). The most significant feature of this passage for our purposes, however, appears at 140C3-4, where it is remarked that if Unity is incommensurable (μὴ σύμμετρον) with other things, then (with implicit reference to equinumerous measures on the part of these other things) "it will have larger measures on the one hand, smaller on the other" (τῶν μὲν σμικροτέρων, τῶν δὲ μειζόνων μέτρων ἔσται). Obvious as the proposition may be that of two given incommensurable magnitudes evenly divided into the same number of measures, the measure of the larger will be greater than the measure of the smaller, this proposition is never explicitly derived in the *Elements*. What is significant about 140C3-4 is the very attempt itself to extend this treatment of greater and smaller in terms of measure to incommensurable magnitudes. The reason it is significant is that Book v of the *Elements* has been recognized since antiquity as containing a general theory of proportions, "the discovery of Eudoxus, the teacher of Plato,"[66] applicable to commensurable and incommensurable magnitudes alike. This theory constitutes a solution to the problem of incommensurability that had plagued the early Pythagoreans, which solution was likened by Dedekind himself[67] to the definition of number known as the "Dedekind cut." The nature of this solution will be examined in the following chapter. For the while it is enough to remark that this explicit reference to incommensurable as distinct from commensurable quantities at *Parmenides* 140C2 is further evidence that Plato was aware of the mathematical developments leading to Book v of the *Elements* when he wrote this passage on the topic of equality.

Under Hypothesis II, preparation for the topic of equality begins at 148D with a discussion of various considerations regarding contact and containment. The general conclusion under this topic comes with the statement at 151B6-7 that Unity (this time a Unity admitting relationships with other things) is equal to, greater than, and less than, both itself and the others. Then, as if by way of coda to a conclusion already established, Parmenides again introduces the topic of comparative measure.

Regarding this Unity which is greater and less and small, he says, "it would be of greater and lesser and equal measures, both to itself and to others; and if of measures then of parts" (ἴσων ἂν εἴη μέτρων καὶ πλειόνων καὶ ἐλαττόνων αὑτῷ τε καὶ τοῖς ἄλλοις, ἐπειδὴ δὲ μέτρων, καὶ μερῶν: 151B8-C2).[68] This single passage repeats exactly what was said in the pair of passages 140B7-8 and 140B9-10 earlier, but without specific limitation to commensurable magnitudes. The interesting innovation in this later context comes at 151C2-5, where Parmenides introduces comparisons in number on the basis of comparisons in measure. "Being of equal, greater and lesser measures," he says, this Unity "would be lesser and greater than both itself and the others in number also, and equal to itself and the others in the same respect" (Ἴσων μὲν ἄρα μέτρων ὂν καὶ πλειόνων καὶ ἐλαττόνων, καὶ ἀριθμῷ ἔλαττον ἂν καὶ πλέον εἴη αὐτό τε αὑτοῦ καὶ τῶν ἄλλων καὶ ἴσον αὑτῷ τε καὶ τοῖς ἄλλοις κατὰ ταὐτά). The reason is that if it is greater than something it would have more measures, and hence parts, and if lesser, fewer, and if equal, the same (151C5-8). And having equal parts, it would be equal in quantity, and having more and fewer it would be greater or lesser in number (ἀριθμὸν: 151D4). The final conclusion of this section also is expressed in terms of number: thus it seems that "Unity will be equal, greater and lesser in number, both to itself and to the others" (τὸ ἓν καὶ ἴσον καὶ πλέον καὶ ἔλαττον τὸν ἀριθμὸν αὐτό τε αὑτοῦ ἔσται καὶ τῶν ἄλλων: 151E1-2).

This movement from comparisons in measure to comparisons in number is interesting for several reasons. One is that this extension of comparisons in magnitude to comparisons in number parallels in a general fashion the extension in the *Elements* from the treatment of magnitudes in Book v to the treatment of numbers in Book vii. Despite this general parallelism in sequence between the two approaches, however, one difference is particularly noteworthy. It is generally recognized that the treatment of proportions in Book vii,[69] and indeed the entire treatment of number in that book, is limited to commensurable numbers. This as a consequence of the definition of number upon which the treatment of this book is premised: A number is a multitude composed of units. Thus what Euclid says about numbers in terms of measures applies only to commensurable numbers. Plato, on the other hand, has introduced number at 151C in such a fashion that it does not require limitation to commensurable numbers alone. At 140C he has provided a manner in which incommensurable magnitudes can be compared with respect to measures—not in terms of different multiples of the same measure, as in the case of commensurables, but in terms of the same multiples of different measures. One magnitude is larger or smaller than another incommensurable with it if the two are measured equal times over by measures which are larger or smaller than each other, as the case might be. There is no reason why this comparative technique should not be extended, in the general manner of 151C, to provide a means for comparing incommensurable numbers as well. Two incommensurable numbers would be greater or lesser if measured equal times over by greater or lesser measures. Indeed, there is an intuitively clear interpretation of Eudoxus' theory of proportions (by De Morgan[70]), which we will examine in the next chapter, that relies upon exactly this device for comparing incommensurable numbers.

Yet another point to note in this connection is that the conception of number which surfaces at 151C is not the same as that at 144A-E. In this earlier context, the numbers generated out of Unity and the Unlimited Multitude are provided limits in terms of ordinary arithmetical operations. At 151C, numbers take on arithmetical properties (are comparable as equal, greater, or lesser) which are explicated in terms of measure. As we shall see, it is just this conception of measure as limiting factor that appears to have been involved in Eudoxus' treatment of incommensurable numbers. From the viewpoint of the picture beginning to emerge of Plato's later ontology, it is no accident that the concept of limit plays a featured role in the *Philebus*.

One further hint of the direction Plato seems to be moving during this transitional period appears in the corollary on temporal becoming at 155E-157B. Given that the Unity of the second hypothesis has been shown to partake of all the opposing characters, a question arises about the nature of its transition from one to another. In general, for any character in which it comes to partake, there is a time when it partakes and a time when it does not. When having been in motion it comes to rest, or having been at rest it comes to move, for instance, during the transition "it cannot occupy any specific time at all" (μηδ' ἐν ἑνὶ χρόνῳ εἶναι: 156C3). The reason is that between the time when it ceases to be at rest (or in motion) and the time it begins to be in motion (or at rest), it is neither in motion nor at rest. But "there is no time during which a thing, all at once, is neither in motion nor at rest" (Χρόνος δέ γε οὐδεὶς ἔστιν, ἐν ᾧ τι οἷόν τε ἅμα μήτε κινεῖσθαι μήτε ἑστάναι: 156C6-8). Therefore there is no time during which Unity (or any one thing at all) could make the transition from movement to rest, or from any state whatever to another state. "But is there then this queer thing, in which it would be, when changing" (Ἆρ' οὖν ἔστι τὸ ἄτοπον τοῦτο, ἐν ᾧ τότ' ἂν εἴη, ὅτε μεταβάλλει: 156D1-2)—(Aristotle interrupts)[71]—the instant (Τὸ ἐξαίφνης: 156D3)? For 'instant' seems to mean that in which change occurs from something to something else. Although indeed there is no change from rest while the thing is still at rest, nor from motion as long as it is still in motion, the instant—this thing of paradoxical nature (φύσις ἄτοπός: 156D7)—lies as a mean (μεταξὺ: 156D7) between motion and rest. In this position "it occupies no time at all" (ἐν χρόνῳ οὐδενὶ οὖσα: 156E1).

By the same account, in passing from one to many, from combining to separating, from like to unlike, or vice versa, a thing makes its transition at an atemporal instant that stands as a mean (μεταξὺ: 157A2) between its opposing characters. Finally, a thing going from small to great or equal, or in the opposite direction, is neither small, great, nor equal as the change occurs.

Contrary to an otherwise natural presumption of mathematical irrelevance on the part of this discussion of temporal notions, there is reason to expect that Plato's conception of time would be related to his conception of number. For one thing, Eudoxus' theory of proportions applies to magnitudes in general, and thus applies to times and numbers alike.[72] If this theory is a prominent feature of the background against which Plato's treatment of number at 151C-D should be understood, as suggested above, then it might naturally pertain to this treatment of time as well.[73] Further indications that number and time were closely associated in the thinking of the fourth-century Greeks appear in the Aristotelian corpus. At *Posterior Analytics* 74a18-25, for instance, where he is discussing a proof of proportionate alternation, Aristotle remarks that although previously this property had been proved separately for numbers, lengths, solids and durations, now the proof is commensurately universal, in virtue of the common character shared by all these quantities. A more explicit instance occurs in the *Physics* where, in a discussion of the "now" (νῦν) similar in several respects to Plato's treatment of the instant, Aristotle speaks of time as continuous (συνεχής: 220a5,26), with the "now" as limit (πέρας: 220a21) but not as part (μόριον: 220a19). In that respect, the "now" both is like the numerical unit (μονὰς ἀριθμοῦ: 220a4) and itself is number (ἀριθμός: 220a22). Furthermore, Plato himself explicitly associated number and time in the well-known passage at *Timaeus* 37D5-8, where time is described as the moving image of eternity "proceeding according to number" (κατ' ἀριθμὸν ἰοῦσαν: 37D7-8).

Let us recapitulate. In the Pythagorean-inspired discussion following Hypothesis II, Plato shows both that numbers can be generated from the ἄπειρον πλῆθος and Unity, and that if numbers exist, then so possibly might sensible things. This reminded us of Aristotle's remark in the *Metaphysics* that, whereas the Pythagoreans thought that numbers and sensible things come from the ἄπειρον and Unity, Plato thought they come from the Great and the Small and Unity instead. Guided by the conjecture

73

that what Plato called the ἄπειρον πλῆθος in the *Parmenides* he might have called "the Great and the Small" in some other context, we examined two aspects of the dialogue that might help explain this possible change in terminology. First is the treatment of the equal and unequal following Hypotheses I and II, which strongly suggests that Plato was aware of then current developments in the mathematical theory of incommensurables which led to Definition 5, Book V, of Euclid's *Elements*. This is the theory that Dedekind in the past century cited as anticipating his own definition of irrational numbers as sections or "cuts" in a continuum of lesser and greater numbers. Plato's probable awareness of this theory is indicated, secondly, by his discussion of temporal becoming in which time is treated as a continuum of before and after (lesser and greater elapsed duration) sectioned by the "paradoxical" instant. In brief, while the early Pythagoreans had conceived both number and sensible things as coming from Unity imposed on the ἄπειρον, and whereas Plato himself in the *Parmenides* showed how both could come from Unity imposed on the ἄπειρον πλῆθος, current mathematical research generated both numbers and things in time (= sensible things) from unique "cuts" imposed on a continuum of greater and lesser. If Plato did in fact sometimes refer to these basic ontological principles as "the Great and the Small and Unity," as Aristotle reports, then it appears he may have had a mathematical precedent.

These observations regarding otherwise disparate passages in the second part of the *Parmenides* do not establish that Eudoxus' theory of proportions is the key to Aristotle's baffling remarks about the Great and the Small in Plato's philosophy, nor that the solution to the problem of incommensurables provided by this theory plays an essential role in the development of Plato's later philosophy itself. The effect of these observations is to recommend further investigation of the possibility that such may be the case. This is the purpose of the following chapter.

CHAPTER TWO

HISTORICAL GLIMPSES AT
THE EMERGING THEORY

1. Plato's "So-Called Unwritten Teaching"

This chapter is sharply limited both in scope and purpose. Its purpose is to provide a probable historical background for the *Philebus*, against which the more recalcitrant ontological passages of this dialogue will become intelligible. Its scope includes various mathematical developments of the fifth and fourth centuries B.C., and various reports on Plato's philosophy by subsequent commentators, but in either case only reports and developments that appear to contribute importantly to this historical background.

The merely probable character of this background should be understood in advance. First and foremost, it is merely probable because it deals with intellectual events for which only very few and very sparse primary sources are still available. Since these events have been of considerable interest to scholars of several diverse disciplines—notably classics, classical philosophy, and the history of mathematics—the paucity of primary sources has resulted in ever-expanding bodies of conjectural and interpretive literature. Necessarily, this literature provides an important access to the developments in question. Yet to become deeply involved with this literature would be both imprudent and impractical. It would be imprudent because this literature, even within isolated areas, shows little tendency toward consensus. Every conclusion accepted on one authority could be countered by another, with the result that what was intended as a sketch of a circumscribed period of intellectual history would be under pressure to become a history of interpretive controversy instead.

It would be impractical, moreover, because of the prohibitive expenditure of research time and printed space that would be required to make a fair representation of even the major interpretive alternatives.

Given the purpose noted above, our course is best guided by the principles of seeking out secondary sources that are authoritative if not definitive, and of avoiding engagement in controversial issues that appear extraneous to our interest in the *Philebus*.

The structure of argument in this chapter is basically hypothetical. In the case of a few conjectured historical developments, I attempt to show (a) that if things happened in about this way we might expect to find certain consequences reflected in Plato's very late thought, (b) that it is plausible to think that things happened in about this way, and hence (c) that it is reasonable to look for these consequences in the *Philebus*. The actual search for these consequences is left for the final chapter. Success of the present chapter thus is to be measured in terms of interpretive fertility, without concern for historical completeness.

There is no better illustration of the constraint this approach dictates than that provided by the issue of the "esoteric teachings." This issue centers on a series of remarks by Aristotle and certain early commentators about a lecture (or lectures) given by Plato on the topic of the Good.

In his review of the natural philosophers in Book 1 of the *Physics*, Aristotle refers parenthetically to the Great and the Small of Plato (187a17), which Plato treats as matter with the One as Form. Commenting on this passage, Simplicius (the sixth-century Neoplatonist) remarks that Aristotle, in his (now lost) work on the Good, had recorded Plato's doctrine that "the Indefinite Dyad, which is called Great and Small" (ἡ ἀόριστος δυάς, ἣν μέγα καὶ μικρὸν ἔλεγεν: 151.7-8),[1] along with Unity are principles of all things, including the Ideas themselves, and says further that the same information could be got from the written reports of Speusippus and Xenocrates, who with Aristotle had attended "Plato's lecture on the Good" (τῇ Περὶ τἀγαθοῦ Πλάτωνος ἀκροάσει: 151.10). Later in the same commentary, Simplicius alludes to Plato's discourses (plural λόγοις: 453.28) on the Good, which were attended by Aristotle and other named companions of Plato who recorded his "enigmatic utterances" (ῥηθέντα αἰνιγματωδῶς: 453.30). In these discourses, Simplicius said, Plato made the Indefinite Dyad and Unity principles of sensible things, located the Indefinite Dyad in the domain of the mind, and referred to it (or the Great and [the] Small) by name as ἄπειρον (453.27,28). Simplicius then goes on to quote a rather lengthy passage from Porphyry, discussing the reports of Plato's listeners (which Porphyry thought might be in accord with the *Philebus*: 454.19), and another from Alexander, which Simplicius also thought agreed with Plato's talk on the Good (454.20). Among other statements Porphyry represents Plato's listeners as reporting is that Unity and the (Indefinite: 454.8,16) Dyad are elements of number (454.15). The Indefinite Dyad, Porphyry says, was also called by Plato the Great and (the) Small (453.36). And although the comments attributed to Alexander are somewhat garbled, he is represented as saying unequivocally that each of the numbers participates (μετέχει: 455.7) in Unity and in the Indefinite Dyad (ἀορίστου δυάδος: 455.7-8), and that Plato said that the Ideas are numbers (455.8). Another source is Aristoxenus, who tells of the story that Aristotle, his mentor, used to relate about Plato's lecture on the Good, concerning such matters as numbers and geometry, which led up to the claim that the Good is Unity, and which thereby confounded his unsuspecting audience.[2]

A reference to clearly related matters by Aristotle himself occurs at *Metaphysics* 988a7-17, where Aristotle summarizes certain Platonic doctrines which he has just finished reviewing. At the end of this summary, Aristotle adds that Plato assigned Unity and the Great and (the) Small as causes of good and evil, one to each, leaving to the reader the obvious inference that Unity somehow is the cause of good. At *Metaphysics* 1091b13-14, moreover, Aristotle says explicitly that some who admit an unmovable substance say that Unity is the Good itself, suggesting that this position is held by those for whom the Forms are numbers (1091b26). Since elsewhere (e.g., *Metaphysics* 991b9, *De Anima* 404b24) Aristotle says that Plato identified Forms with numbers, the implication seems to be that Plato also identified

Unity with the Good. Moreover, *Physics* 209b15 alludes explicitly to Plato's "unwritten teachings" (ἀγράφοις δόγμασιν), while at *De Anima* 404b19 there occurs a passage which *might* (see below) be read to refer to Plato's "lectures on philosophy." Further weight is lent to Aristotle's apparent reference to "unwritten doctrines" by the later commentators Themistius, Asclepius, and Philoponus.[3]

These texts pose severe problems for Platonic scholarship. Here on the authority of Aristotle, a close associate of Plato for about twenty years, are doctrines attributed to Plato that generations of careful scholars have been unable to locate within the dialogues themselves. We seem to be confronted with a vexing dilemma. One alternative is to conclude that much of what Aristotle purports to tell us about Platonic doctrine, in these passages and many others like them, is simply mistaken—despite the fact that Aristotle appears to have been in the best possible position to know what Plato taught and believed. Otherwise we seem driven to the conclusion that Plato's thoughts on such ultimate matters never found their way into writing, with the discouraging implication that the dialogues which have inspired philosophers for twenty-five centuries are devoid of the true Platonic vision. Neither alternative is very appealing; yet each has been defended by formidable scholars.

Many commentators who have become convinced of the existence in the Academy of an "esoteric teaching" have attempted to reconstruct its doctrinal content. Prominent attempts in this century include those of Robin, Burnet, Frank, Stenzel, Gaiser and Kraemer, and Findlay.[4] Since the textual evidence upon which such reconstructions are based is confined to references by Aristotle and his early commentators that are no more direct than those cited above, and since the doctrines they attempt to reconstruct are assumed to deviate from anything to be found in the dialogues proper, the reconstructions offered by these scholars are widely at variance. To review them critically would require a whole book by itself. A paradoxical consequence that all these approaches share, nonetheless, is that we cannot discover what Plato "really believed" in the Platonic corpus, but must rely primarily upon the writings of Aristotle instead.

Since Aristotle was notoriously unreliable in reporting the views of his predecessors, however, we might expect a strong case to be available for the contrary alternative. The standard case to this effect has been made by Cherniss. The upshot of Cherniss's argument is that Aristotle's claims about Platonic doctrine are not based on oral teachings at all, but instead are based upon the written dialogues which Aristotle frequently misinterprets. In Cherniss's view, the very notion of an unwritten doctrine is "a hypothesis set up to save the phenomena of Aristotle's testimony," which "has come to be treated as if it were itself part of the phenomena to be saved."[5]

If Plato reserved his "innermost" philosophic thoughts for private communication to his pupils and other associates in the Academy, Cherniss argues, then it would be reasonable to assume (a) that Aristotle would rely upon these communications rather than upon the dialogues in his discussions of Plato's views, (b) that when in doubt about what was meant in the dialogues he would have checked with Plato directly, and (c) that Plato's associates would have been in general agreement at least about the contents of the master's teaching. As Cherniss shows point by point, however, there is evidence that none of these assumptions corresponds to what actually happened. Even the seemingly direct reference to "unwritten teachings" at *Physics* 209b15, he urges, is subject to various interpretations. What Aristotle says in this passage is that, although the account of the participant in the *Timaeus* differs from that in the "so-called unwritten teachings," Plato's views about space in the latter were in accord with his views in the *Timaeus*. Particularly noteworthy about this passage are the facts (a) that Aristotle refers to the "unwritten teachings *so-called*" (λεγομένοις: 209b14), as if the reference were in some way peculiar; (b) that the reference draws attention to a point of agreement between written and unwritten sources, contrary to the tradition of basic differences between the two sets of teachings; and (c) that this is the sole unambiguous reference to "unwritten teachings" in the entire Aristotelian corpus. Against this single mention of such teachings must be listed several dozen explicit references to the dialogues themselves,[6] a set of statistics out of harmony with the hypothesis that Aristotle relied primarily upon unwritten sources in his characterization of Plato's views. The conclusion Cherniss reaches on the basis of such considerations is that neither Aristotle nor other members of the Academy had resources for the interpretation of Plato's thought beyond the dialogues themselves upon which we also rely.[7] The single reference to "unwritten teachings" at *Physics* 209b15 is to be read instead as referring either to the lecture on the Good itself or just to opinions Plato may have expressed in conversation with his associates.[8]

On this view that there were no unwritten doctrines to supersede the written dialogues in forming Aristotle's conception of Plato's philosophy, the awkward problem arises of accounting for the considerable disagreements between what most commentators find in the later dialogues and what Aristotle records in the *Physics* and the *Metaphysics*. Cherniss faces this problem head-on by maintaining that the theory there attributed to Plato derives, not from private conversation or a careful reading of the dialogues, but from what Aristotle inferred Plato must have meant on the basis of his own interpretive theory.[9] Since this procedure so often resulted in misinterpretation of Aristotle's subjects,[10] Cherniss concludes that the alleged Platonic doctrines in question stem from Aristotle's misunderstanding of Plato's written dialogues.[11]

Cherniss's position leaves a number of basic questions unanswered. For one, what attitude are we to take toward the lecture on the Good? Despite any suspicions we may entertain about Aristotle's reliability as an interpreter of Plato, there is no reason to doubt the report of his pupil Aristoxenus that he used to talk about Plato's discourse on the Good, or the later reports of Alexander, Simplicius, and Philoponus,[12] each of whom refers to a work (now lost) in which Aristotle discusses what Plato said on this particular occasion. Cherniss himself accepts the existence of this lecture on the Good, his concern in this connection being merely to argue against the inflation of this particular event into a series of lectures.[13] In fact, there is no reasonable doubt about the occurrence of this particular discourse, or about its treatment of the Good in a mathematical fashion. But it is equally sure, on the same grounds, that what Plato said on this occasion most of his listeners found puzzling.[14] And if what he said were not apparently different from what could be found in the dialogues, then Speusippus and Xenocrates (Plato's successors to headship of the Academy) and his other associates who attended the lecture presumably would not have been surprised by what they heard. In point of fact, the characterization of the Good as Unity reported to have been made on this occasion is so radically different from anything said about the Good in the *Republic* and the *Symposium* (and prima facie in the *Philebus* as well, the only other dialogue mentioning the Good explicitly) that it cannot reasonably be written off merely as an Aristotelian aberration. Simply to misinterpret the views of another philosopher is not to alter them beyond recognition.

No more credible is the hypothesis that, during the approximately twenty years Aristotle was associated with the Academy, Plato never discussed in the former's presence philosophic issues also treated in the dialogues. Although we should agree with Cherniss that Plato did not impose doctrines upon members of the Academy, and that in Plato's view a student cannot acquire knowledge merely by listening to the master's discourse,[15] it simply is not credible that Plato never discussed serious philosophic issues with his close associates. Indeed, if he did not then his most probable reasons for founding the Academy would have been thwarted from the outset.

I believe that Cherniss has established his case that there is no "unwritten doctrine" to be reconstructed on the testimony of Aristotle and his commentators which has any justifiable claim to override the clear testimony of the dialogues themselves. It is what is written in the dialogues that should guide our understanding of Aristotle's commentary, rather than vice versa.[16] On the other hand, Cherniss surely has overstated his case in suggesting that the testimony of those who associated with Plato on a regular basis should be given no weight in our attempts to understand his thought during his later years in the Academy. It is incumbent upon us to attempt to make sense of the reputed content of the lecture on the Good, and of the puzzlement it caused its audience, without falling back upon some notion of "esoteric teachings."

A middle ground is needed between Cherniss and his recon-structionist adversaries. Cherniss and his adversaries agree in their supposition that nothing corresponding to Aristotle's de-scription of Plato's ontological principles in the first book of the *Metaphysics* can be found in the written dialogues. Their dis-agreement begins with their differing views about how this ap-parent discrepancy is to be explained. A middle ground is ac-cessible by rejecting this common supposition, and in effect denying that there is any major discrepancy between written and alleged "unwritten teachings" that requires explanation. For this middle course to be defensible, certainly, we must be able to find passages in the later dialogues that lend themselves to interpretation in terms of Aristotle's description. And for this middle course to be persuasive, both the passages in question and Aristotle's de-scription itself must become more fully intelligible in light of their congruence. If these conditions can be met, we will have reason to reject both (a) the implausible hypothesis that Aristotle and his commentators provide the most reliable approach to Plato's thought and (b) the even more implausible hypothesis that his associates did not learn anything about Plato's thought in conversation. What emerges in their place is the quite unre-markable hypothesis that Plato wrote into his dialogues various passages which were no better understood by some of his im-mediate associates than by his more recent commentators, and which were intended to represent thoughts he saw fit to represent in other ways during verbal exchanges with members of the Academy.

Suppose that relatively early in the development of these thoughts Plato decided to "try them out" in a public[17] lecture attended by such associates as Aristotle, Speusippus, Xenocrates, Hera-clides, and others who, hearing these thoughts for the first time, found them paradoxical and enigmatic. Upon subsequent ex-posure to these thoughts in various forms on various occasions, however, Aristotle came to feel that he understood what Plato was getting at and found opportunity to record these "Platonic teachings" in his own written work. Other associates went on record with interpretations which did not always agree with Aristotle's,[18] but which for polemical purposes he sometimes grouped together with Plato's thoughts as he understood them, with vague attributions to "the believers in Forms," "the moderns," or "those who posit Ideas as causes."[19] Being preoccupied with his own purposes in dealing with the views he attributed to Plato, Aristotle did not consider it a matter of top priority to check his interpretations with Plato himself.[32] Indeed, we may conjecture, Aristotle's relations with Plato were not uniformly cordial, for he was more ready to react to Plato as an opponent than as a philosophic mentor. Public reference to another's central philosophic thesis as "meaningless prattle,"[21] needless to say, is not conducive to congenial personal intercourse. Moreover, the things Plato had to say about the Forms and their relations to other things tended to drift in the direction of what we might call "higher mathematics," for which Aristotle seemed to have little taste or talent.[22] So all in all, despite his frequent reference to Plato's views in his own writings, Aristotle never realized whatever natural potential he may have had as a reliable expositor of the other's philosophy.

For all this, Aristotle had neither the audacity nor the incentive completely to falsify the views he heard Plato expounding. Even though he sometimes failed to understand what Plato said except in general outline, his reports of what Plato said in general outline for the most part were probably accurate. Thus when Aristotle said at *Metaphysics* 988a10-14, for example, that Plato (not "the moderns," or "the believers in Forms," but Plato himself) declared that Unity is predicated of the Dyad in the case of the Forms, that the Forms are predicated of the Dyad in the case of sensible things, and that the Dyad in question is the Great and (the) Small, this report should not be written off as an Aristotelian fabrication. Problems remain about what Plato might have meant in saying these things, and about how these sayings relate to the written dialogues, but the fact that Plato said something of this general character should be taken as sufficiently certain to require explanation.

The hypothesis guiding the remainder of this work is that, although there was no "esoteric teaching" in the Academy that Plato withheld from his later dialogues, he did talk philosophy at least occasionally with close associates, and that although

Aristotle was not adept in discriminating the exact meaning of Plato's discussions, at least he got them right in general outline. In accord with this hypothesis, we may expect the views Aristotle ascribes directly to Plato in the *Metaphysics* to correspond in general drift to views discernible in the *Philebus*, which almost every commentator agrees is one of Plato's latest dialogues. If it can be shown in following up this implication that certain perennially puzzling passages in the *Philebus* become intelligible in light of Aristotle's ascriptions, then a number of salutary results will have been accomplished. The so-called "Riddle of the Early Academy" will have been at least partially solved, Aristotle's testimony in this respect will have been at least partially vindicated, and most importantly a better understanding will have been achieved of the elusive *Philebus*.

2. ARISTOTLE'S DESCRIPTION OF PLATO'S ONTOLOGY

Although references to Platonic philosophy are scattered throughout Aristotle's work, the richest and most provocative concentration appears in the first book of the *Metaphysics* where Aristotle compares Plato's views with those of the Pythagoreans. Most of the theses reported in this context are echoed elsewhere in the corpus, but this one extended discussion contains all the claims in Plato's behalf that will figure prominently in our subsequent consideration of the *Philebus*. For that reason we will concentrate on this context to the exlusion of various other passages that would require notice if we were undertaking a complete examination of Aristotle's testimony about Plato's philosophy.

Several sentences from this context have already been discussed in isolation. To gather a sense of its radical impact overall, however, it will be helpful to have before us a translation of the major portion of the sixth section of Book I of the *Metaphysics*. The philosophy of Plato, Aristotle says, follows that of the Pythagoreans in most respects, but had distinguishing features of its own. For:

having first become familiar in his youth with Cratylus and the Heraclitean doctrines, that all sensible things are always in flux and that there is no knowledge of them, he held the same in later years [ἐκ νέου τε γὰρ συνήθης γενόμενος πρῶτον Κρατύλῳ καὶ ταῖς Ἡρακλειτείοις δόξαις, ὡς ἁπάντων τῶν αἰσθητῶν ἀεὶ ῥεόντων καὶ ἐπιστήμης περὶ αὐτῶν οὐκ οὔσης, ταῦτα μὲν καὶ ὕστερον οὕτως ὑπέλαβεν: 987a32-b1]. Socrates meanwhile was busying himself with ethics, seeking the universal in this connection, and for the first time directing attention to definitions, but neglecting nature as a whole (Σωκράτους δὲ περὶ μὲν τὰ ἠθικὰ πραγματευομένου περὶ δὲ τῆς ὅλης θύσεως οὐθέν, ἐν μέντοι τούτοις τὸ καθόλου ζητοῦντος καὶ περὶ ὁρισμῶν ἐπιστήσαντος πρώτου τὴν διάνοιαν: 987B1-4). Plato followed this approach, but thought it led not to sensible things but to things other than becoming, since it is not possible to formulate a common definition of sensible things that are always changing [ἐκεῖνον ἀποδεξάμενος διὰ τὸ τοιοῦτον ὑπέλαβεν ὡς περὶ ἑτέρων τοῦτο γιγνόμενον καὶ οὐ τῶν αἰσθητῶν· ἀδύνατον γὰρ εἶναι τὸν κοινὸν ὅρον τῶν αἰσθητῶν τινός, ἀεί γε μεταβαλλόντων: 987b4-7]. Things of this other sort he called Ideas, and said that all sensible things are both dependent upon them and named after them [οὗτος οὖν τὰ μὲν τοιαῦτα τῶν ὄντων ἰδέας προσηγόρευσε, τὰ δ᾽ αἰσθητὰ παρὰ ταῦτα καὶ κατὰ ταῦτα λέγεσθαι πάντα: 987b7-9]. For the many exist by participation in the Forms that share names with them [κατὰ μέθεξιν γὰρ εἶναι τὰ πολλὰ τῶν συνωνύμων (τοῖς εἴδεσιν)²³: 987b9-10]. The name 'participation' was the only new thing [τὴν δὲ μέθεξιν τοὔνομα μόνον μετέβαλεν: 987b10-11]. For the Pythagoreans say that things exist by imitation of numbers, while Plato says it is by participation, thus changing the name [οἱ μὲν γὰρ Πυθαγόρειοι μιμήσει τὰ ὄντα φασὶν εἶναι τῶν ἀριθμῶν, Πλάτων δὲ μεθέξει, τοὔνομα μεταβαλών: 987b11-13]. But what participation or imitation of the Forms might be they jointly neglected to inquire into [τὴν μέντοι

85

γε μέθεξιν ἢ τὴν μίμησιν ἥτις ἂν εἴη τῶν εἰδῶν ἀφεῖσαν ἐν κοινῷ ζητεῖν: 987b13-14.]

Like Socrates, Plato sought universal definitions, but believed they were to be found with respect to Forms rather than sensible things. The assertion that Plato held this even in his later years indicates that Aristotle has the later doctrines of Plato in view (see also *Metaphysics* 1078b9-12). In most respects other than this search for definitions, however, Plato followed the Pythagoreans. The first major departure on Plato's part from Pythagorean philosophy that Aristotle mentions is that whereas they say that things exist by imitation of the numbers, Plato says it is by participation instead. Aristotle then complains that neither Plato nor the Pythagoreans explained what they meant by participation or imitation of the *Forms*, as if the change from ἀριθμῶν at 987b12 to εἰδῶν at 987b14 was incidental. Here is the first hint in the present context that Plato in some manner identified Forms and numbers.[24] Further, Aristotle claims:

he said that besides sensible things and Forms, located between them, there are objects of mathematics [παρὰ τὰ αἰσθητὰ καὶ τὰ εἴδη τὰ μαθηματικὰ τῶν πραγμάτων εἶναί φησι μεταξύ: 987b14-16]. These differ from sensible things in being eternal and unchanging, and from Forms in being many alike, whereas each Form is one uniquely [διαφέροντα τῶν μὲν αἰσθητῶν τῷ ἀΐδια καὶ ἀκίνητα εἶναι, τῶν δ᾽ εἰδῶν τῷ τὰ μὲν πόλλ᾽ ἄττα ὅμοια εἶναι τὸ δὲ εἶδος αὐτὸ ἓν ἕκαστον μόνον: 987b16-18].

That this constitutes a further difference between Plato and the Pythagoreans is made explicit at 987b28-29. The same tenet is again attributed to Plato by name at 1028b19-21, by explicit description ("the first to suppose the Forms exist") at 1086a11, and by apparent implication at no less than seven other locations within the *Metaphysics*.[25] It is clear that, in Aristotle's opinion at least, Plato distinguished the objects of mathematics from the Forms themselves. But what sense is to be made of this distinction, and what weight given to Aristotle's opinion?

The question of sense is relatively easy, for in the context of the theory of Ideas the mathematician cannot be said to deal in his typical practice with the Forms of numbers or of geometrical figures themselves. Although unquestionably it is part of the theory as developed in the middle dialogues that Unity, Duality, and so forth, exist as Forms,[26] these cannot be the objects the arithmetician is concerned with in the equation '1 + 1 = 2', etc. For one thing, Duality itself is not composed of a pair of unities, being one Form in itself. For another, there is only one Form of Unity, and not the pair that would be required to make sense of the equation above. On the other hand, it is not of sensible objects (like apples and pebbles) that the arithmetician speaks in affirming '1 + 1 = 2', for his meaning is independent of what can be counted. That is, the objects with which the arithmetician deals are eternal, like Forms but unlike sensible things, and at the same time indefinitely numerous, like sensible things and unlike Forms. Similar distinctions are required in the case of geometry, for similar reasons. This is exactly the description given by Aristotle at 987b14-18, so no problem exists regarding the sense of this passage.

A more lively issue arises with the question whether any distinction of this sort can be found in the Platonic dialogues. Numerous commentators have argued vigorously and at length that the notion of mathematical objects does not appear in Plato's writings, under motivation in part of freeing Plato from any responsibility for the "intolerable scholasticism" of the *Metaphysics*.[27] Cherniss's stake in the issue is somewhat different; he is concerned to show that Plato did not teach a doctrine of mathematical objects, and so to remove this as a credible example of the imputed "unwritten teachings." To this end he claims that "it has been positively proved over and over again that Plato does not anywhere in his writings recognize mathematical numbers and figures as entities separate from sensibles on the one hand and from ideas on the other."[28] A careful examination of the "positive proofs" Cherniss cites, however, shows that they deal almost exclusively with the context of the Divided Line and the Cave in the *Republic*, and do nothing to establish the case for the later dialogues.[29] In point of fact, there is a passage in the *Philebus* which indicates unequivocally that Plato was aware

87

that arithmetic deals with units which in many instances are entirely the same. At 56C, Socrates divides all arts into two classes, according to degree of exactness, and points out an important difference between two arts of calculating as an example. Whereas the ordinary arithmetician deals with unequal units, like two armies or two cows, etc., his more exact counterpart will have nothing to do with him unless he admits that "every unit among countless instances differs not at all from any other unit" (μονάδα μονάδος ἑκάστης τῶν μυρίων μηδεμίαν ἄλλην ἄλλης διαφέρουσάν: 56E3-4). A similar distinction is recognized at 56E-57A between practical and philosophical geometry. Here is an unimpeachable statement of the difference between changeable sensible objects that can be enumerated and mathematical entities that although many are the same in each case. Then at 61E, Socrates extends the distinction according to degrees of exactness to different modes of knowledge, one pertaining to objects that come into being and perish, the other to objects eternally the same and changeless. As examples of the former he cites the human spheres and circles involved in construction, of the latter "the divine sphere and circle themselves" (κύκλου μὲν καὶ σφαίρας αὐτῆς τῆς θείας: 62A7-8). Here in turn is an unmistakable indication of the difference between changeable geometrical figures and the singular geometrical Forms that are eternal and changeless. Within a span of scarcely five pages, Plato has referred unambiguously to all three levels of mathematical entities distinguished by Aristotle in the *Metaphysics*, the disputed "intermediate mathematicals" included.[30]

Not only is the notion of the mathematical objects between Forms and sensible things intelligible in itself, but moreover it can be clearly identified within the dialogues. For this reason it is best to dissociate claims about these mathematical objects from other doctrines attributed to Plato in the passages immediately following, most of which are problematic in both respects.

Aristotle continues his remarks on Plato by saying:

Since the Forms were causes of other things, he thought their elements were the elements of all things [ἐπεὶ δ' αἴτια τὰ εἴδη τοῖς ἄλλοις, τἀκείνων στοιχεῖα πάντων ᾠήθη τῶν ὄντων εἶναι στοιχεῖα: 987b18-20]. As matter, the Great and the Small were principles, as essence, Unity [ὡς μὲν οὖν ὕλην τὸ μέγα καὶ τὸ μικρὸν εἶναι ἀρχάς, ὡς δ' οὐσίαν τὸ ἕν: 987b20-21]; for from these, by participation in Unity, come the [Forms or]³¹ numbers [ἐξ ἐκείνων γὰρ κατὰ μέθεξιν τοῦ ἑνὸς (τὰ εἴδη) εἶναι τοὺς ἀριθμούς: 987b21-22].

That Plato considered the Forms to be causes of other things is a familiar doctrine from the time of the *Phaedo* at least. However, a startling new dimension appears with reference to *elements* of the Forms, as if the Forms were thought no longer to exist just in and by themselves but rather to be constituted by more basic principles. In the next sentence the principles apparently in question are identified as the Great and (the) Small and Unity, but Aristotle's focus seems to have shifted again from Forms to numbers. The first explicit assertion of a novel philosophic thesis on Plato's behalf is the claim that (for him) numbers come from participation of the Great and (the) Small in Unity.³² This passage also contains the first mention in this context of the Great and (the) Small as a basic ontological principle. In the next section I will review other designations Aristotle used for this principle, and will examine several attempts by recent commentators to make this principle intelligible. At any rate, it is clear that we must understand what the Great and (the) Small amounted to in the Platonic context before we can understand the thesis that the numbers exist by its participation in Unity.

Further information about this principle is provided as Aristotle continues to cite other points of agreement between Plato and the Pythagoreans:

In saying that Unity is substance, and not a predicate of something else, he agreed with the Pythagoreans, and also in saying that numbers are the causes of the existence of the other things [τὸ μέντοι γε ἓν οὐσίαν εἶναι, καὶ μὴ ἕτερον γέ τι ὂν λέγεσθαι ἕν, παραπλησίως τοῖς Πυθαγορείοις ἔλεγε, καὶ τὸ τοὺς ἀριθμοὺς αἰτίους εἶναι τοῖς ἄλλοις τῆς οὐσίας ὡσαύτως ἐκείνοις: 987b22-25]. But to make the indefinite two instead of one—to make the indefinite from the Great and Small—is peculiar to him (τὸ δὲ ἀντὶ τοῦ ἀπείρου ὡς ἑνὸς δυάδα ποιῆσαι, τὸ δ' ἄπειρον ἐκ μεγάλου καὶ μικροῦ, τοῦτ' ἴδιον: 987b25-27].

From this passage we learn that the Great and (the) Small for Plato somehow corresponds to the ἄπειρον of the Pythagoreans, but that Plato made it a dual principle instead of singular. Since at 987a13-19 Aristotle had reported the Pythagorean dictum that the ἄπειρον and Unity are principles basic to other things, and that this is why number is the substance of everything, this correspondence harmonizes with the remarks in Plato's behalf at 987b18-22 that the Great and (the) Small and Unity, as elements of the Forms, are elements of all things, and that the numbers come from the Great and (the) Small by participation in Unity. Moreover, this correspondence suggests that Plato himself, under Pythagorean inspiration, might on occasion have used the term ἄπειρον with about the same meaning that Aristotle intended by 'the Great and (the) Small', a suggestion of particular relevance to the *Philebus*. We should note in passing yet a further indication that Forms now are considered by Plato to be numbers, since here he is alleged to agree with the Pythagoreans in saying that numbers are the causes (of the being) of other things, whereas essentially the same claim was made regarding the Forms at 987b18-19.

Continuing his account of Plato's divergence from the Pythagoreans, Aristotle mentions again that Plato, unlike them, placed objects of mathematics between the Forms and sensible things, and said that numbers are apart from sensible things, whereas the Pythagoreans said that such things *are* numbers. This divergence, Aristotle suggests, along with Plato's introduction of the Forms in the first place, was due to his study of definitions. Further:

he made the other nature a dyad because the numbers, except the primes, could easily be produced from it as from something plastic [τὸ δὲ δυάδα ποιῆσαι τὴν ἑτέραν φύσιν διὰ τὸ τοὺς ἀριθμοὺς ἔξω τῶν πρώτων εὐφυῶς ἐξ

αὐτῆς γεννᾶσθαι ὥσπερ ἔκ τινος ἐκμαγείου: 987b33-
988a1].

In the previous chapter a possible connection was pointed out
between this reference to the "other nature" and that at *Parmenides* 158C6-7, where the ἑτέραν φύσιν is explicitly called
ἄπειρον πλῆθος. Since the "other nature" at 987b33 is the dyad
of the Great and (the) Small, this suggests a possible connection
between the dyad of Aristotle's account and the Unlimited Multitude of the *Parmenides*, as already noted. Also noted in the
previous chapter was the plausible association between the production of the numbers "except the primes" at 987b34, and the
generation of numbers at *Parmenides* 143C-144A by a technique
that appeared incapable of yielding the primes. The only relevant
feature of this passage not previously discussed is its clear implication that Plato himself, and not just the Pythagoreans, thought
that its ability to generate the numbers was reason to adopt this
dyad as a basic principle.

Following a rather unenlightening criticism of this theory he
is attributing to Plato, based on analogies from carpentry and
biology, Aristotle closes the section with what apparently was
intended to be a summary of Plato's ontological position:

Plato thus declared himself on the matters in question (Πλάτων
μὲν οὖν περὶ τῶν ζητουμένων οὕτω διώρισεν: 988a7-8).
It is evident from what has been said that he provided only
two causes, that of the essence and that pertaining to matter
[φανερὸν δ᾽ ἐκ τῶν εἰρημένων ὅτι δυοῖν αἰτίαιν μόνον
κέχρηται, τῇ τε τοῦ τί ἐστι καὶ τῇ κατὰ τὴν ὕλην:
988a8-10]—for the Forms are the causes in essence of other
things, and Unity that of the Forms [τὰ γὰρ εἴδη τοῦ τί
ἐστιν αἴτια τοῖς ἄλλοις, τοῖς δ᾽ εἴδεσι τὸ ἕν: 988a10-
11].

Taken out of context, this passage would appear to contain little
more startling than Aristotle's notorious and ill-founded[33] com-
plaint that Plato recognized only two of his four causes, with
the afterthought that Unity somehow is the essential cause of the
Forms, as the Forms are of other things. It is with the final few

remarks of this section that Aristotle irrevocably parts company with the standard theory of Forms, and opens up the perspective that in the following chapter will be seen to illuminate the *Philebus*:

And the underlying matter of which the Forms are predicated in the case of sensible things, and Unity in the case of the Forms, [it is evident] that this is a dyad, the Great and the Small (καὶ τίς ἡ ὕλη ἡ ὑποκειμένη καθ᾽ ἧς τὰ εἴδη μὲν ἐπὶ τῶν αἰσθητῶν τὸ δ᾽ ἓν ἐν τοῖς εἴδεσι λέγεται, [φανερὸν] ὅτι αὕτη δυάς ἐστι, τὸ μέγα καὶ τὸ μικρόν: 988a11-14). Moreover, he assigned the causation of Good and Evil to the elements, one in each case, as we say some of the earlier philosophers tried to do, like Empedocles and Anaxagoras [ἔτι δὲ τὴν τοῦ εὖ καὶ τοῦ κακῶς αἰτίαν τοῖς στοιχείοις ἀπέδωκεν ἑκατέροις ἑκατέραν, ὥσπερ φαμὲν καὶ τῶν προτέρων ἐπιζητῆσαί τινας φιλοσόφων, οἷον Ἐμπεδοκλέα καὶ Ἀναξαγόραν: 988a14-17].

Here in rapid sequence are enumerated three theses totally foreign to the middle dialogues. One is that the Great and (the) Small is the matter of which the Forms are predicated in the case of sensible things. At 988a10-11 the Forms are identified as essential causes in this regard. Thus in claiming that for Plato the Forms are predicated of the Great and (the) Small, Aristotle is not referring to the ascription of incidental properties. The predication in question has to do with the essence of sensible things, that which makes them what they are. Nor is this predication equivalent to the participation of the middle dialogues, for participation is a relationship between Forms and sensible objects—likened to imitation at 987b13. In Aristotle's account, the predication in question is an ontological relationship between material and formal cause. Sensible things come into being by the interaction of the Forms and the Great and (the) Small. The role of the Forms in the production of sensible things, of course, is familiar from the standard theory. What is utterly unprecedented in the dialogues prior to the *Philebus* is the Great and (the) Small in the role (as Aristotle puts it) of underlying matter.[34] One thesis that Aristotle asserts on Plato's behalf, then, is that sensible things are constituted by the Forms and the Great and (the) Small.

Even more radical in contrast with the standard theory of Forms is the companion claim that Unity is predicated of the Great and (the) Small in the case of the Forms. For one thing, this claim is directly opposed to the standard theory of the middle dialogues in clearly implying that the Forms are composite. According to the standard theory, Forms are ontologically basic and simple in that they exist in and by themselves, not depending upon other things in being what they are. According to the account Aristotle is ascribing to Plato, however, the Forms are composed of more basic ontological principles. Their "material principle" is the Great and (the) Small, their essence ("formal principle") Unity. In some sense the Forms themselves are generated. They exist because of these two principles. Prima facie, it is unclear even what Aristotle is trying to say in this regard. The fact that nothing approximating this conception of the Forms appears explicitly in Plato's writing (although as we shall see it is only partly veiled in the *Philebus*) lends credibility to the notion of an "esoteric teaching." On the other hand, the fact that this conception of the Forms is so radically opposed to the standard theory of the middle dialogues helps explain the fervor with which scholars who accept the standard theory as canonical for Plato's entire career[35] reject Aristotle's testimony as unreliable. Both positions are undercut by the *Philebus*.

A further implication of this claim, which at first glance appears simply unintelligible, is that the Great and (the) Small enters twice in the constitution of sensible things. One time is with the composition of sensible things from the dyad and the Forms, the other with the composition of the Forms as such. It is one of our tasks in the following chapter to make this implication intelligible. For the moment, it is enough to note that this dual role of the dyad does not necessarily involve two separate processes. Another possibility is that the Great and (the) Small enters into the constitution of sensible things in two different respects instead.

Yet another apparent consequence of this claim is the paradoxical thesis, of which evidence was found in earlier passages of this section, that the Forms are numbers. We have already considered Aristotle's claim at 987b21-22 that Plato thought the numbers come from the Great and (the) Small by participation in Unity. But here at 988a11-14 he gives essentially the same characterization of the source of the Forms. What is only implied in this section, moreover, is stated explicitly elsewhere in the *Metaphysics*. At 1086a10-11, for instance,[36] he refers to the first person who said that the Forms exist and that the Forms are Numbers, obviously referring to Plato. At *De Anima* 404b23-27, moreover, the same thesis is mentioned twice over with Plato expressly named (404b16), as the claim that numbers and Forms are the same (ἀριθμοὶ τὰ εἴδη αὐτὰ) and the claim that these very numbers are the Forms of things (εἴδη δ' οἱ ἀριθμοὶ οὗτοι τῶν πραγμάτων). Although it is clear from other contexts (*Metaphysics* 991b9 and 1082b23-24) that Aristotle found this view untenable, it is equally clear that in his opinion this was the view of Plato.

The final thesis to be considered from this context is that the Good is Unity. Like some of his predecessors, Aristotle says, Plato assigned his principles as causes of Good and Evil. The two principles in question, of course, are Unity and the Great and (the) Small. Against the Pythagorean background of the discussion it is apparent that Unity is the cause assigned to Good. A more direct statement of Plato's position in this regard occurs at 1091b13-14, where Aristotle says explicitly that of those who maintain the existence of unchangeable essences, some (including Plato himself[37]) hold that "Unity itself is the Good itself" (αὐτὸ τὸ ἓν τὸ ἀγαθὸν αὐτὸ εἶναι).

This thesis, accordingly, must be added to the list of problematic ontological claims made in Plato's behalf in Book 1, section 6, of the *Metaphysics*. First is the thesis (1) that numbers come from participation of the Great and (the) Small in Unity. Second is the thesis (2) that sensible things are constituted by the Forms and the Great and (the) Small. The third thesis is (3) that the Forms are composed of the Great and (the) Small and Unity. The fourth thesis, only implied in this context but explicitly stated elsewhere, is (4) that the Forms are numbers. Fifth and final is the thesis (5) that the Good is Unity. A cursory review of the testimony of Simplicius and Aristoxenus regarding Plato's lecture on the Good, reported at the beginning of this chapter, will show the almost exact correspondence of these theses to the reported contents of that lecture.

As already emphasized, this section from the *Metaphysics* is not the only place in the Aristotelian corpus where these theses appear, and there are other theses attributed to Plato by Aristotle which do not number among these.[38] As far as I can see, however, these five are all that relate directly to the *Philebus*. Since the concern of this chapter is to gain some control over developments in the later years of Plato's Academy that bear upon the contents of that dialogue, and not to consider Aristotle's views on Plato's philosophy as such, we may be excused from a more complete review of Aristotle's opinions.

Theses (1), (2), and (3) refer explicitly to the Great and (the) Small, and (4) and (5), as will be seen, do so by implication. To understand these theses, accordingly, it will be necessary to identify that principle.

3. The Great and (the) Small

Among contemporary scholars engaged in the controversy over Plato's so-called "unwritten teachings," some have considered it unnecessary to state exactly what they understand by the expression 'the Great and (the) Small', perhaps assuming that its meaning is somehow self-evident. Others have attempted to specify what Aristotle and his commentators understood by the expression, with results that show its meaning to be far from self-evident. Until it is reasonably clear what this key expression means, however, there is little hope of being able to settle the issue whether the so-called "unwritten teachings" in which it figures actually appear in the later dialogues. Since commentators on both sides of the controversy assume that in fact none of these doctrines appear in the dialogues at all, this unclarity about the meaning of 'the Great and (the) Small' is yet another reason for circumventing that controversy in the present study.

In the final chapter I attempt to show that when the meaning of this expression has been made clear, then most of the doctrines in question can be found in the *Philebus*. A consequence is that the question why Aristotle's account of Plato's teachings in the *Metaphysics* does not accord with the dialogues is a question that should not have arisen in the first place, and that the mighty set-to between Cherniss and his German opponents has been a contest more of wits than of philosophic substance.

A precondition of any successful effort to understand the nature of the Great and (the) Small is to realize that this principle was designated by a rather wide variety of different expressions in the writings of Aristotle and his commentators. Although the most common in Aristotle was probably 'the Great and (the) Small', he also referred to it occasionally as the 'Indefinite Dyad' (ἀόριστος δυάς).[39] This same expression was used frequently by Simplicius[40] in discussing Aristotle's comments on Plato, and occurs also in Alexander[41] and Theophrastus.[42] Neither 'the Great and (the) Small' nor the 'Indefinite Dyad', however, can be found in this application within the extant writings of Plato himself.

Another expression used infrequently for this purpose by Aristotle,[43] but more commonly by Simplicius,[44] is the 'Unlimited' (ἄπειρον). An interesting variant also used by Simplicius is the 'Unlimited Nature' (ἀπείρου φύσιν).[45] This expression is particularly interesting in that identically the same expression occurs three times in the *Philebus*, in what appear to be very similar applications.[46] There too it occurs as a variant of the 'Unlimited', which latter term is particularly prominent in early sections of the *Philebus*. Two other variants to be found in Simplicius are 'the Indefinitely Unlimited' (τὸ τῆς ἀπειρίας ἀόριστον)[47] and 'the Indefinite and Unlimited' (τὸ ἄπειρον καὶ ἀόριστον),[48] both of which appear to be hybridizations of the 'Indefinite Dyad' and the 'Unlimited'.[49]

The most intriguing characterization of this principle to be found among the commentators, however, occurs in several passages of Simplicius where he is discussing the views some of his predecessors held on Plato's teachings. Porphyry, for one, said that Plato "made the More and Less to be the Unlimited Nature" (τὸ μᾶλλον καὶ τὸ ἧττον . . . τῆς ἀπείρου φύσεως εἶναι τίθεται: 453.32-33) because they "pass on into the Indefiniteness of the Unlimited" (πρόεισιν εἰς τὸ τῆς ἀπειρίας ἀόριστον: 453.34-35). The same holds, says Porphyry, of "the Greater and Smaller, and as Plato calls them the Great and the Small" (τὸ μεῖζον καὶ τὸ ἔλαττον καὶ τὰ ἀντ᾽ αὐτῶν λεγόμενα ὑπὸ Πλάτωνος τὸ μέγα καὶ τὸ μικρόν: 453.35-36). Much the same, according to Simplicius, was reported by Alexander, according to whom Plato "called the Dyad the Unlimited Nature" (τὴν δὲ δυάδα τοῦ ἀπείρου φύσιν ἔλεγεν: 455.9-10), since "neither the Great and Small nor the Greater and Smaller are bounded, but involve the More and Less which pass on into Unlimitedness" (οὐχ ὥρισται τὸ μέγα καὶ μικρὸν ἤτοι τὸ μεῖζον καὶ ἔλαττον, ἀλλ᾽ ἔχει τὸ μᾶλλον καὶ ἧττον, ἅπερ εἰς ἄπειρον πρόεισιν: 455.10-11). According to Porphyry and Alexander, in brief, there is reportedly a close connection between the Great and (the) Small, the Greater and Smaller, and the More and Less. As far as one can tell from these passages, indeed, the three expressions in question may well have been alternative ways of referring to the same basic Platonic principle. The intimate association among these expressions is stressed, albeit at considerable remove, in yet another passage in the same commentary, where Porphyry is quoted as saying that Dercylides said that Hermodorus, a friend of Plato's, thought it clear that Plato considered matter "to exhibit the More and the Less, along with the Great and the Small" (μᾶλλον καὶ τὸ ἧττον ἐπιδεχομένων, ὧν καὶ τὶ μέγα καὶ τὸ μικρόν ἐστιν: 248.1).[50] Porphyry goes on to explain this by observing that things "called comparatively Great and Small all involve the More and the Less" (μέγα πρὸς μικρὸν λεγόμενα πάντα ἔχειν τὸ μᾶλλον καὶ τὸ ἧττον: 248.5-6).

Insofar as Simplicius' oblique reports are to be relied upon, it would appear, Plato was just as likely to refer to his Unlimited principle as "the More and Less" as "the Great and Small." The reason this is particularly noteworthy, of course, is that Socrates says explicitly in the *Philebus* that the mark of the Unlimited Nature (τῆς τοῦ ἀπείρου φύσεως: 24E4) is "becoming more and less" (μᾶλλον . . . καὶ ἧττον γιγνόμενα: 24E7-8), and that all things possessing this mark belong to the class of the Unlimited (τὸ τοῦ ἀπείρου γένος: 25A1). Here is prima facie evidence, which commentators involved in the "unwritten teachings" controversy have consistently overlooked, that the principle of the Great and Small does indeed appear within that dialogue. Before we can proceed to explore the significance of this passage, however, it is necessary to gain some insight into what Plato understood by this principle.

What might Plato have meant by the Great and (the) Small? There are a number of false leads to be disposed of first. One, sponsored by Aristotle himself (*Metaphysics* 1082a13-15, 1083b36), is that Plato's Great and Small, or Indefinite Dyad, is simply the principle of numerical doubling. This simplistic notion has found its way into recent commentary. Cornford, for example, finds evidence of such a principle at *Parmenides* 143A-144C, where an indefinite multitude of numbers is generated from the interaction of the pair Unity and Being. Cornford's reasoning, as we have seen, is that this multitude "is what Plato calls the Indefinite Dyad, because . . . it 'always proves to be two and never is one'."[51] Taylor is even more explicit in attributing this sense to Plato. Although he believes that Plato was wrong in assigning this function to the Indefinite Dyad, Taylor finds it "clear that the 'doubling' of 2 was supposed to be the first example in the integer series of the working" of this principle.[52] As a basis for interpreting the several allegedly Platonic theses identified in the previous section, however, this notion is deficient in several respects. For one, although duality might be conceived as a matter of doubling, application of the function "times two" within the number series always results in numerical increase; thus if this were a proper sense of 'the Indefinite Dyad' it would be inappropriate to refer to this principle alternatively as 'the Great *and* (the) *Small*'. Secondly, although as Taylor illustrates there are algorithms by which the number series can be generated by doubling and "equalizing" (taking the arithmetical mean, e.g., between 2 and 4),[53] there appears no conceivable sense in which sensible things might come to be by participation of an "indefinite doubler" in the Forms. Finally, there is no conceivable sense either in which the Forms can be composed of an "indefinite doubler" participating in Unity.

Another interpretation suggested by Cornford is that "of the

Indefinite Dyad of great and small . . . extending without limit in both directions."[54] The mathematical illustration he offers is the pair of unending series $1/2$, $1/3$, $1/4$, . . . $1/n$, and $2/1$, $3/1$, $4/1$, . . . $n/1$, both diverging from the unit $1/1$ that he calls 'the One'. The same interpretation is endorsed by Ross, in commenting on Aristotle's remark at *Physics* 206b27. Quoting Aristotle, Ross writes "Plato made the indefinites two in number for this reason, that the indefinite is thought to exceed and to proceed to infinity both in the direction of increase and in that of diminution."[55] This interpretation makes sense of the alternative designation 'the Great and (the) Small', but appears hopeless in the face of the first three theses listed in the previous section. That is, (1) there is no sense in which the numbers could come from this pair of series by participation in Unity, since the numbers (the integers) are presupposed as part of the two series themselves; (2) there is no apparent sense in which sensible things could be generated out of these series by participation in the Forms;[56] and (3) it is simply unintelligible to claim that the Forms themselves come from these two series by participation in Unity.

Yet a third interpretation proposed by Cornford comes closer to the mark.[57] Commenting on the use of πλήθει ἄπειρα at *Parmenides* 158b7, Cornford says that it refers to the Indefinite Dyad, which in the case of magnitude is "the large-and-small," but which in the case of sensible qualities appears as "indefinite continua, like hotter-and-colder, always admitting of the more-and-less."[58] Thus according to this interpretation the Great and (the) Small consists of "a continuum of maniness, along which you can mark off any number of units or measures."[59] More exactly, it consists of a whole variety of such continua, quantitative for magnitudes, qualitative for sensible properties, and so on. A similar interpretation is put forward by Ross,[60] and something apparently like it can be found in Stenzel's "general principle of extension."[61] This interpretation is promising as far as it goes. It distinguishes the production of sensible properties (out of qualitative continua like hotter-and-colder) from that of numerical magnitudes (out of larger-and-smaller), and it gives a rough idea of what production in either case amounts to (imposition of limit). It is inadequate, however, in providing no suggestion of how Forms might be produced from this principle by participation in Unity. And it tells us nothing about how production of either sensible things or numbers might be accomplished. An adequate account of the Great and (the) Small, it is reasonable to expect, must tell us something about how this principle can be subjected to limit. In view of the relatively advanced state of mathematics at the time, moreover, we should expect that Plato's conception of the Great and (the) Small would make explicit provisions at least for the generation of number.

The most promising suggestion to date of how numbers might be generated from the Great and (the) Small is the mathematical interpretation of A. E. Taylor. This interpretation is based upon a garbled but enthusiastic description in the *Epinomis* of the sciences supposedly leading to wisdom and piety. The study producing such virtuous results, according to this source, is astronomy, itself containing several mathematical disciplines. First is the science of number, of the generation of the odd and even, and of what they are able to contribute to the nature of things;[62] next, the "God-given miracle" (geometry) that assimilates, by reference to areas, numbers by nature dissimilar; and third, that "amazing device of God's contrivance" (solid geometry) that accomplishes the same thing for dissimilar solids. These sciences lead men to consider how "all nature models Form and Kind according to each of these proportions" (καθ' ἑκάστην ἀναλογίαν εἶδος καὶ γένος ἀποτυποῦται πᾶσα ἡ φύσις: 990Ε4-991Α2)[63] by "the constant revolution around the double of power and its opposite" (περὶ τὸ διπλάσιον ἀεὶ στρεφομένης τῆς δυνάμεως καὶ τῆς ἐξ ἐναντίας ταύτῃ: 990Ε3-4). In a discussion sharing the enthusiasm of the original author, Taylor focuses upon two aspects of these miraculous sciences. One is that they appear to deal with the well-known problems concerning incommensurable[64] numbers, particularly the quadratic and the cubic surds. Readers of the *Meno* will recall the former from the problem posed to the slave boy of finding the side of the square double in area to a square with side of unit length, the answer to which, of course, is the diagonal of the unit square, or $\sqrt{2}$. Although 1 and $\sqrt{2}$ are themselves incommensurable, they become commensurable in the second power ("by reference to areas"). Both quadratic and cubic surds, in turn, are mentioned at *Theaetetus* 148A-B, as the young respondent provides an example from mathematics of the sort of definition sought for "knowledge" in the ensuing dialogue. The second feature of the passage emphasized by Taylor is its concern with the double and its various progressions. The primary example of the ratio of the double, it points out (991A), is that of 1 to 2, or ½, which doubled again and again yields the ratios 1/4, 1/8, and so forth. These two features of the *Epinomis* passage lead Taylor to think that its author has in mind the problems of finding general solutions for the functions $\sqrt{n}$ and $\sqrt[3]{n}$, which solutions would extend the number system into the domain of what subsequently came to be known as the real numbers.

Taylor's interest in this passage stems primarily from the fact that an arithmetical solution of the "square root of the double" was known to the Pythagoreans.[65] This technique could approximate the value of $\sqrt{2}$ to any specified degree of accuracy, and is graphically illustrated by the so-called "table of sides and diagonals."[66] This table yields two unending series of fractions which approach $\sqrt{2}$ as a limit from opposite sides, the first by becoming progressively greater and the second by becoming progressively smaller.[67] These series, Taylor claims with complete conviction,[68] are what was meant by 'the Great and (the) Small'. The Great and (the) Small is a series of fractions approaching the irrational number in question by way of limit. Since two subseries are involved in this approach, and since each extends without end, the principle in question may appropriately be described as an "Indefinite Dyad." The irrational number thus is defined by the unique limit approached by both series—that is, by the imposition of Unity upon the Indefinite Dyad.

Although Taylor's interpretation offers the most precise explanation yet to appear in the literature of how Plato might have conceived numbers to be produced from the Great and (the) Small, there are difficulties that surely disqualify it from being a fully adequate account. One uncertainty is whether the *Epinomis* passage can support all the mathematical detail Taylor reads into it; presumably it would not suggest his interpretation to someone who had not arrived at it through other channels of insight.

Another problem, familiar from the discussion above of competing proposals, is that his account gives no hint of how the Great and (the) Small might yield Forms by participating in Unity. Nor does there appear to be any intelligible sense in which the mathematical series in question could yield sensible things by participation in the Forms. Unfortunately, moreover, Taylor's account cannot even explain the production of the integers themselves. As Taylor himself recognizes,[69] the integers are essentially involved in the series used to define $\sqrt{2}$ and other quadratic surds; hence the integers cannot be defined by similar methods. Yet in talking about the generation of numbers by the participation of the Great and (the) Small in Unity, Aristotle obviously intended to include the integers.[70] Helpful as Taylor's account has been, it is necessary to seek further clarification regarding the Great and (the) Small.

An adequate explanation of the Great and (the) Small would make sense of all the theses incorporating that principle which Aristotle attributed to Plato in the sixth section of the first book of the *Metaphysics*—namely, (1) that numbers come from participation of the Great and (the) Small in Unity, (2) that sensible things are constituted by the Forms and the Great and (the) Small, and (3) that the Forms are composed of the Great and (the) Small and Unity. Among sustained attempts to clarify this principle in contemporary literature, we have found one (Cornford, Ross, Stenzel) that seems promising with respect to thesis (2), another (Taylor) that makes progress on thesis (1), but none that shows much promise regarding (3).[71] An explanation that satisfies all three desiderata in fact is available. In the remainder of this section I articulate this explanation and attempt to demonstrate its plausibility in connection with thesis (1). In the final chapter I attempt to show how the interpretations it provides of theses (2) and (3) in turn yield precisely the insights needed to make sense of the perennially puzzling remarks at the beginning of the *Philebus*. Thus, although this explanation is no more capable than any other of being deduced from what remains of the ancient sources, it does admit textual support of an inductive nature. If the argument below is successful, it will show (i) that theses (1) through (3) above (taken from the first book of the *Metaphysics*) can be given a literal and sensible interpretation, (ii) that armed with this interpretation we not only can make good sense of the methodological and ontological remarks in the *Philebus* but moreover can find in that dialogue the meaning of theses (4) and (5), and hence (iii) that Aristotle's report of Plato's ontology in the *Metaphysics* is basically credible.

As Taylor foresaw, the key to an adequate understanding of these matters is most likely to be found in the mathematics of the period. This is so for several reasons. One is the simple fact that mathematical concepts figure prominently in three of the five theses in question. Another is that mathematics was more highly developed at this time than any other discipline that might have been expected to contribute to Plato's ontological thinking. A third is that Plato's increasing sympathies with Pythagoreanism during his later years (cf. chapter 1) would tend to encourage experimentation with ontological viewpoints in which mathematical entities are somehow basic. A consequence is that we should expect to find an explanation of thesis (1) which is more fully developed and articulate than any explanation available for the other theses. Nonetheless, explanations of the other theses should be expected to follow the same general pattern.

The mathematical key that unlocks the meaning of the five ontological theses is Definition 5, Book v, of Euclid's *Elements*. As shown in the last section of Chapter 1, this definition almost certainly shares its origin with the discussions of equality at *Parmenides* 140B-D and 151B-D, and also appears to have something to do with the treatment of the temporal instant at 156D-E. The key mathematical development in either case is Eudoxus' theory of proportions, which provided a general solution to the problem of incommensurable magnitudes.[72]

Important as it is for our purposes, Definition 5 bears repeating verbatim:[73]

Magnitudes are said to *be in the same ratio*, the first to the second and the third to the fourth, when, if any equimultiples whatever be taken of the first and third, and any equimultiples whatever of the second and fourth, the former equimultiples alike exceed, are alike equal to, or alike fall short of, the latter equimultiples respectively taken in corresponding order.

The meaning of this definition can be made clear through a numerical analogue.[74] Consider any four numbers a, b, c, and d, standing in the ratios a/b and c/d. The definition establishes necessary and sufficient conditions for these ratios' being equal. For any number m multiplying a and c, and any number n multiplying b and d, the ratios a/b and c/d are equal if and only if one of the following is the case: (i) ma and mc are greater than nb and nd, respectively, (ii) ma and mc are equal to nb and nd, respectively, or (iii) ma and mc are less than nb and nd, respectively.

Another analogy[75] shows how this definition applies to commensurable and incommensurable magnitudes indifferently. Suppose a series of equally spaced columns extending indefinitely in a straight line from a starting base, which serves also as the starting base for a series of equally spaced railings extending indefinitely along a line parallel to the first, with different spacings for the two series (C and R, respectively). Now consider a model of this construction in which the columns and railings are equally spaced at distances c and r, respectively. The model is proportionately an exact replica of the original—i.e., the ratios C/R and c/r are the same—if and only if, for any m and n, it is the case either (i) that the mth column of the original and of the model alike come after the nth railing of the original and of the model respectively, (ii) that the mth columns coincide in distance with their respective nth railings, or (iii) that the mth columns come before the nth railings in their respective constructions.

In this analogy, of course, C/R and c/r are ratios of lengths, which might be either commensurable or incommensurable. If commensurable, there will be values of m and n such that the mth column coincides with the nth railing in the original construction, and also in the model if it is proportionately equivalent. If the ratios in question are of lengths that are not commensurable, however, there is no place along the two lines indefinitely extended where a column and a railing are exactly coincident. This means that no mth multiple of C has a value exactly equal to any nth multiple of R, from which it follows that C and R have no common measure. Nonetheless, it is possible to express one in terms of the other within any given limit of accuracy, however narrow. For example, let R be a magnitude representing the numerical unit and C be a magnitude representing $\sqrt{2}$ ($= 1.41421\ldots$). A simple imagined construction of the C and R series with these values will show the first C falling between the first and second R, the 10th C between the 14th and 15th R, the 100th C between the 141st and the 142nd R, the 1,000th between the 1,414th and the 1,415th, and so forth. In this manner, the value of the quantity $\sqrt{2}$ can be expressed as the 10^nth part of an $n + 1$ digit multiple of the unit R, with accuracy increasing with the value of n.

Eudoxus' theory of proportions thus provided a means of approximating the value of a magnitude in terms of another incommensurate with it, with no limit in accuracy of approximation. In this respect, it is similar to the method of "sides and diagonals" used by the ancient mathematicians to approximate certain irrational quantities. An important difference, however, is that whereas this latter method applies only to certain classes of irrational quantitities,[76] the approximating technique provided by Eudoxus' definition applies to any irrational quantity whatever.[77] According to this technique, any irrational quantity can be represented as falling between two ordered sets of quantities expressed in terms of unit measures, one set containing indefinitely many members each smaller than the irrational in question but approximating it without limit of accuracy, the other containing indefinitely many larger members approaching without limit of accuracy from the other direction. As Kline puts it, Euclid's definition "amounted to dividing the rational numbers m/n into two classes, those for which m/n is less than the incommensurable ratio a/b of the magnitudes a and b and those for which m/n is greater."[78]

The close parallel between Eudoxus' definition of proportional magnitudes and Dedekind's definition of irrational numbers has been noted by several historians of mathematics. Heath, for instance, remarks that "the definition of equal ratios in Eucl. v, Def. 5 corresponds exactly to the modern theory of irrationals due to Dedekind."[79] Struik refers to the "great similarity between the 'Dedekind cut' with which modern mathematics . . . defines irrational numbers and the ancient Eudoxus theory as presented in the fifth book of Euclid's *Elements*."[80] Further indication of the correspondence between the two theories comes from Dedekind himself, with the observation that "if . . . one regards the irrational number as the ratio of two measurable quantities, then is this manner of determining it already set forth in the clearest possible way in the celebrated definition which Euclid gives of the equality of two ratios (*Elements*, v., 5)."[81]

What Struik referred to as the "Dedekind cut" is Dedekind's technique for defining irrational numbers as divisions between classes of rational numbers. A cut exists between any two classes so composed that all members of the first class (A_1) are less than all members of the second (A_2). If A_1 contains a largest member n (alternatively, if A_2 contains n as a smallest member), then that pair (A_1, A_2) demarcates the rational number n. There are other cuts, however, established by pairs of classes such that A_1 has no largest member and A_2 has no smallest. An example is the pair of classes demarcating the square root of 2, each such that for any integer or ratio of integers within the class another can be specified which is closer in value to the square root in question. A cut produced by any pair of classes (A_1, A_2) such that A_1 has no largest and A_2 no smallest member corresponds to an irrational number, of which of course there are infinitely many. The brilliance of Dedekind's theory consisted in showing that both rational and irrational numbers can be conceived as cuts in this fashion, and that so conceived they admit the rigorous application of all standard arithmetical operations.

The correspondence between Eudoxus' and Dedekind's theories is so striking that some recent observers credit Eudoxus with the discovery of a rigorous definition of irrational numbers.[82] Indeed, Dedekind himself notes that before his work irrational numbers were usually introduced on the basis of extensive magnitudes, and were explained "as the result of measuring such a magnitude by another of the same kind"[83]—exactly the procedure provided by Eudoxus.

Nonetheless, there is reason to resist the conclusion that Eudoxus anticipated Dedekind's definition of the irrational numbers.[84] Dedekind's definition of the irrationals is accomplished, by explicit intention,[85] strictly in terms of the rational numbers. As presented in Definition 5, however, Eudoxus' definition is in terms of magnitudes, with no mention of number whatever. A separate definition of proportionality is provided for number in Book VII of the *Elements* (Definition 20). The reason separate definitions are provided for magnitudes and for numbers is that in the tradition represented by Euclid magnitudes are continuous and numbers are discrete.[86] Accordingly, whereas Dedekind's definition applies to numbers explicitly, Eudoxus' definition applies only to magnitudes, and from the viewpoint of a tradition in which numbers and magnitudes are different kinds of quantity the two definitions could not be conceived as equivalent. Ascription of Dedekind's theory to Eudoxus is an anachronism to be avoided.

But if so, how can Eudoxus' theory of proportions afford any insight into the identity of the Great and (the) Small? To put the question more specifically, granting (as it appears we must) that Eudoxus' theory—like Dedekind's—provides for the definition of both rational and irrational quantities in terms of descending and ascending series, and granting (as it appears we may) that these series might appropriately be labeled "Great" and "Small," respectively, how can we conclude that series of this sort had anything to do with Plato's principle "the Great and (the) Small"? For Plato's principle was supposed to generate *numbers*, as well as planes and solids.

The answer to this question must be carefully formulated and carefully interpreted. To begin with, it is clear that we cannot conclude with certainty that Eudoxus' theory and the definition it provides of rational and irrational quantities in terms of descending and ascending series has anything to do at all with Plato's principle. Historical data is too sparse, and the problems of interpreting it too critical, to draw completely firm conclusions either about Plato's relationship to the tradition that generated the treatment of irrationals represented by Euclid's work or about the identity of his principle "the Great and (the) Small." Indeed, the chapter began with a notice of this limitation.

Nonetheless, there are two lines of plausible conjecture that suggest a close connection between Plato's principle and Eudoxus' definition. Either way leads to an interpretation of the Great and (the) Small that not only avoids the difficulties of alternative accounts as reviewed above but also provides a fruitful basis for interpreting the difficult ontological and methodological passages of the *Philebus*. My interest in developing these conjectures is not to show that either is historically accurate (although this remains an open possibility), but rather to establish the credentials of this particular conception of the Great and (the) Small as one worthy of being developed further in application to this puzzling dialogue.

One line of conjecture begins with various reports in antiquity of an arithmetical approach to the problem of irrationals, as distinct from the geometrical approach represented by Euclid. In the *Definitiones* of Hero, for instance, there is reference to "arithmetic elements" (ἀριθμητικὴ στοιχείωσις) which distinguish irrational from rational quantities, in a manner contrasted with that of Euclid's *Elements*.[87] The sense of there being more to fourth-century arithmetic than appears in Euclid is reinforced by a passage in Pappus' commentary on Book x of the *Elements*, which credits Theaetetus with the discovery of irrational quantities that could be formed by arithmetical operations.[88] Beyond this, there is direct mention in the *Elements* themselves of "arithmetical books," which cannot be identified with any part of Euclid's treatise.[89] Indefinite as this evidence may be, it should at least make us comfortable with Knorr's conclusion that the existence of a (now lost) "arithmetic compilation . . . pertaining to incommensurables" is a "necessary . . . complement to the geometric theory of incommensurable magnitudes."[90] Since at least part of the work on these "arithmetic elements" must have taken place during Plato's lifetime in the Academy (Theaetetus is cited as a major contributor), it is entirely credible that Plato himself would have been aware of these developments. If we may credit the testimony of some ancient authorities,[91] moreover, he may even have contributed to them.

But what form might an arithmetic treatment of incommensurable magnitudes have taken? Again, of course, the only safe answer is that we do not really know. But a plausible conjecture is that this treatment would have related rather closely to the geometrical treatment of the *Elements*. This conjecture is plausible (i) because it would have been foolish for the arithmetical theoreticians involved to have ignored what had already been accomplished in this regard from a geometrical standpoint, (ii) because, as we have seen in tracing the parallels between the theories of Eudoxus and of Dedekind, the geometrical approach so readily admits an interpretation in terms of numbers instead of magnitudes, and (iii) because all the sources cited above that point to an independent arithmetical treatment speak of this treatment in connection with treatment of the *Elements*. As we have already seen, however, the geometrical approach epitomized in Euclid provides for the definition of both commensurable and incommensurable magnitudes in terms of limits approached by decreasing (but always greater) and increasing (but always smaller) series.

The upshot of this line of conjecture is (a) that there existed in Plato's time arithmetic techniques for defining both rational and irrational numbers, (b) that these techniques involved the concept of series of quantities which are exclusively Great and Small in relation to the limit that they approach from opposite directions, and (c) that Plato was well aware of these techniques. According to this conjecture, in brief, when Plato spoke of the Great and (the) Small, at least one thing he might have meant is a continuous series of quantities divided into mutually exclusive parts by a limit (or "section" or "cut").

A second line of conjecture that leads to the same result is based upon the concept of number as measure, which was a familiar concept in Greek mathematics generally. Among the Pythagoreans, Philolaus and Eurytus apparently had attempted to save the thesis that things are composed of numbers by emphasizing the role of numbers in measuring boundaries.[92] Euclid himself often speaks of numbers in terms of measures, as for example in Definitions 3 ("A number is a part of a number, the less of the greater, when it measures the greater") and 13 ("A composite number is that which is measured by some number") of Book VII. In the *Protagoras*, moreover, Plato refers to arithmetic explicitly as the science of measure (356E9-357A3), and in the *Philebus* he talks indifferently about the studies of number and of measure in the course of distinguishing practical from philosophic arithmetic (57D6).

Even more striking evidence of the equivalence during this period of at least one concept of number with the concept of measure may be found in Aristotle's *Physics*. After distinguishing number in the sense of what is counted from the number with which we count (an indication in itself that the term ἀριθμός carried more than a single meaning), Aristotle goes on to discuss the relationship between time and motion. The aphoristic conclusion of this discussion is that "time is the measure of motion in respect of before and after." What is particularly significant for our purposes is that two terms are used interchangeably in this formulation, each over a half dozen times between 219b and 222a. At 220b24, 32, 221b7, et passim, time is termed the μέτρον of motion. At 220a15, 221b2, 11, et passim, however, the term used is ἀριθμός. In the only two places in which the full formulation of the aphorism is given (219b1-2 and 220a24-25), in fact, the actual reading is "time is the number of motion in respect of before and after." With regard to its role in the demarcation of things in motion, in brief, time is indifferently the number or measure. The terminological lesson is clear, and for our purposes important: in one of its well-established senses at least, the term ἀριθμός was used as a synonym of μέτρον, or measure.

The second conjecture is that when Aristotle said that for Plato the numbers come from the Great and (the) Small by participation in Unity, he meant that numbers in the sense of *measures* were supposed to come in this fashion. If this in fact was the meaning intended, then Plato's principle is even more closely related to Euclid's Definition 5 than under the previous conjecture. For, as we have already seen, that definition is expressed in terms of equimultiples, and the relation of multiple is defined in Definition 2 (Book v) in terms of measure. Thus Eudoxus' theory of proportions as enshrined in Definition 5 yields directly a sense in which number (as measure) can be understood as deriving from the imposition of singular limits (or "cuts" or

110

"sections") between series of ever decreasing (the Great) and ever increasing (the Small) constituents. According to this conjecture, once again, when Plato spoke of the Great and (the) Small, he meant a continuum of factors divided into mutually exclusive sections by the imposition of Limit, or Unity.

The difference in effect between this and the previous conjecture is as follows. According to the previous, the thesis that numbers come from the Great and (the) Small by participation in Unity pertains to numbers in the sense of the positive integers, their ratios, and the irrationals interpolated to make up a continuum, and the manner in which this is accomplished is provided by the (conjectured) extrapolation of Eudoxus' theory from magnitudes to numbers so conceived. According to the present conjecture, that thesis about the origin of numbers is understood instead, in a manner befitting Plato's Pythagorean ancestry, as pertaining to measures, which can be defined in the requisite fashion by a direct application of Eudoxus' theory. In either case, the Great and (the) Small is conceived as a continuum divisible into mutually exclusive parts by "cuts" or "sections."

Although this result has been reached on the basis of plausible conjecture, the conception of the generation of number which results is not entirely without textual support. In fact, there are obscure references in the later commentators Proclus and Iamblichus which may be interpreted so as to reflect a conception of numbers as sections within an ordered series. Iamblichus, in his book *In Nicomachi Arithmeticam Introductionem Liber* (ed. Pistelli, p. 10, lines 17-20), remarked that Eudoxus, the Pythagorean (!), said that number is πλῆθος ὡρισμένον. Now the term ὡρισμένον might be read as 'bounded' or 'limited', rendering the whole expression a reference simply to a finite collection. This reading appears unlikely, however, on the basis of a quotation from Nichomachus himself[93] using the same expression in *contrast* with μονάδων σύστημα, which does explicitly mean "collection of units." Another meaning for ὡρισμένον is 'divided'. If this meaning is adopted, then the full expression might be read as equivalent to 'sectioned multitude', a fair description of the sense of number offered in Plato's behalf above.

The other ancient source in question is Proclus' *In Euclidem*, where Proclus cites Eudoxus as (among other accomplishments) having increased the number of theorems about the section (τομήν) which took their start with Plato.[94] The meaning of the term τομήν here has been debated over the last hundred years or so, and no definite sense has been reached of its meaning. The most favored interpretation is that Proclus is attributing to Eudoxus some new theorems about the so-called "golden section," in which Plato himself was almost certainly interested. It remains an open possibility, however, that the term τομήν may be read as 'section', in the sense of 'partition'.[95] Read this way, Proclus' report suggests that the conception of number as a "cut" or "section" might actually have been developed by Eudoxus himself. The conjecture that this was so is worth serious consideration.

4. Looking Ahead to the *Philebus*

The second section of this chapter listed five ontological theses attributed by Aristotle to Plato in the first book of the *Metaphysics*. In the following chapter I attempt to show that each of these five theses plays a prominent role in the *Philebus*, although not always in the formulation that Aristotle reported. By way of preparation for a close textual examination of relevant passages in that dialogue, it will be helpful to indicate briefly the particular form in which each thesis may be expected to appear.

Thesis (1) is that numbers come from participation of the Great and (the) Small in Unity. Pursuant to the conjecture that this thesis traces back to Eudoxus' theory of proportions, I identified two possible ways in which it might be interpreted. One is that arithmetical numbers (including the irrationals, which the orthodox mathematician of the period would not be prepared to call numbers as such) can be defined as unique limits imposed upon a continuum of magnitudes, dividing the continuum into two sections of exclusively greater and smaller members. The other is that the ἀριθμοί in question are measures, in the sense previously illustrated from Aristotle's discussion of time in the *Physics*, and that numbers in this sense are unique limits imposed upon continua of progressively larger and smaller constituents. In either case, the Great and (the) Small is a continuum that admits division into exclusive sets of greater and smaller factors, and a given number is identical with a unique segmentation of the continuum. By virtue of its uniqueness—its participation in Unity, that is to say—a point on the continuum of the Great and Small takes on the identity of a particular number.

Although different, these two interpretations are not mutually exclusive, for the first may be construed as a specification of the second. If the Great and (the) Small is conceived generally as a continuum of elements ordered by the relationship of greater and smaller, then there are as many varieties of that general principle as there are varieties of things ordered by that relationship. One such variety, of course, is a series of constituents related as greater and smaller merely with respect to serial order. Since this relationship is purely ordinal, admitting neither spatial nor temporal dimensions, appropriate imposition of limit along the continuum generates the arithmetic numbers of the first interpretation.

Conceived in this more general fashion, however, the Great and (the) Small can also serve in the generation of geometrical magnitudes. Given a continuum of constituents related as greater and smaller in a single spatial dimension, imposition of limit in the form of unique segmentations produces lines thereby comparable in terms of length. Another set of continua then can be conceived in which length is constant, with ordered increase and decrease in a second spatial dimension. Imposition of unique limits along these continua yields simple plane figures. And given specific plane figures in two dimensions, continua ordered in the third spatial dimension can be made to generate geometrical solids. It is certainly noteworthy in this respect that Eudoxus' theory of proportions, on the basis of which this tentative conception of the Great and (the) Small was developed, was recognized by some early commentators as applying "to geometry, arithmetic, music, and all mathematical science" indifferently.[96] Being measures under this interpretation, however, specific lines, figures, and solids must also be describable as "numbers," the propriety of which is supported by Aristotle's remark at *Posterior*

Analytics 75b4 that the magnitudes studied by geometry are numbers.

Under this interpretation, moveover, similar treatment should be possible of temporal dimensionality. Given a set of events related along a continuum of earlier and later, distinct moments in time can be defined as limits partitioning the continuum into before and after. The appropriateness of this conception of time is clear from Aristotle's discussion of time and the "now" at *Physics* 220a. Time, says Aristotle, is continuous (συνεχής: 220a5,26), with the "now" as limit (πέρας: 220a21). This "now" both divides (διήρηται: 220a5) the temporal continuum and marks out (ὁρίζει: 220a9) events as before and after. In this respect, the temporal "now" both is like the arithmetic unit (μονὰς ἀριθμοῦ: 220a4) and itself is number (ἀριθμός: 220a22). It was the very similar treatment of the "instant" in time at *Parmenides* 156D, discussed in Chapter 1, that led to the characterization of that passage as an anticipation of the Indefinite Dyad. The rationale for this characterization is now apparent. For it is just this notion of the "instant" as an external limit demarking a point along the temporal continuum that we would expect Plato to favor while experimenting with this general conception of the Great and (the) Small.

Lines, plane figures, solids, and temporal durations are all magnitudes, as (for someone in the Pythagorean tradition, at least) were numbers themselves. And the measures these magnitudes provide are all quantitative in character, generated out of the Great and (the) Small by the imposition of unique partitions or limits. The quantitative character of these particular measures is due to the mathematical nature of the limits imposed. It is important to note that the continua out of which these measures are generated are not quantitative themselves, independently of the limits imposed upon them. In other words, the Great and (the) Small does not take on quantitative characteristics until subjected to limits of a mathematical sort. No reason has emerged why this general ontological principle of the Great and (the) Small might not provide ordered series qualified to receive limits of a nonmathematical character. A possible candidate is the continuum of hotter and colder, which when appropriately segmented yields a scale of temperature intervals. Although an interval of temperature (e.g., a degree) can be assigned a numerical designation, the degree of temperature itself is not a mathematical measure. Another candidate is the continuum of musical sounds. Although again the intervals that comprise the musical scale can be described in terms of mathematical ratios, the octave and the third (etc.) themselves are qualitative measures. These two cases of "the hotter and colder" and "the higher and lower in pitch," to be sure, are among several examples of such continua mentioned in the *Philebus*—examples of what there is called "the more and the less."

As it appears in the *Philebus*, the Great and (the) Small comprises whatever "becomes more or less, and admits being strongly, slightly, or very so-and-so" (μᾶλλόν τε καὶ ἧττον γιγνόμενα καὶ τὸ σφόδρα καὶ ἠρέμα δεχόμενα καὶ τὸ λίαν: 24E7-8), etc. In the context of the *Philebus*, that is to say, the Great and (the) Small comes to be designated "the More and Less" instead. An alternative designation is simply "the Unlimited" (τὸ ἄπειρον: as at 25A1). It is just this principle, Socrates points out at 25B, that submits to number (ἀριθμός), or measure (μέτρον), or whatever comes under the principle of limit (πέρας). For reasons we shall presently be able to appreciate, moreover, more than one ancient commentator on the *Philebus* (notable Alexander and Porphyry[97]) maintained that the Unlimited received Limit by participating in Unity.

As a consequence of these various terminological shifts, I shall argue in the following chapter, the first thesis attributed to Plato in the *Metaphysics* takes on a formulation for which Aristotle does not adequately prepare us. As Aristotle puts it, the thesis is that numbers come from participation of the Great and (the) Small in Unity. As it appears in the *Philebus*, it is the thesis that numbers (in the sense of measures, including but not limited to arithmetical numbers) come from the Unlimited by participation in Limit.

Readers of the *Philebus* will recognize the Unlimited and the Limit as two of four basic ontological kinds figuring in the discussion between Socrates and Protarchus. A third basic kind comprises those things that come into being as progeny of the first two, resulting from those measures brought about by Limit (26D8-10). Examples offered by Socrates are "music as a whole" (26A4) and measured states of heat and cold (26A7-9). Although the terms ἰδέα and εἶδος do not see much service in this dialogue, the measures that establish the art of music (pitches and notes: 17C11-12) and those identified with moderate heat and cold (degrees typical of the seasons: 26B1), as well as with "countless other things such as beauty and strength and health" (26B6), are what in almost any other dialogue would be labeled 'Ideas' or 'Forms'. Yet musical notes, the moderate temperatures of the seasons, bodily strength and health, and so forth, themselves are paradigm examples of sensible things.

As Aristotle puts the second Platonic thesis, sensible things are constituted by the Forms and the Great and (the) Small. As it figures in the *Philebus*, this is the thesis that the third, or mixed (23D1), class (including sensible things at least) comes from a combination of the Unlimited with Limit.

The third and fourth theses attributed to Plato in the *Metaphysics* are (3) that the Forms are composed of the Great and (the) Small and Unity, and (4) that the Forms are numbers. The sense of these formulations in the context of the *Philebus* follows almost immediately from the observations above. Given that what would be called 'Forms' or 'Ideas' in an earlier dialogue are here referred to as 'measures', and given that numbers in thesis (1) are equivalent to measures, we are led directly to the identification of Forms and numbers. The numbers in question, however, are not exclusively (or even primarily) the integers of arithmetic. They are the measures which provide limit in any domain admitting ratio (25B1) and order. Given the equivalence between Forms and numbers in this sense, moreover, it follows immediately from thesis (1) that Forms are composed from the Great and (the) Small and Unity. Or, in the formulation of the *Philebus* itself, measure comes from the participation of the Unlimited in Limit, which in effect is the participation of the Unlimited in Unity.

The final thesis, which led to such a quandry among Plato's contemporaries and to such dissension among his modern commentators, is that the Good is Unity. Tracing down the significance of this thesis will carry us to the end of the *Philebus*. What appears there is that the Good which Socrates and Protarchus have been seeking to identify is to be found in measure (66A7) instead of pleasure or intelligence. But measure, we will have seen, is a form of Unity.

CHAPTER THREE

THE *PHILEBUS* AND THE GOOD

1. A GIFT OF THE GODS

The apparent purpose of the *Philebus* is to examine the competing claims of pleasure and of intelligence to be identical with the Good.[1] As in so many dialogues, however, pursuit of the apparent purpose provides occasion for raising issues of more general philosophic significance. After a few opening maneuvers, indeed, it becomes clear that neither pleasure nor intelligence would win the competition, but not before Socrates has had opportunity to describe a method which he proclaims extravagantly to be a gift of the gods. These methodological remarks have proven far more baffling to commentators by and large than the results finally reached regarding intelligence and pleasure.[2] Particularly puzzling is the repeated reference to the principles of Limit and the Unlimited, marking a departure from otherwise similar methodological remarks in the *Sophist* and the *Statesman*.

Reference to this "godly method" comes about in the following fashion. Protarchus (priority of principle) has taken over from Philebus (loving youth) responsibility for the argument that pleasure is good. Socrates suggests instead that what is good is intelligence. Since not all pleasures are equally good, however, and since knowledge itself admits contrary instances, Socrates advises that they reach agreement first on the troublesome issue of the one and many (14C). What he has in mind, says Socrates, is not the commonplace and childish problem (as at *Phaedo* 102B) how one individual can have many opposite properties, like being both large and small, or heavy and light. Nor is it the problem (as at *Republic* 525A) how a single thing can be an ensemble of many parts, or how many parts can constitute a single whole. These are problems about things that come into being and perish (τῶν γιγνομένων τε καὶ ἀπολλυμένων: 15A1-2), and hence are not even worth debating. The important problem is about such "ones" as Man, Ox, Beauty, or the Good itself.[3] And concerning these, two (broadly conceived) questions arise. First is the question whether we should accept these unities (μονάδας: 15B1) as having genuine existence (ἀληθῶς οὔσας: 15B2) at all. Assuming an affirmative answer, we face the further question how each unit, being always the same and admitting neither generation nor destruction, can nonetheless be dispersed among the unlimited (ἀπείροις: 15B5) things that come into being—as if, which seems impossible, the selfsame unity came to be at the same time both in one and in many. More directly put,[4] the second question is how a Form, which does not change, can become involved with many changing particulars without losing its unity. These are the questions about the one and the many, Socrates says, that will bring most benefit if properly settled.

Having thus identified the one-many problem worth pursuing as a problem about the unity of Forms,[5] Socrates recommends a way of approaching the issue. Although not difficult to set forth, he says (with undue optimism), it is very difficult to apply. Yet it is to this method that we owe our discoveries in any undertaking requiring skill (τέχνης: 16C2). Indeed, the method appears to be a gift of the gods to man. Our forebears,[6] Socrates continues, who were superior to us in having lived closer to the gods, passed on the tradition that:

> those things that are always[7] said to exist are composed of one and many, having Limit and the Unlimited within themselves connaturally[8] [ἐξ ἑνὸς μὲν καὶ πολλῶν ὄντων τῶν ἀεὶ λεγομένων εἶναι, πέρας δὲ καὶ ἀπειρίαν ἐν αὑτοῖς σύμφυτον ἐχόντων: 16C9-10].

Since this is the way things are disposed (διακεκοσμημένων: 16D1), Socrates says, we ought to do so-and-so—thereupon beginning his description of the "godly method."

Rather than rushing headlong to contend with the puzzling

description that follows, let us reflect upon the significance of this "old tradition." For one thing, the tradition left by our forebears contains an ontological thesis. Although a certain methodology is supposed to follow from it, the tradition explicitly is about the way things are constituted. The things always said to exist originate from (ἐξ) the one and many, and the sense in which this is so is that they have within themselves connaturally (σύμφυτον) Limit and the Unlimited. Another thing to note is that "being one and many" and "having Limit and the Unlimited within them" are not named as two separate modes of composition. Having Limit and the Unlimited within them is the manner in which these things are composed of one and many. Indeed, this is very nearly what Aristotle said at *Metaphysics* 1004b32-34, presumably in Plato's behalf,[9] when he remarked that the Limit and Unlimited named by some thinkers as principles are reducible to unity and plurality.[10] As already noted on various occasions, the account of Plato's ontology in the *Metaphysics* stresses the close similarity of Platonic and Pythagorean doctrine in this regard. Association of *Philebus* 16C9-10 with the Pythagoreans is also suggested at *Metaphysics* 986a23-24, where unity and plurality are listed in close sequence after limit and the unlimited in Aristotle's version of their table of opposites. Returning to the topic of basic principles at 987a13-19, moreover, Aristotle substitutes unity for limit in opposition to the unlimited, and goes on to say at 987b25-27 that Plato agreed with the Pythagoreans save in making his Unlimited two—the Great and (the) Small—instead of a single principle.

These considerations in themselves suggest the possibility that the reference at *Philebus* 16C9-10 to these apparently closely related ontological principles, one and many, and Limit and Unlimited, may have something to do with that basic ontological opposition explicitly attributed to Plato in the *Metaphysics*— Unity and the Great and (the) Small. The hypothesis that the Great and (the) Small of Aristotle's account is none other than the Unlimited of the *Philebus*, indeed, was advanced on independent grounds in the preceding chapter, and will be defended at length when Plato's own characterization of the Unlimited is

discussed in the section following. Since part of my argument
for this hypothesis is the coherent interpretation it enables us to
provide of various baffling passages in the *Philebus*, let us accept
the hypothesis on a provisional basis and see what can be made
of the "godly method."

In stating that the things always said to exist are naturally
constituted from one and many—i.e., from Limit and the Unlimited—we now understand Socrates to be saying that all such
things are constituted from Unity and the Great and (the) Small,
otherwise called the Indefinite Dyad. This is entirely consonant
with the pair of ontological theses regarding Forms and sensible
objects attributed to Plato by Aristotle, namely that sensible
things are constituted by the Forms and the Great and (the) Small
and that the Forms are composed of the Great and (the) Small
and Unity. If Forms are composed of the Dyad and Unity, and
sensible things in turn from Forms and the Dyad, it would be
an intelligible abbreviation to say simply that both Forms and
sensible things—both always said to exist—come from the two
basic principles. So far, of course, no distinction has been made
in the *Philebus* regarding the modes of composition of Forms
and of sensible things, and none will be made until Socrates
attempts to provide general characterizations of the Limit, the
Unlimited and what results from their mixture. His immediate
concern at 16D is not to expand upon the ontology of the "old
tradition," but rather to elucidate the methodology this ontology
dictates.

Since this is the way things are constituted, Socrates goes to
say, we ought:

> in each and every case always to assume a single Form and
> to enquire into it—if one is there we will find it[11]—and,
> laying hold of that, after one to look for two, if two
> are there, or if not for three or some other number [ἀεὶ
> μίαν ἰδέαν περὶ παντὸς ἑκάστοτε θεμένους ζητεῖν—
> εὑρήσειν γὰρ ἐνοῦσαν—ἐὰν οὖν μεταλάβωμεν, μετὰ
> μίαν δύο, εἴ πως εἰσί, σκοπεῖν, εἰ δὲ μή, τρεῖς ἤ τινα
> ἄλλον ἀριθμόν: 16D1-4].

121

Then we ought to treat:

> each of these ones in the same way in turn, until we see that the original one is not merely one or many or indefinite, but also how many it is [τῶν ἐν ἐκείνων ἕκαστον πάλιν ὡσαύτως, μέχριπερ ἂν τὸ κατ' ἀρχὰς ἐν μὴ ὅτι ἕν καὶ πολλὰ καὶ ἄπειρά ἐστι μόνον ἴδη τις, ἀλλὰ καὶ ὁπόσα: 16D4-7].

But one ought:

> not characterize the multitude as unlimited[12] until one recognizes the entire number between the unlimited and the one [τὴν δὲ τοῦ ἀπείρου ἰδέαν πρὸς τὸ πλῆθος μὴ προσφέρειν πρὶν ἄν τις τὸν ἀριθμὸν αὐτοῦ πάντα κατίδη τὸν μεταξὺ τοῦ ἀπείρου τε καὶ τοῦ ἑνός: 16D7-E1]. Then each one of this entirety can happily be given up to the unlimited [τότε δ' ἤδη τὸ ἐν ἕκαστον τῶν πάντων εἰς τὸ ἄπειρον μεθέντα χαίρειν ἐᾶν: 16E1-2].

This, Socrates repeats, is the method of inquiring, learning, and teaching one another that the gods have passed on to us. But the wise men of the day are both quicker and slower than they should be in haphazardly producing their one and many; for in proceeding "directly from the one to the indefinite" (μετὰ δὲ τὸ ἐν ἄπειρα εὐθύς: 17A2-3) they let the intermediates escape their grasp. And it is the intermediates that make the difference between a dialectical and an eristic discussion.

As Gosling has recently remarked in his helpful book on the *Philebus*, this "whole passage has proven extremely recalcitrant to interpretation."[13] A major problem is what to make of the several occurrences of the term ἄπειρον in the description of the method. If it were not for repeated reference to this factor, indeed, the method would appear essentially the same as the procedure of collection and division in the *Sophist* and the *Statesman*. In that method, we recall, the dialectician first looks for a common character in several examples of the thing he wants to define, and then having found (by collection) a single common character proceeds to qualify until a set of characters has been articulated (by division) that together mark off the thing in question from other things resembling it. This final set constitutes a group of interacting Kinds or Forms, participation in which is both necessary and sufficient for being an instance of the Kind defined. Relying upon this method of collection and division as a guide, it seems natural enough to construe the first step at 16D1-2 as a matter of looking for a single Form within the range of things under inquiry, and if one is found (by some procedure equivalent to collection) seizing upon that Form as the basis of further investigation (by some process equivalent to division). Further investigation would consist of seeking out two (or three or more, as the case may be[14]) Forms that effect a dichotomous (or trichotomous, etc.) division of the original Form, and to treat these additional Forms in the same manner as long as additional specification is needed to mark off uniquely the thing being investigated. The final result of the investigation, as 16D5-7 puts it, is to see the original Form as neither simple nor indefinitely numerous, but rather as containing a definite number of specifically identified Forms.

One problem with this easy assimilation of the "gift of the gods" to the method of collection and division is that the latter as described in the *Sophist* involves no reference to the ἄπειρον that figures so prominently in the description of the former at 16D-17A. Another is that there appears to be no way of adapting the description at 16D-17A to fit the method of collection and division without imposing different meanings on ἄπειρον at 16D6, 16E1,2, and 17A2, from that apparently required in the ontological statement that precedes the description. At 16C10, ἄπειρον refers to an ontological principle of considerable generality, and most certainly not to indefinite numerosity or to individual sensible things. In the reading directly above, however, ἄπειρον at 16D6 was interpreted as "indefinitely numerous," in contrast with both one and a definite number. The only interpretation that appears available for the occurrences at 16E1 and 2, moreover, is that of individual sensible objects, of which indefinitely many may fall under a single Form. This is the sense that appeared most natural for 15B5, and also the sense invited by the occurrence at 17A2, inasmuch as the problem with the wise men of the present is that they (like Socrates in the *Phaedo*) recognize no intermediate Forms between individual sensible things and the single Forms responsible for their various characteristics.

There is, of course, no reason generally why Plato should not have used one term in three different senses within less than two pages. But such variation is objectionable in this particular case for several reasons. One is that the ἄπειρον is treated subsequently as a kind admitting a unique characterization (25A4). Another is that the manner in which the ἄπειρον is introduced at 16C10 leads us to expect that it will play an important role in the description of method which follows, an expectation that is frustrated if the term takes on entirely different meanings in subsequent occurrences. Yet another is that the reading of 16D-E above is premised on the assumption that the description of the "gift of the gods" differs from that of the method of collection and division only in its several references to the ἄπειρον, and this assumption appears less innocuous if these references in fact are to different things. A reading which brought these seven occurrences of ἄπειρον (15B5, 16C10, 16D6,7, 16E1,2 and 17A2) into mutual relevance would be preferable, to say the least.

Under the hypothesis we have accepted provisionally for interpreting the ontological statement at 16C9-10, ἄπειρον there refers to what Aristotle called "the Great and (the) Small." One thesis incorporating this principle that Aristotle attributed to Plato is that sensible things come into being by participation of the Great and (the) Small in the Forms. If the ἄπειρον of the *Philebus* is the Great and (the) Small, this means that particular objects are composed of the ἄπειρον and the Forms. Viewed another way, this means that if particular objects somehow were deprived of their relationship to the Forms, they would be indistinguishable from the ἄπειρον itself. Considered in abstraction from their formal element, that is to say, particular objects are unlimited not only in the sense of being indefinitely numerous but also in the sense of being without character or limit.

Exactly the same duality of sense appeared with the expression ἄπειρον πλῆθος as used in the *Parmenides*.[15] At 144A6 following the "generation" of number, for instance, the expression refers to the indefinitely many numbers of the series of integers, each of which is one in itself and distinct from any other. At 143A2 before the numbers have received unique positions in the integral series, on the other hand, the expression refers to a multitude which is unlimited in the sense of lacking determinate members. The nature of the ἄπειρον πλῆθος is further explored in the derivations following Hypotheses III and VII, the upshot being that the limit making sheer unlimited multiplicity into numerically distinct entities is Unity itself. Following Hypothesis III, in which Unity is assumed to exist, what participates in Unity (ὄντα τοῦ ἑνὸς μεθέξει: 158B1-2), and hence is different from it, is called many (πολλά: 158B3). Like the number series in particular, that is to say, things other than an existing Unity are an unlimited multitude in the sense of being indefinitely many. Following Hypothesis VII, in which Unity is assumed not to exist, by contrast, things will only appear to be one and many (164C4-5). That is, while they will appear to have limit relative to each other (165A5-6) when considered uncritically, upon closer consideration (165C1) they will appear to be an unlimited multitude in the sense of having no limits at all.

This close association in the *Parmenides* between limit and the ἄπειρον πλῆθος on the one hand, and Unity and the many on the other, amounts to yet a further reason for suspecting that the discussion in the *Parmenides* may help unravel some of the difficulties we have encountered with the "godly method," since the ontological statement with which this method was introduced stresses an almost identical association. The only difference is that the *Parmenides* refers to an ἄπειρον πλῆθος, while the *Philebus* passage in question refers to an ἄπειρον simply. What would the "godly method" look like if we read ἄπειρον as having the two interrelated senses attached to ἄπειρον πλῆθος in the *Parmenides*?

The method begins, as before, with the search for a common character among examples of what the dialectician wants to define—always assuming that a single Form (a common character) is there to be found. Having found his single character, the dialectician procedes by dichotomous (or trichotomous, etc.) division, stage by stage, until a set of characteristics is found which distinguishes the thing in question from all other things similar to it. When this happens the original character has been articulated in terms of a specific number of other characters. Hence we see that the original character is not just one by itself, but a plurality, and not just an indefinite (16D6) plurality, but one of specific numerosity (ὁπόσα: 16D7). In this way we will recognize the entire number of Forms between the single character we started with and the indefinitely (16E1) many individual instances of the thing we have defined. Then and only then each one of this entirety can be thought of as one of indefinitely (16E2) many things of that type—in effect, characterizing the multitude as unlimited (16D7). The trouble with the wise men of the present day is that they (like Socrates of the *Phaedo*) think they can explain the properties of particular things with reference to single Forms—proceeding directly from the one to the indefinitely (17A2) many—without attending to the Forms in between.

In this reading, that is to say, ἄπειρον at 16D6 and 7, 16E1 and 2, and 17A2, receives the same interpretation as at 15B5—that of indefinitely many single things—while the reading of the Great and (the) Small—i.e., Indefinite Multitude—is retained at 16C10. According to this reading, the "godly method" is just the method of collection and division of the *Sophist* and the *Statesman*, combined with the ontological tradition stated at 16C9-10. The term ἄπειρον in this statement is taken in two interrelated senses, identical to those unquestionably conveyed by ἄπειρον πλῆθος in the *Parmenides* which we found antecedent reason[16] to associate with what Aristotle called the Indefinite Dyad or the Great and (the) Small.

Are we assuming too much in relying upon these two interrelated senses of ἄπειρον πλῆθος in the *Parmenides* as a guide in interpreting the use of ἄπειρον in the *Philebus*? The answer, I think, is that we are not; for that very expression—ἄπειρον πλῆθος—appears in the passage immediately following as Socrates undertakes to illustrate the "godly method." In response to Protarchus' call for clarification, Socrates offers a series of illustrations. And the first illustration he chooses is that of the letters, Plato's favorite example in discussing the nature of knowledge.[17] The sound that comes from our mouths, he says, is a single thing (μία: 17B3) for each and all of us, yet is indefinitely multitudinous (ἄπειρος αὖ πλήθει: 17B4). However, we are not knowledgeable by these things alone—by knowing it "either as indefiniteness or as unity" (ὅτι τὸ ἄπειρον αὐτῆς ἴσμεν . . . ὅτι τὸ ἕν: 17B7). What makes each of us "lettered," rather, is knowing "how many sounds there are and their properties" (ὅτι πόσα τ' ἐστὶ καὶ ὁποῖα: 17B7-8).

Before developing this particular illustration further (at 18B3ff.), Socrates introduces a second and related illustration from the area of music, and then repeats his general admonition about the results of failure to deal with a one-many relationship in the proper fashion. If one fails to grasp the number (τὸν ἀριθμὸν: 17C12) between the one and the many, then one becomes "disqualified from understanding" by the indeterminateness of it all. Somewhat more literally:

> the indeterminate multiplicity in and of particular things [τὸ δ' ἄπειρόν σε ἑκάστων καὶ ἐν ἑκάστοις πλῆθος: 17E2-3] makes each thought indeterminate and neither reputable nor numbered [ἄπειρον ἑκάστοτε ποιεῖ τοῦ φρονεῖν καὶ οὐκ ἐλλόγιμον οὐδ' ἐνάριθμον: 17E3-4], seeing that one can never give the number of anything [ἅτ' οὐκ εἰς ἀριθμὸν οὐδένα ἐν οὐδενὶ πώποτε ἀπιδόντα: 17E4-5].

The appearance of ἄπειρον . . . πλῆθος at 17E2-3 echoes that at 17B4, and carries the same meaning. In fact, this passage might be taken to illustrate both senses attached to the expression in the *Parmenides*, one being that of indefinitely many particulars, the other that of an indefinitely multitudinous principle which in itself admits no numeration at all. The problem one gets into by attempting to explain the presence of a common character in many individuals with reference to a single Form (as in the *Phaedo*) is not merely that the individuals are likely to be indefinitely numerous. The problem more importantly is that such an explanation tells us nothing about the manner in which limit is brought to the ἄπειρον. In terms more directly related to the formula for the constitution of sensible things attributed to Plato in the *Metaphysics*, such an explanation tells us nothing about how the Great and (the) Small receives the Forms that cut it up into individual sensible things—about how the ἄπειρον in the sense of the Indefinite Dyad yields the ἄπειρον (indefinitely numerous) sensible things that result when it submits to limit.

According to the "godly method" of 16C6, the proper explanation will say something about the number (ὁπόσα) of Forms between the single Form (with which Socrates in the *Phaedo* would have been satisfied) and the indefinite multitude of particulars. But as the second illustration makes clear, it is not the number of intervening Forms in itself that makes one knowledgeable, but rather the way these Forms relate to the ἄπειρον in which they come to be instantiated. The result of such instantiation is not merely a number of different intermediate Forms, but rather a set of Forms that provide number in the sense of measure.

The second illustration also has to do with vocal sound, but as divided into pitches rather than vowels and consonants. Just knowing the distinctions between high and low and sameness of pitch, of course, will not make a musician (17C). But when one comprehends:

the quantity of intervals—the number there is between high and low pitch [τὰ διαστήματα ὁπόσα ἐστὶ τὸν ἀριθμὸν τῆς φωνῆς ὀξύτητός τε πέρι καὶ βαρύτητος: 17C11-D1]—and what they are [καὶ ὁποῖα: 17D1], and the limits of their intervals [καὶ τοὺς ὅρους τῶν διαστημάτων:17D1), and how many scales are formed from them [καὶ τὰ ἐκ τούτων ὅσα συστήματα γέγονεν: 17D1-2]—noticing these things our ancestors have instructed us their successors to call them 'scales' [ἃ κατιδόντες οἱ πρόσθεν παρέδοσαν ἡμῖν τοῖς ἑπομένοις ἐκείνοις καλεῖν αὐτὰ ἁρμονίας: 17D2-4], and observing other similar features in bodily movements [like marching or dancing?] they said these should be numerically measured and called rhythms and meters [ἔν τε ταῖς κινήσεσιν αὖ τοῦ σώματος ἕτερα τοιαῦτα ἐνόντα πάθη γιγνόμενα, ἃ δὴ δι' ἀριθμῶν μετρηθέντα δεῖν αὖ φασι ῥυθμοὺς καὶ μέτρα ἐπονομάζειν: 17D4-6]—

when one comprehends this, that is to say, one realizes that this is the proper way to deal with every one-many relationship (παντὸς ἑνὸς καὶ πολλῶν: 17D7).

Despite the cumbersomeness of his description, Socrates here makes tolerably clear what it is to grasp the number between the one and the many. The "one" in question is the vocal sound that is identified with the production of music—broadly speaking, the class of musical sound. By way of contrast, there are the indefinitely many musical notes sounded in individual performances. Without the structure imposed by the intervals of the musical scale(s), the sounds of the performer would be indefinitely multitudinous, in the sense of being devoid of limit. Given the measure provided by the intervals, however, these sounds take on the structure of definite musical pitches, which can be exactly numbered and arranged in the systems of sounds we have learned to designate as musical scales. Because of their similarity to the measured cadence of marching or dancing (supposedly), we have come to call these numerically measurable elements 'rhythms' and 'meters'.

The dialectician's task, of course, is not that of the musician. It is not his business actually to divide the indefinite continuum of musical sound into definite systems of notes, either by way of original discovery (as the Pythagorean ancestors were thought to have discovered musical scales) or by way of individual performance. The dialectician's task is to distinguish the precise number of different intervals and systems of intervals that make up musical sound, and moreover to distinguish the various numerically distinct ways these elements can be arranged by rhythm and meter. In one possible way of putting it at least, the dialectician divides Musical Sound into Octave, Fifth, Fourth, etc., or alternatively into A, B, C, etc., and also into what we would call (3/4), (4/4), etc., by way of meter. Being able to do this to an appropriate level of specificity makes a man knowledgeable in music.

Socrates' lightly veiled reference to the Pythagorean origin of the musical scale, however, indicates that he is concerned with more than musical knowledge of a dialectical sort. The "gift of the gods" these wise men passed on is not merely the method of collection and division. It is this method coupled with an ontological principle regarding the constitution of things. According to this principle, all things we say exist are composed of the one and the many, of limit and the unlimited. And it is because things are so disposed that the dialectician in search of knowledge is instructed to seek out the precise number between the one and the unlimited many. The different Forms isolated by the dialectician in the process of division, we might surmise, should somehow correspond to the natural lines of demarcation by which the ἄπειρον is limited in the original constitution of those things that are relevant to the dialectical inquiry. To put it crudely, the structure of Forms with which the dialectician is concerned must correspond to the structure of elements out of which the relevant things are constituted by πέρας and ἄπειρον.[18] In the case of musical sound, this means simply that the formal divisions among intervals and meters that yield knowledge of music must correspond to the audible divisions by which the early Pythagoreans supposedly were able to bring numerical order to the otherwise indefinite range of higher and lower sound. In a sense, the Pythagoreans *created* music (after all, they were better than us, and lived closer to the gods: 16C7-8). In terms of the fourfold division of all things introduced later in the dialogue (23C-D), the Pythagorean discoverers of the numerical ratios that make up the musical scale provided the intelligence by which the appropriate mixture of πέρας and ἄπειρον was brought about. To put the above point (even more crudely) in yet another way, the order of knowledge must correspond to the order of creation.

When Socrates returns to the alphabetical illustration at 18B, emphasis has shifted from knowing (ἴσμιν: 17B7) the letters to actually separating (διεστήσατο: 18C2-3) them out of the Unlimited (ἀπείρῳ: 18B9) in the first place (πρῶτος: 18B8). As Socrates puts it directly, in the previous case we begin by grasping the one, and are warned "not to look to the indefinite nature immediately, but rather to some number" (οὐκ ἐπ' ἀπείρου φύσιν δεῖ βλέπειν εὐθὺς ἀλλ' ἐπί τινα ἀριθμόν: 18A8-9). In the present and opposite (ἐναντίον: 18A9) case, when one "is forced to take the ἄπειρον as a beginning" (τις τὸ ἄπειρον ἀναγκασθῇ πρῶτον λαμβάνειν: 18A9-B1), one ought not to look to the one immediately (μὴ ἐπὶ τὸ ἓν εὐθύς: 18B1), but should discern some number embracing each plurality [ἀλλ᾽ ἐπ᾽ ἀριθμὸν αὖ τινα πλῆθος ἕκαστον ἔχοντά τι κατανοεῖν: 18B1-2], and from all these end up at the one (τελευτᾶν τε ἐκ πάντων εἰς ἕν: 18B2-3).

In the previous case, that is to say, the dialectician began with the unspecified Form, Musical Sound, and works his way by successive division to the several intervals and rhythms instantiated in a multitude of individual performances. In the present case, we are to begin instead with the ἄπειρον (or φωνὴν ἄπειρον: 18B6) and work our way in the other direction toward the one. The intelligence by which this latter is accomplished is not that of the mortal dialectician, but rather that of some god or godlike man (18B6-7). In Egyptian lore, the intelligence in question is attributed to the god Theuth, who in the *Phaedrus* is credited also with the invention or discovery (εὑρεῖν: 274C8) of number and the various skills that go with it (calculation, geometry, and astronomy) as well as of writing. It was Theuth also, according to the present story, who first apprehended (κατενόησεν: 18B9) the vowels in the Unlimited (ἀπείρῳ: 18B9) with which he began—not just one but several vowels—and then noticed others that are not vowels but could be sounded, of which also there are a particular number (ἀριθμὸν . . . τινα: 18C1-2). Next he

separated a third class of articulate sound that we now call mutes [τρίτον δὲ εἶδος γραμμάτων διεστήσατο τὰ νῦν λεγόμενα ἄφωνα ἡμῖν: 18C2-3]. After that he distinguished the mutes or soundless ones down to the level of the individual [τὸ μετὰ τοῦτο διῄρει τά τε ἄφθογγα καὶ ἄφωνα μέχρι ἑνὸς ἑκάστου: 18C3-4), and did the same with the vowels and the intermediates [the semivowels] [καὶ τὰ φωνήεντα καὶ τὰ μέσα κατὰ τὸν αὐτὸν τρόπον: 18C4-5]. Finally when he had got the number of them all, he gave to them individually and collectively the name 'element' [ἕως ἀριθμὸν αὐτῶν λαβὼν ἑνί τε ἑκάστῳ καὶ σύμπασι στοιχεῖον ἐπωνόμασε: 18C5-7].

Realizing that none of us would ever grasp one of these letters in isolation from the whole group, he considered this to be a unifying bond making them all somehow one and, speaking accordingly, said that they constituted the singular "art of letters" (γραμματικὴν τέχνην: 18D2).

This distinction between accomplishments in the former and in the present case is stressed in the dialogue and should not be neglected. The accomplishment in the former case belongs to the dialectician. He begins with Vocal Sound already conceived as a unity, and is counseled to seek the number and kinds of intermediate sounds and to avoid proceeding directly to the unlimited range of particular instances. The dialectician "knows his letters" when he knows the several Forms between Vocal Sound and the grammatical vocalizations of individual speakers. In the opposite case the task is to begin with sound totally undifferentiated (φωνὴν ἄπειρον: 18B6) into phonetic elements—that is, with a vocal ἄπειρον devoid of any unity—and hence to distinguish by a creative act of discrimination the various phonetic sounds we call "vowels," "semivowels," and "mutes." The final stage in this creative process is to enumerate all the Forms of sound thereby distinguished as phonetic elements, recognizing the systems of elements thus composed as belonging to a single art of letters. To proceed in this creative manner from the vocal ἄπειρον to the single Form, Phonetic Sound, is the accomplishment, not of the dialectician as such, but of a god or godlike intelligence capable of imposing Limit on the Unlimited, and producing a system of intelligible sound as a result. Although (as *Phaedrus* 265E stresses) there may well be natural lines of division to be followed as the godly intelligence separates the phonetic elements out of the ἄπειρον, the result nonetheless is an act of creation on its part. The dialectician, by contrast, does not create the lines of demarcation followed in his divisions, but rather seeks to discriminate limits imposed by an intelligence other than his own. While Socrates has not yet (foreshadowing 23C-D) provided the classification in terms of which this point can be made, the role of Theuth in the story is to serve as Intelligent Cause by which Limit is imposed upon the Unlimited in the production of the phonetic elements as "Mixed" result.

The "gift of the gods" is both ontological and epistemological in character. Corresponding to the general ontological principle that all existing things are composed of one and many, or Limit and the Unlimited, there is the example of Theuth, representing divine intelligence, actually constructing the phonetic system by an appropriate imposition of limits upon the ἄπειρον. Corresponding to the methodological instructions following that principle at 16D, in turn, is the example of the dialectician dividing the general Form, Vocal Sound, into the precise number of Formal elements that constitute this phonetic system. The "godly method" of dialectic is neither more nor less than the reverse counterpart of the "godly method" of creation by which the system of Forms studied by the dialectician is originally composed.[19]

The dialectical aspect of the method is further illustrated at 23C-D where Socrates divides "all that exists in the present universe" (Πάντα τὰ νῦν ὄντα ἐν τῷ παντὶ: 23C4) into the forms (εἰδῶν: 23C12 also 23D2) or kinds (γένους: 23D5): Unlimited, Limit, Mixture, and Cause.[20] Its ontological aspect is further illustrated by a more explicit elaboration of the results of mixing Limit with the Unlimited. These matters are the topics of the following two sections, respectively.

2. Limit and the Unlimited

Forms like those of musical intervals and rhythms, and of phonetic mutes and vowels, are constituted by the imposition of Limit upon the sheer Unlimited. The result is a system of musical or phonetic elements that are one in being singular and unique, and also many in being manifest in countless particular sounds or utterances. But there is a sense as well in which Limit and the Unlimited themselves are one and many (ἓν καὶ πολλὰ: 23E6). Starting with the Unlimited, Socrates shows first that it is "splintered" (ἐσχισμένον: 23E4) into many different manifestations, like hotter and colder and "exceedingly and slightly" (τὸ σφόδρα . . . καὶ τό . . . ἠρέμα: 24C1-2). It is one, nonetheless, in that each of these manifestations shares a single characteristic—the

"mark of the nature of the Unlimited" (τῆς τοῦ ἀπείρου φύσεως . . . σημεῖον: 24E4-5). The mark of the Unlimited is that
it admits "becoming more and less (μᾶλλόν τε καὶ ἧττον γιγνόμενα: 24E7-8). All things admitting "more and less," accordingly, are to be put "under the single kind of the Unlimited"
(εἰς τὸ τοῦ ἀπείρου γένος ὡς εἰς ἕν: 25A1-2). In short, we
are "to mark such things by a single nature" (μίαν ἐπισημαί-
νεσθαί τινα φύσιν: 25A4).

Things not admitting these features, on the other hand, but
rather admitting their opposites—

first equal and equality [πρῶτον μὲν τὸ ἴσον καὶ ἰσότητα:
25A8]; and after equal, double [μετὰ δὲ τὸ ἴσον τὸ διπλάσιον: 25A9], and everything that relates as number to
number or measure to measure [καὶ πᾶν ὅτιπερ ἂν πρὸς
ἀριθμὸν ἀριθμὸς ἢ μέτρον ἢ πρὸς μέτρον: 25A9-B1]²¹—

all these things ought to be reckoned as coming under Limit.
Although Socrates has not cited specific examples of Limit as he
did with the Unlimited (a fact which he recognizes at 25d), it is
clear that the characterization "relating as number to number
or measure to measure" picks out a mark of this class just as
"becoming more and less" does for the class of the Unlimited.

According to the account of the previous section, Musical
Sound is both one and many in the sense of being a single Form
manifest in an indefinite number of particular instances. In a
prima facie similar fashion, Limit and the Unlimited themselves
now appear to be one and many. Does this mean that the Unlimited, for example, itself is a Form, of which hotter and colder,
exceedingly and slightly, and so forth, are particular manifestations? The question is complicated by the fact that Plato uses
terminology here which in earlier dialogues would naturally be
understood as referring to the Forms, and to the dialectical process by which they are known. At 23C12, and by implication
23D2, Limit and the Unlimited are called εἰδῶν (compare 16D7),
and the term γένος is used in this connection several times within
the next few pages (23D5, 25A1, 26D2, 26E2, 27A12, 30B1).
Moreover, the term συναγωγή, which is the very term used at
Phaedrus 266B4 for the process of collection, is used in appar-

ently the same application at 23E5 and 25A3 (and by implication, 25D6,7), where Socrates speaks of collecting the varieties of the Unlimited together in order to discern their common character. And the companion procedure of division seems to be mentioned at 23D, where Socrates disingenuously apologizes for his sorting of things into classes (κατ' εἴδη διϊστὰς: 23D2). The inference initially invited by this terminology is that Socrates here is engaged in a particular application of collection and division, thereby treating Limit and the Unlimited as intelligible Forms.[22]

Nonetheless, there are weighty reasons why this inference should be resisted. For one thing, we have seen no evidence yet that the Forms as understood in the middle dialogues—eternal, self-sufficient objects, radically distinct from the sensible things that participate in them—even appear in the *Philebus*. Scruples on this ground are not out of order, inasmuch as we are working in the shadow of Aristotle's pronouncement that for Plato the Forms are numbers. If there is any sense in which this formula holds for the *Philebus*, clearly we cannot count the Unlimited at least among the Forms, since the Unlimited is the very opposite (ἐναντία: 25A8) of what admits number. A related consideration is that whatever Forms might be in the context of the *Philebus*, if they are to be recognizable as such at all they must impart definite characteristics to the things that participate in them. But such things as hotter and colder, or extremely and slightly, which we have been tempted to think of as instantiations of the Unlimited, are themselves unlimited precisely in not exhibiting definite characteristics. Whatever the relationship between the Unlimited "in general" and hotter and colder "in particular," it cannot be the relationship between Form and instantiation.

Another telling reason why this cannot be so is that dialectical division as characterized in the "godly tradition" follows in reverse order the distinctions created by the "godlike" intelligence responsible for subjecting the Unlimited to Limit. Form, that is to say, results from the imposition of Limit upon the Unlimited. But it is entirely unthinkable that Limit and the Unlimited themselves result from the imposition of Limit upon the Unlimited. Hence these two principles themselves cannot be Forms.

To think of Socrates' treatment of these two basic principles between 23D and 25C as somehow of a piece with the dialectical method recommended at 16D is an entirely unpromising approach. This is so despite the remark at 23E6 that Limit and the Unlimited themselves are one and many. The tenor of that remark, in fact, is such as to suggest on the face of it that the sense in which these principles are one and many is not the same as that obtaining with Forms and their instances. The challenge posed at 23E6 is to attempt to see "how in the world" (πῇ ποτε) each of these things is one and many. And the manner in which this is so, inadequately understood as it may yet be, has nothing to do with Forms and particulars.

A further indication that this is so, if one is needed, is that the division undertaken by Socrates at 23D is not dialectical at all. Limit and the Unlimited are not further articulated in an effort to reach the defining characteristics of the thing being considered. If there is any specific method by which "becoming more and less" is reached as the "mark of the nature of the Unlimited," it is nothing more procedural than a simple examination of cases at point. The division of "all that exists in the present universe" into the four kinds—Limit, Unlimited, Mixture and Cause—to be sure, is rather like that at *Timaeus* 48E, where Pattern, Imitation, and Receptable are distinguished as primordial principles.[23] Although the terms εἶδος (48E3) and γένος (48E4) figure in that division as well, there is no temptation to think of the principles thus distinguished (with the exception of Pattern, of course) as like Forms in the traditional sense.

If the first two principles into which "all that exists in the present universe" are divided are not Forms, then what are they? The answer to which my line of interpretation is committed, of course, is that they are what Aristotle called "the Great and (the) Small" and "Unity," respectively. My primary argument for this interpretive approach is that it makes considerably better sense of the difficult methodological and ontological passages of the *Philebus* than do alternative approaches. I have already examined its results in connection both with the "godly method" and with the illustrative examples from music and the phonetic alphabet. It remains to spell out the consequences of this approach for the equally difficult passages between 23E and 27B. Before the case from this approach can be made complete, however, it will be necessary to examine the major alternatives and to identify their shortcomings. A reason for undertaking this examination at the present juncture is that some of these alternatives contain insights that will help make the notion of "the Great and (the) Small" itself more intelligible.

Attempts to catalog available interpretations of Limit and the Unlimited in the *Philebus* have been made by Crombie (1963), Striker (1970), and Gosling (1975). Gosling's treatment is particularly helpful, both in being more recent and comprehensive and in providing specific lists of desiderata (to which I will turn later) on which competing views can be evaluated. As Gosling sees it, there have been two main lines of interpretation among twentieth-century commentators, to which his own is added as a more promising third.

According to the first interpretation (which Gosling attributes in one form or another to Jowett, Ross, Taylor, Hackforth, et al.), Limit and the Unlimited are to be thought of as anticipations of Aristotle's Form and Matter. The Unlimited is "the undetermined potentiality for manifesting certain properties."[24] Inasmuch as objects can be described as having certain temperatures, weights, and so on, there must exist in them something with capacity for taking on these determinations. That is to say, there must exist "a material receptacle with these potentialities, waiting for the imposition of a form to produce some object with these qualities."[25] Limit, in turn, includes those numbers or proportions (cf. 25A9-B1) the presence of which constitutes a Form. As Gosling notes, the material principle in question need not be thought of as pure potentiality, capable of any determination whatever. That which becomes a definite temperature has heat already in some indeterminate manner, involving constant change and instability. Its potentiality is to take on a specific and relatively fixed temperature, which is accomplished by the imposition of Form or Limit. A more accurate characterization of the Unlimited, accordingly, is that as material principle it "is not potentiality to receive a certain character" per se, as was Aristotle's Prime Matter, but rather "something with that character in flux with the potentiality to have it in a precise degree."[26] As with Aristotle's Form and Matter, however, the mixture of Limit with the Unlimited is supposed to produce sensible things with particular properties.

One difficulty with any view like this which makes Limit and the Unlimited constituent principles of particular sensible things is that it seems hard to reconcile with 25E-26B. The problem is that Limit in these passages (and at 30B-C as well) seems to be a principle of positive value, in opposition to disorder, which is portrayed as defective. That is to say, the contrast between Limit and the Unlimited in this context appears not to be a contrast between the formal and the material element constitutive of particular objects in general, but rather that between good and bad states in which particular objects might in fact exist. This sense that Limit and the Unlimited are somehow value-laden in character is conveyed primarily by a list of products supposedly arising from a mixture of the two, but is hinted at as well in a second characterization of the class of Limit at 25E.[27] The family of the Limit, says Socrates, is

> that of the equal and double [Τὴν τοῦ ἴσου καὶ διπλα-σίου: 25D11], and whatever stops opposites conflicting with one another [καὶ ὁπόση παύει πρὸς ἄλληλα τἀναντία ·διαφόρως ἔχοντα: 25D11-E1], making them commensurate and harmonious by the introduction of number [σύμ-μετρα δὲ καὶ σύμφωνα ἐνθεῖσα ἀριθμὸν ἀπεργάζεται: 25E1-2].

As examples of desirable mixtures brought about by the "harmony producing" influence of Limit upon the "conflicting opposites" of the Unlimited, Socrates cites health, "music as a whole," the seasons, "all that is beautiful," and "countless other things" (26B5). As Gosling interprets these examples, "measure and proportion emerge always as what constitute fineness and excellence," which "entails that a poor mixture is not in the required sense a mixture at all, and so not all states of objects are mixtures"[28] of Limit and the Unlimited as this interpretation maintains.

A second difficulty for this interpretation, in Gosling's estimation, is that when Socrates does talk explicitly about the constitution of particular things at 29A-C he mentions the traditional four elements (earth, air, fire, and water) but says nothing at all about Limit and the Unlimited. On the other hand, we do have an explicit example of things being constituted out of the Unlimited and number at 18B-D with Theuth's discrimination of the vowels and mutes; and in this case what is thereby constituted apparently are not particular things at all but rather specific Forms of phonetic sound.

It is because of problems like this that Striker[29] and others have been led to formulate an alternative view, which Gosling treats as second among the major existing interpretations. According to this interpretation, the Unlimited is a set of concepts and has nothing directly to do with sensible objects at all. In saying at 24A-25A that hotter, colder, slightly, and so forth, are all Unlimited in admitting "becoming more and less," Socrates is saying that the concepts "hot," "cold," and so forth, can be qualified by such terms as 'more', 'less', and so on.[30] But if the Unlimited element consists of concepts, so too must the mixture of Limit and Unlimited. This means that the concept of health, for instance, can be analyzed into concepts of indeterminate properties having to do with bodily functions, and into formal or numerical factors having to do with how these properties are related in a healthy person. Although as Striker points out[31] Plato had no technical expression for "concept," his concern in these passages was with the analysis of concepts applying to particular objects rather than with the constitution of such objects themselves.

One possible difficulty with this interpretation is that, even if some concepts belong to the class of the Unlimited, surely this is not the case with concepts generally. For instance, the concept "health," being a mixture of Limit with the Unlimited, cannot belong to the Unlimited just by itself. Anticipating this problem, Striker provides a criterion for determining membership in the Unlimited, to the effect roughly that only concepts qualify which in application to an individual object imply that there are other objects more or less fully endowed in the relevant respect than the object in question.[32] For example, unless there are some things more or less hot than a given object, it is uninformative to call that object hot itself.

Another problem is posed by the fact that several passages[33] suggest strongly that particular objects or states of affairs are to be included in the class of the Unlimited, whereas this interpretation finds room there for concepts only. Striker attempts to forestall this difficulty by suggesting that since in Plato's estimation the class of cold things is included in the Unlimited, members of the former are considered members of the latter as well[34]—in effect, a confusion of class inclusion with class membership. Hence he would find it appropriate to mention particular pleasures, for example (52C), as instances of the Unlimited.

What Gosling considers the most serious difficulty of this interpretation, however, is that it involves an essentially different use of the term ἄπειρον at 23C and following than its advocates usually read into the "godly method" at 16D-E. In Crombie's analysis, for instance, ἄπειρον at 16D-E refers to "the *indefinite* number of variants, or instances," of a specific universal.[35] To read the term as designating a classification of concepts instead in this later context is to assume that Plato has shifted the meaning of a key term radically in just a few pages, quite contrary to what we are led to expect by the transitional remarks at 23C. This objection could have been appended to another that Gosling might well have made, to the effect that this second interpretation seems unduly forced and complicated. Unless no other alternatives are available, we cannot rest happily with the suggestions (1) that, in a passage purporting to explain how "things that come to be" are constituted from Limit and the Unlimited, Plato really was concerned primarily with concepts, even though he had no vocabulary in which concepts could be discussed, and (2) that he did not realize that talking about concepts was not to talk about "things that come to be," because he confused class membership and class inclusion.

Yet another objection against Gosling's second interpretation is that several of the alleged problems with the older interpretation (Gosling's first) that provided its motivation in fact are rather easily resolved. Since these same problems might be raised also against the interpretation based upon Aristotle's notion of "the Great and (the) Small" which I am attempting to develop, it is appropriate to look at them a bit more carefully.

One difficulty with the first interpretation, we recall, is that it seems unable to cope with the fact that the examples of mixture at 26A-B all appear to be cases in which the results are especially desirable. Since not all particular objects or states of affairs are desirable, it seems to follow that the mixture of Limit with the Unlimited cannot be responsible for all particular things. Two points should be made in response. First, the difficulty is not easily generated if one attends carefully to Plato's exact language at 25E7 and following. What he says there is not that combining Limit and Unlimited invariably produces health, music, or other desirable things, or that it produces these only when these in fact are produced. What he says is that their combination produces something in each case (ἐφ' ἑκάστων αὐτῶν: 25E4), that the *right* combination (ὀρθὴ κοινωνία: 25E7) generates health in the case of sickness, and that in the cases "of high and low, and of fast and slow—indeterminate things" (ὀξεῖ καὶ βαρεῖ καὶ ταχεῖ καὶ βραδεῖ, ἀπείροις οὖσιν: 26A2-3)—the introduction of members of the family of limit[36] "both expresses Limit perfectly and comprises music as a whole in full completeness" (ἅμα πέρας τε ἀπηργάσατο καὶ μουσικὴν σύμπασαν τελεώτατα συνεστήσατο: 26A3-5). It is sensible on the one hand to question whether all combinations of Limit and Unlimited are right combinations. On the other, it remains possible that certain normative (right) combinations, say that of equal and double with the indeterminate high and low to produce musical pitches (perfectly exact middle C, etc.), might also establish ranges of instances (e.g., notes in actual performances) which although imperfect are identifiable and nameable with reference to these norms. In either case, the listing of only desirable cases at 26A-B is compatible with the interpretation according to which the "things that come to be" at 27A11-12 include both Forms (norms) and sensible things (instances judged by those norms).

The second point to be noted in this connection is that Aristotle identified the Great and (the) Small and Unity as causes of Bad and Good, respectively, but was not thereby prevented from saying in Plato's behalf that both Forms and sensible things are constituted from these two principles. It is reasonable to expect that an interpretation that explains how this is possible in the *Metaphysics* will explain the parallel possibility in the *Philebus*, and vice versa. According to the interpretation presently being developed, of course, the cases are identical. To explain how the principles of Good and Bad can nonetheless be constitutive of all sensible things is a major goal of the final sections of this chapter.

Another objection raised by Gosling against the first interpretation was that, in his words, if Plato "meant physical objects in all states to be mixtures, then he missed a golden opportunity of making this clear," for when at 29A and following "he compares the constitution of our bodies to that of the universe at large," he mentions the traditional four elements only, with no suggestion of "any connection between, say, fire and the hotter or any *apeiron* mentioned earlier."[37] In response to this objection it may be pointed out that, although Plato might have mentioned some connection between the Limit and Unlimited constitutive of "all things that come to be" (27A11) and the traditional four elements if he had seen fit to do so, the fact that he does not do so is no indication that he does not mean what he says at 27A11. The list of earth, air, fire and water at 29A10 is presented as a popular view regarding the constituency of "the corporeal nature of all living bodies" (τὴν τῶν σωμάτων φύσιν ἁπάντων τῶν ζῴων: 29A9-10), in the course of a highly rhetorical argument that mind is (or belongs to the category of: 30E1) the cause of all things. Since Protarchus obviously is not yet comfortable with the notion of Limit and the Unlimited as constituents of all that comes into being, it is good tactics for Socrates to formulate this particular argument in more traditional terms. Quite apart from the dynamics of this particular interchange, however, we should be able to see that the citation of the traditional four elements as constituents of "the corporeal nature of all living bodies" is not incompatible with the more general claim that "all things that come to be" are constituted of Limit and the Unlimited. It is no more incompatible, at least, than a modern listing of various protein molecules as constituents of all living organisms is incompatible with a general theory to the effect that everything in the universe is composed of electrons and protons, subatomic particles, force fields, or what have you.

Yet another problem for the first interpretation pointed out by Gosling, which in fact he considers "perhaps the most serious" of all, is that the illustrations at 17B-18D concern "general phenomena of vocal sound"—what we have called the Forms of musical intervals, vowels, mutes, and so forth—and not, as the interpretation would lead us to expect, "the constitution of individual objects."[38] This remains a serious difficulty for any interpretation aspiring to draw any connection between these illustrations and the remark at 27A11 that "all things that come to be" are composed of Limit and the Unlimited. For the reference of this latter remark seems clearly to include individual sensible objects, while the illustrations just as clearly pertain to Forms. We should bear in mind, however, that 27A11 is only a partial restatement of 16C9-10, which claims that Limit and the Unlimited are constituents of "those things always said to exist." And this very general claim, which in fact is the keynote of the "godly tradition" itself, seems clearly to refer to Forms as well as sensible objects. The illustrations at 17B-18D, as I have suggested, include examples both of dialectical method and of creative art or skill (τέχνης: 16C2)—just what we would expect as illustrations of the "godly method." As such, these examples deal both with the constitution of Forms from Limit and the Unlimited, and the method by which connections among these Forms are traced by the dialectician. In the section beginning with 25E, on the other hand, Socrates is dealing with the class of mixtures of Limit and Unlimited, and according to the illustrations there, this certainly includes individual sensible things. These two sections would appear not only harmonious but complementary if we could see that the "godly tradition" is about the constitution both of Forms and of sensible objects. A clue that this in fact is the case is provided by Aristotle's (increasingly less) mystifying report that for Plato both Forms and sensible things are composed from the Great and (the) Small—in the first case by imposition of Unity, in the second by imposition of Form. The task of showing just how this all works out in the *Philebus* is one to which we turn in the following section.

In the meanwhile, we can only agree with Gosling's estimation that neither of the two major alternative interpretations of πέρας and the ἄπειρον are without serious difficulties. The third interpretation he considers is one of his own devising. A remarkable thing about this interpretation is that it comes close to opening up the resources of the *Metaphysics* and of the Aristotelian commentators, and yet never quite turns the corner that brings these resources into view.[39] This interpretation warrants a careful examination.

Gosling's own account begins with a series of relevant observations about the "godly tradition." For one thing, "the terminology of *peras* and *apeiron* is characteristically Pythagorean."[40] For another, it "is hard to resist the conclusion that the Prometheus referred to at 16c6 is Pythagoras" himself. In addition, there is "the stress laid on number, which . . . would have obvious Pythagorean echoes." And at 31A9-10, "*apeiron* receives the traditional Pythagorean characterization as that without beginning middle or end." An additional point is that "it is highly probable that in the *Philebus* we have Plato's reaction to the repercussions of Eudoxus," whom Gosling on the authority of Diogenes Laertius considers to have been associated with the Pythagoreans. In particular, Eudoxus made notable contributions to the problem of irrationals, which had caused considerable consternation among Pythagoreans and other mathematicians during the first half of the fourth century.

Now while Eudoxus was most distinguished as a mathematician, he also maintained an ethical theory about pleasure being the good. Gosling is able to argue effectively that Plato's critique of hedonism in the *Philebus* is aimed at this theory. Part of the argument is to point out that much of the terminology that runs through the treatment of Limit and the Unlimited in the *Philebus* is taken from the vocabulary in which the problem of irrationals had traditionally been discussed.[41] Against this background, Gosling then asks what connection there might have been in Plato's mind between Eudoxus' interest in irrationals and his hedonism as the *Philebus* represents it.[42] Gosling's account, in effect, is an answer to this question.

After a brief presentation of the problem of irrationals in terms of a geometrical example, Gosling observes in summary that "the discovery of irrationals was the discovery that a continuum can be divided *ad infinitum (eis apeiron)*, that is that there is no length in terms of which to measure all divisions of a continuum."[43] Setting the mathematical issue aside,[44] he then argues that the illustration at 17B-D can be understood as showing one way in which the variety of musical sounds can be represented as distributed along a continuum of higher and lower. Discovery of musical scales (by our Pythagorean forebears) was discovery of limits by which this continuum can be divided into mathematically describable intervals, and musical skill is the ability of a composer or performer to deal with musical sound in terms of these intervals. Although there are various ways in which the continuum of sound pitches can be subdivided, and accordingly various systems of musical sound (various scales) with which a musician might deal, no system can possibly incorporate all points along the continuum. Like all ranges of phenomena representable by a continuous line, the range of musical sound is infinitely divisible, and hence remains Unlimited even after the assignment of Limit.

According to Gosling's interpretation, the "godly method" is a way of dealing with such phenomena on a mathematical basis. When Socrates says at 25A8-B1 that Limit is that which admits "equal and equality, . . . double and every proportion of number to number or measure to measure" (Gosling's translation), he means that the limits imposed upon a continuum by anyone following this method are literally mathematical in character. The *technai* that the "godly method" makes possible—like music and (potentially[45]) grammar—all depend, in Gosling's view, upon the possibility of mathematical representation.[46]

In defending the thesis that pleasure is the Good, Protarchus in the dialogue (and presumably Eudoxus in real life) is putting forward a principle which, if defensible, should provide some kind of *techne* by which human life could be systematically and intelligently organized (although Gosling does not say so, perhaps something like the "hedonic calculus" of the *Protagoras*). Just as "a musician is expected to produce an account of the rules for combining notes," so Protarchus, if his position is defensible, should be able to "tell us how pleasures are to be combined"[47] and unified in a single, mathematically articulated system of human conduct. Implausible as this may seem on the face of it, "only in this way can Eudoxus' interest in irrationals be related to his doctrine on pleasure."[48]

According to Gosling's account, in brief, the Unlimited comprises various ranges of phenomenon that can be represented as mathematical continua, and Limit comprises any of various ways in which such phenomena can be subdivided so as to be subject to mathematical treatment. The *technai* made possible (16C) by the "godly method," accordingly, are ways of imposing Limit upon the Unlimited that produce combinations of these phenomena subject to mathematical treatment. The mixed class of things described at 25D-26B, in his estimation, are "combinations produced by a techne," that is, "proportions of measures on a particular continuum."[49] In speaking of Limit, the Unlimited, and things resulting from their mixture, Plato is concerned with the development of mathematically based *technai*, and not in any sense with the constitution of objects.[50]

Gosling has brought us a considerable distance toward what I believe is the correct interpretation of the terms ἄπειρον and πέρας in the *Philebus*. Yet his account remains subject to several objections, some of which he anticipates. The problem Gosling himself seems most preoccupied with stems from his interpretation of the "godly tradition," and derivatively from his understanding of the one-many problem. At the beginning of his discussion with Protarchus, Socrates points out that the pleasures of immoral and of sensible persons seem opposed to each other, raising the question of how a single thing (pleasure) can appear in several opposing forms. Since similar questions arise about knowledge, both candidates for the Good seem threatened from the outset, and Socrates offers some observations about "the one and the many" as a general problem. Although a straightforward reading of 15B suggests that the problem Socrates had in mind is how one Form can be instantiated in many particulars—in effect, the problem of participation—Gosling decides that the problem is how pleasure, and so on, can take on various different and sometimes opposed forms.[51] This interpretation governs

Gosling's account of the "godly method," which Socrates says (15D) is the proper way to deal with the one-many problem. In effect, the problem is solved in the case of a particular ἄπειρον (e.g., vocal sound) when a *techne* has been achieved that systematizes diverse phenomena in the field by a single bond of unity (e.g., the *phone*, p. 172). The difficulty Gosling sees in this connection is that there appears another "one-many problem" a few pages later to which the "godly method" seems inapplicable. For at 23E-24A the ἄπειρον itself is said to be both one and many, and Gosling rightly sees that there is no mathematical bond of unity by which the several varieties of ἄπειρον at 24A-25A can be unified. Their common mark instead is "becoming more or less," which is precisely the opposite of any mathematical unity. Gosling's problem here would be solved if he were to recognize that the "godly method" is basically the method of collection and division, and that what Socrates calls "collection" at 23E5 is just that—a collection of different varieties of ἄπειρον with an eye to discerning their common feature.[52]

There is another set of difficulties concerning his conception of the "godly method" which Gosling acknowledges, but seems to consider relatively incidental. One is that the method as he interprets it has practically no resemblance to any other method in the dialogues, despite the fact that at 16B Socrates describes it as a method to which he has always been devoted. Gosling solves this (halfheartedly) by observing that Plato showed signs of favoring mathematical techniques as early as the *Republic*.[53]

Another is that mathematical approaches of the sort Gosling suggests seem singularly inappropriate in connection with most of the fields of skill to which the "godly method" either directly or by implication is supposed to be applicable in the *Philebus*—such as grammar, beauty, health, strength and "fair weather." The only case in which it appears applicable at all is music, and this to a limited degree only (a person totally innocent of mathematics could still be a good musician). Gosling's conjecture that Plato in these cases believed that mathematical techniques might one day be found[54] seems a superficial response to the problem.

Perhaps the most serious difficulty with his account, however, is one that Gosling seems to have suppressed completely. As we have seen, his conception of the "godly method," and of the role ἄπειρον and πέρας play within it, leads him to deny that these two principles have anything to do with the constitution of particular things. Yet there are no fewer than five passages between 14 and 28 (the section of the dialogue receiving the giant share of his commentary) which say more or less specifically that the opposite is the case. The first, already examined above in detail, occurs at 16C9-10, asserting that "those things that are always said to exist" have "Limit and the Unlimited within themselves connaturally." Although there remains room for debate on this issue, it seems reasonably clear that particular objects are among things always said to exist.⁵⁵ The second, which has also been noted, is the reference at 27A11 to Limit and the Unlimited as constitutive of "all things that come to be." Third, there is mention at 25E4 of things coming to be by a mixture of these two principles. Fourth, there is reference at 26D9-10 to whatever "comes into being from the measure introduced by limit" as the progeny of Limit and the Unlimited. And fifth, at 27B7-9 there is mention of a third class whose "existence is brought about" as a mixture of these same two principles. Clearly these last two passages, which are central to the discussion of the following section, refer to individual sensible objects.

Gosling's interpretation of Limit and the Unlimited, it seems to me, goes wrong primarily in his attempt to assign a literal mathematical significance to the term πέρας. Although he is very probably right in tracing Plato's use of ἄπειρον and πέρας back to Pythagorean origins, the latter term should not be confined in application to mathematical measures exclusively. By nature, Limit includes "everything that relates as number to number or measure to measure" (25A8-B1). But there is no necessity that the numbers or measures in question be mathematical in any strict sense. Among numbers might be temporal moments, which according to *Physics* 219b1-2 are numbers of motion. And among measures might be those of moderation, which according to *Statesman* 284B1 accounts for the effectiveness of weaving and statecraft. By similarly broadening Gosling's conception of the Unlimited, moreover, we ought to countenance under that heading not only ranges of phenomena that can be represented by a mathematically continuous line as such, like musical tones, but also phenomena that exhibit indefinite divisibility in other forms as well. An example would be vocal sound itself which, although a prime illustration of the Unlimited in the *Philebus*, can scarcely be conceived as a linear continuum. The mark of the Unlimited according to the dialogue, after all, is not linear continuity as such but "becoming more or less," and any range of phenomena should qualify that possesses that mark.

Thus construed, the Unlimited of the *Philebus* in its primary meaning[56] is what Aristotle (in comparing Plato with the Pythagoreans) referred to as "the Great and (the) Small," or the "Indefinite Dyad." Textual evidence that this is the case comes with the intelligibility that can be achieved by applying this interpretation to passages of the dialogue that notoriously have been most difficult to understand. Before returning to the task of marshaling this evidence, however, there is evidence of another sort that takes on added interest in light of Gosling's remarks about Pythagorean origins. In point of fact, direct support for this mathematically inspired interpretation can be found in the commentary by Simplicius on Book III of the *Metaphysics*.

To begin with, there is a passage pertaining to *Physics* 207a18 in which Aristotle is cited as having reported that Plato, in his remarks on the Good, said that the Great and (the) Small was matter, that it was unlimited (ἄπειρον: 503.13), and that it contained all sensible things, which were unknowable because of their material, fluid, and unlimited nature (ἄπειρον . . . τὴν φύσιν: 503.15). Parallel to this is a passage in Alexander's commentary on *Metaphysics* 987b33, saying that Plato spoke of his Dyad as being both Indefinite and Unlimited (ἀόριστον τε καὶ ἄπειρον: 56.20). Since this claim, like that of Simplicius above, traces back to Plato's lecture on the Good (56,35), by our hypothesis it may be judged relevant to his doctrine in the *Philebus*.

All uncertainty about this matter of relevance vanishes when we turn to a series of comments by Simplicius on *Physics* 202b36. Since the paths of thought into which these comments lead are somewhat tortuous, it may be helpful to state in advance what a careful reading will show us. From these passages by Simplicius, we will learn (1) that in the estimation of several early commentators (not only Simplicius himself) the Indefinite Dyad or Great and Small of which Plato spoke in his lecture on the Good is identical with the Unlimited of the *Philebus*, (2) that this Dyad can take the form of a mathematical continuum, but (3) that it can occur also in sensible things. Although this passage falls short of being an eyewitness account, it comes closest of material still available to being a straightforward historical report.[57] The effect of this report is both to establish the *Philebus* as an access to the content of Plato's ill-fated lecture, and to help illuminate some of the more baffling passages of that dialogue itself.

The passages in question consist largely of quotations (or summaries) from the earlier commentators Alexander and Porphyry (briefly mentioned in Chapter 2), which Simplicius introduces with some remarks of his own. These introductory remarks purport to convey what Aristotle heard at the lecture on the Good, which he attended with other of Plato's companions whom Simplicius mentions by name. Although Plato denied that the Ideas are in space, Simplicius tells us, "he asserted nonetheless that the Unlimited is in sensible things and in the Ideas" (τὸ μέντοι ἄπειρον καὶ ἐν τοῖς αἰσθητοῖς εἶναι φησι καὶ ἐν ταῖς ἰδέαις: 453.24-25). Expanding on these two points in sequence, the report goes on to say that Plato asserted that "Unity and the Indefinite Dyad were principles of sensible things" (ἀρχὰς γὰρ καὶ τῶν αἰσθητῶν τὸ ἓν καὶ τὴν ἀόριστόν . . . δυάδα: 453.25-26), and also "located the Indefinite Dyad in the realm of thought, saying it was Unlimited" (τὴν δὲ ἀόριστον δυάδα καὶ ἐν τοῖς νοητοῖς τιθεὶς ἔπειρον εἶναι ἔλεγε: 453.26-27). "In his discourse on the Good, he made the Great and the Small principles, calling them Unlimited" (τὸ μέγα δὲ καὶ τὸ μικρὸν ἀρχὰς τιθεὶς ἄπειρον εἶναι ἔλεγεν ἐν τοῖς Περὶ τἀγαθοῦ λόγοις: 453.27-28).

Two claims made in these passages are relevant to the *Philebus*. One is that the Indefinite Dyad is present both in Forms and in sensible things. The other is that Plato himself called the Indefinite Dyad, or the Great and (the) Small, by the alternative title "Unlimited." Exactly the same points are made by Aristotle in the passage upon which Simplicius is commenting, where we are told that for Plato (in contrast with the Pythagoreans) "the Unlimited is dual, the Great and the Small" (δύο τὰ ἄπειρα, τὸ μέγα καὶ τὸ μικρόν: *Physics* 203a15-16), and that "the Unlimited is present not only in sensible things but also in Ideas" (τὸ μέντοι ἄπειρον καὶ ἐν τοῖς αἰσθητοῖς καὶ ἐν ἐκείναις [τὰς ἰδέας] εἶναι: 203a9-10). As far as Simplicius and Aristotle are concerned, it is clear the Great and (the) Small was sometimes called by Plato simply "the Unlimited," and that this is the same principle said elsewhere to be constitutive both of Forms and of sensible objects.

Connection with the *Philebus* is established directly, as Simplicius, after naming Aristotle and others who were present at Plato's lecture and wrote down his "enigmatic utterances," goes on to quote from a work by Porphyry which he identifies explicitly as concerning that dialogue. Since the more and less (τὸ μᾶλλον καὶ τὸ ἧττον) and the strong and mild (τὸ σφόδρα καὶ τὸ ἠρέμα) "do not stay put nor set bounds to what participates in them" (οὐχ ἵσταται οὐδὲ περαίνει τὸ μετέχον αὐτῶν: 453.34), Porphyry says, Plato "held that they are the Unlimited Nature" (τῆς ἀπείρου φύσεως εἶναι τίθεται: 453.32-33). The same is the case, he continues, with "the greater and smaller, or as Plato calls them the Great and the Small" (τὸ μεῖζον καὶ τὸ ἔλαττον καὶ τὰ ἀντ' αὐτῶν λεγόμενα ὑπὸ Πλάτωνος τὸ μέγα καὶ τὸ μικρόν: 453.35-36). Because of this, these opposites "pass on into the indefiniteness of the Unlimited" (πρόεισιν εἰς τὸ τῆς ἀπειρίας ἀόριστον: 453.34-35). Three things are particularly noteworthy thus far in Porphyry's commentary. For one, although both ἀόριστον and ἄπειρον occur in application to the Great and (the) Small, precedence seems to be given to the latter expression: the opposites pass into the "indefiniteness of the Unlimited" rather than into "the unlimitedness of the indefinite." For another, the Great and (the) Small are referred to alternatively as "the greater and the lesser," and associated not only with the particular opposition "strong and mild" but also with the more general "the more and the less." For the moment, however, let us focus upon the third noteworthy fact about Porphyry's report, that the Great and (the) Small are described as the Unlimited Nature.[58] The same expression occurs twice again in the two pages immediately following.

Having identified the Unlimited Nature with the Great and (the) Small, Porphyry illustrates this principle with a mathematical example. Take a "limited magnitude" (μέγεθος πεπερασμένον: 453.37)[59] like a cubit, he says, and divide it into two halves, further dividing one part and adding half of it to the other. Continuing to diminish the smaller portion by further halvings, we can separate the original cubit into a greater and a smaller without limitation (ἀτελευτήτως: 454.3). We never reach the indivisible by such segmentation of parts, since a cubit is "continuous and always divides into divisibles" (δὲ συνεχὲς διαιρεῖται εἰς ἀεὶ διαιρετά: 454.5). This "unintermittent sectioning reveals a certain Unlimited Nature" (ἀδιάλειπτος τομὴ δηλοῖ τινα φύσιν ἀπείρου: 454.5-6) reposing in the cubit, "perceived as an Indefinite Dyad" (ἡ ἀόριστος δυὰς ὁρᾶται: 454.8).

This passage reinforces the identification of the Unlimited Nature with the Great and (the) Small, here designated in alternative form as the Indefinite Dyad. The Unlimited Nature is said to "lie hidden" (κατακεκλεισμένην: 454.6) in the cubit, and to be revealed in the course of segmentation. A cubit, of course, is a definite length, or what Porphyry called "continuous body" (συνεχέσι σώμασι: 454.9-10), and as such is perceptible in a way numbers themselves cannot be. If we can think with Porphyry of the Indefinite Dyad as being revealed in lengths by segmentation, so too we should be able to conceive a reverse "process" by which sensible magnitudes are constituted from the Indefinite Dyad by an appropriate imposition of limit or measure. After a problematic attempt to provide a similar illustration regarding number,[60] the quotation from Porphyry concludes with the remark that "Unity and the Dyad therefore are principles of numbers, the one limiting and productive of Form, the other indefinite in excess and defect" (στοιχεῖα οὖν καὶ ἀριθμῶν τὸ ἓν καὶ ἡ δυάς, τὸ μὲν περαῖνον καὶ εἰδοποιοῦν, ἡ δὲ ἀόριστος καὶ ἐν ὑπεροχῇ καὶ ἐλλείψει: 454.15:16). The term εἰδοποιοῦν here is particularly interesting. In light of the undoubted fact that Porphyry was familiar with Aristotle's thesis that for Plato Forms were numbers, the passage above appears to be an effort on his part to be somewhat specific about how numbers are produced from the Dyad and Unity. Since the Dyad (mistakenly conceived as the numerical two; see n. 60) "does not stay put" (οὐχ ἵσταται: 453.34) in its excess and defect (perhaps like the two of *Parmenides* 142E7), the limiting role of Unity is required to make a Form (or definite number) out of it. If we read εἰδοποιοῦν in this literal fashion, and no reason appears why we should not, we find in this passage a surprisingly candid acknowledgment of the Aristotelian thesis that for Plato Forms were constituted—literally produced—from the Great and (the) Small by participation in Unity. Within the scope of a few lines, Porphyry has adverted to three of Aristotle's claims about Plato that perennially have caused most trouble among commentators, and done so in a context explicitly pertaining to the *Philebus*. The three claims, to repeat, are (a) that sensible things are constituted by Forms and the Great and (the) Small, (b) that Forms are composed of the Great and (the) Small and Unity, and (c) that Forms are numbers.

Terminating his report from Porphyry, Simplicius remarks that this report sets forth the enigmatic utterances made at the lecture on the Good, and that this report agrees with what Plato wrote in the *Philebus*. He then turns to Alexander's account of Plato's lecture, as "recorded by Aristotle and other companions of Plato" (ἱστόρησαν Ἀριστοτέλης τε καὶ οἱ ἄλλοι τοῦ Πλάτωνος ἑταῖροι: 454.21).

After a brief summary of certain probably confused notions about the number two in relation to the Indefinite Dyad (not unlike those of Porphyry, for which see n. 60), paralleling a more verbose treatment of the same topics in his own commentary on the *Metaphysics*,[61] Alexander is quoted as saying that Plato called the Indefinite Dyad by that particular name because it is a case of "the more and the less" (τὸ μᾶλλον καὶ τὸ ἧττον: 454.36). For these, he says, pass on into "the indefiniteness of the Unlimited" (τὸ τῆς ἀπειρίας ἀόριστον: 455.2), exactly the same wording as earlier attributed to Porphyry. After another series of muddled remarks about the two and other numbers, the quotation from Alexander ends with the expressed opinion that Plato said the Dyad was the Unlimited Nature (ἀπείρου φύσιν: 455.10), since neither the Great and (the) Small nor the greater and lesser are bounded, but rather involve "the more and less" (τὸ μᾶλλον καὶ ἧττον: 455.11). This, Simplicius concludes, is what Aristotle had to say about the Unlimited in the case of the Pythagoreans and Plato.

Let us arrange the disclosures of Simplicius' commentary in an intelligible order. For one thing, both Porphyry and Alexander are quoted as referring to the Great and (the) Small as the Unlimited Nature. This is especially noteworthy for our purposes because exactly the same expression (ἀπείρου φύσιν) appears three times in the *Philebus*, each time in a context related to the report of Simplicius. Once is at 18A8 where, preparatory to his illustration involving Theuth, Socrates says that when a person employing the "godly method" has grasped the one (Form) under consideration, it is proper to look to a number instead of to the Unlimited Nature. Another appearance is at 28A2, where Socrates advises that we must look to something other than the Unlimited Nature to allow pleasure a share of the Good. Most striking, however, is the occurrence at 24E4, where Socrates concludes his collection over the Kind of the Unlimited by proposing that the mark of the Unlimited Nature is "becoming more and less." At 25A1, this mark is attributed to the Unlimited *simpliciter*. But the same characterization, in almost the same words, is made of the Great and (the) Small by both Porphyry and Alexander. This, in conjunction with the fact that Porphyry also found this principle in the *Philebus*, allows us to conclude with practical certainty that the Unlimited of this dialogue is none other than the Great and (the) Small. The Dyad of which Plato spoke in his notorious lecture on the Good also appears in at least one of his writings.[62]

A further consideration stemming from Simplicius' commentary that is important for the *Philebus* is that the Great and (the) Small can take forms other than those appropriate to mathematical entities. In the passages we have been examining, Simplicius mentions the opposition "strong and mild," which also is mentioned at *Philebus* 24C1-2. In an earlier passage of the same work, he also cites in the same connection "the heavy and light" (248.7-8), and "the broad and narrow" (248.7). In the *Metaphysics* Aristotle himself mentions in Plato's behalf not only "the broad and narrow" pertaining to planes, but also "the long and short" pertaining to lines and "the deep and shallow" pertaining to bodies (992a13-19, 1085a9-12). All are varieties, Aristotle there says, of the Great and (the) Small. "The hot and cold" is added at *Philebus* 24B5-6. The unequivocal conclusion is that the Great and (the) Small is not confined to mathematical applications, but also includes features attributed to sensible bodies. This conclusion is confirmed by *Metaphysics* 1090b37-1091a1, where Aristotle says explicitly that the Great and (the) Small generating spatial magnitudes for Plato is other than that principle as it produces the numbers.

The answer to the question regarding the identity of the Unlimited in the *Philebus*, which modern commentators have debated at such length, is almost surely that it is none other than the Indefinite Dyad or Great and Small about which Aristotle has so much to say in the *Metaphysics*. This principle is constitutive not only of arithmetical number, as was surmised in Chapter 1, but also of lines, solids, and planes in the realm of geometry, and of sensible bodies inasmuch as they are hot and cold, heavy and light, and so forth. In effect, the Great and (the) Small, or the Unlimited as the *Philebus* has it, comprises all ranges of qualitative differences that are continuous in the sense of admitting more or less in degree at any given point.[63] Limit, in turn, comprises all numbers and measures by which such continua can be subdivided into determinate elements. It is part of the task of the following section to argue that such limits are what in another dialogue Plato would have called Forms, but with a very important ontological difference. For these Forms do not exist separately from sensible things.

3. THE CONSTITUTION OF FORMS AND OBJECTS

In one of its aspects the "godly method" discussed above is ontological, having to do with the division of the Unlimited into determinate characters that can be manifested in individual sensible objects. An explicit illustration is given at 18B-D with the tale of Theuth, who separated out vowels, semivowels, and mutes from the Unlimited of vocal sound. Another illustration perhaps is implicated in the case of the Pythagorean ancestors at 17D, who first imposed limits in the form of numerical ratios upon the indefinite range of musical tones. The skill of Theuth in the first case produced not only the formal elements of spoken language that make possible the science of grammar, but also the phonetic patterns that form the basis of intelligible speech. In like fashion, the skill of the early Pythagoreans provided both for the scientific treatment of musical sound in terms of intervals and meters, and for the systematic measure of actual sounds produced by voice and instrument. To put it traditionally, these godlike personages contributed both to the demarcation of Forms germane to their particular skills and to the orderly identification of sensible things in which these Forms are (imperfectly) exhibited. With regard to the latter specifically, in the language of the *Philebus* instead, they contributed the Cause by which appropriate forms of Limit (musical measures) were imposed on Unlimited musical sound, with reference to which individual sounds could be constituted with recognizable identities.

This recipe for the constitution of sensible things is formulated explicitly at 26D8-10. Having characterized the Unlimited as comprising what admits "becoming more and less" (25E7-8), and Limit as "everything that relates as number to number and measure to measure" (25A9-B1), and whatever accordingly "stops opposites from conflicting with one another" (25D11-E1), Socrates provides the following characterization of things generated (γενέσεις: 25E4) by the mixture of these two principles. This third kind, he says, is

> a unity constituted by all the progeny of these [other two kinds] [ἓν τοῦτο τιθέντα τὸ τούτων ἔκγονον ἅπαν: 26D8-9]—[all] coming-into-being from the measures established by Limit [γένεσις εἰς οὐσίαν ἐκ τῶν μετὰ τοῦ πέρατος ἀπειργασμένην μέτρων: 26D9-10].

The term γένεσις appearing here, and at 25E4 preceding, is the very one used at *Timaeus* 52D3, *Republic* 509B3, *Phaedo* 70D9, and many other places where undoubted reference is to sensible things in the realm of Becoming. Whatever else we are to make of it, the clear message here is that things which become—that is, sensible things—are produced by the interaction of Limit and the Unlimited.[64]

Immediately preceding this passage, however, occur the remarks noted above which several commentators believe rule out the thesis that Limit and the Unlimited are being represented in the *Philebus* as constitutive of sensible things. After Protarchus remarks that he understands Socrates to be saying that the mixture of these two principles "results in something coming to be in each case" (γενέσεις τινὰς ἐφ' ἑκάστων αὐτῶν συμβαίνειν: 25E4), an understanding Socrates explicitly accepts, a number of illustrative cases are mentioned. In each case the state of affairs that comes into being from this mixture is highly desirable, or in some other way of positive value. The distinctly positive character of these illustrations has led the commentators to conclude that the mixture of Limit and the Unlimited cannot produce sensible things generally, since many particular objects and states of affairs are in no way desirable. For example, if Limit is productive of health when imposed upon the Unlimited, then these two principles cannot also be responsible for sickness, which is a particular state of affairs no less than any other.

In response to this argument I have already pointed out that, according to 25E7-8, it is the "right combination" (ὀρθὴ κοινωνία) of these principles that is responsible for health, leaving open the possibility that other combinations might have less favorable results. Another possibility is that all combinations of members of the "family of Limit" (τοῦ πέρατος γένναν: 25D3) with the Unlimited count as "right combinations," yielding norms or standards by which deviant instances can be identified. Thus the combination of equal and double with the Unlimited of musical sound, for instance, might be said to "express Limit perfectly" (πέρας . . . ἀπηργάσατο: 26A3-4) and thereby to "comprise music as a whole in full completeness" (μουσικὴν σύμπασαν τεχεώτατα συνεστήσατο: 26A4-5). The exact ratios (octaves, fifths, etc.) resulting from these combinations serve as standards by which the sounds of individual performances are given musical identity, thereby constituting these individual sounds as musical entities.

According to the first possibility, in brief, certain limits yield desirable results in combination with the Unlimited, while others are less fortunate in their consequences. According to the second, all impositions of limits (as at 25D3) upon the Unlimited are "right combinations," resulting in fixed standards by which diverse instances can be measured and thereby identified—much as the Standard Meter provides a measure for diverse spatial magnitudes.

The first possibility was stressed by Jackson, in an article now over one hundred years old,[65] who draws attention to the distinction at *Philebus* 24C between definite quantity (ποσόν) generally and the particular quantity called due measure (μέτριον). Both are in opposition to the "more and less" characteristic of the Unlimited, but their effects upon being introduced into various indefinite ranges of qualities admitting "more and less" are not the same. The effect of introducing due measure into hotter and colder, Jackson argues, "is to produce in actuality an equable temperature which is neither θερμόν nor ψυχρόν." But when any other quantity is introduced into the hotter and colder, "the effect is to produce in actuality a temperature diverging . . . from the equable temperature" on the side either of the hotter or the colder. While the mixture of hotter and colder with any ποσόν produces some temperature or another, only mixture with the μέτριον produces what we identify as being just the right temperature (ὥρα). Although these many other temperature states do not in this interpretation gain their identity in turn with reference to the μέτριον, Jackson nonetheless suggests that "all other actual temperatures must be measured from it." The problem I find with this interpretation is that definite quantity can be present only in conjunction with number, and there is no indication in the *Philebus* of how the presence of number in different instances can have qualitatively different results. It would be preferable if we could retain Jackson's suggestion that due measure serves as a fixed standard of comparison, without being committed to qualitatively different membership in the "family of Limit."

The apparent tension between these two possibilities can be resolved in light of some parallel passages in the *Statesman*, wherein the Stranger distinguishes two types of measurement. On the one hand is measurement of "greatness and smallness" (τοῦ μεγάλου καὶ τοῦ σμικροῦ: 283E8-9) "relative to each other" (πρὸς ἄλληλα: 283E9-10), on the other measurement "according to the norm or mean" (πρὸς τὸ μέτριον: 283E11). It is the latter, he says, that is necessary for coming-into-being (literally, "the necessary being of becoming," τὴν τῆς γενέσεως ἀναγκαίαν οὐσίαν: 283D8-9). Or, as he puts it at 285A1-2, the latter is the "measurement involved in all that comes into being" (μετρητικὴ περὶ πάντ᾽ ἐστὶ τὰ γιγνόμενα). The two interdependent consequences drawn from this discussion are that "the arts as a group exist" (τὰς τέχνας πάσας εἶναι: 284D4-5), and that the "greater and smaller" (μεῖζον . . . καὶ ἔλαττον: 284D5) are measurable "not only with respect to one another, but also with respect to attaining the norm or mean" (μὴ πρὸς ἄλληλα μόνον ἀλλὰ καὶ πρὸς τὴν τοῦ μετρίου γένεσιν: 284D5-6).

In point of fact, several aspects of the Stranger's discussion of measurement are relevant to our present concern with the *Philebus*. Of particular interest is the fact that the expressions (i) μεγάλου καὶ σμικροῦ ("greatness and smallness") at 283E8-9 and (ii) μεῖζον καὶ ἔλαττον ("greater and smaller") at 284D5 both appear in Simplicius' account of the relationship between Plato's lecture on the Good and the contents of the *Philebus* (*Commentaria*, Vol. 9, 453.35, 454.3, 35-36). Indeed, one passage (453.35-36) cites (ii) as equivalent to τὸ μέγα καὶ τὸ μικρόν ("the Great and [the] Small"), and yet another (454.35-36) treats both (i) and (ii) as equivalent to ἀόριστον δυάδα ("the Indefinite Dyad") and to τὸ μᾶλλον καὶ τὸ ἧττον ("the more and less," named the mark of the Indefinite in the *Philebus*). In view of these terminological overlaps, it is not incautious to assume that the distinction between types of measurement in the *Statesman* also pertains to the *Philebus*, and that the sense in which measurement is involved in all that comes into being (*Statesman* 285A1-2) is related to the sense in which all coming-into-being is progeny of the measures established by Limit (*Philebus* 26D8-10).

What we learn from this passage in the *Statesman* regarding our problem with *Philebus* 25E-26B is that not all measures are normal or "right measures," but at the same time that these "right measures" are responsible for the existence of everything accessible to art. Similarly, "right measure" (μέτριον) is mentioned at *Philebus* 24C8 as standing in contrast with the more and less, and later is identified specifically (ἔμμετρον: 26A8) as a result of the introduction of limits into the Unlimited. An entirely reasonable conjecture is that the reference to "right combination" of limits with the Unlimited at 25E7 is intended to convey about the same meaning as reference to "right measure" in the surrounding passages of the *Philebus* as well as in the *Statesman*. In line with this conjecture, "right combination" should be construed, not in contrast with some problematic "bad combination" of limits with the Unlimited, but rather in contrast with the measurement of things that are more or less (i.e., members of the Unlimited) with respect to themselves alone. The introduction of "right measure," says the Stranger in the *Statesman*, is responsible for the arts (284D4-5) and is involved in all that comes into being (285A2). Similarly, as Socrates puts it in the *Philebus*, "right combination" of limits, like equal and double, with the Unlimited results in the art of music (26A4-5), and has as its progeny all coming-into-being (26D9). In the case of music particularly, however, what comes into being is not just the ideal ratios that define the various intervals and tones (in an earlier terminology, the Forms Octave, Middle C, etc.), but the musical character of whole ranges of sounds that now can be identified with reference to these norms (the octaves and notes of individual performances). In some sense, the sounds existed before, as part of the characterless "more and less," or Unlimited. But now they exist as identifiable musical entities, accessible to the devices of the musical art.

This dual emphasis at *Philebus* 25E-26A and at *Statesman* 284A-285A upon the "right combination" or "right measure" as the basis of arts and skills invites comparison with the passage immediately preceeding the statement of the "godly method," to the effect that it is to this method that we owe our success in any enquiry requiring art or skill (16C2-3). In spelling out the sense in which this is so, Socrates then describes (in different terms) the method of collection and division from the *Sophist* and the *Statesman*. Because things are constituted from Limit and the Unlimited, he says, we start in each case with a single Form (ἰδέαν: 16D1), and then go on to look for two or more, and so on. At *Statesman* 285A, similarly, after reiterating that all arts and skills involve measurement in some form or other, the Stranger then attributes failure to see this on the part of some learned persons as "failure to study things by dividing them according to Forms" (τὸ μὴ κατ᾽ εἴδη . . . σκοπεῖν διαιρουμένους: 285A4-5). Although reference to Forms does not figure prominently in the discussion of the "godly method," and although Plato's conception of the Forms may well be undergoing change during this period, these passages bespeak a close relationship in his thinking between measure, Limit, and what he often called Forms.

In the preceding attempts to come to grips with Aristotle's characterization of Plato's ontology in the first book of the *Metaphysics*, five theses were distinguished that capture most of what he was claiming there in Plato's behalf. First was the thesis (1) that numbers come from participation of the Great and (the) Small in Unity. A reconstruction of what this probably meant was presented and defended in the previous chapter. The next three theses in order are:

(2) that sensible things are constituted by the Forms and the Great and (the) Small;

(3) that the Forms are composed of the Great and (the) Small and Unity; and

(4) that the Forms are numbers.

Since the Forms are not mentioned explicitly in any of the ontological passages in the *Philebus*, we cannot expect to find these theses represented there in just those terms. With the help of three auxiliary propositions, however, the dialogue can be seen to contain equivalent doctrines represented in alternative terminology. One is the proposition that what Aristotle called "the Great and (the) Small" is what Plato called "the Unlimited Multitude" in the *Parmenides* and simply "the Unlimited" in the *Philebus*. This proposition was established in the preceding section. Second is the proposition that Unity cannot be instantiated independently of some other character, and that no character can be instantiated independently of Unity. This is to say, in effect, both (i) that no particular thing can have the character of being one alone but must be one man or one stone, and so on, and (ii) that no particular thing can have the character of being man or stone, and so on, without being one man or one stone, and so forth. To put it more briefly, an instantiation of Unity in a particular thing of a given character is indistinguishable from an instantiation of that character in a single particular thing. Although this proposition, I believe, is demonstrated in the *Parmenides*,[66] for present purposes it may be accepted as simply obvious. Whatever else we are to make of the relationship between Forms and particulars, its nature is such that instantiation of any Form depends upon the presence of Unity as well. The third auxiliary proposition, finally, is that the Unity and the Limit mentioned (at 16C9 and 10, respectively) in the ontological statement prefacing the description of the "godly method" are in effect one and the same ontological principle. Before arguing the merits of this third proposition, let us consider the implications for theses (2), (3), and (4) above.

If Unity and Limit are ontologically equivalent, then the second auxiliary proposition above (that Forms bring Unity to their instantiations and that this is the only way Unity is instantiated) converts to the proposition that it is by Forms and Forms only that Limit is brought to sensible things.[67] A consequence is that the frequently repeated claim in the *Philebus* (25E4, 26D9, 27A11, 27B8) that things which come into being (i.e., sensible things) are constituted by Limit and the Unlimited translates into the thesis that sensible things are constituted by imposing Forms upon the Unlimited. Since by the first auxiliary proposition above (already demonstrated) the Unlimited of the *Philebus* is the Great and (the) Small, this can be restated as the Aristotelian thesis (2) that sensible things are constituted by the Forms and the Great and (the) Small.

In the context of the *Philebus*, however, the Forms that bring Unity to their instantiations do not exist independently in and by themselves. The four kinds comprising "all that exists in the present universe" (23C4) are listed as Limit, the Unlimited, Mixture, and Cause—a list conspicuously lacking any reference to Forms. Although, as I have argued, Forms somehow serve a limiting function, they no more qualify for ontological independence than do equal, double, and the various other measures by which (according to *Philebus* 25A8-B1) Limit is represented. An instructive parallel may be found in the reconstructed account of number tentatively attributed to Eudoxus in section 3 of Chapter 2. According to this account, numbers (rationals and irrationals alike) are conceived as unique limits or "cuts" imposed on a continuum indefinitely divisible into great and smaller components. The continuum in this case was identified as a manifestation of the Great and (the) Small in the field of quantity, thus providing an interpretation of the first Aristotelian thesis that for Plato numbers came from the participation of the Great and (the) Small in Unity. What Unity provides in this case, of course, is the uniqueness of the limits or "cuts" with which the numbers individually are uniquely identified. What exists independently in this case, as it were, are Unity and the Great and (the) Small. Numbers exist only derivatively, as the result of the participation of the latter in the former. Given our third auxiliary proposition from the *Philebus* that Unity and Limit are ontologically equivalent, the parallel in question is that Forms, in similar fashion, exist derivatively by the participation of the Great and (the) Small in Unity—or, in terms proper to the *Philebus*, by the participation of the Unlimited in Limit. The difference is that we were concerned before with the constitution of arithmetical numbers out of a quantitative continuum appropriate to this branch of mathematics, whereas we are concerned now with the constitution of nonmathematical Forms out of continua (like the hotter and colder) appropriate to the domain of sensible objects. For a specific example, we are concerned with the constitution of such Forms as Freezing and Boiling, and the Forms of Spring and Summer (ὧραί: 26B1) and so on, that establish a just measure between inordinate cold and stifling heat (χειμῶσι καὶ πνίγεσιν: 26A7). In the ontology of the *Philebus*, these Forms do not exist independently. Their existence rather is due to the interaction of Limit and the Unlimited. But by the auxiliary propositions above, these two principles are equivalent to Unity and the Great and (the) Small. Thus it is, in the terminology of Aristotle's thesis (3), that Forms are composed of the Great and (the) Small and Unity.

The further consequence of note from our three auxiliary propositions is the following. Second among these is the proposition that Unity is imparted to particular things by the instantiation of Forms. By the third proposition, this amounts to the thesis that Limit is imparted by the instantiation of Forms, which supports an interpretation of the Aristotelian claim in Plato's behalf that sensible things are constituted by Forms and the Great and (the) Small. In line with *Philebus* 25A8-B1, as already suggested, this means in turn that Forms provide the "proportions of numbers and measures" by which Limit is imposed upon the Unlimited. To put it summarily, Forms are the numbers and measures by which the Great and (the) Small is made definite and determinate. Although there is indeed a sense of the term ἀριθμός in which it was seen to be important to distinguish numbers and measures,[68] there is another sense in which the term is synonymous with μέτρον. This latter sense is amply illustrated, as noted in the third section of the last chapter, by Aristotle's discussion of time in the *Physics*, where in repeated statements of the formula that "time is the (measure/number) of motion" the two terms are used interchangeably without change in sense.

In the apposition of the two terms at *Philebus* 25B1, similarly, there is no reason to understand the terms as differing in reference. When Socrates says that Limit consists of "anything that relates as number to number or measure to measure," I suggest, he is saying in effect that Limit consists of numbers (= measures) that permit proportional comparison—that is numbers which introduce commensurability. In fact, he says this explicitly in his second characterization of Limit at 25E1-2, in saying that the opposites (of the Unlimited, or as we may now say, the Great and [the] Small) are made commensurate (σύμμετρα) and harmonious by the introduction of number. Since Forms are the numbers (or measures) by which this result is accomplished, a summary way of expressing what is said at 25E1-2 is to say that Forms are numbers. Aristotelian thesis (4) above is that Forms are numbers—not numbers in the sense of arithmetical elements, but numbers in the sense of determinate measures.

Thus, if the third auxiliary proposition above can be sustained, there are available interpretations for Aristotelian theses (2), (3), and (4) which both (a) make them intelligible in themselves as attributed to Plato and (b) show them present in the text of the *Philebus*. The third auxiliary proposition is that Limit and Unity are ontologically equivalent. For evidence that Plato in his later years conceived Limit and Unity as ontologically equivalent we again may resort to Aristotle and his later commentators.

Several passages in the *Metaphysics* suggest that, in Aristotle's way of thinking, Plato conceived of Limit and Unity as equivalent, or at least closely related. Indirect evidence to this effect appears at 1054a29-31 and 1087b33-34, when read with *Philebus* 25A8-B1 in mind (the full statement there that Limit comprises "first equal and equality; and after equal, double, and everything that relates as number to number and measure to measure"). In the former passage, Aristotle says that the equal belongs to Unity, referring back to his discussion of the contraries at 1004a which we know from Alexander (Vol. 1, 250.20) was associated with his report on Plato's lecture on the Good. In another discussion of the topic in the latter passage, which relates explicitly to Plato and other members of the Academy, Aristotle says that for these thinkers "Unity apparently means measure" (τὸ δ' ἓν ὅτι μέτρον σημαίνει, φανερόν; see also 1053a18-19). In these two passages, Aristotle characterizes as coming under Unity two of the factors that Plato in the *Philebus* characterized as coming under Limit. In their involvement with equality and measure, at least, Unity and Limit appear equivalent. Positive association of this equivalence with Plato comes at 1004b32-34, with the remark that the contraries πέρας and ἄπειρον admitted by some thinkers (the *Philebus* provides a clear example) are reducible to τὸ ἓν and πλῆθος. It was on the strength of this remark that I first proposed the hypothesis that the juxtaposition of the opposed terms ἑνὸς and πολλῶν with πέρας and ἀπειρίαν in the ontological statement at *Philebus* 16C9-10 might in fact amount to an apposition of equivalents—in effect that Unity and Limit are the same ontological principle.

Further evidence to this effect is available from the Aristotelian commentators. In the previous section I dwelt at some length on what Simplicius quotes from Porphyry in his commentary on the *Physics*. In the midst of his attempt to explain how numbers are generated from the Indefinite Dyad, Porphyry remarks that although the Dyad is indefinite "it is limited by participating in Unity" (ὡρίσθη δὲ τῇ τοῦ ἑνὸς μετοχῇ: 454.14). As an element of number, he says, Unity is "limiting and Form-making" (περαῖνον καὶ εἰδοποιοῦν: 454.16).[69] In the same text from Simplicius, commenting on the same topic, Alexander is cited as saying that each number, insofar as limited, "participates in Unity" (τοῦ ἑνὸς μετέχει: 455.7). Abstracting from the apparently (as previously noted) confused efforts of these earlier authors to make out some intelligible sense in which arithmetical numbers can be generated from the Indefinite Dyad, one finds here explicit statements of the way in which arithmetical numbers (and maybe numbers in the sense of measures) receive the limitation that separates them from the Great and (the) Small.[70] For numbers to participate in Unity, says Porphyry, is for them to receive Limit; and for numbers to receive Limit, says Alexander, is for them to participate in Unity. What one says is necessary the other says is sufficient. As far as numbers are concerned at least, to come under Limit is the same thing as to come under Unity. Extension of this conclusion from numbers to Forms explicitly is accomplished in yet another statement of Porphyry quoted by Simplicius. As he puts it, the Dyad "in itself is indefinite, receiving limit by participating in Unity" (καθ᾽ αὐτὴν μὲν ἀόριστος, ὡρίσθη δὲ τῇ τοῦ ἑνὸς μετοχῇ: 454.13-14); "for the Dyad is limited by having a single Form" (ὥρισται γὰρ ἡ δυὰς καθ᾽ ὅσον ἕν τι εἶδός ἐστι: 454.14-15).

One further bit of evidence comes from Plato himself. Among the consequences of the third hypothesis in *Parmenides II*, I have noted, is that the "nature other than the Forms" (τὴν ἑτέραν φύσιν τοῦ εἴδους: 158C6-7), considered just in and by itself, in indefinitely multitudinous (ἄπειρον . . . πλήθει: 158C7-8). However, when each single part becomes a part, they all have limit (πέρας: 158D1) with respect both to themselves and to the whole. What provides limit in the context of this hypothesis, of course, is the Unity assumed to exist at 157B5. Thus, as Parmenides points out, the "consequence for the things other than Unity . . . is that from the combination of themselves with Unity something else comes to be in them—amounting to limit with respect to each other" (Τοῖς ἄλλοις δὴ τοῦ ἑνὸς συμβαίνει ἐκ μὲν τοῦ ἑνὸς καὶ ἐξ ἑαυτῶν κοινωνησάντων . . . ἕτερόν τι γίγνεσθαι ἐν αὐτοῖς, ὃ δὴ πέρας παρέσχε πρὸς ἄλληλα: 158D3-6). In brief, Unity is the principle by which limit is imparted.

Although evidence of this sort is not conclusive, and probably never could be by the nature of the case, the auxiliary proposition that Unity and Limit are equivalent ontological principles is strongly supported (1) by testimony of Aristotle expressly relevant to the *Philebus*, (2) by the perception of commentators some sixteen hundred years closer than we to Plato whose sources include Aristotle's notes on Plato's lecture on the Good,[71] and (3) by a text in the *Parmenides* that previously has been shown directly germane to the content of the *Philebus*. If better evidence is available, it must come in the form of interpretive results notably more satisfactory than any provided by alternative hypotheses.

Results under two headings have already been demonstrated that show the advantages of the present interpretive approach over available alternatives. Our earlier discussion of the very difficult passages at *Philebus* 16C-18E and 23C-27B has shown that a unified and fully intelligible account can be given of their contents on the basis of the interpretive hypothesis that the Unlimited and Limit correspond to what Aristotle called the Great and (the) Small and Unity. No previously available interpretive approach has been able to accommodate these passages without notable lapses.[72] As shown directly above, moreover, this hypothesis in conjunction with two additional auxiliary propositions, both of which themselves receive considerable support from ancient texts, makes relatively straightforward sense of three of the five theses attributed to Plato by Aristotle in the *Metaphysics*, and reveals the presence of these three theses in the *Philebus* itself. Since these theses have proven perennially baffling to commentators on both Plato and Aristotle, and since the assumption that they cannot be located in the dialogues has generated what some day may be judged one of the more futile controversies in Platonic studies, the discovery that in fact they appear in the *Philebus* (as Porphyry had maintained) might be enough in itself to recommend the interpretative hypotheses that led to this discovery.[73]

In point of fact, however, another bit of interpretative evidence is available. The three auxiliary propositions above, and in particular the proposition that Limit and Unity are ontological equivalents, also enable us to assign an intelligible interpretation to the remaining Aristotelian thesis (5) that the Good is Unity, and to show that this thesis as well is contained in the *Philebus*.

4. UNITY AS THE GOOD

That Plato actually delivered a lecture on the Good seems beyond plausible doubt. Even Cherniss accepts the lecture as historical fact,[74] although he argued vigorously that it should be not multiplied into a whole series of lectures presenting an "unwritten teaching" not to be found in the dialogues. Aristotle himself is said to have attended the lecture,[75] but apparently found it puzzling, as did the rest of the audience.[76] What puzzled the audience in particular was its preoccupation with numbers, and the claim in which it culminated that the Good is Unity.[77] Although Aristotle was perplexed by this claim, he was not thereby prevented by recording what Plato said in a now lost work entitled "On the Good,"[78] or from making reference in the *Metaphysics* to the apparently related Platonic teaching that Unity and the Great and (the) Small are the causes of Good and Evil, respectively (988a14-15).

Speculation on the significance of Plato's remarks in this lecture has come in recent years to constitute a major industry of Platonic studies and has generated one of the more spirited controversies in contemporary philosophy.[79] Reasons for my resolve not to become enmeshed in this controversy as such have already been given (Chapter 2, section 1), and this is not an occasion for breaking resolutions. Nonetheless, it is fitting to address now the fifth thesis mounted by Aristotle in Plato's behalf, since (i) an interpretation flows naturally from the discussion of the other four theses and (ii) thus interpreted this thesis also appears in the *Philebus*. The thesis in question is (5) that the Good is Unity. Although I should not suspect that the interpretation in question will quench the controversy to the satisfaction of all participants, it may at least prove salubriously deflationary, for what it makes of this thesis is not particularly mysterious. What it makes of it, in fact, is equivalent to the conclusion Socrates arrives at the end of the *Philebus*, regarding the relative merits of the various contenders for the title "the Good."

Having distinguished the four basic kinds—the Unlimited, Limit, Mixture, and Cause—and having located pleasure and intelligence in a general fashion under the first and fourth, respectively (31A), Socrates turns to a more detailed examination of these two original contenders. The examination of pleasure that follows in the next twenty-four pages, despite its involvement with certain dubious theses (for example, that pleasure, like opinion, admits truth and falsehood), effectively disqualifies any claim of pleasure to be the Good itself. But intelligence must be subjected to an equally rigorous test. Like pleasure, it must be examined in the purest form possible. And the purest forms of knowledge are those involving "techniques of number and measure" (ἀριθμητικὴν . . . καὶ μετρητικὴν: 55E1-2), with the exactitude (ἀκρίβειαν: 56B5) that results from their use. These, of course, are the skills of arithmetic.

But the skills of arithmetic admit further division. On one hand are the methods of those arithmeticians who deal with "unequal units" (μονάδας ἀνίσους: 56D10), pairing cows at one time, armed camps at another, or any two things whatever, be they "smallest or biggest of all" (τὰ σμικρότατα ἢ καὶ τὰ πάντων μέγιστα: 56E1-2). On the other hand is the person who holds that "every unit among countless instances differs not at all from any other unit" (μονάδα μονάδος ἑκάστης τῶν μυρίων μηδεμίαν ἄλλην ἄλλης διαφέρουσάν: 56E3-4).[80] Thus when we compare the calculation and measuring of the shopkeeper and builder with the numerical reasoning of the philosopher, we have two classes of knowledge, one purer than the other. In general, Socrates continues, when there is a distinction of this sort to be made between philosophic and nonphilosophic skills, those of the philosopher pursued "in reference to measure and number" (περὶ μέτρα τε καὶ ἀριθμοὺς: 57D2) are far superior to the other in "exactness and truth" (ἀκριβείᾳ καὶ ἀληθείᾳ: 57D1-2).

This repeated reference to exactitude and measure in the *Philebus* is reminiscent of the strikingly parallel passage at *Statesman* 284D-E, where essentially the same distinction is made between two kinds of measurement. One kind includes "all arts by which number, length, depth, breadth or velocity of things are measured by their opposites" (συμπάσας τέχνας ὁπόσαι τὸν ἀριθμὸν καὶ μήκη καὶ βάθη καὶ πλάτη καὶ παχύτητας πρὸς τοὐναντίον μετροῦσιν: 284E4-5). The other includes arts concerned with due measure (τὸ μέτριον: 284E6), which hold to a "mean removed from the extremes" (μέσον ἀπῳκίσθη τῶν ἐσχάτων: 284E7-8). This distinction reflects the prior division at 283D-E between measure "according to relative greatness and smallness (κατὰ τὴν πρὸς ἄλληλα μεγέθους καὶ σμικρότητος: 283D7-8), and that according to "the nature of due measure" (τὴν τοῦ μετρίου φύσιν: 283E3) which is said to be necessary for coming-into-being. That this latter kind of measure is possible, the Stranger says by way of explication at 284D, is a condition of the existence of all arts and skills. And the manner after which due measure is applied to the arts and skills, he continues, involves studying them by "dividing them according to classes" (κατ᾽ εἴδη ... διαιρουμένους: 285A4-5). This reference to division (which in the context of the *Statesman* inevitably brings to mind the method of collection and division), in association with the discussion of due measure as playing a role both in the arts and skills and in the coming-into-being of things out of "relative greatness and smallness," calls to mind the way in which these several themes are brought together in the early passages of the *Philebus*. When the Stranger says at 284D that this principle of due measure will some day be necessary when we come to the "demonstration of exactness itself" (αὐτὸ τἀκριβὲς ἀπόδειξιν: 284D2), it is hard to resist the conclusion that this time is now at hand in the final pages of the *Philebus*. For it is here that the exactness yielded by measure earns measure a place in the domain of the Good.

Although it is the "power of dialectic" (διαλέγεσθαι δύναμις: 57E7) that produces knowledge with its attention to "exactness and truth at its fullest" (τἀκριβὲς καὶ τὸ ἀληθέστατον: 58C3), however, knowledge by itself cannot be understood as "the wholly Good" (τὸ παντάπασιν ἀγαθὸν: 61A1-2). As was apparent at the outset of the dialogue (61B), the Good must be sought rather in a life that is mixed. In making up this mixture, Socrates counsels, we should include not only the knowledge of eternal and immutable things, but also that of things that come into being and perish (62B). Not even true opinion or guesswork should be excluded (62C). Pleasure, however, cannot be dealt with so generously. Only the purest forms can be admitted, such as those accompanying health and temperance, if we are to come upon a mixture to teach us what is "naturally Good in man and in the world at large" (ἔν τ᾽ ἀνθρώπῳ καὶ τῷ παντὶ πέφυκεν ἀγαθὸν: 64A2-3) and how "its Form might even be divined" (ἰδέαν αὐτὴν εἶναί ποτε μαντευτέον: 64A3-4). As a further ingredient, Socrates says, we should add truth to the mixture, else nothing truly can come to be.

Given this mixture, he then asks matter-of-factly, might we be "even now on the threshold of the Good" (τοῖς τοῦ ἀγαθοῦ νῦν ἤδη προθύροις: 64C1)? Protarchus agrees that this is the case.

Although the Good thus is a mixture of several things, one thing contributes most to the worth of the mixture. This is the complement of "measure and proportion" (μέτρου καὶ . . . συμμέτρου: 64D9). And since these qualities invariably constitute "beauty and excellence" (κάλλος . . . καὶ ἀρετὴ: 64E7), as well as being responsible for exactness and truth (57D1-2), beauty and excellence also are part of the mixture.

Thus we see that "the Good cannot be traced to a single character" (μὴ μιᾷ δυνάμεθα ἰδέᾳ τὸ ἀγαθὸν θηρεῦσαι: 65A1-2). Nonetheless, we may regard the conjunction of beauty, proportion, and truth as a particularly excellent form of Unity (οἷον[81] ἕν: 65A3). It is this element of unity, says Socrates, that we

"should rightly hold responsible" (ὀϱθότατ' ἂν αἰτιασαίμεθ':
65A3)—"it is because of this as something good that the mixture
itself becomes good" (διὰ τοῦτο ὡς ἀγαθὸν ὂν τοιαύτην αὐτὴν
γεγονέναι: 65A4-5). The Good thus resides in a trio of superlative characters, so related as to comprise a Unity that is uniquely
excellent.

Neither intelligence nor pleasure is the Good itself. The final
step in the contest between these two ill-fated contenders is to
order them along a scale of qualities approximating the Good.
In something approaching a triumphant meeting of minds, Socrates asks Protarchus to measure each contender in turn against
the superlative trio, and to proclaim the results for the world to
hear (66A5-6). The highest of all possessions falls "within the
region of measure, the mean, and what is appropriate" (πεϱὶ
μέτϱον καὶ τὸ μέτϱιον καὶ καίϱιον: 66A7-8). Second is the
"region of proportion and what is beautiful, complete, satisfactory, and so forth" (πεϱὶ τὸ σύμμετϱον καὶ καλὸν καὶ τὸ τέ-
λεον καὶ ἱκανὸν καὶ πάνθ' ὁπόσα: 66B1-2). Only third in order
come intelligence and wisdom, and fourth the skills accompanied
by true opinion. The fifth and final ranking is reserved for the
so-called "pure pleasures," with those of a baser sort receiving
no ranking at all. On this note of agreement, the dialogue ends.

Let us recapitulate the steps taken by Socrates and Protarchus
after reaching the doorstep of the Good at 64C. What makes
any mixture good is measure and proportion (64D-E). As previously characterized at 25A-B and 26D, measure is introduced
by the imposition of Limit. At 25E proportion (σύμμετϱος, the
same word as at 64D9) is characterized as being produced by
number, and number is identified at 25B as coming under Limit.
At 26A, moreover, proportion is mentioned directly as resulting
from Limit. Thus both characters cited at 64D as being responsible for making any mixture good are characters achieved by
the imposition of Limit.

With the introduction of beauty and truth along with proportion at 65A as the ingredients of the mixture best exemplifying
the Good, Plato appears to be bringing onto stage for final ap-
plause the lead actors in his earlier attempts to delineate the
Good. At the end of the Book VI of the *Republic*, where the

Good so extravagantly is likened to the sun as sovereign over the intelligible and the visible worlds, respectively, the relationship between the intelligible and the visible is represented by a line "divided with regard to truth and falsehood" (διῃρῆσθαι ἀληθείᾳ τε καὶ μή: 510A9-10). The clarity with which its various sections can be presented to the mind is a function of the truth of their respective objects (511E3-5).[82] In the speech of Diotima in the *Symposium*, on the other hand, there are strong intimations that the Good is the Beautiful. What all lovers of the Good long for is to make the Good their own forever (206A). And in describing the pursuit of this longing, Diotima divides into several stages (suggestive of stages of the Divided Line) man's successive approach to the Beautiful itself (211C9). Perhaps with these earlier contexts in mind, Plato has Socrates deny at *Philebus* 65A that the Good can be identified as a single character. Rather, the Good in some sense is a synthetic unity, incorporating not only truth (from the *Republic*)[83] and beauty (from the *Symposium*) but also proportion (which has been central in the discussion of the *Philebus*). Indeed, proportion is cited at 64E, along with measure, as being responsible for the constitution of beauty and excellence.

When the final results are announced to the world at 66A-B, however, measure has been singled out for highest honors, with proportion and beauty taking second place. And truth seems to have slipped to third, insofar as truth is the object of intelligence and wisdom. As Socrates proposes, and as Protarchus is to proclaim, the Good which is the highest of all possessions falls within the domain of measure and the mean.

But we know from 25A-B that measure is achieved by the imposition of Limit. And as argued earlier in this chapter, Limit and Unity are ontologically equivalent. So the following deduction is now available. Whereas measure is the primary ingredient of the Good, and whereas measure is achieved by the imposition of Limit, which in this role is equivalent to participation in Unity, for something to be good is for it to participate in Unity. For Plato in the *Philebus*, the Good is Unity. As Socrates puts it at 65A3-5, it is because of Unity that a mixture becomes good.

According to Aristoxenus, the audience of Plato's lecture on

the Good came expecting to hear about such recognized goods
as health and strength, but were confounded when Plato talked
about mathematics and stated "finally that the Good is Unity"
(τὸ πέρας ὅτι ἀγαθόν ἐστιν ἕν: 122.13-14). Aristotle was as
confused as the other listeners (Simplicius, 453.28-30). He ought
not to have been, however, if he had studied the *Philebus*. For
health and strength are explicitly mentioned at 26A-B among
the recognized goods resulting from the imposition of Limit—
resulting, that is to say, from participation in Unity.

5. PLATO'S FINAL THEORY OF FORMS

According to *Metaphysics* 987a32-33, Plato's youthful theory of
Ideas was influenced by Cratylus and Heraclitus, who contributed the view that sensible things are always in flux. Heraclitus
also is cited in this connection at *Metaphysics* 1078b, where,
however, a distinction is made between the theory "originally
understood by those who first maintained that the Ideas exist"
(ἐξ ἀρχῆς οἱ πρῶτοι τὰς ἰδέας φήσαντες εἶναι: 1078b11-
12) and a later version "connected with the nature of numbers"
(συνάπτοντας πρὸς τὴν τῶν ἀριθμῶν φύσιν: 1078b10-11).
The parties of the first part almost surely include Plato in the
Phaedo and the *Republic*. On the basis of the argument preceding, we may now identify the later version of the theory as that
of the *Philebus*, in which the conception of the Forms as numbers
(= measures) plays a prominent role, along with other theses
attributed to Plato in the first book of the *Metaphysics*.

Among the several difficulties Plato came to recognize in the
former theory, and undertook to remedy in the *Theaetetus* and
the *Sophist*, the one that remained most recalcitrant was the
problem of participation. As most clearly shown in the *Timaeus*,
the problem basically was one of explaining how eternally unchanging principles can give rise to a world of changing sensible
objects. The problem was diagnosed in the *Parmenides* as arising
from the notion of radical separation between Forms and objects,
and the several eristic points made in the first part of that dialogue
indicate particular respects in which this notion gets the theory

into trouble. In the second part of the *Parmenides* we find a lavish defense of Pythagorean ontology against Eleatic attack, and at the same time an exploration of the conditions of a more adequate theory. A sure sign that Plato was still preoccupied with the problem of participation appears in the early pages of the *Philebus*, where Socrates identifies the important version of the one-many problem as that of explaining how a unified Form can nonetheless come to be in many particular things. The theory described in the ensuing sections gives an account, among other things, (1) of how Forms come to be from the interaction of Limit and the Unlimited, and (2) of how sensible things come to be from the interaction of the Unlimited and the Forms.

This, in briefest summary, is the upshot of the argument of the pages preceding. What remains is to examine more closely the relationship indicated in this account between Forms and sensible things, and to see the sense in which ontologically they are no longer separate. Finally, I will compare the account of the *Philebus* with the earlier theory, and show how little was lost by giving up the notion of ontological separation.

Behind the constitution of both Forms and sensible things, as we have seen, are the basic ontological principles Limit and the Unlimited—or as Aristotle put it, Unity and the Great and (the) Small. Existing apart from members of "the family of Limit," the various ranges of continuous qualitative differences that comprise the Unlimited contain neither Forms nor particular sensible objects. Imposing Unity or Limit upon these continua results in fixed and unique reference points which admit quantitative comparison. These unique reference points are the equivalent in the *Philebus* to what in earlier dialogues were called Ideas or Forms, and, like the latter, can be precisely characterized and known independently of particular instances. Given the presence of an appropriate set of fixed Forms along a given continuum, in turn, other states along the continuum can be referred to the Forms they most nearly approximate. These other states have no determinate characteristics in and by themselves, and hence no independent identity. With reference to appropriate Forms as norms, however, these states become identifiable and numerable, and take on the names of the Forms themselves. Thus individual sensible things come into being as determinate objects by participation in the Forms; as Aristotle puts it, they are constituted by the Forms and the Great and (the) Small. Unlike the Forms, however, sensible things cannot be independently known. This is because they admit fixity (i.e., partake of Unity) only with reference to the Forms, but otherwise are lacking in self-identity. As the description of the "godly method" emphasizes, individual sensible things are both indeterminate in themselves and indefinitely numerous in their instantiations of a given Form.

A useful (albeit anachronistic) illustration is provided by the unlimited range of hotter and colder, which is invested with "number and measure" by the discovery of one of the temperature scales devised as part of modern thermometry. Whereas relative differences in hot and cold comprise an effectively limitless range of thermal states, by imposing scales based on natural[84] limits corresponding to the freezing and boiling points of water modern physicists have made possible comparison of temperatures in terms of "equal," "double," and other numerical ratios. Before the imposition of these so-called "ratio" scales upon the continuum of thermal qualities, temperature differences could be compared only as hotter and colder, whereas now they can be compared with reference to due measure. In this illustration, to be sure, we have a plurality of due measures between freezing and boiling[85] (99 on the Celsius scale). But this does not prevent our distinguishing between a finite number of determinate cuts along the temperature continuum and an indefinite number of actual temperature states falling within the intervals marked off by these cuts. Whereas the former can be defined and characterized—that is, can be known—independently of any actual temperature state, the latter are knowable only in comparison with the former as standards.

An equally apt illustration is provided by Plato's own example of musical sound. Our Pythagorean ancestors, Socrates says in effect, have taught us how to discriminate the number of intervals between high and low pitch, and to comprehend the scales that can be formed from these intervals. But the fact that a musical scale is based (for example) upon twelve determinate tones does not prevent the production of indefinitely many other notes in actual musical performance. As every violin player knows, the sounds that can be produced by an unfretted string constitute an effectively continuous range of pitches between higher and lower, and part of the skill he or she must master to become an accomplished player is to be able to pick out just those pitches that have a place within the musical scale. Part of our Pythagorean inheritance is the ability to define, and hence to know, these pitches and intervals independently of any actual musical performance, whereas by contrast the sounds produced in actual performance can be known only relatively to these mathematically fixed intervals.

Fixed points of reference such as these which are established along various continua of the Unlimited (e.g., the indefinitely higher and lower in temperature and musical sound) by the imposition of Limit according to due measure, correspond to fixed types in a well-ordered world of nature (such as might be brought into being by the Pythagoreans, Theuth, or some other godlike intelligence). As Jackson observed, these fixed types are "just what the Ones spoken of at 15B were supposed to be"[86]—such Unities as Man, Ox, Beauty, or the Good itself—what in earlier dialogues were called Ideas or Forms.[87]

Granted that the case with temperature scales and musical intervals is relatively intelligible, the problem remains of how a more complex Form might be constituted from Limit and the Unlimited. Although Plato does not give us much explicit help in answering this question, the manner presumably is not far removed from that in which Man (and Stone, and any Living Creature or other Kind) is said at *Theaetetus* 157C1-2 to be an assemblage of sensible qualities. In that earlier context, sensible qualities were conceived as springing pairwise (with perceptions) from the intercourse between active and passive powers, the basic constituents of the world of becoming. Although the account in the *Theaetetus* is not necessarily inconsistent with that of the *Philebus*, the ontological emphasis has shifted in the latter dialogue. In the *Philebus* there is no particular concern with the constituency of the world of becoming as such. Indeed, there is no sharp distinction between the world of becoming and the world of being as separate realms of existence, inasmuch as "all things that come to be" (27A11, 16C9)—including both Forms and sensible things—are constituted from Limit and the Unlimited. Aristotle was somewhat more helpful in his explanation that Forms are composed from the Great and (the) Small (the Unlimited) and Unity (Limit), while sensible things are composed from the Great and (the) Small and Forms in turn. As Aristotle helps us see, although both Forms and sensible things are composed out of Limit and the Unlimited, the manner of their composition is not the same. In order to understand the composition of full-bodied sensible things in the *Philebus*, we must first understand something of the composition of complex Forms themselves.

Characteristic of any particular man are certain features of height, breadth, weight, age, color, and so forth and so on. As we know from *Metaphysics* 1085a9-12 (also 992a11-12), the long and short is one variety of the Great and (the) Small. The same is said of the broad and narrow and the deep and shallow. This means, in the case of the long and short, that determinate lengths are defined within the range of the indefinitely longer and shorter by the imposition of limit, according to one or another system of measurement (yards, meters, cubits, etc.). Although the lengths of any two sensible objects may be assumed to vary by some minute amount at least (as pointed out in effect at *Phaedo* 74A), those sufficiently close in magnitude can be compared and called "equal" with reference to a fixed standard which they both approximate. In a typical case, the length of a sensible object is not measured exactly as it is in itself, but rather is measured with reference to a fixed point of comparison that has an exact relationship to other points ordered along a standard measurement scale. These fixed points thus ordered constitute a set of norms or paradigms that enable us to assign determinate lengths to sensible bodies, which otherwise we could compare only as longer and shorter.

In the case of musical sound, as noted earlier, standard reference points are established along the scale of higher and lower tones by the imposition of mathematical limits. These reference points are given names such as 'C', 'D', and so on, designating ideal or paradigmatic pitches that the performer attempts to match in his or her production of actual sounds. In the terminology of the earlier dialogues, the notes C, D, and so forth, would be called Forms instead of measures. But the role they are conceived to play with respect to sensible sounds would be essentially the same, inasmuch as both Forms and fixed measures serve as paradigms with reference to which sensible sounds are assigned determinate pitches. In a similar manner, the fixed reference points along a scale of linear measurement constitute a set of Forms with reference to which sensible bodies can be assigned determinate lengths. And parallel accounts could be given of our standard systems for measuring breadth and depth as Aristotle mentions, these being sets of Forms generated respectively from the Broad and Narrow and the Deep and Shallow—both varieties, as Aristotle says, of the Great and (the) Small—by the imposition of Limit. Since Limit, as we have seen, is ontologically equivalent to Unity, the Forms Length, Breadth, and Depth alike are composed from Unity and the Great and (the) Small.

Another variety of the Great and (the) Small is designated by Simplicius (248.7-8) as the Heavy and Light, from which Weight is generated by the imposition of Unity. Yet another relevant example is provided at *Physics* 220a, where Aristotle speaks of the "Now" as a limit (πέρας: 220a21) imposed on continuous (συνεχής: 220a5,26) temporal duration, whereby Time comes to be designated "the number (or measure) of motion with respect to before and after." Further Forms presumably constituted in a similar way are cited in the *Philebus* itself, as Socrates speaks of Beauty, Strength, Health, and many fine attributes of mind (26B6-7) generated by the mixture of Limit and the Unlimited.

It is with reference to the Forms of Length, Weight, Time, Beauty, Health, and so forth, that individual sensible things are characterized as being of such-and-such particular length, weight, age, appearance, or physical condition. These particular states of the individual, like the fixed reference points provided by the Forms, occupy positions along the relevant continua of the Great and (the) Small. But these states, unlike their fixed counterparts, have no definite place along their respective continua just in and by themselves. In and by itself, that is to say, the height of a particular individual is comparable to the height of another by the indefinite relationship of "taller or shorter" at best. It is only insofar as both heights can be assimilated to fixed points along a standard scale of measurement that they can be compared with each other in a determinate manner.

For Plato in the *Philebus*, observations of this sort have an ontological as well as a methodological significance. As Forms are brought into being by the imposition of Unity on the Great and (the) Small, so the characteristics of particular sensible things are brought into being by the Great and (the) Small submitting to the Forms as measures. Albeit in different fashions, both Forms and sensible things are composed from the Unlimited or the Indefinite Dyad. One respect in which their mode of composition is different, as previously noted, is that Forms might exist independently of sensible things, inasmuch as a musical scale, for instance, could exist as such without musical sounds actually being produced in temporal sequence. But musical sounds as we know them could not exist without the Forms or measures of the musical scale. Thus Forms have a mode of existence distinct from that of sensible objects. Nonetheless, their ontological role is to serve as standards or paradigms by which sensible things are characterizable as being what they are. It is part of the very nature of the Forms in Plato's final ontology that they exist for comparison with individual objects. This is made possible by the provision at the very heart of this ontology according to which both Forms and sensible objects are generated, as Aristotle puts it (*Metaphysics* 988a10), from the same material cause—the Indefinite Dyad or the Great and (the) Small. By removing the condition of radical separation of Forms and objects that held sway throughout the middle dialogues up through the *Timaeus*, Plato has finally provided an answer to the problem of participation. For changing and inconstant sensible things to participate in Forms is for Forms to serve as fixed standards or measures with reference to which these sensible things can be assigned determinate characteristics, despite their indefiniteness and constant change.

As in the *Theaetetus*, a particular man is an assemblage of sensible properties. These properties, however, are not such as might be generated according to a theory of becoming which takes active and passive powers as ontologically primitive. They rather are properties that by nature are identifiable as such only with reference to a set of fixed paradigms imposed along indefinite continua of comparative qualities. They are, in short, properties generated by the Great and (the) Small submitting to the measures of the appropriate Forms. With this basic ontological adjustment, we may continue to conceive individual sensible things after the manner proposed in the *Theaetetus*—as an assemblage of many things, to which assemblages people give the names 'man', and 'stone', and those of other living creatures and of all other kinds. An individual man is an assemblage of otherwise indefinite qualities, made determinate by participation in relevant Forms.

But what can be said about the manner in which the Form Man itself is subject to composition? Considerable help is available in Gosling's speculation about the conception of health operating at *Philebus* 25E8. What Plato seems to have in mind, Gosling suggests, is a matter of fixed proportions between such physiological factors as "degrees of heat, solidity, size, and so on,"[88] that constitute a healthy state of the body for a person of a given age or stage of growth. Since these proportions will change with increasing years, "to remain healthy would be to be in a constant process of changing proportions between elements."[89] Inasmuch as the Form Man may be presumed to be that instantiated in a normally healthy mature person, however, we may conceive of the Form Man itself as the set of proportions among constituent elements that characterizes such a person. Thus conceived, the Form Man serves as a fixed standard or paradigm against which the states of health of individual persons can be compared and measured, and can exist as such even though no particular person ever instantiates the healthy state in a wholly perfect manner. Without reference to this Form, on the other hand, the states of health of individual persons could be compared only indefinitely as more or less healthy, and could never be subject to the type of knowledge we would like to think a skilled physician might possess.

Textual evidence that Plato indeed had something like this in mind appears in a frequently misunderstood passage at *Philebus* 32A-B. By way of summing up his preceding discussion of the causes of pleasure and pain, Socrates offers the following general statement:

> when the Form (or particular state) of the living, naturally produced as I said before from the Unlimited and Limit, is disrupted, this disruption is pain [τὸ ἔκ τε ἀπείρου καὶ πέρατος κατὰ φύσιν ἔμψυχον γεγονὸς εἶδος, ὅπερ ἔλεγον ἐν τῷ πρόσθεν, ὅταν μὲν τοῦτο φθείρηται, τὴν μὲν φθορὰν λύπην εἶναι: 32A9-B3]; while return to the proper manner of being, by contrast, is always a pleasure [τὴν δ᾽ εἰς τὴν αὐτῶν οὐσίαν ὁδόν, ταύτην δὲ αὖ πάλιν τὴν ἀναχώρησιν πάντων ἡδονήν: 32B3-4].

Whereas some translators have found the term εἶδος at 32B1 so awkward as to suppress it entirely[90] (presumably as a result of the general uncertainty how anything at all could be produced from Limit and the Unlimited), we are now prepared to make tolerably clear sense of this puzzling passage. In fact, there are two possible interpretations. One is to translate εἶδος as "particular state" or "condition," and to construe disruption of this state as a departure from the proper proportions among its elements that render any organism alive and healthy. In this interpretation, the proper proportions are those particular measures or limits imposed upon the Unlimited that are established "according to its nature" (κατὰ φύσιν) or Form. A second interpretation is to translate εἶδος as the Form (Living Thing) itself. In this case the passage says, in effect, that when the proper relationships among its elements are disrupted—that is, when the arrangement of its elements departs from the due measure established by the Form Living Thing—an individual organism suffers pain as a result of this disruption; and that, by contrast, when the arrangement among its parts returns to this natural order—thus returning to "their proper manner of being" (τὴν αὐτῶν οὐσίαν ὁδόν)—the result for the organism is always pleasure. This second interpretation gains credibility by comparison with *De Anima* 404B, where Aristotle cites his "On Philosophy" (or else a lecture by Plato of that title, in either case tracing back to oral remarks of Plato), and pronounces in Plato's behalf that Animal itself (τὸ ζῷον ἐξ αὐτῆς: 404b20) is composed of Unity and "the primary length, breadth, and depth" (τοῦ πρώτου μήκους καὶ πλάτους καὶ βάθους: 404b20-21). If by "the primary length, breadth, and depth" we may understand (after *Metaphysics* 1085a9-12) the basic opposites out of which length, breadth, and depth are constituted, which opposites we have seen to be varieties of the Great and (the) Small, this remark from the *De Anima* about the constitution of the Form Animal strongly suggests that *Philebus* 32a9-B1 may incorporate a parallel claim about the genesis of the Form Living Thing as well.

By understanding the frequently repeated terms ἄπειρον and πέρας in the *Philebus* as referring to what Aristotle designated "the Great and (the) Small" and "Unity," respectively, we have seen how straightforward and intelligible interpretations can be provided for even the most puzzling passages of that dialogue. Moreover, we have seen how the ontological doctrines contained in these passages thus interpreted correspond almost exactly to the theses claimed by Aristotle at *Metaphysics* 987b to be characteristic of Plato's later ontological thinking. Since the concerned sections of these two documents heretofore have resisted wholly intelligible interpretation, the fact that both sets of passages become clear under the account developed in the foregoing pages offers perhaps the best evidence available that this account is correct in general outline. Correction of details and further exploration of particular ramifications of the account, needless to say, will require much additional labor.

The theory of Forms embodied in this later ontology differs in two fundamental respects from the theory ranging from the middle dialogues through the *Sophist* and the *Timaeus*. In the earlier theory, for one, the Forms are absolute, both in the sense of being themselves incomposite and in the sense of not depending for what they are upon other things. This character of the Forms is severely compromised as early as the *Sophist*, where Forms are seen to combine with other Forms, and hence to depend upon each other for being what they are. By the time of the *Philebus*, however, Plato's thinking in this regard has so changed that the Forms are no longer conceived even to be ontologically basic. Like sensible things, Forms in this later context are conceived as being constituted from two more fundamental ontological principles—in the case of the Forms, the Great and (the) Small and Unity. The main difference between Forms and sensible things with respect to their constitution is that Forms must be constituted prior to the latter, inasmuch as sensible things are composed of the Great and (the) Small and the Forms in turn. The fact that both Forms and sensible things are constituted from the Great and (the) Small bespeaks the second fundamental deviation of the later from the earlier theory. Since both Forms and sensible things come to be by the imposition of measure upon the same basic ontological principle, their respective modes of being can no longer be conceived as radically distinct. Thus Plato's later theory avoids that one aspect of the earlier which we saw in the *Timaeus* and the *Parmenides* caused the most difficulty for the earlier theory—the radical separation of Forms from sensible objects.

In other respects, however, the two theories are basically similar. According to the theory of the *Phaedo* and the *Republic*, Forms are standards or paradigms by which sensible objects are given names and identified, inasmuch as objects share the names of the Forms in which they participate. The trouble with the notion of Forms as standards or paradigms in the earlier dialogues is that this notion there never amounted to much more than a metaphor, as Plato seems to have realized while writing the *Timaeus*. In the theory of the *Philebus*, by contrast, the doctrine of the Forms as paradigms is given a literal and relatively unproblematic sense.[91] Just as the strict numerical ratio of the octave provides a paradigm against which to measure the octaves of actual vocal or instrumental performance, and just as the numerically exact interval of the meter, yard, or cubit provides a standard against which to measure the length of individual sensible objects,[92] so Forms generally provide paradigms or standards against which to measure the related characteristics of objects that accordingly we call "beautiful," "healthy," or "good." In the case of health, for instance, the Form Healthy constitutes a set of exact relationships among elements of an ideal living organism that provide a norm against which corresponding relationships in an individual organism can be measured and evaluated. To the extent that the state of the individual approximates that norm in relevant respects, the individual itself is described as "healthy."

Because Forms provide paradigms by which sensible things can be characterized as having certain properties, moreover, there is a sense in which Forms cause individual things to be what they are. Just as it is because of the standard meter that a particular object can be characterized as a meter long, or because of the numerically exact "Middle C" that a particular vocal sound has the corresponding character, so it is because of the Form Healthy that an individual organism is healthy. And so on for the other characteristics (Fair Weather, Beauty, Strength, etc.) with which the *Philebus* is concerned. Whether this is the sense of cause in which Forms were considered causes in the *Phaedo* is not wholly evident, inasmuch as the sense of cause in that earlier context was never made entirely perspicuous. In the *Philebus*, however, there is another sense of cause in which Forms patently are not causes themselves. This is the sense of the fourth basic principle or kind, which is the Cause of the mixture of Limit and the Unlimited. Inasmuch as Forms themselves result from such mixture, they cannot themselves be the Cause by which they are generated. The fact that the Intelligence or Mind that plays the role of Cause in the *Philebus* appears closely analogous, in its creative role, to the Intelligence of the *Timaeus* suggests that Plato had given up the notion of Forms as causes in this latter sense before the *Philebus*, if in fact he had ever held it.

Most important, however, is a third respect in which the later remains faithful to the earlier theory. The hallmark of the Forms in the *Phaedo* and the *Republic* is that they can be directly known, in a manner independent of sense perception. It was just this provision of the early theory, of course, that enabled it to respond to Plato's primary concern (as Aristotle says at *Metaphysics* 1078b15-16) with questions of knowledge and its ontological requirements. As was the case with other key features of the earlier theory, however, the sense in which Forms could be directly known was never made wholly explicit. With the theory of the *Philebus* Plato finally achieved a precise conception

185

of the sense in which some Forms at least can be known independently of the changeable things that participate in them. As Middle C can be known by a precise mathematical characterization, and as the standard Yard can be known in numerical proportion to other linear measures, so the Forms Health, Beauty, and so forth, can be known by exact specification of the due measure by which they are constituted. So, at least, Plato seems to believe in the *Statesman* and the *Philebus*. For us to say just how the relevant measures in these latter cases could actually be specified, however, would require more resources than these dialogues provide. Perhaps it was Plato's vision that a new "godly intelligence" someday would appear to answer such questions, after the manner of the Pythagoreans in the case of music.

KNOWLEDGE AND ONTOLOGY IN THE INTERMEDIATE DIALOGUES

Against the common view that Plato's ontology reaches its final expression in the *Sophist* and the *Timaeus*, I have argued that a new and radically different theory appears in the later *Philebus*. The ontological passages of the *Sophist* and the *Timaeus* should be viewed instead as phases of an attempt during the intermediate ("early late") period to repair the theory of the *Phaedo* and the *Republic*. One major defect of this earlier theory is that it never progressed beyond the level of metaphor in its treatment of the ontological requirements of knowledge (said at *Metaphysics* 1078b15-16 to be Plato's main concern behind the theory of Forms). Another is that this theory provided no account of how sensible objects can receive fixed names and persist through time. Part of the difficulty in this respect is that the early theory remained silent on the nature of participation, by which changing objects receive characters from unchanging Forms. Beyond this is unclarity about the status of sensible objects as such—regarding the manner of their existence and how they are constituted. These three problems (the status of sensible objects, the ontological requirements of knowledge, and the nature of participation) are addressed in the *Theaetetus*, the *Sophist*, and the *Timaeus*, respectively. Seen from this viewpoint, it was the failure of the *Timaeus* to provide a coherent notion of participation that led finally to Plato's rejection of his earlier ontology.

187

Although acceptance of this viewpoint is not essential to the foregoing discussion of the *Parmenides* and the *Philebus*, it provides a perspective on the ontology of the intermediate dialogues that may be of interest in its own right. One purpose of this appendix accordingly is to trace Plato's efforts through the intermediate dialogues to provide coherent answers to the problems besetting his earlier ontology. Another purpose is to gain insight into why that ontology was finally rejected.

EARLY DEVELOPMENTS IN THE ONTOLOGY OF KNOWLEDGE

In the standard textbook approach to Plato's teachings, the theory of Forms is closely associated with the doctrine of recollection. The lineaments of this association are roughly as follows. Since the Forms are changeless they are beyond sense perception, which admits only the mutable among its objects. Sense perception instead is an impediment to knowledge, being a major source of distraction and false opinion. Knowledge of the Forms can be initiated only when this impediment is absent, which requires that the knowing mind exist apart from the body. What is called "learning" accordingly is not the inception of knowledge but rather the recollection of previously known objects that were forgotten under the influence of bodily diversions. Since the knowing mind thus is capable of incorporeal existence, it is incomposite, imperishable, and hence immortal. A feature often added in the textbook account is that Plato maintained this doctrine throughout his career.

Edifying as this account may be, it distracts from the core epistemological elements of the doctrine of recollection. These are the elements that enable us to understand (1) the role this doctrine actually played in the *Meno* (the dialogue in which it was introduced), and (2) why Plato relinquished this theory by the end of the *Phaedo* (the second and only other dialogue in which it has a role). Its absence in the *Republic* appears virtually certain when we attend to the epistemological developments within these three dialogues.

The doctrine of recollection is introduced at *Meno* 80C, where a torpified Meno poses a garbled version of the well-known "learner's paradox."[1] Socrates sets the problem straight, and responds with his story of immortality and foreknowledge. The problem is to explain how inquiry is possible. For one must inquire into either what is known or what is unknown; and whereas learning is not possible where one knows already, with the unknown one is ignorant of what the inquiry concerns. In either case, inquiry would appear to be pointless.

A serious difficulty lies behind this sophistical puzzler. To seek knowledge about some specific thing, a person must in some sense know the thing already for this to be the thing about which knowledge is sought. And to achieve articulate knowledge about a specific object, a person must know what the thing is already to recognize this as the thing about which knowledge is gained. In its most general form, the problem is to explain how knowledge is possible originally, inasmuch as gaining knowledge requires something previously known. To resolve the problem would be to identify a "ground level" of cognition that does not require antecedent knowledge in turn. Plato's answer in the *Meno* is to the effect that the "ground level" of cognition is the mind's direct awareness of the Forms themselves. Although this initial awareness is eroded by sense experience, the mind is capable of recalling what it once knew explicitly; hence learning is possible as a result of inquiry.

One core element of this account thus is its acceptance of the (foundationalist) requirement that there be a "ground level" of knowledge which does not rely upon prior knowledge in turn. Another is that knowledge on this fundamental level be present within the mind before the onset of experience. This second requirement reflects a number of assumptions about sense experience which Plato in the *Meno* accepts without question. One is that no form of experience provides an access to knowledge. This assumption rules out induction as a source of knowledge, as for example in Book II of the *Posterior Analytics*. A more restrictive assumption is that bodily experience actually is hostile to knowledge, and is the cause of the mind's forgetting upon incarnation. The effect of these two assumptions is that sense experience has nothing positive whatever to contribute to inquiry

189

(an attitude which appears to soften considerably in the *Republic* [523B through 525A] and even in the *Phaedo* [74B]). A further assumption which seems less problematic is that the influence of sense perception begins at birth. The upshot of all three assumptions together is that knowledge in some manner must be present in the mind before it begins its career of bodily experience. The proposal of the *Meno* is that this knowledge is obtained during a state of mind prior to incarnation. We should note carefully, however, that postulation of an incorporeal state of existence is not a necessary response to the problem as it stands. A response which would do just as well, and which would sound more plausible to some modern philosophers at least, is that knowledge somehow is present in the mind innately, but in a manner not relying upon prenatal states of awareness.

A third core element, essential to the theory but often overlooked, is that recollection can be accomplished by nullifying the effects of those influences that caused forgetting in the first place. The influences are those of bodily experience; and their effects—in the cognitive realm at least—are deception and false opinion. Following from these considerations is a distinctive prescription for the conduct of inquiry. What is necessary to bring about recollection of the previously known Forms is removal of the falsehoods engendered by bodily experience. Insofar as the theory tells the whole story about how inquiry leads to knowledge, moreover, this is all that is required for recollection. The Socratic method of elenchus, or refutation, is tailored expressly to serve this function. Insofar as the essential purpose of Socratic refutation is the removal of false opinion, the result of its successful application should be a return of the subject to an explicit state of knowledge. This fact undoubtedly is connected with the allegedly inconclusive character of several of the Socratic dialogues that commentators perennially have found so frustrating. If the process of elenchus has been successfully applied (in the *Euthyphro*, for instance, or the *Laches*, or the *Charmides*), then no explicit statement of the result (the nature of Piety, Courage, Moderation, or whatever) is called for—since the result will be present already in the mind of the subject. If the theory of recollection provides an adequate account of inquiry, in other words, elenchus is a unidirectional process,[2] adequate in itself for the recovery of knowledge.

But the theory of recollection was not an adequate theory, and it is clear that Plato had given it up by the time of the *Republic*. The theory was inadequate for at least two reasons. One is that it was basically incoherent. An essential part of the theory is that the mind first comes to apprehend the Forms in a direct and hence unmediated fashion, which means that the mind so situated must exist in the immediate presence of the Forms themselves. But the realm of the Forms is atemporal. To be in the immediate presence of the Forms, accordingly, the mind itself must exist atemporally. And there is no intelligible way the mind can exist atemporally *before* entering the body, since what is atemporal does not enter into temporal relationships.

This difficulty could perhaps be skirted by emphasizing the nonliteral character of the theory—which after all was attributed to religious seers and poets (*Meno* 81A-C)—and interpreting talk of "preexisting" knowledge as referring more accurately to innate mental capacities, along the lines indicated above. But there are no signs that Plato even considered this option.

The second reason for rejecting the theory, moreover, would be conclusive even under a "nativist" interpretation. As a straightforward matter of fact, removal of false opinion is not sufficient for bringing the mind to a state of knowledge. The elenctic art of Socrates may be necessary to rid the mind of certain impediments to knowledge. But refutation itself, however artfully practiced, does not bring knowledge in its wake. In a word, elenchus may be necessary, but it is not sufficient. Despite the strictly elenctic character of the *Euthyphro*, for instance, it remains a stubborn fact that neither Euthyphro nor we as readers are brought to a state of knowing the nature of piety as a result of exposure to Socratic refutation.

There are two reasons in turn for being almost certain that Plato was aware of this particular shortcoming. The difficulty, to repeat, is that the theory of recollection gives conditions which are necessary at best, but not sufficient, for reaching a state of explicit knowledge. One indication of Plato's loss of confidence in the theory is that in the second of the only two dialogues in which it does any work—the *Phaedo*—it is replaced before the dialogue is over with another account of how to arrive at "the truth about things" (99E6), which explicitly provides both necessary and sufficient conditions for knowledge. I will turn shortly to an examination of this successor theory.

The most direct reason for believing that Plato was aware of this shortcoming, however, is that he in effect makes the same criticism himself in a later dialogue, the *Sophist*. At the very beginning of that dialogue, after a few introductory comments, Socrates turns over the argument to a Stranger from Elea, who in the course of the discussion following develops seven distinct definitions of the sophistic art. The first five definitions are inadequate characterizations (giving only sufficient but not necessary conditions) of sophistry as it is generally understood, while the seventh gives an adequate account of that particular calling. The sixth definition, however, is not of sophistry as normally understood at all, but rather of a purgative art designated "sophistry of noble lineage" (ἡ γένει γενναία σοφιστική: 231B9). As the physician separates better from worse in bodily disease, the practitioner of this form of sophistry effects a comparable separation in afflictions of the soul. Indeed, the maladies that the sixth sophist cures are just those brought about by sophistry in its other forms—errors of intellect (229C6) and empty conceit of wisdom (231B7). In summary, as the Stranger puts it (230B4-C2), these sophists

> cross-examine a man's false impressions who, thinking he is saying something, says nothing instead, and easily proves by scrutiny the errors of his opinions. These they marshal by reasoning[3] and, placing them side by side, show that they are contrary to each other regarding the same things and in the same respect. Seeing this, the man becomes dissatisfied with himself and more considerate of others, and thus is delivered from gross and obdurate opinions, in a manner delightful to the hearer and auspicious for himself as patient.

Commentators who consider this passage have not infrequently seen in it an entirely apt characterization of Socratic elenchus.[4] What makes this characterization particularly notable in the pres-

192

ent regard is that it seems expressly intended to show up the limitations of that particular practice. The "sophist of noble lineage" prepares the mind of his patient for an "approach to learning" (προσφερομένων μαθημάτων: 230C8-D1), but is not capable of bringing about knowledge by his own devices. Even the ascription of "noble lineage" to this form of sophistry is a doubtful compliment, since the nobility in question is a matter not of genealogical but of definitional kinship. That is, whereas the other six forms of sophistry are defined by means of an initial distinction between productive and acquisitive arts, the definition of this beneficial form shows that it, like the dialectic of philosophy, is concerned with the separative as distinct from the combining arts. The all-important difference is that the beneficial form of sophistry separates better from worse in mental matters, while the science of dialectic separates like from like (*Sophist* 253D). Socratic elenchus is essentially a purgative art. Its great deficiency as a method of philosophy is that, while it contributes what is often[5] necessary for the achievement of knowledge, by itself it is not sufficient. Such at least is the clear implication of Plato's own description, in the very dialogue where Socrates retires as major interlocutor.

After the *Phaedo*, there is only one other reference to recollection (ἀνάμνησις) in any sense remotely connected with the doctrine of immortality.[6] This occurs at *Phaedrus* 249C2, in which context ἀνάμνησις is identified with the quite different method of collection and division. A few other occurrences of the term in the very late dialogues (*Philebus* 34B2; *Laws* 732B8) appear entirely removed from this earlier sense.

In his final philosophic remarks before taking the hemlock, at any rate, Socrates recommends a quite different method of inquiry. Although described initially as a "next best way"[7] of proceeding, this method dominates the methodological discussions of the *Republic* and is applied explicitly (although not discussed) in the *Theaetetus*.[8] In the *Phaedo* it is identified as the procedure anyone will follow who is a philosopher (102A1), and in the *Republic* as the dialectic of reason by which one pursues the nature of each thing (αὐτὸ ὃ ἔστιν ἕκαστον ὁρᾶν: 532A7) including the Good itself (αὐτὸ ὃ ἔστιν ἀγαθὸν: 532B1).

193

The procedure begins in each case by assuming a proposition (λόγον: 100A4) or hypothesis (ὑποθέσεως: 101D4) that one judges soundest (ἐρρωμενέστατον: 100A4). Having thus laid down the best starting point available in the context of inquiry, the philosopher deals with his hypothesis in two distinct stages. First he determines whether it could possibly be true. This is done by considering whether its consequences (ὁρμηθέντα[9]: 101D5) are consistent or not. If the consequences are found consistent amongst themselves (and with other propositions essential to the context in question), then and only then[10] the philosopher undertakes to give an account of the hypothesis itself. To do this, he proceeds in the same way (ὡσαύτως: 101D7), positing a higher (ἄνωθεν, in the sense of "by which the first is generated:" 101D8) hypothesis, the best (βελτίστη: 101D8) to be found, and continuing until one is reached that is satisfactory (ἱκανὸν: 101E1). To be satisfactory in this regard, presumably, is to be such that no further justification is called for within the context, in the sense that the axioms of geometry cannot be geometrically proved.

The first stage of this method is to establish the necessary conditions for the truth of the hypothesis—that it be consistent, or possibly true. After this is established, the second stage is to provide sufficient conditions, in the form of another hypothesis which (1) is also consistent, (2) includes the initial hypothesis among its consequences, and (3) itself requires no justification in the context of inquiry. Whereas Socratic elenchus deals only with necessary conditions for the truth of a thesis, and hence could never establish it as true, the method of hypothesis aims at conditions that are both necessary and sufficient for truth.

Having described this method to the satisfaction of all concerned (102A), Socrates proceeds to apply it in a fourth and final (and, unlike the first three, valid) argument for the soul's immortality (103C-105E). His very last philosophic comment to Simmias before the myth that preceded his leave-taking is that the initial hypotheses of the argument call for more clear examination, and that in analyzing them adequately "you will be following the argument as far as man is able" (ἀκολουθήσετε τῷ λόγῳ καθ᾽ ὅσον δυνατὸν μάλιστ᾽ ἀνθρώπῳ ἐπακολουθῆ-

194

σαι: 107B6-7). Reaching surety in this analysis, says Socrates, "your inquiry will be over" (οὐδὲν ζητήσετε περαιτέρω: 107B8). As Plato depicts his final hour, Socrates himself has come to see that success in philosophic inquiry is more than recollection.

Despite the enthusiastic expressions of satisfaction from his Pythagorean associates (102A), however, we have ample reason for being dissatisfied with the method of hypothesis as formulated in the *Phaedo*. The method appears to be modeled after the then fairly common geometrical method of analysis, which deals exclusively with mutually convertible propositions. A characteristic of two such propositions in the geometrical context is that they both are consistent with each other and imply each other, and moreover are consistent only if mutually implicative. This is just the relationship necessary to make sense of Socrates' instructions at 100A, to the effect that he accepts as true any proposition which "agrees" (συμφωνεῖν: 100A5) with the hypothesis he initially judges to be strongest, and takes to be false any proposition which does not agree.[11] Although intelligible in a geometrical context, the application of these instructions as part of a general philosophic method is unclear at best, since philosophy does not typically deal with convertible propositions.

Another difficulty with the description as it stands is that no indication is provided of what exactly it is for a "higher" hypothesis to be "satisfactory." In his application of the method of analysis, the geometer traces out a series of (mutually implicative) propositions until he finds one that is axiomatic or that can be independently proven. A "satisfactory" proposition for a geometer thus would be one for which the question of justification either did not arise or had been antecedently settled. But since philosophic argument (both then and now) usually is not axiomatic in structure, it is not clear what the philosopher should be looking for in seeking a hypothesis that is "satisfactory." Another way of putting the difficulty relates to Socrates' instructions to Simmias and his associates at 107B, that they should follow up the argument "as far as man is able," at which point they will reach surety and their inquiry will be over. Just how far can a person pursue the assumptions of an argument? And what is it to arrive at an assumption that is entirely sure?

The general problem behind these difficulties is that Plato appears to be adopting a mathematical method for philosophic purposes, without considering either the differences between mathematics and philosophy or the implications of these differences for philosophic inquiry. Perhaps this was deemed appropriate for the *Phaedo*, with its predominately Pythagorean cast of characters. By the time the middle parts of the *Republic* were written, however, Plato obviously had taken these difficulties into account, for the description of philosophic method in that dialogue is essentially a matter of contrast with mathematical procedures.

Book VI of the *Republic* contains the last explicit discussion of method in the middle dialogues.[12] Mathematics and philosophy herein are alike in that both relate to the intelligible as opposed to the visible domain. The visible is divided into images (shadows, reflections, etc.) and the objects that are imaged (animals, human artifacts, etc.), in a manner corresponding to the division of the intelligible into mathematics and philosophy. The relationship between all four domains is represented by a mathematical construction—a line subdivided into four parts such that the ratio of the first (images) to the second (physical objects) is the same as that of the third (mathematics) to the fourth (philosophy), which in turn is the same as that of the visible (images and physical objects) to the intelligible (mathematics and philosophy). The primary symbolism of the ratio is to express a division with respect to truth and its opposite (διῃρῆσθαι ἀ-ληθείᾳ τε καὶ μή: 510A9-10): as images are less true than what they image, so objects of opinion (visible objects) are less true than objects of cognition (intelligible objects).

The clear implication is that the objects of mathematics are less true than those of philosophy. What is meant by 'true' here is not a value of propositions (in correspondence with fact, opposed to erroneous), but rather an excellence of status (opposed to "only apparent")—that is, the objects of mathematics somehow are less *real* than the objects of philosophy. One respect in which the objects of mathematics are less real than those of philosophy is that the former, unlike the latter, can be studied only through the use of images. Indeed, the mathematician relies for examples and illustrations upon objects of the very sort which themselves are imaged in reflections and shadows. While he relies upon diagrams and other constructions as visible representations, however, it is the square and diagonal as such that are objects of the mathematician's thought.[13]

The second aspect of mathematics which makes it defective in truth or reality is that mathematicians posit their objects hypothetically—the odd and even, various figures, the three kinds of triangles, and so on (510C4-5)—and then regard them as known and obvious to everyone, beyond any need of further accounting. In philosophy, by contrast, the mind proceeds from hypotheses to a nonhypothetical principle (ἀρχὴν ἀνυπόθετον: 510B7). The hypotheses it begins with are taken, not as unjustifiable axioms or primitives, but as points of departure from which it can rise to the "principle of all" (τὴν τοῦ παντὸς ἀρχὴν: 511B7) which is beyond hypothesis. Having grasped this highest principle, the mind then proceeds downward with its consequences, remaining always with Ideas without sensible imagery. While mathematics is exclusively "downward" (deductive) in its procedures, that is to say, philosophy involves both an "upward" and a "downward" moment, the former of which leads the mind to a starting point intrinsically beyond justification.

Beyond its avoidance of imagery, there are two ways in which philosophic method of the Divided Line differs from the quasi-mathematical method described in the final pages of the *Phaedo*. Both methods are concerned with drawing out the consequences of the hypotheses with which they begin (i.e., with necessary conditions for the truth of those hypotheses), and both are concerned with the justification of these hypotheses (i.e., with sufficient conditions). According to the instructions of the *Phaedo*, however, justification of the initial hypothesis can begin only after the consequences of the hypothesis have been checked for consistency, while in the *Republic* the procedure is first to justify the hypothesis by "ascent" to a first principle, and only then to draw out the consequences. The second and more basic difference

197

may explain why this is permissible. Whereas justification in the *Phaedo* is said to terminate when the philosopher reaches a hypothesis that is "satisfactory"—presumably meaning one that does not call for an account in the particular context of inquiry—in the description of the Divided Line the philosopher continues the "upward path" of justification until he reaches a principle that is not hypothetical at all, regardless of context. Since this nonhypothetical starting point is the "principle of all things," a hypothesis flowing from it presumably does not require an independent consistency test.

This is all Plato says about the nonhypothetical principle, in the *Republic* or elsewhere. A tantalizing question left unanswered is whether this principle is intended to be identified with the Good, the alleged source of being and truth so extravagantly praised in analogy with the sun in the passages preceding. Since most commentators seem inclined to the conjecture that the nonhypothetical principle and the Good are one and the same, it is important to see why this is problematic. First and foremost, there is no explicit identification of the two superlative factors, whereas the close proximity and common subject matter of the sun analogy and the Divided Line would have made it entirely natural for Plato to have asserted their identity if this was his intention. Second, in a recapitulation following his prescriptions for the education of the guardians, Socrates again characterizes dialectic as the process of inquiry that proceeds to a principle beyond hypothesis (533C10-534A1), by which process one is able to grasp an account of the nature of each thing (τὸν λόγον ἑκάστου λαμβάνοντα τῆς οὐσίας: 534B3-4), the idea of the Good (τὴν τοῦ ἀγαθοῦ ἰδέαν: 534B9-C1) included. But it makes little sense to talk of giving an account of the idea of the Good by tracing it back to itself, which would be required if the first principle and the Good were identical. Finally, there is no intelligible sense in which the Good appears capable of establishing mathematical postulates (cf. 510C), or any other starting points of any other inquiry, on a nonhypothetical basis. For all we know about the Good from the *Republic*,[14] it is much too amorphous a principle to generate the determinate starting points of the particular sciences.

On the other hand, the final apprehension of dialectic at the limit of the intelligible (τῷ τοῦ νοητοῦ τέλει: 532B2) is said to be of the essence of the Good (αὐτὸ ὃ ἔστιν ἀγαθὸν: 532B1), a characterization that also occurs in the summary of the allegory of the cave (517B8-9). Another consideration supporting the alleged identification of the two superlative factors is that the epistemological powers of the Good are emphasized in the analogy with the sun (as the sun is the source both of existence and visibility in the realm of the sensible, so the Good is the source both of truth and knowability in the realm of the intelligible), and that the Divided Line (with its nonhypothetical principle) is introduced explicitly as a further clarification of these powers. Other considerations permitting, one could argue plausibly that Plato assumed the reader would automatically identify the superlative principles of these two passages, and did not think it necessary to state what is obvious.

An especially appealing conjecture is that Plato, in associating the idea of the Good with the foundational principles of knowledge, is attempting to rescue his method of hypothesis from the so-called "next best" status accorded it in the *Phaedo*.[15] If knowledge of all things could be shown to depend upon the source of the right and beautiful (as the idea of the Good is characterized at 517C), then Plato would have succeeded where Anaxagoras failed (cf. *Phaedo* 97B-99C)—in establishing reasoning about causes on a teleological basis. A serious obstacle to this conjecture is that (a) the Good in analogy with the sun is endowed with epistemological and ontological powers only and, although cited as inconceivably beautiful in that context, has no explicitly normative status, (b) there is nothing morally right or aesthetically beautiful about the goal of dialectic in the Divided Line account[16], and (c) no further plausibility or intelligibility would be added to this account if such factors were grafted onto it.

On balance, the only proper conclusion regarding the question of the relationship between the first principle and the Good is that the question is moot. Moreover, the question is not as urgent as some self-styled Platonists insinuate, since neither superlative factor appears in any dialogue after (or for that matter, before) the *Republic*. This is not to say that Plato abandoned his efforts to develop an intelligible account of the ultimate grounds of knowledge, for that attempt continues with new vigor in the *Sophist*. Nor is it to say that Plato never again was concerned to relate axiological considerations to epistemology and ontology, for that concern is pursued with striking results in the *Philebus*. It is to say merely that the notion of the Good conceived in analogy with the sun, and the notion of the nonhypothetical first principle as the ground of knowledge, go the way of the notion of recollection from the *Meno* and the *Phaedo*. None of these celebrated factors of textbook Platonism remains active in Plato's writing after the middle period. To maintain the contrary is to espouse a nondevelopmental conception of Plato's thought that cannot be supported conjointly with a careful reading of the dialogues.

This brief review of Plato's conception of philosophic method in the middle period helps clarify one aspect of the so-called "early theory of Forms" that Plato apparently found particularly troublesome—the doctrine that the Forms are directly knowable. The part of this doctrine that is not problematic for Plato is the disclaimer that knowledge of the Forms depends in any essential way upon sense perception. Regarding the question of what positive steps must be taken for the mind to arrive at this knowledge, however, Plato seems to have experimented with a variety of answers during the middle period. Let us briefly review these answers, and note their ontological consequences.

The first and simplest answer appears in the *Meno*, where Socrates (rather tentatively; see 86B) suggests that coming to know is a process of recollecting what the mind has apprehended[17] in a previous existence. As the remainder of the dialogue makes clear, what is supposed to be required for recollection is the removal of false opinions born of bodily involvement. Methodologically, the doctrine of recollection went hand in hand with the technique of Socratic elenchus, uniquely adapted to the removal of erroneous opinion. Ontologically, it was accompanied with a conception of the Forms as entirely incomposite entities, in the sense of being what they are without essential relationship to other things. This is stated most explicitly in the early part of the *Phaedo* where, in a series of descriptive passages immediately following the second reference in the corpus to the theory of recollection, the Forms are referred to repeatedly as invariable (μονοειδὲς: 78D5, passim), changeless (ὡσαύτως: 78C5, passim), and self-identical (ἑαυτῷ ὁμοιότατον: 80B2).

By the end of the *Phaedo*, however, this all begins to change. With the new and considerably more sophisticated method of hypothesis, we are introduced to the novel conception of Forms as intrinsically interrelated. In the final proof of immortality, for instance, Cebes is convinced that soul brings life and does not admit death, on the analogy of the Form Three which necessitates participation in the Form Odd and excludes the Form Even. Similar cases, Socrates says, are Two and Odd, Fire and Cold, and many others (104E7-8). As part of their very nature, in brief, Forms admit relations akin to entailment and inconsistency. This is not to say that Forms no longer are conceived as invariable or changeless; rather, they are conceived no longer as entirely simple,[18] but as admitting internal relations among themselves. It would seem to follow that knowing the Forms would require knowing about these relations, which would require an application of logical (hence discursive) reason.[19]

Another dimension of complexity is added in the *Republic*. Logical relationships among the Forms are still a factor, inasmuch as mathematicians are said to inquire in a consistent manner (ὁμολογουμένως: 510D1) about "the Square and the Diagonal as such" (τοῦ τετραγώνου αὐτοῦ . . . καὶ διαμέτρου αὐτῆς: 510D6-8), along with other such things. Philosophers also are concerned with reasoning in terms of consequences (καταβαίνῃ: 511B9). The added dimension is that the philosopher is not content to treat his initial suppositions as principles beyond need of further support, as the mathematician postulates the odd and even, and so forth (510C4-5). The philosopher instead seeks to relate these suppositions to a principle that by nature transcends hypothesis. Attaining this nonhypothetical principle, he then proceeds to draw consequences from it, moving from Form to Form and ending with Forms (511C1-2). Since philosophic reasoning deals with Forms exclusively, we must surmise that both the initial suppositions and the nonhypothetical principle (whether the Good or something else) themselves are Forms. The crucial point is that the highest Form which transcends hypothesis relates to other Forms in a manner beyond mere consistency and entailment; it also provides a ground by which the existence of these other Forms can be accepted nonhypothetically. In other words, the domain of Forms is characterized by a hierarchical ordering, one Form supporting others in a nonreciprocal manner. This ontological structure is reflected in the philosopher's method, as he reasons first ("upward") toward and then ("downward") from this ultimate principle. That his mode of grasping the Forms is discursive is a necessary consequence.

Thus from the first appearance of the theory of recollection in the *Meno* to the final discussion of the method of hypothesis in the *Republic*, Plato's thought undergoes significant development with respect both to the character of philosophic method and to the nature of the philosopher's apprehension of the immutable Forms. More important for present purposes, however, is the concomitant change in his conception of the relationships among the Forms in their own domain. While he was experimenting with the theory of recollection, Plato seems to have conceived the Forms each as self-sufficient unto itself, simple in the sense of admitting no internal relations. By the end of the middle period with the *Republic*, however, Forms of necessity must be thought of, not only as admitting quasi-logical relations like consistency and entailment, but also as being ordered in relationships of ontological dependency, which it is the philosopher's business to grasp by reason.

A major problem with this scheme from the reader's point of view is that no further clues remain either about the identity of the highest principle or about how specifically it is supposed to relate to the rest of the Forms. Although it is tempting to surmise that the nonhypothetical principle is the Form of the Good, for reasons examined above, this surmise does nothing to help us understand how the philosopher should set about gaining knowledge in actual circumstances. As Aristotle has said (*Metaphysics* 1078b15-16), however, Plato's primary concern with the theory of Ideas was with questions of knowledge and its ontological requirements. The practical inapplicability of his theory as it stands in the *Republic* therefore must be understood as a serious impediment from Plato's point of view as well as from the reader's. Although the method of hypothesis itself finds further employment in the *Theaetetus*, the particular ontological trappings it receives in the *Republic* have entirely dropped from view in the later dialogues. When Plato returns to these problems in the *Sophist*, the realm of the Forms has been invested with a different ontological structure.

Another basic problem with the theory of the middle period is that the notion of participation upon which it relies remains little more than a suggestive metaphor.[20] In one manner of speaking, participation is accepted as primitive within the early theory, with no effort to explain how it might possibly come about. At the same time, of course, Plato obviously had some thoughts about what participation must amount to, if it is to play the role required by the general theory. One role is in the causation of sensible things. As previously noted, an integral part of the theory is that Forms are causes, in the sense that participation in a given Form is both necessary and sufficient for a sensible object to have the corresponding attribute. To take an example from the *Phaedo*, any sensible thing is beautiful that participates in Beauty (participation in Beauty is sufficient for being beautiful), and only things are beautiful that so participate (such participation is necessary for being beautiful). The Form Beauty somehow is the source of beauty, and participation is the manner in which the source is tapped. Accordingly, beauty must be present in the Form Beauty in a more fundamental manner than it comes derivatively to be present in sensible things. The theory does not require (in fact, does not even permit) that beauty be a property of the Form in the manner in which it is a property of a beautiful object.[21] Nor, for similar reasons, is the Form identical with the property beauty as such, since the beauty of things is a sensible property and the Form itself is never sensibly present.[22] The manner in which beauty is supposed to be present in Beauty, rather, may be something like the manner in which a nation's wealth might reside in its mineral resources—its resources are its source of wealth, without being either wealthy or identical with wealth themselves.

Another role required by the theory is that participation must provide for the identification of sensible things. Forms establish criteria by which an object warrants this or that particular designation. As Aristotle indicates (*Metaphysics*, 987b8-9), according to Plato all sensible things are named after Ideas. It is because a thing participates in Beauty, for instance, that we call it a thing of beauty, for it comes thereby to share the designation of the Form itself. Moreover, Aristotle continues (987b9-10), the many sensible things exist by participation in the Forms with which they share their names. Thus the name 'beauty' belongs first and foremost to the Form Beauty itself; but because of participation it belongs to beautiful things as well. In brief, by providing criteria for naming, the Forms serve as standards by which any given sensible object can be identified as one thing distinct from another.

Given these roles for participation to play in the general theory of Forms, a number of important consequences follow regarding the relationship between Forms and sensible objects. One is that the assignment of names to particular things is not arbitrary, or a matter of convention only, but ought to reflect the nature of the thing named. That Plato was aware of this consequence of his theory, and not wholly uncomfortable with it, is indicated by the subject matter of the *Cratylus*, a key remark of which is that names can be instruments both of communication and of distinguishing natures (388B13-C1).[23]

Another consequence is that sensible things are inferior to Forms not only ontologically but also with respect to those very features by which alone they make their presence known. That is, not only are sensible things changeable (hence not knowable), receptive of opposites (hence not fully real), and in general dependent for what they are upon the Forms (hence not absolute), but moreover the very characteristics by which they are identified in sense perception are subordinate to features of the Forms themselves. It is the beauty inherent in the Form Beauty that makes a particular thing beautiful, and the perfection of that former beauty is that it is not derivative from anything else. The effect is a sharp gradation in status between Forms and sensible things. As Plato reiterates several times at *Phaedo* 74D-75A, sensible objects are lacking (ἐνδεῖ) in comparison with Forms;

for example, sensible equals are inferior (φαυλότερα: 75B7) aspirants (προθυμεῖται: 75B5-6) to the Equal itself. Although this "degrees of reality" aspect of Plato's theory does not have explanatory power in itself, and hence does not appear an essential part of the basic theory,[24] it clearly is a consequence of the basic features of the theory. An explicit recognition of this aspect of the theory on Plato's part appears in the ratio of the Divided Line, which is said to represent a division between truth (ἀλήθεια: *Republic* 510A10) and its opposite—not just propositional truth and falsehood, but truth in the sense of reality opposed to appearance (cf. 508E3-4).

A third consequence of the role assigned participation in the early theory is that Forms in some sense admit characterization in terms of the same features as those they impart (by participation) to sensible things. Being the source of beauty, in some sense the Form Beauty possesses beauty in itself. As Socrates insists in the *Phaedo*, a necessary condition of anything else possessing beauty is that it participate in the Form of Beauty, the only exception being the Form itself (100C4-6). The sense in which the Form possesses beauty, however, cannot be the same as with sensible things. For one thing, the beauty of sensible things is sensibly manifest. For another, it is unthinkable that the Form Beauty be lacking in beauty, while this certainly is not the case with any beautiful object. In a parallel passage at *Protagoras* 330D8-E1, Socrates proclaims with unusual emphasis that nothing else could be holy if not the Holy itself. In whatever sense it might be that the Holy is holy, in that sense the Form is its own "perfect instance."

At least two major defects afflict this conception of participation as it stands at the end of the middle period. One is that the notion of a Form being a "perfect instance" of itself is not really intelligible. Although in our illustrative cases there have been analogies available to lend the notion a semblance of plausibility (beauty is in Beauty, as a country's wealth is in its natural resources), there are other cases in which the notion seems to make no sense at all. Since oddness is a mathematical property belonging only to numbers, and since the Form Oddness is not a number, in what conceivable sense can Oddness be odd? Again, since Forms are in every respect changeless, in what sense can the Form Change itself possess change? And for that matter, inasmuch as being tangible is a property only of things that might be present to touch, how can the Form Tangibility be in possession of that property? Similar cases abound when one begins looking for them.

A second, albeit related, deficiency is that Plato in the middle dialogues never set about to clarify what exactly it is for an object to participate in a Form. Neither allusions to the Forms as paradigms (e.g., at *Euthyphro* 6E6, or *Republic* 472C5, passim) which objects resemble, nor reference to objects as copies or imitations of Forms (e.g., at *Phaedo* 76E2, or *Phaedrus* 250B4), are very helpful as long as we are not told how it is that Forms might share properties with objects in the first place. And there are the additional difficulties of understanding how the atemporal Form can become involved with temporal processes, and what happens with respect to participation when an object manifests change in sensible properties (is there a moment at which it participates in two opposing Forms at once?).

The problem of reaching a coherent conception of participation thus joins that of clarifying the conditions of knowledge in the budget of problems remaining after the middle period. The former is addressed in the ontological passages of the *Timaeus*, while the latter is the subject matter of the *Theaetetus* and the *Sophist*. A prior problem is to provide an account of sensible objects, which despite their defects enjoy some mode of existence. This problem also is taken up in the *Theaetetus*.

BECOMING IN THE *Theaetetus*

Although Plato playfully attributes the theory at *Theaetetus* 156A-157C to Protagoras and various unnamed persons who maintain that all is motion, the theory is usually considered to have originated with Plato himself. A separate question is whether Plato himself accepted the theory. And this in turn can be decided only if two other questions are answered first. One is the question of what exactly the theory says, which is aggravated by ambiguities in Plato's account. The other is the question of just what purpose the theory serves within the dialogue. My case for an affirmative answer to the first question, in effect, is that the theory is developed in considerably more detail than required for its purpose within the dialogue proper, and that the additional particulars are just what Plato needed to respond to certain problems in the early theory of Forms.

The theory in question is what Cornford referred to as a theory of sense perception.[25] In fact, it is a theory both of sense perception and of sensible objects, with the latter receiving primary emphasis. The first principle upon which the theory is based, says Socrates, is that "all is motion and nothing other than motion" (τὸ πᾶν κίνησις ἦν καὶ ἄλλο παρὰ τοῦτο οὐδέν: 156A5). This remark follows a series of arguments purporting to establish that no object of sense perception (including number and size, which we would call "primary" properties) possesses self-identity independently from its appearances, the upshot of which Socrates sums up with the sweeping conclusion that "there is no one thing in and by itself" (μηδὲν αὐτὸ καθ' αὑτὸ ἓν ὄν: 153E4-5).[26] The principle that everything is motion upon which the theory is based, accordingly, cannot be understood as affirming merely that every physical thing is *in* motion, as if physical things might exist apart from their motions. The principle rather is that only motion exists, with the implication soon to be drawn that physical things are mere collections of motions.

In the realm of becoming, according to the theory, motion is ontologically basic. However,

> these motions are two in kind, each indefinitely numerous [τῆς δὲ κινήσεως δύο εἴδη, πλήθει μὲν ἄπειρον ἑκάτερον: 156A5-6], one having the power to act, the other that of being acted upon [δύναμιν δὲ τὸ μὲν ποιεῖν ἔχον, τὸ δὲ πάσχειν: 156A6-7]. From the intercourse and friction between these arise offspring paired as twins, themselves indefinitely numerous ['Εκ δὲ τῆς τούτων ὁμιλίας τε καὶ τρίψεως πρὸς ἄλληλα γίγνεται ἔκγονα πλήθει μὲν ἄπειρα, δίδυμα δέ: 156A7-B1]—the object of perception, and the perception which always is generated and

comes to be with the perceptual object [τὸ μὲν αἰσθητόν, τὸ δὲ αἴσθησις, ἀεὶ συνεκπίπτουσα καὶ γεννωμένη μετὰ τοῦ αἰσθητοῦ: 156Β1-3].

To the perceivings, Socrates continues, are given names such as 'seeing', 'hearing', 'smelling', 'feeling cold', and 'feeling hot', and like names for pleasures, pains, desires, fears and so forth. A corresponding variety of colors, on the other hand, arise with the seeings, and sounds with the hearings, and so on for other kindred pairs of perceivings and objects.

Passsing over for a moment the puzzling passage from 156C4 to E7, we find the account of sensible objects continued as follows:

So we must think of hardness, hotness, and all the rest [Καὶ τἄλλα δὴ οὕτω, σκληρὸν καὶ θερμὸν καὶ πάντα, τὸν αὐτὸν τρόπον ὑποληπτέον: 156E7-8]. As we said before, no one of them is just by itself [αὐτὸ μὲν καθ᾽ αὑτὸ μηδὲν εἶναι, ὃ δὴ καὶ τότε ἐλέγομεν: 156E8-157A1]. All of them of whatever kind are generated by motions in intercourse with one another [ἐν δὲ τῇ πρὸς ἄλληλα ὁμιλίᾳ πάντα γίγνεσθαι καὶ παντοῖα ἀπὸ τῆς κινήσεως: 157A1-3]. For as they say, there is no definite thought of either agent or patient existing as just one thing itself [ἐπεὶ καὶ τὸ ποιοῦν εἶναί τι καὶ τὸ πάσχον αὐτῶν ἐπὶ ἑνὸς νοῆσαι, ὥς φασιν, οὐκ εἶναι παγίως: 157A3-4].

What follows from all this, Socrates repeats, is that "nothing is a single thing in and by itself, but always is coming to be for something" (οὐδὲν εἶναι ἓν αὐτὸ καθ᾽ αὑτό, ἀλλά τινι ἀεὶ γίγνεσθαι: 157A8-9).

Reading this much as an ontology of becoming, we find no room for determinate objects of any sort that might exist independently of the perceptual transaction, as required by several standard interpretations of this theory.[27] In particular, there is no room either for physical objects of perception or for physical organs of perceiving, capable of maintaining identity apart from the perceptual process. The world of becoming contains exclusively parent motions—active or passive depending upon their interaction—and generated motions that arise in inseparable pairs. In each case, the object of perception is one of the twins, and not an independent physical thing that acts upon a sense organ; and the patient upon which the active motion acts is a passive motion, and not an independently existing organ of sense affected by a physical thing. Thus far, that is to say, the interpretation that glosses the active and passive motions as physical objects and organs of perception, respectively, is entirely without foundation.

The ambiguity that makes this common interpretation initially credible arises in the passage omitted above, beginning at 156C4. The relevance of this to all that has gone before, Socrates says, is that all things are moving:

But there is quickness and a slowness in these movings [τάχος δὲ καὶ βραδυτὴς ἔνι τῇ κινήσει αὐτῶν: 156C8]. The slow stays put and moves in relation to things that approach it, thereby generating offspring [Ὅσον μὲν οὖν βραδύ, ἐν τῷ αὐτῷ καὶ πρὸς τὰ πλησιάζοντα τὴν κίνησιν ἴσχει καὶ οὕτω δὴ γεννᾷ: 156C8-D1]. The offspring, however, are quicker, with their natural motion in being brought from place to place [τὰ δὲ γεννώμενα οὕτω δὴ θάττω ἐστίν· φέρεται γὰρ καὶ ἐν φορᾷ αὐτῶν ἡ κίνησις πέφυκεν: 156D1-3]. When an eye and something else nearby and commensurate with it give birth to whiteness and its associated perceiving, neither of which would have been produced if either of them had approached something else ['Επειδὰν οὖν ὄμμα καὶ ἄλλο τι τῶν τούτῳ συμμέτρων πλησιάσαν γεννήσῃ τὴν λευκότητά τε καὶ αἴσθησιν αὐτῇ σύμφυτον, ἃ οὐκ ἄν ποτε ἐγένετο ἑκατέρου ἐκείνων πρὸς ἄλλο ἐλθόντος: 156D3-6], then when the vision from the eyes and the whiteness from the other thing that joins in producing color pass in between [τότε δὴ μεταξὺ φερομένων τῆς μὲν ὄψεως πρὸς τῶν ὀφθαλμῶν, τῆς δὲ λευκότητος πρὸς τοῦ συναποτίκτοντος τὸ χρῶμα: 156D6-E2], the eye becomes full of sight and sees, becoming not the power of seeing but a seeing eye [ὁ μὲν ὀφθαλμὸς ἄρα ὄψεως ἔμπλεως ἐγένετο καὶ ὁρᾷ δὴ τότε καὶ ἐγένετο

οὔ τι ὄψις ἀλλ᾽ ὀφθαλμὸς ὁρῶν: 156E2-4], while its partner in producing color is filled with whiteness, and become
not whiteness but a white thing; [τὸ δὲ συγγεννῆσαν τὸ
χρῶμα λευκότητος περιεπλήσθη καὶ ἐγένετο οὐ λευ
κότης αὖ ἀλλὰ λευκόν: 156E4-5]—whether stick or stone
or whatever else becomes colored in this way [εἴτε ξύλον
εἴτε λίθος εἴτε ὁτουοῦν συνέβη χρόα χρωσθῆναι τῷ
τοιούτῳ χρώματι: 156E6-7].

Why has Plato shifted his account in this passage, and begun
talking about sticks and eyes as partners in the production of
offspring, whereas active and passive motions are assigned this
function in the surrounding passages? A possible answer that
has nothing to recommend it is that he changed his mind twice
in the course of writing down the theory, first and finally assigning ontological priority to motions exclusively, with a brief
interim endorsement of physical objects. Another unlikely possibility is that Plato was unaware of this discrepancy, after taking
such care to identify the principle (156A) upon which his account
would be based. Much more plausible is that one of the two
apparently competing descriptions is intended to be literally accurate, while the other is figurative and not literally intended.
The question to be answered, then, is which description of the
cooperating partners is intended to be literally accurate—that
identifying them with physical objects and organs of perception,
or that identifying them simply as active and passive motions?

The case for taking the description in terms of physical objects
and organs of perception as literal, it seems to me, is exhausted
by two considerations: (1) that an apparently similar account of
sight in the *Timaeus* (45B-46C, 67C-68D) also mentions eyes
and external objects as contributing factors, and (2) that in a
brief recapitulation of the theory at 159A-E Socrates cites his
own person and the wine he drinks as patient and agent, respectively, in the production of sensory offspring. With regard
to (1), however, it may be argued (a) that we have no a priori
reason for assimilating the accounts of the *Theaetetus* and the
Timaeus, (b) that the latter might be figurative as well as the
former, and (c) that, at any rate, physical objects in the *Timaeus*

account are not ontologically basic.²⁸ Regarding (2), it should be pointed out (i) that reference to the person Socrates as patient (rather than his sense organs, or some indefinite slow motion), if taken literally, yields yet a third version of the theory, and (ii) that there is no more reason to take this version literally than the earlier version in terms of organs of perception.

A much more substantial case is available for the remaining alternative. For one thing, the basic principle of the theory—that all is motion and nothing else (156A5)—rules out permanence of the sort implicated in literal reference to eyes and sticks as causes of perception. That the disclaimer "and nothing else" is to be taken seriously is indicated by the repeated remainder that nothing *is* one thing just by itself (153E4-5, 156E8-157A1, 157A8-9). Furthermore, the very difficulty we are facing with this reference to eyes, sticks, stones, and such, at 156D-E seems to be anticipated and answered in the passages immediately following. Having observed that everything is in a process of becoming for something, Socrates continues with the admonishment that

being is to be ruled out entirely [τὸ δ᾽ εἶναι πανταχόθεν ἐξαιρετέον: 157A9-B1], even though by habit and inadvertence we have used the term several times only just now [οὐχ ὅτι ἡμεῖς πολλὰ καὶ ἄρτι ἠναγκάσμεθα ὑπὸ συνηθείας καὶ ἀνεπιστημοσύνης χρῆσθαι αὐτῷ: 157B1-2]. But we ought not to have done so, as these wise men say [Τὸ δ᾽ οὐ δεῖ, ὡς ὁ τῶν σοφῶν λόγος: 157B2-3]. Nor should we accede to the expressions 'something', 'someone's', 'my', 'this', or 'that', or any other word that brings things to a standstill [οὔτε τι συγχωρεῖν οὔτε του οὔτ᾽ ἐμοῦ οὔτε τόδε οὔτ᾽ ἐκεῖνο οὔτε ἄλλο οὐδὲν ὄνομα ὅτι ἂν ἱστῇ: 157B3-5]. Instead we should speak, according to nature, of coming to be, being produced, ceasing to be,²⁹ and altering [ἀλλὰ κατὰ φύσιν φθέγγεσθαι γιγνόμενα καὶ ποιούμενα καὶ ἀπολλύμενα καὶ ἀλλοιούμενα: 157B5-6]. For those who in their talk bring things to a standstill are easily refuted [ὡς ἐάν τί τις στήσῃ τῷ λόγῳ, εὐέλεγκτος ὁ τοῦτο ποιῶν: 157B6-7]. And we ought to speak of things this way either severally or in collections of many, to which collections are given the names of man, stone, or any living creature or kind [Δεῖ δὲ καὶ κατὰ μέρος οὕτω λέγειν καὶ περὶ πολλῶν ἀθροισθέντων, ᾧ δὴ ἀθροίσματι ἄνθρωπόν τε τίθενται καὶ λίθον καὶ ἕκαστον ζῷόν τε καὶ εἶδος: 157B7-C2].

The answer to the difficulty above is that 'eye' and 'stick' and (expressly) 'stone' are words that bring things to a standstill, which we have been using inadvertently but, strictly speaking, should refrain from using. Such words refer to collections of things properly named only in a vocabulary of becoming—that is, to collections of motions.

Considerable uncertainty has prevailed among commentators regarding the membership of these collections. The view generally accepted by those who have paid particular attention to this passage has been that Plato here is putting forward the thesis that particular things are collections of sense qualities.[30] On this basis, some have even spoken of it as a Berkeleyan thesis.[31] The equivalent description in Plato's own terms would be that things in the world of becoming are collections of fast motions; specifically, of those motions which as objects of perception are generated pairwise with individual perceivings. The mistake in this view, we may now observe, is that it misrepresents the role of such collections in the theory. Whatever the ontological status of particular things, their role in the theory remains that of contributing to the production, pairwise, of sensory offspring. At 159C-E, where the theory is being applied, it is Socrates (or his tongue: 159E2) as patient, and wine as agent, that give rise to sweetness and the sensation accompanying it. And in the initial statement of the theory itself, at 156C-157A, it is the eye as patient, and stick or stone as agent, that generate colors and seeings by their interaction. As Socrates is careful to note, however, what is patient in one case may be agent in another; for example, the eye can be seen as well as see. In short, physical things play the role of generative factors, which elsewhere in the theory is assigned explicitly to motions with the power of acting and being acted upon. If particular things are collections of motions, as the theory seems clearly to indicate, then they must be composed of the slow motions that generate offspring, and not of the colors and other fast motions that are paired with particular acts of perception. In fact, there is no other way to make sense of the provision that what is patient on one occasion might be agent on another. If the eye consisted of qualities, or fast motions, as the received view has it, then the eye would result from the interaction of various agents and patients, but it could be neither agent nor patient itself.[32] A consequence is that, although particular things have powers to produce colors, sounds, and other sensible qualities, these qualities are not parts of the things that produce them. In a literal sense, particular things are not objects of perception.[33] Knowing this, we should be prepared for the consequence which Socrates adduces in his final refutation of the theory—that in comparing what is hard and what is soft, for instance, it is not within the competence of sensation alone to reveal *what they are* (ὅτι ἐστὸν: 186B6) to be so opposed.

The authorship of this theory is deliberately blurred. At 156A (and maybe 152C) it is represented as a secret held by certain subtle persons who teach that everything is motion. But at 152E this thesis is attributed to a whole series of major poets and philosophers, with only Parmenides excepted. The proximate reason given for introducing the theory at 155D is that it will help us understand the teachings of Protagoras, whereas at 157C Socrates identifies it as Theaetetus' offspring. In the same passage, Theaetetus, who we must assume was familiar with the thought of the major poets and philosophers, wonders whether the theory originated with Socrates himself.

Cornford's diagnosis, following Jackson and Burnet,[34] is that the theory is being constructed by Plato for the purposes of the dialogue, with obvious contributions from Heraclitus and Protagoras. Although this diagnosis seems correct, Cornford's argument in its behalf is not convincing.[35] The argument is that Plato has set about to refute the claim that perception is identical with knowledge, and that any such refutation would be pointless unless it dealt with what Plato thought to be a correct account of perception. Accordingly, says Cornford, Plato "states his own doctrine and takes it to be established for the purposes of the whole subsequent criticism of perception." The attribution of the theory to "a whole succession of wise men who notoriously had never taught anything of the kind" was a transparent device for dramatic purposes.

One problem with this argument is that it confuses the question of authorship with the question of acceptance. Since Plato could perfectly well have accepted an account of perception which he did not originate himself, the most Cornford's argument could show is that Plato accepted the theory. It is also conceivable, however, that Plato was responsible for major details of the theory, but at the same time did not intend it to be literally correct. Cornford's argument does not rule out even this possibility. The reason is that Cornford, despite his concern with the dialectical method employed in the dialogue, has misinterpreted the structure of Plato's refutation of Theaetetus' first hypothesis. A careful analysis of Plato's argument against the hypothesis that knowledge is perception shows that whether he accepted the account of perception is quite irrelevant to the argument.

In my previous discussion of methodology in the middle dialogues, I traced the steps by which the theory of recollection and the method of elenchus associated with it were superseded by a much more explicit method of hypothesis. Although attempts to link this method to a doctrine about ultimate grounds yielded results that were nebulous at best (a "satisfactory hypothesis" in the *Phaedo*, and a "nonhypothetical first principle" in the *Republic*), the method itself was made quite specific. The philosopher begins by laying down the thesis he judges to be soundest. Since his first step then is to test this hypothesis for consistency, we may assume that the "soundest" thesis is one in which all key terms have been adequately defined. After assuring that the thesis is consistent, and hence possibly true, the philosopher next attempts to derive it from a more general hypothesis which has been shown consistent in turn, and so on until he reaches a hypothesis not requiring further accounting. The stepwise procedure, accordingly, is (1) to lay down a hypothesis to be tested, (2) to clarify all key terms in the hypothesis, (3a) to test its consequences for mutual consistency and (3b) likewise for consistency with accepted fact, and finally, if thereby shown possibly true, (4) to attempt to deduce it from more general hypotheses.

This is precisely the method followed in the *Theaetetus*.[36] Three hypotheses are posed in all, each falling short at a different stage of the procedure. The first hypothesis, identifying perception and knowledge, fails at step (3a) inasmuch as it entails consequences that are not mutually consistent. The hypothesis identifying knowledge with true judgment in turn is shown inadequate with respect to (3b), entailing consequences incompatible with accepted fact. Finally, the hypothesis affirming the identity of knowledge with true judgment accompanied by λόγος is dropped before its consistency can even be tested, failing in respect (2) to be provided an adequate definition of λόγος.[37] Our particular concern at the moment is with the initial hypothesis, which arises as follows.

Having mentioned to Socrates his general definition of incommensurable numbers, the young mathematician is charged with "arriving at a similar formula for the many kinds of knowledge" (τὰς πολλὰς ἐπιστήμας ἑνὶ λόγῳ προσειπεῖν: 148D6-7). Guided by the thought that one knows what one perceives, he lays down the hypothesis that knowledge is perception (step [1]). Since the term αἴσθησις carries many different meanings, Socrates helps Theaetetus develop an account of perception in terms of which the hypothesis can be tested. If the hypothesis is to have any chance of succeeding, the account must show perception to have the essential features of knowledge—it must "always be of what exists, and be infallible" (τοῦ ὄντος ἀεί ἐστιν καὶ ἀψευδὲς: 152C5). Borrowing heavily from Protagoras and Heraclitus, Socrates formulates for the other's acceptance a theory of perception carefully constructed to provide for the infallibility of perception. This completes step (2) of the procedure. After further arguments limiting the sense of 'knowledge' in question, and separating Theaetetus' thesis from the theses of his two predecessors, Socrates finally shows that perception so understood does not have what exists among its objects (186E2-5). The upshot is perfectly clear: the price for meeting one necessary condition of the hypothesis (that perception be infallible) is failure to meet the other (that perception be of what exists). The two cannot be true simultaneously. The hypothesis fails at step (3a), entailing consequences that are mutually inconsistent.

In other words, the hypothesis identifying knowledge and perception is not refuted by showing it false in the sense of contrary to fact. It is refuted by showing it inconsistent, and hence not even possibly true. For the latter purpose it is irrelevant whether Plato or anyone else accepts as factually accurate the theory of perception upon which the refutation is based. If we are to be convinced that Plato himself accepted this account of perception, it must be on other grounds than those advanced by Cornford.

Such grounds appear in the fact that the theory of perception contains considerably more detail than is required for its role in the *Theaetetus*, conjointly with the fact that these details are of the very sort we should expect Plato to be preoccupied with, given the problems we have seen in his early theory of Forms. Consider first the matter of detail. The salient details of the theory are as follows. Fundamentally, (1) all that exists in the sensible universe is motion. There is (2) a distinction between active and passive motions, (3) both of which are indefinitely multitudinous. Further, (4) motions that are passive under some circumstances might be active under others. In any case, (5) the role of such motions is to cooperate in the generation of offspring, (6) which latter are fast in contrast to the slow parent motions. These offspring (7) are produced in pairs each consisting of one perceiving and one perceived object, (8) so related that no perceiving can be paired with a different object and no perceived object can be paired with a different perceiving. Since these fast motions are constantly changing, (9) the objects of perception can be spoken of accurately only in terms of "becoming," while terms of "being" are precluded altogether. Finally, (10) collections of slow motions constitute both animate and inanimate objects— the sort of things that inhabit the sensible world of becoming.

All that is required to refute the first hypothesis of the *Theaetetus* is that objects of perceiving be generated pairwise with unique acts of perceiving (to assure infallibility), and that these objects change so rapidly as to rule out fixed descriptions (to preclude such objects from admitting existence). The former requirement is met by (5), (7), and (8) of the preceding paragraph, while (6) and (9) are enough to meet the latter. In the context of the *Theaetetus* specifically, there is no need to give any account of the parentage of these fast motions. In particular, nothing is accomplished in this context by stressing (1) that *everything* in the sensible world is motion, including (10) ordinary objects like stones and men, nor by distinguishing (2) active and passive motions and then emphasizing (4) that under varying conditions these roles might be reversed. The provision (3) that these motions be indefinitely multitudinous, moreover, seems entirely irrelevant to the purposes of the dialogue.

In the preceding section I identified several problems to be resolved if the theory of Forms of the middle dialogues was to be rendered wholly intelligible. Prominent among these problems was that of clarifying the ontological status of sensible objects, and particularly their failure to be wholly real. Forms, on the one hand, are wholly real in that they are wholly what they are and do not admit their opposites, while sensible things typically are characterized by opposing properties. But what accounts for this ontological deficiency on the part of sensible objects? The answer is provided by items (2) and (4) above. The sensible properties associated with objects in the world of becoming are generated by factors that combine in producing these properties, and which are constantly changing in combination. So complete is the lack of fixity in these combinations that what is active at one time might be passive at another. It is because of total lack of permanence in the conditions generating sensible properties, as Socrates points out at 152D (and repeats at 154B), that a thing which is large or heavy, and so on, under one set of circumstances will become just the opposite when circumstances alter.

An associated problem left over from the middle dialogues is the manner in which sensible things depend upon the Forms for their self-identity. Whereas Forms, that is to say, are absolute in not depending upon other things for being what they are, sensible things have no characteristic features by themselves alone. Although this problem will not be resolved independently of a full-scale theory of participation, the theory of perception specifies what it is about sensible objects that poses the problem initially. As items (1) and (10) make explicit, all objects of the sensible world consist entirely of motions. And what is totally in motion has no characteristics on its own. When Plato sets about in the *Timaeus* to work out an articulate theory of participation, it is sensible objects thus conceived that he must bring to account.

If there is any characteristic typical of such objects by themselves, paradoxical as it may appear, it is that such things have no definite characteristic at all. It is particularly noteworthy that expressions indicating indefinite multiplicity occur three separate times in the initial statement of the theory of perception. The expression ἄπειρον πλῆθος appears at 156A6 and B1, while at 156B6-7 Socrates says that perceivings that have names are very numerous while those that are unnamed are without limitation (ἀπέραντοι μὲν αἱ ἀνώνυμοι, παμπληθεῖς δὲ αἱ ὠνομασμέναι). The term ἀπέραντοι here cannot carry the sense of an indefinitely large number, for that is ruled out by the subsequent stipulation that nothing is just one thing in and by itself (157A8-9). The sense rather is of total lack of determinate character. Without the Forms, the domain of becoming is a mass or multitude with no limitation whatever, whether with respect to number or to characteristic. It is with a world of becoming thus totally devoid of limiting features that Plato must cope in attempting to formulate a coherent theory of participation.

One of the questions behind these considerations was whether Plato himself accepted the theory of perception developed in the *Theaetetus*. The answer must be that he accepted it as an account of the realm of becoming that was sufficiently detailed and plausible to provide the basis for further deliberations regarding the relationship between Forms and sensible objects. At the same time, however, we should be very hesitant to conclude that Plato considered this to be the only or ultimately the best theory of becoming available. For a substantially different theory appears in the very late dialogues.

THE ONTOLOGY OF KNOWLEDGE IN THE *Sophist*

The major ontological contribution of the *Theaetetus* was a new conception of becoming. In the *Sophist* Plato turns to a set of related problems about the nature of being. Although the theory of Forms (= Kinds) that emerges is novel in several obvious respects, commentators have not generally realized how extensively this theory differs from that of the *Phaedo* and the *Republic*. Nor have the motives for the change been generally recognized. Although Plato is not yet ready to break entirely with this earlier theory, his conception of Forms at this point is no less in flux than is his conception of the nature of sensible things. In at least one respect, however, his motivation remains the same: as in the middle period, Plato's conception of the Forms is tailored to meet what he understands to be the requirements of knowledge.[38]

Under the guise of a mere exercise in definition (of the technique of sophistry), the *Sophist* overcomes all the major obstacles set in the *Theaetetus* to arriving at a credible account of knowledge. Most importantly, it provides an elegant explication of truth and falsehood in judgment, it isolates a sense in which knowledge may be said to be true belief accompanied by λόγος, and it both formulates and illustrates a method for achieving philosophic knowledge. The account of the "blending Forms" developed in the dialogue provides just the ontological backing needed to make this method intelligible.

The method of collection and division is not novel with the *Sophist*. It was first mentioned explicitly at *Phaedrus* 266B4 as the practice of the dialecticians, and was alluded to earlier in the same dialogue as providing recollection (ἀνάμνησις: 249C2) of what the soul had previously seen. Not coincidentally, the first mention of collection and division is the last mention of recollection. The alleged (265E3-4) illustrations of the method (Socrates' two speeches on love) in that dialogue, however, are not particularly striking. In fact, the most convincing illustration of the method prior to the *Sophist* appears in the *Theaetetus* itself, with its five attempts to formulate a definition of falsehood.[39] Toward the end of his last sustained attempt to apply the method of hypothesis, Plato begins to employ this new methodological discovery.

Like the method of hypothesis, the method of collection and division includes two procedures that must be followed in a prescribed order. First is collection, which amounts to assembling typical cases in search of common features. In one way or another, these cases are supposed to share characteristics with the thing to be defined, so that by examining them as a group the dialectician can discern what features he should start with in his subsequent division. In the collection preceding the definition of the "Sophist of Noble Lineage" (*Sophist* 226B-231B), for example, the Stranger itemizes a number of arts sharing separation (Διακριτικήν: 226C8) in common; and with that feature he begins the ensuing division. In like fashion, the five abortive definitions of sophistry at the beginning (which themselves fail because not preceded with collections) together serve as a collection for the division finally completed at the end of the dialogue. The function of collection is to disclose features that are necessary ingredients of all cases of the thing to be defined. It is the purpose of division, in turn, to distinguish just those cases from other things which to some extent possess similar features. Thus the division of the angler, for one clear example, distinguishes in succession those who capture what they acquire from those who buy it, those who capture by stealth from those who capture in the open, and so forth, until angling has been uniquely segregated from all other acquisitive arts.[40] When carried through to completion, a proper division exhibits features that in combination are sufficient for being a case of the thing in question. Together, the procedures of collection and division thereby make explicit a set of conditions that all and only things of the type to be defined have in common. The result is a definition in terms of essential properties—that is, properties both necessary and sufficient for being a case of the thing defined.

Definitions of this sort epitomize the philosopher's knowledge. The science of dialectic (διαλεκτικῆς . . . ἐπιστήμης: 253D2-3) is just

> to divide according to kinds [Τὸ κατὰ γένη διαιρεῖσθαι: 253D1], not taking for another a Form that is the same, or for the same one that is another [μήτε ταὐτὸν εἶδος ἕτερον ἡγήσασθαι μήτε ἕτερον ὂν ταὐτόν: 253D1-2].

The outcome of this procedure, properly followed, is a λόγος in the sense of account or definition[41]—just the kind of λόγος called for at the beginning of the dialogue when the Stranger undertakes to find a definition manifesting the nature of the Sophist (ἀπὸ τοῦ σοφιστοῦ . . . ἐμφανίζοντι λόγῳ τί ποτ' ἔστι: 218B8-C1).

As the Stranger puts it somewhat more specifically, the dialectician who is capable of this procedure

> can adequately distinguish one Form everywhere extended through many, each lying apart, and many [Forms] different from one another encompassed externally by the one [μίαν ἰδέαν διὰ πολλῶν, ἑνὸς ἑκάστου κειμένου χωρίς, πάντῃ διατεταμένην ἱκανῶς διαισθάνεται, καὶ πολλὰς ἑτέρας ἀλλήλων ὑπὸ μιᾶς ἔξωθεν περιεχομένας: 253D5-8].

The "many Forms" in this description are the cases collected by the philosopher in search of a common feature, which he discerns as one Form common to the nature of each. These many Forms "lie apart" in the sense of appearing initially to be independent, but then are seen to be encompassed in their independent (external) status by a single Form shared within their several natures. Whereas the five sophists defined at the beginning of the dialogue, for instance, appeared at first to be entirely separated (having different sufficient conditions), upon reconsideration they exhibited productivity as a common feature. Productivity thus was the necessary condition revealed by collection.

Having thus completed his collection, the dialectician next distinguishes

> one Form connected in a unity through many wholes [μίαν αὖ δι' ὅλων πολλῶν ἐν ἑνὶ συνημμένην: 253D8-9], and many [Forms] altogether separated off [καὶ πολλὰς χωρὶς πάντῃ διωρισμένας: 253D9].

In this description of division, the "one Form" previously arrived at by collection is combined with other Forms to provide a series of dichotomous distinctions, each stage of which contributes to the definition of some general class of entity. When developed in the direction of human semblance-making, for example, the combined properties of art and production yield authentic sophistry, while leading to divine creativity in the other direction.

Sophistry and Divine Creation thus are two of "many wholes" (uniquely defined Forms) that are both connected by the relation they share with productivity and sharply separated from each other by their distinctive definitions.

Having reached a definition of this sort, the dialectician is in a position to make a judgment about the nature of the thing defined. If the collection and division were properly executed, moreover, the true nature of the thing will have been revealed. When the dialectician thereby finally reaches a true judgment about the nature of the thing concerned, that judgment, in company with the λόγος upon which it was based, constitutes philosophic knowledge in its purest form (253E5). The formula of the *Theaetetus* is vindicated. Knowledge is true judgment accompanied by λόγος. The λόγος in question, however, is not something added as an afterthought to an independently formulated judgment that happens to be true. The λόγος rather is the source of the judgment, and the ground that renders the judgment true.

The condition that makes philosophic knowledge possible is succinctly stated at 253E1-2. To be able to generate a proper collection and division is

> to know how to distinguish, Kind by Kind, which combinations are possible and which are not [ἥ τε κοινωνεῖν ἕκαστα δύναται καὶ ὅπη μή, διακρίνειν κατὰ γένος ἐπίστασθαι].

In this, the skill of the philosopher is analogous to that of the grammarian. Whereas the skill of grammar is knowing which letters it is possible to join together (253A2) or to combine (253A8), and which not to, the philosopher's knowledge (ἐπιστήμης: 253C4) is to point out "which Kinds are consonant and which will not receive one another" (ποῖα ποίοις συμφωνεῖ τῶν γενῶν καὶ ποῖα ἄλληλα οὐ δέχεται: 253B12-C1).

Philosophic knowledge distinguishes Kinds that combine and those that do not. For knowledge in this paradigmatic sense to be possible, it is necessary for Forms or Kinds[42] actually to exist in these relationships of blending and exclusion. In the language of the *Phaedrus*, the philosopher is guided in his collections and divisions "by the natural articulations among Ideas" (κατ᾽ εἴδη . . . κατ᾽ ἄρθρα ᾗ πέφυκεν: 265E1-2). An ontological requirement of knowledge is that Forms really are related according to these articulations. The far-reaching significance of this requirement can be appreciated only in contrast with corresponding requirements laid out in the middle dialogues.

In the *Meno* and the first part of the *Phaedo*, knowledge is represented as a matter of mental perception (εἴδω: *Meno* 84A5,7,8,9, passim), the objects of knowledge as each "uniform and unto itself" (μονοειδὲς ὂν αὐτὸ καθ᾽ αὑτό: *Phaedo* 78D5), and the ground of knowledge as a process of "causal reasoning or recollection" (αἰτίας λογισμῷ . . . ἀνάμνησις: *Meno* 98A4-5). In the latter part of the *Phaedo* and in Book VI of the *Republic*, where the method of hypothesis is prominent, knowledge is a matter of working out certain relationships among propositions or hypotheses, the objects of knowledge are Forms existing in certain quasi-logical relationships (double will not admit oddness, at *Phaedo* 105A8), and the ground of knowledge is a nonhypothetical starting point (*Republic* 510B7, 511B6-7) possibly identified with the Good itself. By the time of the *Sophist*, however, all these considerations have been realigned around the conception of the blending Forms. Knowledge is a matter of discerning necessary conditions by collection, and then dividing along lines of combination and disjunction to arrive at sufficient conditions. The objects of knowledge are Forms uniquely marked off from one another according to these natural lines of division, and the grounds of knowledge are these natural relationships of combination and disjunction themselves.

Whereas the nature of knowledge as conceived in the early middle dialogues, that is to say, dictated that Forms exist independently both from other Forms and from sensible things, knowledge is so conceived in the *Sophist* as to require that the Forms exist in determinate relationships one to another. So complete is his repudiation of the former view in this later context, indeed, that Plato has the Stranger say at 252A that those who say "the Forms are always the same in all respects" (εἴδη . . . κατὰ ταὐτὰ ὡσαύτως ἔχοντα εἶναί φασιν ἀεί: 252A7-8) are easily refuted (by the fact that Motion and Rest blend with

Existence), and that "λόγος itself originates with the blending together of Forms" (διὰ γὰρ τὴν ἀλλήλων τῶν εἰδῶν συμπλοκὴν ὁ λόγος γέγονεν ἡμῖν: 259E5-6).

Not only are the Forms by nature interrelated, but moreover there is a certain hierarchy in their interrelationship.[43] Whereas (presumably) most Forms combine with some but not all others, there are a few that combine with all Forms, including themselves. In his illustration of this with reference to the five "very important Kinds" (Μέγιστα . . . γενῶν: 254D4), the Stranger points out that while Motion and Rest are incapable in every respect (255E11) of sharing in one another (ἀλλήλοις . . . ἐπικοινωνίας: 252D2-3), "Existence and Difference pervade all [Kinds]" (τό τε ὂν καὶ θάτερον διὰ πάντων . . . διεληλυθότε: 259A5-6), themselves included. While Motion is in no way at rest nor Rest in motion, that is to say, each Form (including Existence itself) exists and each Form (including Difference itself) is different from all other Forms. The same may be said of Sameness, in that every Form (including Sameness) is the same as itself.

There is one further respect in which the conception of Forms in the *Sophist* differs markedly from that in the middle dialogues. In setting up the "battle of giants" (245A4)[44] between those who define reality as body (246B1) and the "friends of the Forms" (248A4-5), the Stranger identifies the latter as those who maintain that being and becoming are separate (χωρίς: 248A7) and that, whereas we have commerce with becoming through the body by sensation, our commerce with the "nature of being" (ὄντως οὐσίαν: 248A11) is through the mind by reflection. This is because becoming constantly varies, while being by its nature "always remains constant in itself" (ἀεὶ κατὰ ταὐτὰ ὡσαύτως ἔχειν: 248A12). Almost exactly the same expression is used at *Phaedo* 78D2 in characterizing what I have been referring to as the early theory of Forms. As Cornford observes,[45] the position of the "friends of the Forms" is none other than Plato's own position in the middle dialogues. In criticizing these unnamed heroes, Plato is finding fault with his own earlier theory.

The problem with this theory is that it ends up contradicting itself. While insisting that being is entirely constant and immovable, the "friends of the Forms" maintain at the same time that mind and Forms "have commerce through reflection" (κοινωνεῖν . . . διὰ λογισμοῦ: 248A10-11). In fact, a primary motivation in conceiving the Forms as changeless in the first place was to make them suitable objects of knowledge, as knowledge was understood in that earlier context. But "knowing is acting upon something" (τὸ γιγνώσκειν . . . ἔσται ποιεῖν τι: 248D10-E1), with the necessary consequence that being known is "being acted upon" (πάσχειν: 248E1-2). By this reasoning:

> being, in being known by an act of knowledge, to the extent that it is known, to that extent alters in being acted upon, [Τὴν οὐσίαν . . . γιγνωσκομένην ὑπὸ τῆς γνώσεως, καθ᾽ ὅσον γιγνώσκεται, κατὰ τοσοῦτον κινεῖσθαι διὰ τὸ πάσχειν: 248E2-4]. And that, we say, cannot be the case with the motionless [ὃ δή φαμεν οὐκ ἂν γενέσθαι περὶ τὸ ἠρεμοῦν: 248E4-5].

Faced with this consequence, the Stranger asks rhetorically, can we be easily convinced that motion—and with it life, thought and understanding—have no place in the wholly real (248E7-249A1)? Since Theaetetus (and we) must agree that this consequence is unacceptable, we must concede that being includes (at least something of) motion and what is moved.

The ontological status of Forms can no longer be distinguished from that of sensible objects with respect to motion and change alone. How then are they to be distinguished? Plato's answer in the *Sophist* includes two parts. First he develops a mark of reality, replacing those of both contenders in the "battle of giants," which applies to Forms and sensible objects alike. Then he leads us to see that Forms possess, but that sensible objects lack, a necessary condition for having a determinate nature. Let us consider first the mark of the real.

The Stranger begins his discussion of reality in the *Sophist* by canvassing the views of his predecessors. One group attempted to delineate the real by identifying it with a specific number of principles, either one and one only (Parmenides) or more than one (242C4-6). In either case, the Stranger argues, at least one more thing will have to exist than was originally claimed. Another group attempted to find a property coextensive with the real, thereby providing a mark by which it could be identified. These are the "giants" who contend against one another that the real is body (σῶμα: 246Β1), on one side, and that it is changelessness ("something always remaining constant in itself," ἣν ἀεὶ κατὰ ταὐτὰ ὡσαύτως ἔχειν: 248Α12), on the other. These worthies are refuted by showing that either party must admit as real various things that lack the mark they champion. The Stranger then proposes an alternative mark, or coextensive property, which both contenders have been shown committed to accept. As he puts it (in a passage to which commentators have given too little attention):

> Whatever naturally possesses power, either to affect another or to be affected, however minimally, by the most insignificant agent, even if only once, all such is real [ὁποιανοῦν τινα κεκτημένον δύναμιν εἴτ᾽ εἰς τὸ ποιεῖν ἕτερον ὁτιοῦν πεφυκὸς εἴτ᾽ εἰς τὸ παθεῖν καὶ σμικρότατον ὑπὸ τοῦ φαυλοτάτου, κἂν εἰ μόνον εἰς ἅπαξ, πᾶν τοῦτο ὄντως εἶναι: 247D8-E3]. I propose concerning the mark that sets the boundary[46] of real things that it is power and nothing else [τίθεμαι γὰρ ὅρον ὁρίζειν τὰ ὄντα ὡς ἔστιν οὐκ ἄλλο τι πλὴν δύναμις: 247E3-4].

Essentially the same characterization is repeated at 248C4-5.

It seems clear that this characterization of reality is Plato's own, after the manner of the characterization of becoming in the *Theaetetus*. This means (i) that the characterization is not taken ready-made from his predecessors, (ii) that there are reasons why Plato would have been motivated to develop it as he did, (iii) that it is not explicitly refuted in the *Sophist* or in later dialogues, and (iv) that he appears to be working with the characterizaton in later contexts (notably, in this case, the *Timaeus*). Several considerations point to this conclusion. One is that both contenders in the "battle of giants"—who alone among Plato's predecessors approach the problem of characterizing the real in the proper way, that of isolating a mark—are themselves committed to accept δύναμις as the mark of being in place of their own proposals. The original advocates of body in this role are explicitly represented as accepting it at 247E, and the "friends of the Forms" accept it in effect when they are forced to admit at 248D-E that the Forms are acted upon in being known. Plato certainly must realize that this result is binding on his present theory of Forms, in whatever direction it has taken him since the middle dialogues. Another consideration is that this characterization matches nicely with his ontology of becoming in the *Theaetetus*. Although the slow motions there, which as we have seen provide the entire constituency of physical objects, cannot be said to exist in any sense that implies fixity, they clearly have reality of some fundamental sort. And this reality is precisely the δύναμις of acting and being acted upon.

Yet another consideration indicating that Plato accepted this mark of the real is that, shortly after proposing it, the Stranger proceeds actually to examine the capacity (δύναμιν: 251E9, 252D2, passim) of Forms to combine with one another, which is the feature of the Forms most emphasized in this particular dialogue.[47]

The primary consideration to the contrary is raised by Cornford,[48] to the effect that the Stranger expresses uncertainty about the nature of the real at 249Eff., and concludes that it cannot be motion (following the advocates of body), nor rest (following the "friends of the Forms"), nor both together. But this observation has very little force when we (i) recall that both motion and rest had been previously disqualified and (ii) reflect that the rejection of motion and rest in whatever combination has no implications whatever for δύναμις as the mark of the real. Presumably the Stranger expresses perplexity about reality at this juncture as a rhetorical move to set up the pretext at 250D that the real (τὸ ὄν; existence, what is) and the not real (τὸ μή ὄν; what is not, not-being) are equally puzzling, setting the stage for his subsequent attack upon the latter problem.

The reality of the Forms no longer consists, as in the *Phaedo*, of their not admitting opposing characters. Their reality consists in their power to combine. But objects in the sensible world possess power on their own. Does this mean that there is no distinction ontologically between Forms and objects? The answer is emphatically negative. Although Forms are no longer conceived as absolute in the sense of being what they are in a manner totally independent of other things, they remain absolute in another important sense. Forms are still conceived as being independent in the sense of having determinate properties in and by themselves. What precise properties a Form has reflects its involvement with other Forms. But that it have some definite property or another belongs to its own nature. Sensible objects, on the other hand, are incapable in themselves of admitting any determinate property whatever—any property, that is, that brings things to a standstill (*Theaetetus* 157B6). This incapacity, as noted above, is highlighted by repeated use of the expression ἄπειρον πλῆθος in those passages of the *Theaetetus* where the theory of the sensible world is first articulated. What is indefinitely multiple by nature cannot itself be determinate.

The reason the Forms are by nature determinate is that each combines with the "very important" Kind Sameness, and hence is one Form in itself. Since sensible objects are constantly changing, however, it is their nature always to be different and never one and the same. Both Forms and sensible objects, in their own ways, participate in Difference. But only Forms participate in Sameness, in and by themselves. In order for sensible objects to be unified and hence to share fixed names with the Forms (a relationship Plato never shows signs of relinquishing), they somehow must gain determinacy from another quarter. How this might occur is one of several problems associated with the notion of participation, which Plato finally confronts in the *Timaeus*.

Before Plato is ready to attempt an integration of his accounts of becoming and of being into a coherent theory of participation, however, another important problem from the *Theaetetus* must be resolved. Although λόγος is made possible by the weaving together of Forms (*Sophist* 259E5-6), not every case of λόγος is a case of knowledge. It is just the difference between true and false discourse, in fact, that ultimately marks the difference between philosophy and sophistry. To complete the "official" mission of the *Sophist*, which is to make the nature of the latter clear, the distinction between truth and falsity in judgment must be firmly established. To complete its account of being, in turn, which is the more substantial purpose of the dialogue, is to show

how the objects of knowledge (the Forms) must be related to make the distinction between true and false judgment possible. To this end Plato develops an account of not-being (of what is not) that remains among his more impressive accomplishments of the intermediate period.

The sophist is a producer of semblance in discourse, which means that he influences our minds "to think things that are not" (τὰ μὴ ὄντα δοξάζειν: 240D9). What we thus understand him as doing, however, is precisely what Parmenides had proclaimed not to be understandable at all. "That it is not," he said, "is not to be said or thought" (οὐ γὰρ φατὸν οὐδὲ νοητὸν ἔστιν ὅπως οὐκ ἔστι);[49] rather, "all that can be thought is the thought that it is" (ταὐτὸν δ' ἔστι νοεῖν τε καὶ οὕνεκεν ἔστι νόημα).[50] Thus to complete his definition of the sophist's art, the Stranger must engage in a form of parricide (241D3),[51] and show that "what is not" can be thought after all.

Plato's discussion of "what is not" between 257B and 259B has raised vexing questions for recent commentators, most notably in regard to (i) what logical relation is intended between τὸ ὄν and τὸ μὴ ὄν, and (ii) how this account of the not-real or "what is not" supports the subsequent definition of falsehood in judgment. One of the most thoroughgoing and judicious treatments of (i) is that of David Keyt, who concludes that Plato's description of the logical relation in question is vague, and perhaps ambiguous.[52] This verdict is undoubtedly correct, insofar at least as the text does not rule out any of the major options in a wholly definitive manner. There is one interpretation, however, which seems to have a strong edge over all other contenders, on the grounds that it makes clear and precise sense of the definition of falsehood that follows. An added advantage of this interpretation is that it seems to follow naturally from a step-by-step reading of the Stranger's argument.

A natural first step is to note that, because each Kind is different from every other Kind, for each Kind there are many things it *is not*. In the illustration involving the five "very important Kinds," for example, Motion is different from the remaining four, and hence *is not* Rest, Existence, Sameness, or Difference themselves. In like fashion, "Existence itself is different from the others" (τὸ ὂν αὐτὸ τῶν ἄλλων ἕτερον εἶναι: 257A1); and given an indefinite number of other things (ἀπέραντα δὲ τὸν ἀριθμὸν τἆλλα: 257A6—not just five, as in the illustration), there is an indefinite number of things it is not. In general, "for each Form, what is not [is] indefinitely numerous" (Περὶ ἕκαστον ... τῶν εἰδῶν ... ἄπειρον δὲ πλήθει τὸ μὴ ὄν: 256E6-7). Assuming that the "indefinitely numerous other things" in question are all and only other Forms,[53] a natural interpretation at this point is that "what is not" in the case of a given Form comprises all Forms other than itself. This in fact is the alternative most commentators adopt as their final interpretation. But at this point the discussion is only beginning, and a number of important qualifications are imposed before a sense of "what is not" is isolated to serve the purposes at hand.

The second step consists of the first important qualification. A point for us to consider, says the Stranger, is that

> when we speak of what is not ... we do not speak of the contrary of what is, but only of something different ['Οπόταν τὸ μὴ ὂν λέγωμεν ... οὐκ ἐναντίον τι λέγομεν τοῦ ὄντος ἀλλ᾽ ἕτερον μόνον: 257B3-4].

For example, when we speak of something as "not large" we do not mean "small" exclusively, but either "small" or "equal" in comparative size (257B6-7). The point is reinforced at 257B9-C2, where the Stranger makes the precise grammatical point that the negative particles οὐ and μὴ, when prefixed to words, indicate not the contrary but rather something different from what is designated by the words themselves. The qualification is quite explicit: when 'A' is the name of a given property (for example, largeness), 'not-A' designates something different (ἕτερος) from A, and not something contrary (ἐναντίος). What is not immediately clear is what exactly Plato means by the contrast between ἕτερος and ἐναντίος.

Of the two terms, ἐναντίος appears less problematic. Throughout the dialogues, Plato uses this term to designate what we might call "polar contraries."[54] To mention just a few examples, from the Lysis we have dry/wet, cold/hot, bitter/sweet, and sharp/blunt (215E); from the Phaedo, hot/cold (103C); from the *Parmenides*, older/younger (155A); and from the *Laws*, hot/ cold and dry/moist (899B). The *Sophist* itself mentions large/ small in this immediate context, as distinct from the opposition of large to small and equal together. A further clue to the nature of this form of contrariety appears at *Protagoras* 332C, where Socrates concludes a list of contraries with the observation that of everything that admits of an ἐναντίον there is one such opposite and one alone. The character of the contrariety in question is what we might characterize more precisely as "nonexhaustive opposition." Hot and cold are nonexhaustive opposites in the sense that they (1) are contrary properties (what is hot cannot be cold in the same respect, and vice versa), but (2) do not together exhaust all alternatives (what is moderate in temperature is neither hot nor cold). The point of ruling out the ἐναντίον, or nonexhaustively opposite, in this specific context is apparent at 258E, which incidentally provides further evidence for the sense in which this term is intended. "What is not," the Stranger says there, is not the "contrary of the existent" (τοὐ- ναντίον τοῦ ὄντος: 258E6), for as far as that contrary is concerned we have long ago "said goodbye" to the question whether or not there is such a thing or whether it can be accounted for. The reference must be[55] to 238C10, where the stranger allows that "what is not just by itself" (τὸ μὴ ὂν αὐτὸ καθ᾽ αὑτό) is unthinkable and unutterable. That is to say, the "polar contrary" of what is cannot even be expressed in intelligible language. To make "what is not" intelligible, we must rely upon the relationship of difference instead. But in what sense of ἕτερος are these instructions intended?

The third step is the first indication that what is ἕτερος with respect to a given Form might not be simply everything other than that Form itself. A point to consider, says the Stranger emphatically is that

> the nature of Difference seems to me to be parceled out in the same way as knowledge ['Η θατέρου μοι φύσις φαί- νεται κατακεκερματίσθαι καθάπερ ἐπιστήμη: 257C6-7].

When asked in what manner, the Stranger explains that although knowledge is undoubtedly one (Μία: 257C9), each part (μέρος:

257C10) of it is marked off by field and given a special name. As a consequence we speak of "many arts and kinds of knowledge" (πολλαὶ τέχναι . . . καὶ ἐπιστῆμαι: 257D1-2). And the same is the case with "the parts of the single nature of Difference" (τὰ τῆς θατέρου φύσεως μόρια μιᾶς: 257D4). The Stranger then proceeds to enumerate several such parts—the not-Beautiful, the not-Tall, and the not-Just, which are said to exist just as much as their positive counterparts.

Two things are emphasized in this comparison that deserve careful attention. First, Difference is like Knowledge in having a single nature. The term φύσις is repeated in this connection several times on the following page (258A8,11, B11, D7). Second, the nature of Difference is parceled out (257C6; again at 258D8) into parts (257D4,7, 258A9,11, E1), in the same way that Knowledge is parceled into the various arts and sciences. Two such "parcels" of Knowledge have already been isolated in earlier passages of the *Sophist*—the "free man's knowledge" and the acquisitive art of the angler. The clear implication is that the not-Beautiful and the not-Tall, and so forth, are related to the nature of Difference much as Dialectic and Angling are related to Knowledge. But Dialectic and Angling have been shown to be definable Forms. It appears to follow that the not-Beautiful and the not-Tall are Forms themselves, a conclusion reinforced by the fact that the Stranger insists several times over (257E10, 258A1,5,8) that these "negative Forms" exist just as much as their positive counterparts. Here is a strong indication that the not-Beautiful is not just everything other than the Beautiful itself, and so forth for the other parts of the nature of the Different. For as the *Statesman* puts it, the divisions of the philosopher do not indiscriminately "separate parts without respect to Forms" (μόριον . . . μηδὲ εἴδους χωρίς: 262A9-B1). The philosopher is concerned "instead with a part which is at the same time a Form" (ἀλλὰ τὸ μέρος ἅμα εἶδος ἐχέτω: 262B1-2). An example of mistaking a part of the first sort for one of the second is dividing the human race into Greek and non-Greek, ignoring the fact that the latter is an indefinite (ἀπείροις: *Statesman* 262D3) class with nothing in common among its members. As the Stranger has already pointed out in the *Sophist*, the class of everything other than a given Form is likewise indefinite (ἄπει-ϱον: 256E7). It appears that the parts into which the nature of the Different are broken up cannot be parts in the sense of *Statesman* 262A9—that is, an indefinite class of everything other than a given Form.[56] They must be parts in the sense of 262B1 instead. That is, they must be Forms in their own right, unified with respect to some common character.

The Stranger's next step provides a hint of what that common character might be. When asked by Theaetetus to explain how the parts of the nature of the Different are like the subdivisions of knowledge, the Stranger stresses in several examples that the part which is different from a given Form in the sense in question is "set against" (some form of ἀντιτίθημι: 257D7, E3,6, 258B1, E1-2) some existing thing. The not-Beautiful, for instance, exists in being marked off from a single Kind; which is to say that it exists in being "set against" (ἀντιτεθὲν: 257E3) an existing thing. The not-Beautiful is not merely different from the Beautiful; it is "set against" the Beautiful in some particular way. Although ἀντιτίθημι has no precise logical significance, a clearer sense of this relationship is given at 258B1, where the Stranger shifts to the logically more determinate term ἀντικειμένων.[57] When a part of the nature of Difference (e.g., the not-Beautiful) and a part of that of Being (e.g., the Beautiful)[58] "contradict each other" (ἄλληλα ἀντικειμένων: 258B1), this "contrast is no less existent than Existence itself" (ἀντίθεσις οὐδὲν ἧττον . . . αὐτοῦ τοῦ ὄντος οὐσία ἐστίν: 258B1-2). The sense of being "set against" in question, this remark tells us, is that of being in logical opposition. And it is just this relationship, the Stranger explains at 258B3-4, that is meant when we speak of what is different from Existence, as distinct from its contrary.

As we are now in position to see, the manner of logical opposition in question has already been illustrated at 257B, where the Stranger noted that the relationship of "difference" in question is like that between "tall," "short," and "equal." Whereas the opposition between "tall" and "short" as "polar contraries" is exclusive but not exhaustive (since there is another alternative, being "equal" in stature), the opposition illustrated by the trio of relative characters is both exclusive and exhaustive. In any comparison with regard to stature, the things compared must be either tall, short, or equal—at least one of these but no more in a given respect. We may refer to this relationship as "opposition in the exhaustive sense."

The final step is to give this relationship a name. This contrast between the respective natures of Difference and Existence, the Stranger observes, is obviously just the "what is not" (τὸ μὴ ὄν: 258B7) for which we have been looking. The not-Beautiful, exhaustively opposed to the Beautiful, the not-Tall to the Tall, and in general the not-A to the A, collectively are the "not-Being" that will enable him to complete his definition of the essential sophist. As such, τὸ μὴ ὄν not only exists and has a nature of its own (258B11), but also is a single Form (εἶδος ἕν: 258C4)[59] among the many things that exist.

In taking a stand against the injunction of Parmenides, the Stranger from Elea says in summary, we not only have shown of things "that are not that they are" (τὰ μὴ ὄντα ὡς ἔστιν: 258D5), but also:

> have brought to light the Form which constitutes not-being [τὸ εἶδος ὃ τυγχάνει ὂν τοῦ μὴ ὄντος ἀπεφηνάμεθα: 258D6-7]. We have shown that the nature of the Different exists, and is parceled out over all existing things with reference one to another [τὴν γὰρ θατέρου φύσιν ἀποδεί-ξαντες οὖσάν τε καὶ κατακεκερματισμένην ἐπὶ πάντα τὰ ὄντα πρὸς ἄλληλα: 258D7-E1]; and of each part of the Different opposed to "what is" we have ventured to say that this itself is really "what is not" [τὸ πρὸς τὸ ὂν ἕκαστον μόριον αὐτῆς ἀντιτιθέμενον ἐτολμήσαμεν εἰπεῖν ὡς αὐτὸ τοῦτό ἐστιν ὄντως τὸ μὴ ὄν: 258E1-3].

With this concept of not-being at his disposal, the Stranger finally is ready for a definition of true and false judgment.

Given that the examination of not-being was initiated expressly to make way for an account of false judgment (240E10), the account finally given is remarkably terse. Every statement, says the Stranger, is about something (τινὸς: 262E6) and is either true or false. Consider the pair of statements "Theaetetus sits" and "Theaetetus flies":

The true one says of things-that-are with respect to you, that they are [Λέγει δὲ αὐτῶν ὁ μὲν ἀληθὴς τὰ ὄντα ὡς ἔστιν περὶ σοῦ: 263B4-5]. The false [says this of] things different from things-that-are [with respect to you] ['Ο δὲ δὴ ψευδὴς ἕτερα τῶν ὄντων: 263B7]. So it states things-that-are-not as things-that-are [Τὰ μὴ ὄντ᾽ ἄρα ὡς ὄντα λέγει: 263B9]. But at any rate [it states] things-that-are, different from things-that-are with respect to you ['Οντων δέ γε ὄντα ἕτερα περὶ σοῦ: 263B11]. For we said that there are many things-that-are with respect to each thing, and also many things-that-are-not [Πολλὰ μὲν γὰρ ἔφαμεν ὄντα περὶ ἕκαστον εἶναί που, πολλὰ δὲ οὐκ ὄντα: 263B11-12].⁶⁰

Although the amount of commentary inspired by this passage is as extensive as the passage is brief, adequate surveys of alternative interpretations are already available.⁶¹ For present purposes, it will be enough (1) to identify criteria of an acceptable interpretation, and (2) to lay out an interpretation that meets these criteria.⁶²

One factor to be taken into account by an acceptable interpretation is the Stranger's remark at 259E that "any statement we make arises from Forms combining with one another" (διὰ ... τὴν ἀλλήλων τῶν εἰδῶν συμπλοκὴν ὁ λόγος γέγονεν ἡμῖν: 259E5-6). However, the three very simple statements he offers as examples ("A man understands," "Theaetetus sits," and "Theaetetus flies") show no grammatical signs of being dependent upon a combination of Forms. The standard explanation is that the dependency in question has to do with the character every statement must have of being either true or false (263A11-B3).⁶³ The first criterion thus is (i) that the interpretation make clear a sense in which the truth and falsehood of judgments depend upon a combination of Forms.

Another factor is that the Stranger's prior account of the Form or Kind of not-Being, with its stress upon what this Form owes to the nature of Difference, was developed for the express purpose of providing a definition of false judgment. Another criterion accordingly is (ii) that an acceptable interpretation show

235

clearly how the Form of not-Being bears upon falsehood in judgment. Since Plato's account of non-Being depends essentially upon the capacity of the Forms to combine, an interpretation satisfying (ii) will satisfy (i) as well.

A further desideratum has to do with the fact that although Plato includes only affirmative statements among his three examples, he is explicitly concerned in this sequence of passages with negative statements as well—for example, with our saying of something that it is not tall (257B6). Any interpretation would be less than wholly satisfactory that did not provide essentially the same definition of falsehood (and, by the same token, of truth) for both affirmative and negative statements. By way of illustration, if one were inclined toward an interpretation according to which "Theaetetus sits" is deemed true simply because Theaetetus happened at the time to participate in a certain Form (Sitting), it would be reason for dissatisfaction with that interpretation that it makes "Theaetetus is not flying" ("Theaetetus is not-flying" or "Theaetetus not-flies") true for exactly the opposite reason—failure to participate in a certain Form (Flying). Converting this desideratum into a requirement, we have as a further criteria (iii) that our interpretation provide the same account of both truth and falsehood for affirmative and for negative judgments.[64]

Another criterion, which has received even less emphasis in contemporary commentary than the two just preceding, reflects the fact that participation of sensible things in Forms is not mentioned as part of the Stranger's account. As we shall see, indeed, there is reason to believe that Plato is unsure at this point of how to conceive that relationship; and it is important to realize that the account of true and false judgment given in the *Sophist* does not share the vicissitudes of participation to be disclosed in later dialogues. Thus, we should accept as a further criterion (iv) that our interpretation not rely in any essential way upon the notion of participation.[65]

The final and obvious criterion is (v) that our interpretation make good sense of Plato's language at 263B. The following account satisfies these five criteria.

A combination (συμπλέκων: 262D4) of nouns and verbs like

236

'Theaetetus sits' "accomplishes something beyond mere naming" (οὐκ ὀνομάζει μόνον ἀλλά τι περαίνει: 262D3-4). It says something (in the sense of propose, proclaim, or assert—εἴπομεν: 262D5) and hence constitutes a statement (λόγον: 262E1); specifically, this statement says something about (περὶ: 263A4,5) Theaetetus. Since Theaetetus actually is sitting, moreover, it says something true. The statement "Theaetetus flies," to the contrary, although it also says something about Theaetetus, says something that is false given his actual circumstances. What difference between these two statements makes them true and false respectively?

At the moment of this particular conversation between the Stranger and Theaetetus, there are many things-that-are (the case) with respect to the latter. There also are many things different from things-that-are (ἕτερα τῶν ὄντων) in this respect. As argued above, however, what is meant by ἕτερα τῶν ὄντων is not the indefinitely extensive class of all things simply other than things that are the case. What is meant rather is the part of the Different which is related to "what is" in his case as "what is not." And "what is not" in a given respect is not merely other than "what is," but is related to "what is" in the sense of what above we called "exhaustive opposition."

Among the several (but limited number of) things exhaustively opposed to Sitting are Running, Jumping, Reclining, Falling, and of course Flying. Flying thus belongs to not-Sitting, and is included in "what is not" with respect to Theaetetus at moments when he is sitting. By reverse token, Sitting belongs to not-Flying; hence, at those moments, not-Flying is among "what is" with respect to Theaetetus. For as the Stranger emphasized in his previous discussion of not-being, "what is not" exists no less fully than anything else. Among the many things-that-are the case with Theaetetus at the relevant moment, in short, are Sitting and not-Flying. And among the many things-that-are-not (i.e., things different from things-that-are the case) at that moment are not only Flying itself but also not-Sitting (including Jumping, Running, etc., as well as Flying).

The statement "Theaetetus sits" is true because it says of things-that-are with respect to Theaetetus that they are (ὡς ἔστιν).

"Theaetetus is not-flying" is true for exactly the same reason. On the other hand, both "Theaetetus flies" and "Theaetetus is not sitting" are false because they say of things-that-are-not (Flying and not-Sitting) with respect to Theaetetus that they are.

In general, a statement saying that X is A (or not-A) is true, given appropriate substitutions of nouns and verbs for 'X' and 'A', if and only if A (or not-A) is the case with X, and is false if and only if A (or not-A) is different from what is the case with X. Or, as the stranger puts it even more succinctly at 263B, a true statement says of things-that-are with respect to its subject, that they are, and a false one says this of other than things-that-are in this respect. As a consequence, it represents things-that-are-not incorrectly as things-that-are.

Commentators may have made the problem of interpreting Plato's account of truth and falsehood in judgment needlessly complicated by failing to observe how closely it parallels that of Aristotle at *Metaphysics* 1011b26-27, which latter never has seemed particularly puzzling. By Aristotle's account, to say of "what is" that it is not, or of "what is not" that it is, is false (τὸ μὲν γὰρ λέγειν τὸ ὂν μὴ εἶναι ἢ τὸ μὴ ὂν εἶναι ψεῦδος); and to say of "what is" that it is, or of "what is not" that is not, is true (τὸ δὲ τὸ ὂν εἶναι καὶ τὸ μὴ ὂν μὴ εἶναι ἀληθές). Plato has prepared the way for Aristotle by providing an intelligible sense in which "what is not" nonetheless is, and can be meaningfully stated. The fact that Plato and Aristotle can agree on the nature of truth and falsehood dramatizes the absence of any dependence in Plato's account upon the concept of participation. If Plato comes eventually to reject participation as a helpful concept, he remains free to maintain this account of truth and falsehood in judgment.

A Story about Participation in the *Timaeus*

The *Timaeus* is a highly controversial dialogue. Perhaps the most certain thing about it is that the task of interpreting Plato's later writings would be considerably easier if the *Timaeus* had never been written. The interpretive problem is complicated by the fact that early Neoplatonists (notably Plotinus and Porphyry) accepted the *Timaeus* and the *Parmenides* together as embodying Plato's most mature thought,[66] while modern commentators tend to emphasize the disparities between these two dialogues.

A focal point of contention among modern commentators, to be sure, is whether the *Timaeus* should be ranked before or after the *Parmenides* in chronological order.[67] Those who argue that the *Parmenides* is earlier appear to be burdened with the formidable task of explaining how Plato could continue to maintain in the *Timaeus* what appears to be essentially the same theory of Forms as propounded earlier in the *Phaedo* and the *Republic*, after criticizing it vigorously in the first part of the *Parmenides*.[68] Those who argue that the *Parmenides* is later, on the other hand, are confronted with a large body of stylometric data which alledgedly indicates that Plato employed stylistic devices in the *Timaeus* that are typical of the *Philebus* and the *Laws*, while the style of the *Parmenides* is reminiscent of the *Phaedo* and the *Republic*.[69] Sufficient literature has been generated on both sides of the issue to ensure that one will be faced with weighty objections regardless of one's position in matters of dating.[70]

At first glance this appears to constitute an unavoidable impasse for any study (like the present) purporting to document major changes in Plato's philosophic viewpoint. For if we cannot determine the order in which key dialogues were written, how can we tell in case of conflict between them which account was intended to be superseded? Formidable as this challenge may appear when stated thus generally, in this particular study I believe it can be avoided. If indeed Plato lost confidence in the earlier theory of Forms primarily as a result of his failure in the *Timaeus* to provide even a metaphorical account of the notion of participation, as proposed in the present section, and if the several arguments in *Parmenides I* amount to little more than a rhetorical exhibition of that theory in its most problematic aspects, as urged in chapter I above, then it makes little difference for interpretive purposes which of these two writings preceded the other. Rather than beg the question of relative dating, in brief, I attempt to deal with the *Timaeus*—as with the *Parmenides* earlier—in a manner not dependent on chronological order.

As a beginning, it will be helpful to assess the consequences of a few facts about the *Timaeus* which most commentators should be prepared to accept at face value, regardless of their thoughts on the order of the dialogues. First and foremost is the fact that the contents of the dialogue are referred to repeatedly as "fictional"—the Greek term being μῦθος.[71] In the preamble of his narration, which also gives Timaeus an opportunity to call upon the gods, his main concern is to make clear that the story will be only probable, and to explain the reason why this is unavoidable. The reason is that the universe, the generation of which is the subject of the story, is only a copy or likeness. Although the pattern of which it is a copy is itself eternal, and hence within the grasp of reason and wisdom (29A7), the likeness is subject only to a form of belief that necessarily falls short of truth (as being is to becoming, so is truth to belief—πρὸς γένεσιν οὐσία, τοῦτο πρὸς πίστιν ἀλήθεια: 29C2-3). As a consequence, Timaeus stresses, the tale he is about to tell must be accepted as reasonable (εἰκότας: 29C1,7) only. Given the nature of the subject matter, we cannot expect more than a likely story (εἰκότα μῦθον: 29D1). This caveat is repeated several times later in the dialogue, where Timaeus refers to his conclusions as reasonable at best (48D2,6, 56D1, 57D6, 59D1,4), and again characterizes his discourse as only a tale (μύθῳ: 69B1) or likely story (εἰκότων μύθων: 59C7). The common translation of εἰκός as 'probable' in this context is misleading, insofar as what is probable is thought of as a candidate for truth. As 29C makes entirely explicit, the sense in which Timaeus' story is probable excludes it from any possibility of being true, in the manner that becoming analogously is excluded from being. The discourse of the *Timaeus* is not an approximation to the truth; it is a story about a subject matter that by its nature cannot be truly described.[72] It is only a diversion or pastime (παιδιὰν: 59D2), offering respite from thoughts about eternal being (περὶ τῶν ὄντων ἀεὶ: 59C8).

As a consequence, whatever ontological significance this dialogue may have, its contents cannot properly be weighed in the same manner as those of the *Phaedo*, the *Sophist*, the *Parmenides*, or the *Philebus*. The methods employed in relevant passages of these latter dialogues, whatever their differences, are all portrayed as properly philosophical (*Phaedo* 102A1, *Sophist* 253C9) or dialectical (*Sophist* 253D2-3, *Philebus* 17A4), or as directed toward the achievement of knowledge (*Sophist* 253C8, D3) and the discovery of reality (*Phaedo* 101E3) and truth (*Parmenides* 136C6).

Insofar as ontology is a study of being in a manner leading to knowledge and truth, the *Timaeus* explicitly disqualifies itself from being read as a statement of Plato's ontology. This is the case regardless of its chronological order relative to the *Parmenides*. Even if *Parmenides I* is understood as a reaction to the ontological theory of the middle dialogues, as clearly as it should be, it is not therefore in any direct sense an argument against the fictional account of the *Timaeus*, for that account is not an ontological theory at all. The doctrinal issue of how Plato could have maintained in the *Timaeus* the very position regarding the Forms that he criticizes in the *Parmenides*, assuming the *Timaeus* is the later of the two dialogues, is not an issue that warrants the heroic attacks and counterattacks it has inspired in recent critical literature. Strictly speaking, Plato is not maintaining any position at all in the *Timaeus*. He is instead presenting a figurative exploration of some ontological topics that at best resemble certain positions developed dialectically in other dialogues.

A second unproblematic fact about the *Timaeus* may throw light upon Plato's motives in undertaking this exercise. Needless to say, this ontological exploration is not the sole topic of Timaeus' discussion. The fact of the matter is that the *Timaeus* is dominated by various themes which Plato wove into other dialogues (both earlier and later), but which never received the careful dialectical treatment accorded the topic of true and false judgment in the *Sophist*, for example, or that of statecraft in the *Statesman*. One such theme quite obviously is that of the role of mind in ordering the universe, which appears in several other middle and late dialogues (*Cratylus* 400A9, *Phaedo* 97C3, *Philebus* 30D8, *Laws* 966E4), but never as the subject of dialectical examination. Another is the role of mathematics in the structure of sensible objects, which lurks behind the symbolism of the Divided Line in the *Republic*[73] and, I have argued, begins to surface in the *Parmenides* and the *Philebus*. Most important for our present purposes, however, is the theme of the interaction between Forms and objects by which the latter receive the characters that make them identifiable. The problem of giving a coherent account of this interaction—specifically, the problem of participation—remained unsolved, as we have noted, in the middle dialogues.

Although these three themes of course are not the only ones involved in the *Timaeus*, they establish a pattern that may help us understand Plato's choice of μῦθον as its medium of discussion. For these themes share two characteristics which Plato obviously found challenging. One is that all three themes have to do with the formation of sensible things which at least appear to remain stable through time. Although falling short of the absolute permanence of eternal objects, these things possess more fixity than can be accounted for by the theory of becoming in the *Theaetetus* alone. That is to say, they fall somewhere between the account of becoming in the *Theaetetus* and the theory of being in the *Sophist*. Second, each of these themes involves some manner of interchange between the realm of the permanent (mind, mathematical entities, Forms) and the realm of change, which Plato simply does not seem prepared to cope with at this stage in his ontological development. In short, the problems of accounting for the seeming permanence of sensible objects through change imposes demands which Plato did not yet appear ready to meet on a dialectical basis.

Plato's predicament at this point was similar to that of Parmenides at the end of the "Way of Truth." Having laid out an account of being and knowing according to which only what is changeless exists as an object of knowledge, but feeling called upon nonetheless to give some kind of explanation of why things appear otherwise, Parmenides shifts mode of discourse and embarks upon a story which he warns his readers is reasonable (ἐοικότα)[74] at best. The "Way of Truth" has been concluded, and what follows cannot be literally true. He labels it instead the "Way of Seeming." Plato's recourse is the same. Having given accounts of being and of knowing according to which only the changeless Forms exist as proper objects of knowledge, but hav-

242

ing done so in the context of a theory according to which Forms are somehow responsible for the ways things appear, Plato recognizes the need of explaining how this comes about. Following the best precedent available, that of the redoubtable Parmenides, Plato formulates his explanation as a reasonable story, and puts it in the mouth of the (probably) fictional Timaeus.

Indeed, a third unproblematic (although generally unremarked) fact about the *Timaeus* is its striking resemblance to the poem of the historical Parmenides. Beyond the characterization of each work by its author as merely reasonable, noted above, there are several substantial parallels in content. To set the stage, being for Parmenides "is now, one, all at once, and connected" (νῦν ἔστιν ὁμοῦ πᾶν, ἕν, συνεχές: fr. 8.5-6), and "never in the past nor yet to be" (οὐδέ ποτ' ἦν οὐδ' ἔσται: fr. 8.5) Similarly in the *Timaeus*, it is "eternal being . . . only to which the term 'is' belongs in true description" (ἀΐδιον οὐσίαν . . . τὸ ἔστιν μόνον κατὰ τὸν ἀληθῆ λόγον προσήκει: 37E5-7), while " 'was' and 'will be' are properly said of things that come to be and proceed in time" (τὸ δὲ ἦν τό τ' ἔσται περὶ τὴν ἐν χρόνῳ γένεσιν ἰοῦσαν πρέπει λέγεσθαι: 37E7-38A1). In brief, being, according to both authors, alone admits the term ἔστιν, while ἦν and ἔσται should be reserved for becoming. Nonetheless, both authors, with due warning, suspend their own proscriptions and proceed to give (necessarily figurative) accounts of the mechanisms of perception and of how things come to change in various mixtures. The basic principles involved in Parmenides' account are the opposites light and dark (φῶς . . . καὶ σκότος: Simplicius, *Physics*, 30.21), although air, fire, and earth also apparently were given prominent status.[75] In the *Timaeus*, of course, the basic elements out of which sensible things are composed are the standard four—earth, air, fire, and water.

In both accounts, moreover, the processes of generation are set in motion by divine agency. In Parmenides' story, it is a goddess who controls all things (δαίμων ἣ πάντα κυβερνᾷ: Simplicius, *Physics*, 31.14, 39.16).[76] In Plato's, it is the Demiurge (δημιουργός: 28A6), who took all that is visible and brought it to order out of disorder (πᾶν ὅσον ἦν ὁρατὸν παραλαβὼν . . . εἰς τάξιν αὐτὸ ἤγαγεν ἐκ τῆς ἀταξίας: 30A2-5). According to Parmenides, the goddess's creative act is according to justice (δίκη: Simplicius, *Physics*, 145.14) and necessity (ἀνάγκη: ibid., 145.17, 146.3).[77] Similarly, when Timaeus comes to that part of his story where the task of creating mortals is turned over to the celestial gods, these lesser gods provide examples of invariant justice (ἀεὶ δίκη: 41C7) for mortal creatures to follow; and when the story turns to the generation of the visible universe, necessity (ἀνάγκης: 48A1) is the dominant factor that the craft of reason must deal with.

To be sure, the creative goddess of Parmenides' poem is not depicted as being guided by mind or reason as is the Demiurge of the *Timaeus*. Even in this respect, however, there are parallels between the two stories. For the goddess of Parmenides was said to be identified with the middle of a series of rings, some of which were made up of unmixed fire (Simplicius, *Physics*, 39.14) or unmixed rareness or density (Aetius, Kirk and Raven, 1962, p. 284), and others of mixtures of light and darkness (ibid.). The middle ring, which is mixed, was said to be the primary cause of motion and of coming to be. In the *Timaeus*, of course, the world soul is composed of a set of rings fabricated from mixtures of Sameness and Difference (which for Plato, we know from the *Sophist*, were opposites more basic than rareness and density), as well as Existence, and endowed with reason and intelligence (λογισμοῦ . . . καὶ . . . νοητῶν: 37A1). Although in the extant fragments of Parmenides' poem he does not attribute mind to the creative principle directly, the shared imagery of the two stories at least is compatible with the conjecture that Parmenides thought of reason as having something to do with creation according to justice and necessity. After all, if everything has some amount of knowledge, as Theophrastus reports that Parmenides maintained (πᾶν τὸ ὂν ἔχειν τινὰ γνῶσιν: Kirk and Raven, 1962, p. 283), then surely the creative principle is preeminently so endowed.

Another image that reinforces the parallelism between the two stories is the description in each of the world as a well-rounded sphere, equidistant from center to extreme in every direction (ἐκ μέσου πάντη πρὸς τὰς τελευτὰς ἴσον ἀπέχον: *Timaeus* 33B5-6; μεσσόθεν ἰσοπαλὲς πάντη: *Simplicius* 146.17). Yet another is the image of the chariots by which the soul of man is conveyed while being shown the nature of all things (τὴν τοῦ παντὸς φύσιν ἔδειξεν: 41E2), which the *Timaeus* shares not only with the *Phaedrus* but with the proem of Parmenides' poem.

Wittingly or not, Plato has followed the lead of the historical Parmenides in constructing a figurative story about a number of related topics which, both men believe, cannot be subjected to a true account. Each of these topics concerns the constitution of sensible things, whether by a creative act of intelligence, by an interaction of eternal principles (the Forms and the receptacle), by the composition and decomposition of sensible bodies themselves, or (in the special case of the human body) according to the functional needs of the composite organism. If these topics could be pursued with reference to being alone, exclusive of becoming and change, they would be subject to discursive treatment corresponding to what we classify as cosmology (and perhaps theology), ontology, chemistry, and biology (including medicine), respectively. Since each deals with things in change, however, none is a proper topic of knowledge in the strict sense of the *Republic*, the *Theaetetus* and the *Sophist*. These topics are subject to belief at best, and (as 29C appears to make clear) not even true belief at that. The only course open to Timaeus in addressing such matters is to narrate a story which, although perhaps more plausible than its alternatives (such as Parmenides' "Way of Seeming" itself), by its nature falls short of being true.

Taking up once again the question why Plato should have written a dialogue of this character during the peak of his later period (otherwise marked by dialogues that are strongly dialectical in character), we see that the answer has to do at least in part with the state of his ontology after the *Sophist* had been completed. One major feature of Plato's ontology during the middle period, as previously noted, is the tenet that Forms are both causes by which sensible things come to manifest certain characters and standards by which such things are named and identified. Another major tenet is that Forms and sensible things are radically disparate in their modes of existence. Given these two tenets in combination, the problem of participation constituted a crucial impediment to a satisfactory completion of Plato's overall ontological vision. Even granted that adequate answers have been given to the problems of the status of sensible things and of the ontology of knowledge in the *Theaetetus* and the *Sophist*, respectively, that is to say, a number of very basic questions remain unanswered. If the Forms are eternal and hence outside the realm of time, how can they be causally related in any way to things that by their nature fall within that realm? If the Forms are changeless, how can they be responsible in any sense for the characters of sensible things that are constantly changing? And if sensible things are constantly in flux, how can they be identified in the first place and be called by the same names as the self-identical Forms? Not coincidentally, we now may observe, it is to questions of this cast that the story of the *Timaeus* responds in its explicitly ontological section between 48E and 53B.

In the cosmological section of the dialogue between 29E and 47E, Plato has discussed, in his unavoidably figurative manner, those aspects of the world that have been brought about by νοῦς (reason, motivated by purpose and a desire for goodness). The dominant theme of this section is that the Demiurge created both the world's body, out of earth, air, fire, and water, and the world soul, out of Existence, Sameness, and Difference in various combinations, following throughout the pattern of the Living Creature, and then turned the project over to the generated gods for the creation of man and other temporally bound creatures. The essential factors in this part of the story thus are (1) the Demiurge, or divine creative force, (2) the created universe in time, and (3) the timeless patterns or Forms after which the universe was fashioned.

But as we move into the ontological section beginning at 48E, the Demiurge fades into the background of the account, and a new factor comes into view to which Timaeus attaches importance equal to that of the Forms and the visible world. As he puts it:

> Our new beginning must be a fuller classification of the universe than the previous one ['Η δ' οὖν αὖθις ἀρχὴ περὶ τοῦ παντὸς ἔστω μειζόνως τῆς πρόσθεν διῃρημένη:

48E2-3]. Then we distinguished two classes, but now must point out a third kind [τότε μὲν γὰρ δύο εἴδη διειλό-μεθα, νῦν δὲ τρίτον ἄλλο γένος ἡμῖν δηλωτέον: 48E3-4].

The two sufficient for the earlier discussion were that of "paradigmatic Form, intelligible and always the same being" (παρα-δείγματος εἶδος ... νοητὸν καὶ ἀεὶ κατὰ ταὐτὰ ὄν: 48E5-6), and that of "copy of this paradigm, generated and visible" (μίμημα δὲ παραδείγματος ... γένεσιν ἔχον καὶ ὁρατόν: 49A1-2). The third now required is a "difficult and obscure" (χαλεπὸν καὶ ἀμυδρὸν: 49A4) sort of thing. What power by nature can we understand it to have? The answer is that "it is the receptacle, or as it were the nurse, of all generation" (πάσης εἶναι γενέσεως ὑποδοχὴν αὐτὴν οἷον τιθήνην: 49A6-7). The role of this third factor, difficult as it is to understand, is in some manner to provide the context within which sensible things come to resemble the Forms they imitate. As Timaeus puts it in repeating his threefold classification at 50C7-50D2, altering the order of mention, we must fix our minds on "that which comes to be, that in which it comes to be, and that which it resembles when what comes to be is produced" (τὸ μὲν γιγνόμενον, τὸ δ' ἐν ᾧ γίγνεται, τὸ δ' ὅθεν ἀφομοιούμενον φύεται τὸ γιγνόμενον).

The answer to the problem of participation that Plato is experimenting with in this passage is that the manner in which sensible things resemble the Forms after which they are named is not a direct two-term relationship, but rather involves a third factor through which the relationship of resemblance is mediated. For a particular sensible thing to participate in a given Form is for the Form to be copied in the receptacle, and for that copy to be associated with that particular thing. This answer, however, is of little value unless the relationships among the several factors involved can be made more specific. In what sense can Forms be copied in the receptacle? And under what conditions is a given copy associated with a given sensible thing?

Familiar as the reader is likely to be with scholarly discussions of the receptacle as a fundamental principle in the *Timaeus*, it is all too easy to overlook the fact that Plato never gets beyond the level of metaphor in his treatment of this factor. Indeed, he employs a number of different metaphors, some of which seem to be at cross-purposes with others. Although Plato typically avoids deliberately precise and technical language even in his most carefully crafted dialogues, and although the *Timaeus* is necessarily given over to figurative discourse, a careful examination of the variety of metaphors employed in this connection should convince us that understanding the role intended for the receptacle poses an unusually difficult task of interpretation.

To begin with, this essential third factor is mentioned under at least seven different titles in less than four pages. First is ὑποδοχὴν (receptacle: 49A6; also 51A6), followed closely by τιθήνην (nurse: 49A7; also 52D5) in the sense of foster mother (cf. 88D7). Since the nurse does not provide the womb in which a child develops, the sense of these two metaphors together must be something like "that which sustains a thing in growth." The image of sustaining factor in the sense of "upholding" or "containing" suggested by ὑποδοχὴν is reinforced by the subsequent occurrence of ἐκμαγεῖον (recipient of an impression, like wax:[78] (50C2) and δεχόμενον (containing vessel: 50D3). The sense of "nurture" suggested by τιθήνην, on the other hand, is reinforced by μητέρα (mother) at 51A5 and τροφὸν (foster mother) at 88D7. The sense of "containment" seems to win favor in the end, however, with reference to the receptacle as ἕδραν (place: 52B1) and χώραν (space: 52D3; also 52B1) in the summary comments of this section.[79]

This tension between images of containment and of nurture carries over into the set of metaphors by which Timaeus characterizes the relationship between the Forms and the receiving element. At 50D2-4 the relationship between receptacle and Form is likened to that between mother and father, with a reproduction of the latter arising as a child between them. In the immediately surrounding passages, however, are the essentially nonbiological images of the wax receiving shape from external objects (50C), and of the base fluid receiving scent in the making of perfume (50E). A related simile at 50A-B invites us to think of the receptacle as a quantity of gold that constantly changes shape as an artisan remolds it. In this connection, Timaeus emphasizes (50B-C) that the receptacle (unlike gold) can have no characters on its own, and hence is enabled to receive all characters externally imposed upon it.[80]

With this latter requirement in mind, indeed, we may find fault with all the images just mentioned, and for the same reason. The womb of the mother, the wax, the perfume base, and the gold, all possess characteristics of their own which make the images impressed within them tend to persist, at least until forcibly replaced by others. The best simile in view of this problem would appear to be that of a mirror, which possesses no retentive capacities whatever. To be sure, it is the mirror, rather than the gold or the wax, that seems best to fit the description at 52C, where Timaeus remarks that

> for an image, since not even the very principle on which it
> has come into being belongs to the image itself, but it is the
> every-moving semblance of something else, it is proper that
> it should come to be *in* something else, clinging to some sort
> of existence on pain of being nothing at all.[81]

The feeling that the complex relationship between (i) mirror, (ii) reflection, and (iii) object reflected, is the best analogy Plato has to offer for the relationship he is trying to capture between (i) receptacle, (ii) sensible thing, and (iii) Form, is encouraged by his choice of terms to express the thing which results from the interaction of receptacle and Form. Three terms that figure prominently in these expressions are μίμημα (imitation, likeness, copy: e.g., 49A1), ἀφομοίωμα (resemblance, impression, reproduction: e.g., 50E4), and εἰκών (image, reflection: e.g., 52C2).

The most apt metaphor Plato seems to have available for expressing the relationship he is trying to articulate in this passage, accordingly, is that of the reflected visual image. Timaeus' account thus can be understood as suggesting that the participation of sensible things in Forms is somehow like the relationship between reflections and objects reflected, with the receptacle corresponding to the mirror in between.[82] Although mirrors of course must have characteristics of their own to provide a reflective surface, no trace of these characteristics appears in the images reflected by a (perfect) mirror. The only exception is that of spatial position, inasmuch as the spatial relationship between mirror and reflected object is an essential determinant of the resulting image.

With this caveat, however, the usefulness of the mirror metaphor is severely compromised. For in the final summing up at 52D, this third factor—the "nurse of generation" (γενέσεως τιθήνην: 52D5)—is referred to as space χώραν: 52D3, repeating 52B1), providing a place or abode (ἔδραν: 52B1) for all created things. And there is no conceivable sense, metaphorical or otherwise, in which the receptacle can both be in space (like a mirror) and be space itself. By the end of the ontological passage we are left with the empty image of space itself, possessing no characteristics on its own, somehow reflecting the Forms to generate sensible things. Impossible as this image appears to be, it is the best aid Plato is able to provide in his entire corpus for understanding the relationship of participation.

Indeed, Plato himself seems to realize the futility of the very enterprise of making sense of this relationship as he remarks time and again that the sense in which the receptacle shares relationship (μεταλαμβάνον: 51A8-B1) with the Forms is very hard to deal with (ἀπορώτατα: 51B1) and exceedingly difficult to comprehend (δυσαλωτότατον: 51B1)—all in all marvelous (θαυμαστόν: 50C6) and hard to express (δύσφραστον: 50C6). The failure of this attempt, in fact, is monumental, inasmuch as no reasonable hope can remain of making literal sense of the notion of participation—which an articulate statement of his ontology at this point would require—if the notion eludes even metaphorical expression.

The results of Plato's imaginative exploration of the notion of participation at *Timaeus* 48E-53B are not entirely negative. One specific question included within the general problem of participation, mentioned previously, is the following: Under what conditions is a given copy (e.g., of a Form in the receptacle) associated with a given sensible thing? What makes a particular reflection in the receptacle, so to speak, an appearance of one perceptual object rather than another? Put yet another way: Given a set of appearances at a given time, what makes them all appearances of one object rather than several, or of no particular object at all? And given a sequence of appearance-sets through time, what makes this sequence a continuing series of appearances of identically the same object, rather than the disappearance of one object and its replacement by another? In response to what is perhaps the first occurrence in philosophy of the so-called problem of individuation, Plato provides an insightful answer at 50B.

The reason the problem arises for Plato's ontology in the first place is that the change inherent in sensible objects prevents their ever being the same in and by themselves. As the *Theaetetus* puts it at 186A, Sameness can be comprehended by soul alone, and not by any faculty of sensation. In the language of the *Sophist*, while every Form is the same as itself, and this because each shares in Sameness, sensible things partake in Difference but never in Sameness. For what is constantly changing cannot be the same in itself. This restriction of the sensible world to the domain of the Different is continued in the *Timaeus*, where it is said at 37B that true beliefs (πίστεις . . . ἀληθεῖς [37B8-C1], as distinct from ἐπιστήμη [37C3]), arise when the circle of the Different (θατέρου κύκλος: 37B7) sends messages of the sensible throughout the soul.

Clearly enough, however, we do speak with cogency about perceptual objects being the same as well as different, and about individual objects retaining their identity through time. Since sensible things do not possess identity in and by themselves, there must be an external source of sameness for such talk to be intelligible. In the *Timaeus* the receptacle is put forth as that source. Regarding this nature that receives all bodies (περὶ τῆς τὰ πάντα δεχομένης σώματα φύσεως: 50B7-8), Timaeus says, "it must be called forever the same" (Ταὐτόν αὐτὴν ἀεὶ προσρητέον: 50B8). The sense of this remark, I suggest, is not that we should always apply the same name to it,[83] or that we should describe it as "always the same," but rather that in speaking of this factor we should never fail to recognize that it warrants being called "the same." It is strictly ταὐτόν. Ταὐτὸν appears to serve here as yet one more metaphor expressing something important about the recipient of sensible images. Whereas these images, being

251

sensible and constantly changing, possess no self-identity on their own, collections of them are designated "the same" from time to time by virtue of appearing at the same place in space, or presumably by virtue of their change through time being a relatively continuous transition across adjacent places. To suggest even this much about the receptacle playing a role in the sensible world, corresponding to that played by Sameness in the realm of the Forms, goes beyond what Plato says in the dialogue itself. Yet it is worth noting that Plato's figurative explorations in the *Timaeus* have made available a perfectly cogent answer to at least one of the basic problems associated with the notion of participation.

But with this designation of the receptacle as strictly ταὐτόν, another problem comes into focus that will block any further attempt to articulate an intelligible relationship between the eternal Forms and mutable sensible objects. The problem has been incipient in Plato's ontological theory of radical separation between Forms and sensibles since its beginning in the middle dialogues. But the *Timaeus* is the first dialogue in which he appears to have confronted it directly. Put simply, the problem is this: How can two (or any number of) unchanging principles possibly interact to generate change? And simply put, the problem is unanswerable.

Being strictly the same, the receptacle "never deviates at all from its natural disposition" (ἐκ γὰρ τῆς ἑαυτῆς τὸ παράπαν οὐκ ἐξίσταται δυνάμεως: 50B8-9). And the Forms as well are eternally changeless. This seems inevitably to require that any relationship between these two principles itself be invariable. But what is invariable can be neither occasion nor cause of what exists at one moment and fails to exist at another. Some other principle than the Forms and the receptacle themselves would be needed for an intelligible account of the genesis of sensible things. Far from solving the problem of how the Forms can contribute to the characterization of sensible things, the receptacle merely adds complications.

The difficulty can be seen in yet another perspective. Time, "made as a moving image of eternity" (εἰκὼ ... κινητόν τινα αἰῶνος ποιῆσαι: 37D5-6), came into existence only with the creation of the universe (37E). But "being and space [the Forms and the receptacle] existed before the heaven was created" (ὄν τε καὶ χώραν . . . εἶναι . . . πρὶν οὐρανὸν γενέσθαι: 52D3-4). Since the Forms and the receptacle are changeless by nature, and hence did not change with the creation of the heavens, it follows that these principles by nature are independent of time. What is not involved in time, however, cannot in any conceivable manner be an adequate cause for what is essentially temporal and variable. Again we see that some other principle than the Forms and the receptacle would be needed for an intelligible account of sensible things.[84]

It is tempting to solve this problem in Plato's behalf by invoking the Demiurge from the previous section of the dialogue, pointing out that motion entered the universe with the creation of the world soul.[85] But the effect of this expedient is only to offer a theological solution when an ontological one is required. For however one might formulate the contribution of the Demiurge (or of any other divine agency for that matter), such a formulation will not constitute an answer to the problem of participation. The problem of understanding participation—the relationship between Forms and sensible things by virtue of which the latter take on characteristics justifying their being named after the former—is not solved by a suggestion merely about how the relationship comes to be instantiated. What we need to understand is the nature of the relationship itself. So even if Plato had said that sensible things come into existence by the Demiurge's bringing about their participation in the Forms, this would not have contributed to our understanding of how things in change can be related to the changeless Forms in the first place.[86] To Plato's credit, however, he does not adopt this expedient. What he does instead, when the problem becomes apparent at 52D, is change his metaphor once again. And the result is totally at odds with what he has said just previously.

In the final passage of this section, just before beginning his physicochemical account in terms of basic triangles, Timaeus likens space (χώραν: 52D3) or the "nurse of generation" (τὴν . . . γενέσεως τιθήνην: 52D4-5) to a sieve or winnowing basket (πλοκάνων: 52E7). Having received the forms (μορφὰς: 52D6) of the basic characters, earth, air, fire, and water, the receptacle receives all the other qualities going with these (ὅσα ἄλλα τούτοις πάθη συνέπεται πάσχουσαν: 52D6-E1). Then

> being thus filled with powers that were neither similar nor equally balanced [διὰ δὲ τὸ μήθ᾽ ὁμοίων δυνάμεων μήτε ἰσορρόπων ἐμπίμπλασθαι: 52E2-3], the receptacle itself was nowhere in balance; but being swayed everywhere unevenly and shaken by these things, it by its own motion shakes them in turn [ἀλλ᾽ ἀνωμάλως πάντη ταλαντουμένην σείεσθαι μὲν ὑπ᾽ ἐκείνων αὐτήν, κινουμένην δ᾽ αὖ πάλιν ἐκεῖνα σείειν: 52E3-5].

In this respect, the receptacle is likened to a winnowing basket, in which heavy and light particles are carried in different directions, and by their shifting mass impel the basket in turn.[87] According to this image, in short, motion enters the realm of sensible objects as a result of the powers imported with the basic characters. After the reciprocal motions between these powers and the receptacle had distributed the characters into separate regions, god (θεός: 53B3) came on the scene and began to fashion these characters by form and number (εἴδεσί τε καὶ ἀριθμοῖς: 53B4-5).

Insofar as this image is intended as a metaphorical device to help us understand how motion can be imparted by participation in the Forms, it suffers the fundamental defect of internal incoherence. The suggestion is that the receptacle, or space, receives characters that are dissimilar and out of balance and, being moved by their shifting, imparts further motion to the characters themselves. What results is a preliminary ordering of the sensible universe, before divine agency takes control with its purposeful plan. This image is incoherent for the simple reason that it represents the receptacle itself as undergoing motion. But the receptacle at the beginning of the passage is identified with space (52D3), and space is the context in which all motion takes place. The notion of the context of all motion itself being in motion is simply unintelligible.

Like the previous images of the nurse and mother, of the characterless recipient, and of space itself, this final image of the winnowing basket is ultimately fruitless as an aid toward understanding how participation is possible. The remainder of the story told by Timaeus is concerned with the physical constitution of familiar substances and the functions of various parts of the body, in which matters the participation of sensible things in Forms apparently has no essential role to play.

This set of passages in the *Timaeus* is Plato's only sustained attempt to come to grips with the problems of participation raised by his theory of the radical separation between Forms and sensible things, characteristic of the middle and certain later dialogues. The upshot of this attempt is that there appears to be no conceivable way in which Forms can account for the changing characters of sensible things, as long as these Forms are conceived as intrinsically removed from the domain of change in and by themselves. If the ontological theory of Forms and sensibles is to be rescued, it would appear, the thesis of radical separation must be relinquished.

It is surely significant in this connection that the thesis of radical separation is expressly rejected in the *Parmenides*, is absent in the *Statesman*, and is replaced in the *Philebus* by a contrary theory. Although the issue of relative dating has not been a factor in the foregoing discussion of the *Timaeus*, this set of facts in itself (apart from matters of stylometric data discussed in Appendix B) suggests that the *Timaeus* was written relatively early within the late period. Far from representing Plato's final ontological views, the *Timaeus* instead is his last serious attempt to deal with the notion of participation as it figures in the middle dialogues.

ON THE STYLOMETRIC DATING OF THE *TIMAEUS* AND THE *PARMENIDES*

"Until 1953," Guthrie observes, "the *Timaeus* and its sequel the *Critias* were universally believed to be, with the possible exception of the *Philebus*, the latest of Plato's works except the *Laws*."[1] This belief was based largely upon the stylometric investigations of Lutoslawski[2] and several other European scholars of the early twentieth century.[3] The event in 1953 that shook this widely held belief was the publication of Owen's "The Place of the *Timaeus* in Plato's Dialogues," which on the basis of a reassessment of the stylometric evidence mounted an argument for the chronological priority of the *Timaeus* over the *Theaetetus* and the *Parmenides*—as well, of course, as the *Sophist*, the *Statesman*, the *Philebus*, and the *Laws*. The salutary advice to which this argument led was that these "profoundly important late dialogues" should be delivered "from the shadow of the *Timaeus*"[4] and left to their own devices.

Although Owen's argument convinced a considerable number of English and American scholars, the spirited rebuttal of Cherniss (1957) had the effect upon others of reinforcing the *Timaeus* in its traditional shadow-casting role. As Cherniss read the stylometric evidence, while the *Timaeus* indeed is earlier than the *Laws*, probably the *Philebus*, and possibly even the *Sophist* and the *Statesman*, it surely is later than the *Theaetetus* and the *Parmenides*. For those whose opinions in matters of dating rest upon the outcome of stylometric studies, the relative position of the *Parmenides* and the *Timaeus* to this day remains controversial.

My reasons for distrusting stylistic measures as final arbiters of chronological order have already been indicated (Appendix A, n. 69). I have also indicated why, in the approach to Plato's late ontology developed in this volume, the issue of the chronological relationship between the *Timaeus* and the *Parmenides* is not of crucial importance. Inasmuch as both the figurative explorations of participation in the *Timaeus* and the forensic attacks in the first part of the *Parmenides* generate reasons for dissatisfaction with the middle theory of Forms, that is to say, it is a matter of relative indifference which came first. Nonetheless, it seems unlikely that Plato would have remained preoccupied with a theory based on the assumption of radical separation between Forms and sensibles (in the *Timaeus*) after beginning work on the foundations of a new theory rejecting that assumption (in the second part of the *Parmenides*). Moreover, even though stylometric evidence should not serve as final arbiter in questions of dating, it surely is not irrelevant in that regard. Hence, it remains a source of uneasiness that a substantial number of stylometrists in this century promulgate an order of composition in which the *Parmenides* as a whole antedates the *Timaeus*.

To counteract this source of uneasiness with finality would be to establish conclusively either (1) that the *Parmenides* as a whole was written after the *Timaeus* or (2) that, while *Parmenides I* might have been written before the *Timaeus, Parmenides II* was written after. Unconvinced as I am of the reliability of stylistic measures in general, I do not believe that either (1) or (2) can be established conclusively by this means. The next best thing would be to show that the evidence upon which stylometrists who believe the *Parmenides* precedes the *Timaeus* rest their case in fact cannot be relied upon to support that belief. To attempt even this much, however, would be too ambitious for present purposes, since it would require a reexamination of the accumulated efforts of over a century of stylometric scholarship.[5] Among realistic alternatives, the best appears to be that of coming to terms with the set of five hundred stylistic measures compiled by Lutoslawski, upon which the view that the *Parmenides* antedates the *Timaeus* originally achieved orthodox status (see n. 2 above). And even here my goal must be severely limited. For both the general strategy and the particular tactics of Lutoslawski's approach have been criticized before,[6] with issues in view much larger than the relative dating of these two dialogues. Since my concern is with this latter issue alone, and since I have no aspiration of contributing to the critical literature of stylometry in general, I shall address Lutoslawski's analysis only as it bears upon that issue and only under the presumption of its general validity. Assuming the general validity of Lutoslawski's method, that is to say, I will examine the question whether indeed it indicates that the *Timaeus* was composed later than the *Parmenides*. The conclusion of my argument will be that it does not.

My purpose, accordingly, is not to develop a new self-sufficient argument on stylometric grounds for an early dating of the *Timaeus*, or to join forces with Owen and others who previously have argued to this effect. Nor is my purpose to generate a critically reasoned assessment of the general reliability of this or that stylistic measure, or to provide a fresh appraisal of individual measures over which recent analysts have found disagreement.[7] My purpose is simply to show that *if* Lutoslawski's measures are taken at face value, after being purged of obvious misunderstandings and inconsistencies, then the effect of these measures is to suggest either (1) that the *Parmenides* as a whole was written after the *Timaeus* or (2) that if *Parmenides I* and *II* are treated separately, then only the former is clearly prior to the *Timaeus*. Either result is consonant with the account of Plato's ontological development presented in this volume, which prescribes at most that the new departure of *Parmenides II* comes after the final efforts in the *Timaeus* to rescue the earlier theory of Forms.

Here a summary description of Lutoslawski's approach may aid the discussion. Both the measures and the data with which Lutoslawski dealt were taken from the work of various predecessors, ranging from that of Engelhardt and Campbell around mid-century to the later results of Campbell in the 1890s. By Lutoslawski's characterization, these measures pertain to such

matters as "numerical proportion between verbs, adjectives, sub-
stantives, and other kinds of words . . ." (p. 70); "length, construction, and interdependence of phrases; the rhythm produced
intentionally or resulting naturally from the order of words selected; . . . avoidance of the hiatus or the repetition of syllables
with the same vowels or consonants; . . . the frequency of rhetorical figures and tropes . . . " (pp. 71-72); and so forth. The
stylistic features these measures pick out are referred to as "peculiarities of later style" (p. 162, passim). From the much larger
number of peculiarities treated by his predecessors, Lutoslawski
selected five hundred that occur in what he assumed from the
start[8] were the six latest dialogues—the *Sophist*, the *Statesman*,
the *Philebus*, the *Timaeus*, the *Critias*, and the *Laws* (pp. 75,
140). These features in turn were divided into four classes with
respect to importance. Least important are those described as
"*accidental* peculiarities, such as words or idioms occurring only
once in a dialogue" (p. 146, author's emphasis). Next in importance are the "repeated peculiarities" (p. 147), occurring from
two to four times in small to larger dialogues, and more than
twice overall but less than once in twelve pages in the two longest
works. Peculiarities occurring more often than these, but less
than once in two pages in the Didot edition, in turn are referred
to as "important" (p. 148). The fourth class, finally, which he
terms "very important" (p. 151), is reserved for words and idioms that occur even more frequently, and for a small number
of other peculiarities described as "most characteristic" (p. 150).

After the tallying of peculiarities in each of the four classes
for a given dialogue, the remaining steps of his method were
entirely mechanical. Each number was multiplied by a weighting
factor of 1 through 4, by order of increasing importance, and
the total of the four products divided by 718 (the total of the
Laws). The resulting quotient was descriptively labeled "*relative
affinity* to the latest group measured on the *Laws*" (p. 162,
passim, author's emphasis). The *Timaeus*, for example, was tal-
lied at 123 accidental, 58 repeated, 44 important, and 14 very
important peculiarities; hence its relative affinity was set at 60
percent (the result of dividing by 718 the sum of 123 × 1, 58
× 2, 44 × 3, and 14 × 4). The *Parmenides*, on the other hand,

with its tallies of 56, 42, 21, and 10, respectively, earned a relative affinity of only 34 percent. On this basis, Lutoslawski concluded that the *Parmenides* is earlier than the *Timaeus* (pp. 188-89).

Perhaps it was Lutoslawski's strict adherence to method that lulled the world of Platonic scholarship into accepting his conclusions. For one thing, he was conscientious in his attempts to test his measures before applying them to difficult cases. The test consisted in a series of applications to relatively unproblematic cases, in each of which the expected result was clearly evident. For example, not only did various parts of the *Republic* turn up in the right order, but also the *Theaetetus* was shown earlier than the *Sophist*, the *Sophist* in turn earlier than the *Statesman*, and the *Parmenides* as a whole antecedent to the *Philebus*. Results such as these were reassuring, and led Lutoslawski to great confidence in his method's general reliability. Another indication of due methodological concern was his awareness of the "influence of the size of a dialogue on the number of stylistic peculiarities found in it" (p. 184), and the resulting counsel of perfection that "only exactly equal amounts of text should be compared in order to give precise conclusions"[9] (p. 143). For practical purposes, however, Lutoslawski thought he could circumvent this problem by varying according to dialogue size the number of occurrences required for the ranking "important." Being a rather long dialogue, the *Timaeus* for example was required to exhibit from 5 to 26 occurrences for a peculiarity to be ranked "important," while occurrences in the considerably shorter *Parmenides* qualified for this ranking by falling within the range 4 to 15. Yet another indication of concern for method was Lutoslawski's insistence that statistical inferences should not be drawn from small sets of data (p. 142). All in all, the stylistic measures he employed covered several thousands of instances, and were sensitive to peculiarities of many different sorts.[10]

Despite Lutoslawski's methodological punctiliousness, however, certain of his results provided immediate indications of faulty technique. One was the great disparity in relative affinity (to the *Laws*) between the *Timaeus* and the *Critias*. Whereas the *Timaeus* produced an affinity rating of 60 percent, thus fulfilling his unquestioned expectation that it would turn up among the very latest dialogues, the *Critias* was rated at only 24 percent—the level of several writings of the middle period (e.g., the *Phaedo* and Books VIII-IX of the *Republic*). Lutoslawski's explanation of this anomaly was that the eleven pages of the *Critias* "are insufficient for a stylistic determination, so long as we deal only with a few hundred stylistic tests" (p. 184). Yet no reason was suggested why eleven pages should provide an inadequate sample with his five hundred measures, or why exactly the number of pages of a given dialogue (as distinct from number of peculiarities entering into a sample) was relevant to his method at all. Lacking such explanations, we should deem it no less reasonable to give the *Timaeus* an early dating on the basis of its obvious relationship to the *Critias* than to date the *Critias* later on the basis of the *Timaeus* (as he did). To be sure, Lutoslawski was well aware that the size of a dialogue has a "great influence . . . on the number of peculiarities found in it" (p. 184)—the only apparent reason being that more pages provide more opportunities for more peculiarities to occur. This being the case, however, the obvious remedy would be to normalize the total count of a given peculiarity by dividing that count by a factor proportionate to the number of pages from which occurrences are drawn—in effect, to expect two or three times more occurrences from one dialogue than from another roughly contemporaneous with it when the first is two or three times longer than the second. In contrast with this obvious and straightforward expedient, Lutoslawski's device of requiring variable counts for the ranking "important" according to dialogue length appears both arbitrary and ineffective. In point of fact, there is no reason at all to think that the effect of the double length of the *Phaedo* over the *Meno*, for example, would be counteracted in relevant respects by making the cutoff between "important" and "very important" 24 for the former and 11 for the latter. Another sign of trouble appears in the strikingly different affinity ratings for the *Republic* overall (57%) and for the several parts that he treats individually (7%, 31%, 36%, 26%, 18%). Since increasing level of affinity rating is supposed to indicate increasing chronological proximity to the *Laws*, it seems quite unaccountable that the dialogue as a whole should rate so much higher than any one of its major parts. The rating of 7 percent for Book 1, in fact, is practically the same as the 6 percent for the *Charmides* (of closely comparable length), while that for the dialogue overall is practically the same as the 56 percent for the *Philebus*. Although Lutoslawski did not address himself to this problem,[11] results that place the whole dialogue at the opposite end of the chronological scale from one of its major parts seem entirely unacceptable. Similar problems appear in the case of other groupings with which he experimented—while the *Theaetetus*, the *Parmenides*, the *Philebus*, the *Timaeus*, and the *Critias* as a group rank at 95 percent, for example, the highest ranking for any one of the five individually is the 60 percent of the *Timaeus*.

A careful look at Lutoslawski's method in operation, in fact, reveals other flaws which, although not accounting for these anomalies directly, at least make it less surprising that they should occur. One has to do with the use made of the classifications "accidental," "repeated," "important," and "very important." The purpose of these distinctions was to allow assignment of extra weight to peculiarities deemed more significant—hence the weighting factors 'x1', 'x2', 'x3', and 'x4', respectively. For the most part, inclusion in one or another class was determined by number of occurrences of a given peculiarity in a given context (with higher cutoff levels, as noted, for longer writings). Independently of these numerical criteria, however, Lutoslawski designated 6 particular peculiarities for the 'x2' weighting (p. 148), 30 for the 'x3' (pp. 149-50), and 18 for 'x4' (pp. 150-51). Apart from the apparent arbitrariness in selection of these special peculiarities, however, there are at least a dozen among them that should not appear on his list of five hundred stylistic peculiarities in the first place. Several (16 through 20) are peculiarities that Lutoslawski himself says "deserve renewed inquiry" and "should be investigated again" (p. 88). Others (206, 308, and 412, for example) appear almost as frequently in earlier as in later dialogues, and hence do not serve to indicate affinity with the very late *Laws*. Yet others (12 though 15, for example) are not stylistic peculiarities at all, and have no obvious relevance to the chronology of the dialogues. The upstaging of Socrates (peculiarity 13), for instance, is not a reliable indicator of an early date of composition, since Socrates is the main protagonist in the unquestionably late *Philebus*. And the fact that the *Sophist* and the *Statesman* (or the *Timaeus* and the *Critias*) are members of an unfinished tetralogy (peculiarity 12) has no obvious bearing on when they were written. Measures such as these are dubious in themselves, and certainly should not be magnified by extra weightings.

Since the purpose of my critique is to evaluate Lutoslawski's conclusion that the *Parmenides* antedates the *Timaeus*, it is appropriate to pay particular attention to several inadequacies in his method that favor the latter and are prejudicial to the former. One is that the five hundred peculiarities contributing to his statistics include only features appearing in what he assumes to be the six latest dialogues—the *Sophist*, the *Statesman*, the *Philebus*, the *Timaeus*, the *Critias*, and the *Laws* (pp. 75, 140). This means that if the *Parmenides* in fact is later than any of these six (the *Timaeus* in particular), this fact would tend to be obscured by the exclusion from the data of those peculiarities appearing in it alone. Since there are approximately three dozen peculiarities on the list that appear only in one of the dialogues among the privileged six, Lutoslawski's question-begging assumption that the *Parmenides* is an earlier dialogue might well have excluded measures that would have increased its affinity rating if duly included. An even more serious handicap dealt the *Parmenides* from the very beginning is that the measures taken over from Campbell, which comprise approximately one-third of the total list of five hundred (peculiarities 29 through 181), are never applied to the *Parmenides* at all. While Lutoslawski projects a rather complicated set of reasons for this startling omission (pp. 89-93), he makes no effort to compensate for its strongly prejudicial effect.[12]

To these considerable reasons for distrusting Lutoslawski's results regarding the dating of the *Parmenides* must be added the fact that, with the exception of the *Critias* (which by strict application of his method appears even earlier than the *Parmenides*), this dialogue is considerably shorter than any other of Plato's later period. To put the matter directly, its 31 (Didot) pages present fewer opportunities for stylistic peculiarities than do the 53 of the *Timaeus*. Since Lutoslawski's method did not incorporate an effective means of counteracting such disparities, his conclusion that the *Parmenides* is the earlier dialogue should be viewed as inconclusive at best.

My purpose in this brief discussion is not to remake Lutoslawski's method into a reliable technique for detecting chronological differences among the dialogues. I doubt that this can be done at all, and surely am not prepared to undertake it myself. Nonetheless, it would be unrealistic to assume that stylistic indicators are of *no* value with respect to chronology; and it would appear to be an interesting exercise in itself to approach Lutoslawski's data with a set of criteria that avoid the shortcomings so evident in his.

One of the more arbitrary aspects of Lutoslawski's method was his assignment of weights, primarily on the basis of frequency of occurrence. Yet clearly some peculiarities are more important than others. And while frequency of occurrence is not irrelevant, other considerations may be more directly informative. Among such considerations are distribution of peculiarities among early and late dialogues, and the distinction between patterns and isolated instances (Lutoslawski's "repeated" and "accidental" occurrences). Let us lay down as general principles of order (1) that shared patterns of peculiarities are better indicators of chronological affinity than sharing of isolated occurrences, (2) that features appearing only in known late dialogues are better indicators of lateness than those appearing also in early dialogues, and (3) that features shared by the *Laws* are better indicators of affinity with that particular dialogue than other features not appearing within it. On the basis of these principles, the following classifications may be listed in order of increasing importance:

> class A: isolated words, idioms, and other features shared
> incidentally by earlier dialogues but more dom-
> inant in later dialogues;
> class B: isolated words, idioms, and other features ap-
> pearing only in later dialogues;

class C: repeated occurrences of features (patterns) dominant in (although perhaps not exclusive to) later
dialogues, not necessarily including the *Laws*;

class D: repeated occurrences of features exclusive to later
dialogues and appearing in the *Laws*.

The ranking of C and D above A and B is secured by principle
(1), that of B above A by principle (2), and that of D above C
by principle (3). For purposes of classification, let us count the
Theaetetus, the *Sophist*, the *Statesman*, the *Timaeus*, the *Critias*,
the *Parmenides*, the *Philebus*, and the *Laws* as later dialogues,
and the *Republic* and prior writings as earlier (without begging
the question with respect to the *Phaedrus* and the *Cratylus*). Thus
conceived, classes A through D will provide our basis for relative
weighting.

To compensate for differences in length, no expedient appears
more suitable than dividing number of peculiarities by number
of ten-page segments (i.e., dividing by length of dialogue divided
by 10). This expedient is applicable, however, only to classes A
and B. Frequently repeated appearances of a peculiarity throughout a dialogue will count as a single occurrence of the pattern
in question, and hence will be classified under either C or D.
Although no precise numerical cutoff seems specifiable in general
between a few isolated peculiarities and the kind of repetition
that constitutes a pattern, clear examples of the latter are easy
to find among Lutoslawski's data (e.g., under items 307, 366,
378, and 453). It is compatible with the degree of precision
expected of the following exercise that the few difficult questions
that arise in this connection be adjudicated on the basis of the
analyst's intuition.

Our formulae for weighting, accordingly, will be the following:

(a) number of occurrences of class A, divided by length of
dialogue divided by 10, times 1;

(b) number of occurrences of class B, divided by length of
dialogue divided by 10, times 2;

(c) number of patterns of class C, times 3;

(d) number of patterns of class D, times 4.

The sum of the products (a), (b), (c), and (d) will be interpreted as indicating the putative proximity of the dialogue in question to the *Laws*. An appreciably higher sum for the *Parmenides* than for the *Timaeus*, in particular, will indicate a later date of composition for the former dialogue.

Two further adjustments are in order before we turn to the data. One is to eliminate measures based on peculiarities that appear with comparable frequency in both early and later dialogues, and hence do not provide indications of relative lateness (1-10, 23, 206, 243-67, 269-77, 279-85, 288-90, 292-94, 296-302, 305, 308, 311, 327, 354, 355, 365, 389, 403, 405, 406, 410-14, 420-22, 424, 440, 441, 443, and 457), as well as those defective in this regard for other reasons noted above (12-20). Another is to eliminate those measures that, although perhaps effective as indicators of relative lateness, were not applied to the *Parmenides* in Lutoslawski's analysis (29-181).

In applying the resulting 248 measures to Lutoslawski's data, I have kept separate tallies for *Parmenides I* and *II* (with Stephanus 135C4 the dividing line). Although Lutoslawski did not distinguish these two parts in compiling his results, with most of these measures the distinction can be made routinely with the help of Brandwood's *A Word Index to Plato* (Leeds, 1976).[13] Table 1 shows the results of these tallies, along with results for

TABLE 1

Tally of Peculiarities in the
Timaeus and the *Parmenides*

	NUMBER OF PECULIARITIES FOR			
CLASS OF PECULIARITY	*Parmenides* *I*[14]	*Parmenides* *II*[15]	*Parmenides* entire	*Timaeus*[16]
A	25	82	107	177
B	9	12	21	47
C	6	21	27	22
D	1	7	8	4
Didot pages	7	24	31	53
Weighted sum	84	135	162	133

the *Timaeus* from the same 248 measures. The weighted totals in the last line are derived by applying weighting formulae (a), (b), (c), and (d) to the counts indicated in the four lines preceding, and summing the results.

Interpreting this table with the qualifications previously discussed in mind, we may arrive at the following conclusions germane to the chronology of Plato's ontological development. (1) On the basis of those measures that are not patently prejudicial against the *Parmenides* and that provide an unambiguous indication of relative lateness, weighted according to formulae less arbitrary in application and more responsive to differences in length than those of Lutoslawski, the data suggest that if the *Parmenides* was composed as a single work then it was written later than the *Timaeus*. (2) Measured and weighted in this manner, however, the data suggest that *Parmenides I* was written substantially before *Parmenides II*. (3) Under the assumption that the two parts of the *Parmenides* were composed at different times, the data suggest that the *Timaeus* was written after the earlier and during roughly the same time period as the later. These three conclusions are wholly consistent with the account of Plato's ontological development presented in this volume.

COMPARISON OF THE PRESENT INTERPRETATION WITH GOSLING'S BY GOSLING'S CRITERIA

Among the signal contributions of Gosling's recent book on the *Philebus* (1975) are two lists of criteria for judging the relative success of alternative interpretations of what he calls the "Heavenly Tradition" and the "Determinant and Indeterminate," and what I have called the "godly method" and the "Limit and Unlimited," respectively.

The first is the longer list, containing predominantly (i) a series of points regarding the description of the "godly method" itself, and (ii) three points regarding the relationship of the method to other important sections of the dialogue. With respect to (i), the first section of Chapter 3 shows that my interpretation of this method, according to which it is basically a synthesis of the method of collection and division from the *Sophist* and the *Statesman* with a Pythagorean ontology (but with two senses assigned to ἄπειρον, corresponding to the two senses of ἄπειρον πλῆθος in the *Parmenides*), provides firm and intelligible answers to all of Gosling's concerns. Since my interpretation is akin to Gosling's own in tracing the method back to Pythagorean influences, it is noteworthy that mine makes clear sense of Socrates' remark at 18B5-6 that he has "always been devoted" to the method, whereas Gosling's involves an overtly mathematical technique unlike anything evident in earlier dialogues. Except for the interpretation attributed to Jowett (which I have urged is erroneously based on

268

a genus-species account of the method of division), however, all approaches do moderately well on these points, so mine gains no more than a modest comparative advantage on this score. It is with respect to (ii) that the available approaches encounter most difficulty, and exhibit most divergence. Gosling judges his own highly mathematical interpretation to falter most notably on the point that the "method is claimed to be of help with the important one/many problems of 15a-b, and so with the problems about pleasure and knowledge of 12-14" (p. 155). By Gosling's account, the "important one/many problem" in regard to pleasure and knowledge is how each can be a single Form (unit) and yet have different and even opposing manifestations—some pleasures being good for instance, and others bad. Given his own account of the "Heavenly Tradition," which seems to have nothing to do with the one/many problem thus interpreted, Gosling arrives at the unsatisfying conclusion that "we just do not know how Plato thought the Heavenly Tradition applied to the initial problem" (p. 177). On my interpretation the explanation here is quite straightforward. The opposition between good and bad pleasures, and similar oppositions mentioned with regard to knowledge, color, and so forth, is nothing more than opposition between parallel lines of specification or limitation in the course of applying the method of division. An illustration from the *Sophist* is the appearance of Sophistry under the opposing guises of the eristic sophists who generate false opinion in their subjects and the "Sophist of Noble Lineage" who removes this affliction. A second point under (ii) is one that Gosling judges gives his account an advantage over the more traditional alternatives, namely that the "illustrations of 17b-18d are introduced as illuminating the doctrine of 16c-17a" (p. 155). Nonetheless, he candidly points out, his interpretation shares an unsolved problem with these others, due to the fact that the example of Theuth "reverses the process described at 16c-17a" (p. 174). As Gosling sees it, 16c-17a describes a process of exposition, while Theuth's accomplishment is an illustration of discovery. In my interpretation, on the other hand, this very reversal of the process exemplified by Theuth was one of the clues that the "godly method" pertains both to the definition and to the creation of the elements basic to a given art or skill, just as we are led to expect by the onto-logical statement with which the method is introduced at 15C9-10. Far from posing a problem for my interpretation, this point contributes to its plausibility. Again my interpretation gains a modest advantage.

The third point under (ii) is that the "doctrine expounded here [16C-18E] is taken up and developed at 23 seq." (p. 155). This point overlaps with the first of the list of points governing Gos-ling's discussion of the later passage, which in fact is one of only two points on that list with which the several available inter-pretations have much difficulty in his estimation. As it appears on the second list, the point is that 23C-27B "is supposed to take certain tools from the earlier one" (p. 186). While pointing out how the other alternatives falter on this point, Gosling is able to make a convincing case that the terms πέρας and ἄπει-ρον are used unambiguously and in the same senses in the two passages in question. As he puts it, the "association *peras*-num-ber-measure has the same process in view, and '*apeiron*' is in both cases used of the continuum" (p. 200). Since this is precisely one of the points on which mine and Gosling's interpretations overlap, mine can claim the same advantages over the more traditional interpretations. The only remaining point of sub-stance on the second list is that in the examples at 25E-26B "*peras* . . . produces only good quantities" (p. 186), which is shown above not to pose a difficulty for my interpretation.

What I take to be the main difficulty with Gosling's account, however, is not represented in either list, but rather involves the suppression of a number of passages no less prominent than any to which his lists respond. As noted above, there are at least five passages (16C9-10, 25E4, 26D9, 27A11, 27B8) in which Soc-rates either says explicitly or strongly suggests that sensible things actually are constituted by the imposition of Limit upon the Unlimited, which Gosling's approach leads him flatly to deny (p. 178). Far from denying them, on the other hand, my account is directed toward an intelligible interpretation of these passages, and finds one available which is of a piece with the interpretations offered of other difficult passages in the first part of the *Philebus*.

On this score, my account at least appears to be more successful overall than other available alternatives, Gosling's included. If so, however, Gosling's account deserves considerable credit, because in a way it serves as a point of departure which makes exposition of the present account considerably less venturesome.

NOTES

INTRODUCTION

1. For reservations on τοῖς εἴδεσιν, see Ross (1924), pp. 161-62.
2. The case for translating ἀφεῖσαν ἐν κοινῷ ζητεῖν as "they set aside as a subject of joint study" in Allan (1960) seems too conjectural. I suggest "they jointly neglected to inquire into."
3. For discussion, see Vlastos (1969) and Sayre (1969), Chapter 1.
4. Here we consider the theory of the middle period exclusively. It is well known that in the *Sophist* a sense is provided in which Forms admit their opposites. Although the Same and the Different are opposites, for instance, the Same is different from other Kinds, and the Different is the same as itself. For discussion of the notion that a particular thing might instantiate opposing Forms, see Rohr (1978), p. 271.
5. Reference, of course, is to Plato's character rather than his historical counterpart. When clarity demands, reference to the latter will be indicated by 'the historical Socrates'; and so for 'the historical Parmenides', etc. One must avoid the common mistake of assuming that Plato's characters speak for actual persons (Plato included).
6. The most sustained discussion of the nature of the Ideas in the middle dialogues is at *Phaedo* 78C-80B. A striking peculiarity about this set of passages, however, is that the term ἰδέα never occurs in it, and that each occurrence there of the term εἶδος (79A6, B2, E1) carries the ordinary meaning of class (hence not of Form).
7. See Vlastos (1969), p. 301, for discussion.
8. The relationship between Socrates' remarks on causation and the method of hypothesis described at 100A and 101E is discussed in Sayre (1969), pp. 3-15.
9. Although Socrates' suggesting this to Hermogenes of course does not show that Plato accepted such a problematic view (see White [1976], Chap. 6, in this connection), it does indicate his interest in conditions of proper naming during his mid-career. Note that some commentators place the *Cratylus* before the middle period (e.g., Taylor [1926], p. 75), others among the later dialogues (e.g., Owen,

as alleged by Cherniss in Allen [1965], p. 339). For yet other conjectures, see Ross (1951), p. 2.

10. The term, however, does not appear in the *Phaedo*; compare n. 6
above.

11. For current representation of this option, see Gaiser (1980).

12. This alternative is most forcefully represented in Cherniss (1945).

13. The explicit attitude of Striker (1970).

14. With Ryle (1939) and Owen (1953) notably.

15. An exemplary case is Gosling (1975).

CHAPTER ONE

1. An example of an argument that should be construed as elenctic,
but often is taken as "doctrinal" as a result of this assumption, is
the so-called "argument for hedonism" at the end of the *Protagoras*.
See Sayre (1963) for reasons.

2. An example is the argument with the "exquisite conclusion" against
Protagoras at *Theaetetus* 170E-171C.

3. This is not to assume, of course, that Plato never unintentionally
made a logical mistake in the dialogues. Plato's skill as a logician,
however, tends to be underestimated by commentators who miss
such masterstrokes as Socrates' refutation of Protagoras (see Sayre
[1963] for analysis) or the refutation of the historical Parmenides
in the second part of this dialogue (to be discussed in this chapter).

4. Socrates for most dialogues, but the Stranger for the *Sophist* and
the *Statesman*, Timaeus for the *Timaeus*, Parmenides for the *Parmenides*, and the Athenian for the *Laws*.

5. After the fashion canonized by Vlastos (1954).

6. A resolute task of Cherniss (1957).

7. There are four more occurrences immediately following at 131A6
and at 131B1, 2, 5, when Parmenides argues that the Forms will
be separate from themselves if in many separate things.

8. At *Sophist* 245A1-2, a whole is characterized as "an ensemble of
parts with the property of unity" (πάθος μὲν τοῦ ἑνὸς ἔχειν ἐπὶ
τοῖς μέρεσι πᾶσιν); at *Theaetetus* 205A4-5 as that from which
nothing is missing. But Forms are incomposite (*Phaedo* 78C6) and
each one in itself (*Republic* 476A6-9). A comparable definition at
Parmenides 137C7-D1) requires that what is strictly one cannot be
many and hence not be a whole. The same is said at *Parmenides*
157C.

274

9. It is Plato, of course, and not Parmenides who prevents pursuit of this insight. Given the likelihood that Plato was aware of the subtleties of the conversation he wrote between these two characters, interpreters of this passage should (i) be sensitive to these nuances and (ii) try to account for them.

10. This aspect of the theory, of course, was modified in the *Sophist*, where a sense was defined in which all Forms, including Sameness, are different from other Forms, each, including Difference, the same as itself, etc.

11. Aristotle, *Metaphysics* 990b17; cf. Alexander, *In Metaphysica* 83.34, 84.5-6.

12. Vlastos (1954), p. 233, gives essentially this translation, but goes on to gloss "by which all appear large" as in effect "in virtue of which we *apprehend* all these things as large." This gloss is dubious, since the point of the theory of participation is to account for how things present themselves as having certain characters, not how we apprehend them as such. As the *Theaetetus* shows, Plato's theory of participation plays no part in his theory of perception.

13. See Cherniss (1944), p. 234. It is argued later here that the expression ἄπειρον (τὸ) πλῆθος is ambiguous in the *Parmenides*, meaning "indefinitely numerous" in some occurrences and "indefinitely multitudinous" in others. The notion of an infinite regression is intelligible only in connection with the former sense. My suggestion is that the use at 132B2-3 involves the latter sense instead. Use of τὸ at 132B2 argues no more for the former sense here than at 143A2 and 144E5.

14. Not all Forms are instantiated in more than one thing (e.g., that of the Living Creature in the *Timaeus*), and nothing in the argument here suggests otherwise.

15. As several commentators have pointed out, this version of the "third man" argument is not logically tight as it stands, and in fact involves various assumptions that Plato by this time might have been inclined to reject. One is the assumption that Forms themselves share the properties which they impart to participating objects; another the assumption that the presence of its typical character in a given Form must be accounted for with reference to another Form in turn. The first of these is called by Vlastos (1954), p. 236, the "Self-Predication Assumption." The second is close in effect to his "Nonidentity Assumption," but worded less deviously. One advantage of the present wording is to make clear that one would be motivated to accept the latter assumption only if already committed to the for-

mer. As Vlastos and many others have seen, the dialogues indicate an ambivalent attitude toward the first, ranging from outright acceptance in some earlier dialogues (e.g., *Protagoras* 330C-E) to implicit rejection in some later (e.g., Motion in the *Sophist*). Since this ambivalence presumably carries over to the latter assumption as well, the problem of why Plato did not produce an explicit rebuttal to the "third man" argument (as in Vlastos [1954], pp. 254-57, and Cherniss [1957], pp. 368-74) is of dubious cogency. Plato is not putting arguments in the mouth of Parmenides that he himself finds puzzling and threatening. He is using Parmenides to raise questions to which the middle theory of Forms never provided cogent answers, and which require attention in subsequent modifications of the theory.

16. As recounted by Aristotle, in *Metaphysics* 1078b12-32; see the Introduction for commentary.

17. It may be noted in this regard that Vlastos' analysis of the alleged "Nonidentity Assumption" behind these arguments in fact does not apply to the version at 132D-133A, since this version has nothing to do with how we apprehend characters (cf. Vlastos [1954], p. 237).

18. Cf. *Metaphysics* 987b9-10, and the Introduction of this work.

19. Despite the imaginative efforts of Vlastos (1954), pp. 254-55.

20. Despite the insistence of Cherniss (1957), p. 374.

21. τὰ πρός τι. *Categories* 7b15-35, in fact, seems to be taking issue with 133C10-D1, in arguing against the complete generality of "the opinion that correlatives by nature exist at one and the same time" (Δοκεῖ δὲ τὰ πρός τι ἅμα τῇ φύσει εἶναι).

22. Aristotle seems to be taking exception with the upshot of this argument when he suggests that "the object of knowledge seems to exist before knowledge itself" (τὸ γὰρ ἐπιστητὸν πρότερον ἂν δόξειε τῆς ἐπιστήμης εἶναι: *Categories* 7b23-24).

23. No commentator who has spent comparable time with each of the five arguments raised in *Parmenides I* should be content with the disproportionate attention given the "third man" argument in recent literature. The difficulty behind the final argument is most devastating of all.

24. As we shall see, relinquishing the tenet of radical separation between Forms and sensible objects does not prevent Plato from continuing to employ the metaphors of "paradeigmatism." Presence of the latter in the *Philebus* does not support the claim that Plato's on-

tology remained unchanged in the later dialogues, contrary to Cherniss (1957), p. 361.

25. The term γυμνάζω appears five times in the following Stephanus page, and has encouraged some commentators to look upon what follows as a particularly strenuous display of mental calisthenics. It is unlikely that Plato would waste thirty pages of discourse by the most formidable character appearing in his dialogues on logical frivolity, however vigorous.

26. When no deep-seated metaphysical issues hang in the balance, I have been guided only by considerations of felicity in translating forms of the verb εἰμί, with no attention to distinctions among uses so diligently explored in Kahn (1973). It is clear, nonetheless, that ἔστιν here has an existential use, expressible alternatively as '(such a thing) is' or 'existence (of such a thing)'.

27. For textual exegesis of these passages, and for an analysis of the method itself, see Sayre (1969), Chapter 1.

28. Another way of improving upon this aspect of the hypothetical method of the *Phaedo* and the *Republic* is the method of division in the *Sophist*. This raises questions about priority of the two improved methods in the development of Plato's thinking. Such questions are complicated by the fact that the *Philebus* describes and illustrates yet another method which, although resembling that of the *Sophist* in general outline, differs from it in important respects. The method of the *Philebus* is discussed in the final chapter.

29. To the best of my knowledge, this important observation is originally due to Cornford (1939), p. 114.

30. Turnbull (1978) maintains an interpretation of "If Unity is" according to which 'Unity' is a "placeholder for any relevant subject-term" and 'is' is "the same for a predicate-term" (p. 757). In this manner, we may read Parmenides' remark at 142C1-3 as pointing out that with Hypothesis II we are to be concerned with the hypothesis, not "If Unity is-Unity," but "If Unity is-. . . ."

31. It is commonly recognized that what Parmenides labels the third argument at 155E4 in fact is an addendum to the second.

32. Precisely this was denied of the others under Hypothesis III at 157C1-2.

33. If the order of Hypotheses V and VI had been reversed, the symmetry would be complete. There is no reason apparent in the dialogue why their order could not be reversed. This schema, and the list preceding, follow equivalent formats in Sayre (1978).

34. Since in most cases this assumption has figured materially in the

interpretations offered, the error in pairing is likely to be reflected in mistaken conceptions of what the hypotheses accomplish—either separately or collectively. Since so many different interpretations have been proposed over the centuries, it must fall beyond the range of this essay to criticize any one of them in detail.

35. Reference to the Forms as unities is even more prominent in the *Philebus*, a topic for discussion in Chapter 3.

36. The refutation here is independent from, and more elegant than, the equally tight refutation of Parmenides' basic thesis at *Sophist* 244B-245E.

37. Greek text reprinted is from Kirk and Raven (1962), originally from Simplicius, *In Aristotelis Physicorum*, Berlin Academy *Commentaria In Aristotelem Graeca*, ed. H. Diels (1882). When texts deviate, Kirk and Raven is followed.

38. This is not to suggest that "Theaetetus sits" is an example of knowledge. It is rather to draw attention to the fact that the Stranger's account of true and false discourse, although developed strictly in terms of Forms and Kinds, is nonetheless illustrated in terms of sensible objects.

39. Pythagorean ontological themes are present in the *Statesman*, and are prominent in the *Philebus*. Whether such are to be found in the *Timaeus*, as commentators often assume, is problematic. The account there of the constitution of the primary bodies out of geometrical figures is uncertain evidence at best, since numbers—not figures—were probably (see Kahn [1974], esp. p. 182) basic constitutive principles for the historical Pythagoreans.

40. Cornford (1939) and Raven (1948) have developed historical accounts of a running dispute through most of the Fifth Century between representatives of the Pythagorean and of the Eleatic schools. These accounts have been vigorously attacked by Vlastos (1953) and Cherniss (1950), among others. In speaking of Plato's involvement in the disagreement between the Eleatic and the Pythagorean viewpoints, I am not taking sides on this historical issue. Quite apart from the course of actual interaction between individual representatives of these viewpoints, it is clear that the viewpoints themselves stood in radical contrast as Plato received them. In taking a position with the Pythagoreans in opposition to the Eleatics, Plato is defending one distinct ontology against another. He may or may not thereby have entered an ongoing controversy between two doctrinely opposed groups of historical figures.

41. Topics treated under Hypotheses III through VIII are subsets of

these, with order reversed under all but vi. Hypothesis ii leads to treatment of exactly the same topics as Hypothesis i, in identical order. Under Hypotheses iv and viii the topic "one and many" replaces "limit and the unlimited." This may foreshadow the *Philebus*, in which Unity is revealed as the principle of limit, and "the many" are characterized as "unlimited multitude."

42. From Simplicius; see n. 37. The translation above is from Kirk and Raven.

43. Being driven anywhere implies time. A more explicit temporal claim is in fragment 5, from Proclus (Kirk and Raven [1962], p. 268): "It is all one to me where I begin, for I shall come back there again in time [πάλιν]."

44. This is the only flat contradiction apparent in *Parmenides II* (cf. Sayre [1978]).

45. This is apparent in Aristotle's definition of place as "the innermost motionless boundary [limit] of the container" (τὸ τοῦ περιέχοντος πέρας ἀκίνητον πρῶτον: *Physics* 212a20). The logical relationship noted in the text above seems to have been anticipated in part by Cornford (1939), p. 119, n. 2.

46. Cornford (1939), p. 138, reads too much into this passage in claiming it "shows that the existence of number follows immediately from the Parmenidean hypothesis itself, understood as positing a One that is not merely one but also has being."

47. Allen (1974) has argued that the unlimited multitude announced at 143A2 is a dense infinity, allied to but distinct from a strict continuum. The argument relies upon the analogy between the unlimited multitude and a line (p. 706), and the assumption that the divisions by unity and being at 142E produce parts corresponding to rational points on the line (p. 706). A line is dense with respect to rational intervals, in that between any two rational points there are yet others to be specified. Analogously, there are further parts of Unity between any two of its parts in Parmenides' derivation of the unlimited multitude. But continuity of a line requires density also with respect to its irrational points, and there is nothing in the derivation to produce irrational parts. What Parmenides derives in his first deduction terminating at 143A, Allen concludes, is a dense multitude that is infinitely numberable (p. 712), but not continuous. This would appear correct save for one crucial deficiency. Density in this sense requires order among points, which is naturally provided in the analogy by distribution along the line. But the parts of Unity which are indefinitely multitudinous as yet have no rela-

tionship of before and after. The derivation of number that Parmenides is undertaking requires both infinity and serial order. These factors are provided by the first and second generative arguments, respectively.

48. In Peano's approach via this general method, the first member of the series was identified with zero. If Plato had employed a similar version (which he does not, contrary apparently to Annas [1976], p. 53), the first member would have been two, since two was considered the first integer by the Greeks (cf. *Metaphysics* 1085b10). In the method of ordering actually employed by Plato at 153C-E, two is taken as the initial element.

49. Allen (1974) suggests that Plato could have relied upon this previous existence proof if he had wished (p. 712). It seems less conjectural to say that he did rely upon it, since (i) he needed it and (ii) it was immediately available.

50. Aristotle remarked at *Metaphysics* 987b34 that according to Plato the numbers could be facilely produced out of the Indefinite Dyad, *except the primes* (ἔξω τῶν πρώτων). If we entitle the constituent that "always necessarily is becoming two" at 142E7-143A1 the "Indefinite Dyad" (with Cornford [1939], p. 144), then Aristotle's remark would fit this passage. A more defensible candidate for the title "Indefinite Dyad," it will be argued subsequently, is the ἄπειρον πλῆθος of 143A2. Aristotle's remark would still fit under this latter interpretation.

51. Any integer not obtainable by successive additions of two to three would be even and hence not prime.

52. This conjecture is not really satisfactory, since the operation in question seems to be "plus one" rather than "plus two," which is needed to get the primes from three. A derivation based on "plus one" would be functionally equivalent to generation by the successor relation, which would render the multiplier operation of the text superfluous.

53. The expression ἄπειρον πλῆθος here cannot mean a "multitude without differentiation into definite constituents" as at 143A2, since definition or limit has been introduced in the form of number. At 144A6 and 144E4 the expression must have the sense of μέρη ἀπέραντα at 144C1—that of an unlimited number of unique parts.

54. Here Parmenides reverses himself with regard to his rhetorical question (never clearly settled) at 131C9-10 whether a single Form could ever be divided. We must bear in mind, when thinking of the legitimacy of this apparent reversal, that in *Parmenides I* a theory of

Forms is under criticism which had firmly maintained the inviolable integrity of the Forms, but that in *Parmenides II* a new theory is under development which might take a different stand on that issue.

55. For reasons that will become clear in the next section, it is noteworthy that equality here consists in identical numbers of membership, whereas at 151B-C it is a matter of identical numbers of measures.

56. Allen (1970). What follows agrees with his observation that the force of Parmenides' argument is hypothetical (p. 33), but on different grounds.

57. Among them, Aristotle (*Metaphysics* 986a20-21); Theophrastus (*Metaphysics* 6a24-25, ed. W. D. Ross and F. H. Fobes [1967]); and Alexander Polyhistor (via Diogenes Laertius, quoted in Cornford [1939], p. 3).

58. Cornford (1939), p. 58; Kirk and Raven (1957), p. 287. In this connection, however, see n. 40 above.

59. Fragment 1, from Simplicius, quoted in Kirk and Raven (1957), p. 288.

60. As Parmenides says at 135D8, the discipline he subsequently demonstrates by mounting arguments on his eight hypotheses takes the same form as the treatise of Zeno. The conditional form of the argument is indicated grammatically by the frequent appearance of the optative with ἄν (e.g., 143E7, 144A5, 144E9-10, 145A1-2, 145B3) when Parmenides begins to draw together his conclusions— i.e., in sentences that relate as apodosis to the original protasis "if Unity exists" (ἐν εἰ ἔστιν: 142B5-6). (See Goodwin and Gulick, *Greek Grammar*, Blaisdell Publishing Co., London [1958], 1393, for the rule.) In view of this, an accurate paraphrase of the overall results thus far under Hypothesis II would be "If Unity exists, then nothing hinders number from existing also, nor hinders this Unity from being both limited and unlimited." The next stage of the argument, it may be noted, builds on the hypothesis, already established conditionally, that "if [this Unity] is whole, then nothing hinders it from having beginning, middle, and end" (εἰ ὅλον, οὐ καὶ ἀρχὴν ἂν ἔχοι καὶ μέσον καὶ τελευτήν: 145A5-6; note also ἔχοι ἂν at 145B1). Cornford (1939) cites the use of the optative at 145A6, and notes that it could be translated 'might have'. This emphasis upon possibility need not conflict with the frequent appearance of ἀνάγκη throughout this section. I suggest that the form of inference is 'If . . . , then necessarily there might be . . .' .

61. The only appearance of the expression in *Parmenides I* is at 132B2-

281

3, in the context of the first "third man" argument. According to the traditional way of reading this particular argument, as leading to an infinite regress, the expression would take the sense of indefinitely numerous. In the first section of this chapter it has been argued that a more satisfactory reading shows the argument to be aimed at proving that the (separate) Forms are incapable of serving a limiting function. To say that the Forms are ἄπειρον πλῆθος is instead to say that they themselves—like the sensible things they are supposed to characterize—are multitudinous and without limit.

62. See Cornford (1939), p. 210, n. 4.

63. Ross (1924), Vol. 1, pp. 171-72, justifies retaining τοὺς ἀριθμούς in favor of τὰ εἴδη.

64. Not "the same number of measures" as in Cornford's translation. The distinction is potentially important because the concept of measure is more basic than that of number in Euclid's *Elements*. Number is first defined in Book VII; the concept of measure figures in certain key definitions of Book V.

65. This is evident in the argument for Proposition 7, Book V, to the effect that equal magnitudes have the same ratio to the same magnitude, and vice versa. A key step in the argument is that if D and E are equimultiples of equal magnitudes A and B, then D and E are equal. Since by Definition 2 a magnitude is a multiple of another when it is measured by that other, then for D and E to be equimultiples of equal magnitudes is for D and E to have the same measures, and hence themselves to be equal. This conception of equality is more explicit in the argument for Proposition 16 of Book VII, a key step in which is that when a given number A measures C and D the same number of times, then the numbers C and D themselves are equal. Malcolm Brown (1972), p. 24, n. 1, finds this definition implicated in Definition 20 of Book VII also.

66. *Euclid: The Elements*, Heath (1947), tr., pp. 112-13.

67. The heart of this solution is Definition 5 of Book V, which Dedekind (1901), pp. 39-40, cites as setting forth "in the clearest possible way" the conception that an irrational number can be "defined by the specification of all rational numbers that are less and all those that are greater," which is the basis of his own definition.

68. Compare Definition 1, Book V, of the *Elements*, relating parts and measures in the case of magnitudes.

69. Heath (1947), tr., p. 113.

70. Ibid., p. 122.

71. The abrupt interruption by Aristotle, which several commentators

have remarked upon, may symbolize the effect of the ἐξαίφνης next mentioned—it is a "cut" in a continuum.

72. Heath (1921), p. 323.

73. Brumbaugh (1961) discusses this section of the *Parmenides* under the title "The Eudoxean Cut," but has little to say about the mathematical background that makes this title appropriate.

CHAPTER TWO

1. *Commentaria In Aristotelem Graeca*, Vol. 9, H. Diels, ed., Berlin, 1882. References to works in this series will cite page and line number, as above. Note that Simplicius here refers to "Great and Small," rather than to "the Great and Small" or "the Great and the Small" as at *Physics* 187a17. Aristotle vacillates, referring to "the Great and Small" on occasion (e.g., *Metaphysics* 1085a12, 1087b8, 1090b36, and 1091a1), but generally preferring to use two articles. By way of compromise, I will henceforth use the expression 'the Great and (the) Small'.

2. ΑΡΜΟΝΙΚΩΝ ΣΤΟΙΧΕΙΩΝ, H. S. Macran, ed., Oxford, 1902, 122.7-14.

3. *Commentaria In Aristotelem Graeca*, Vol. 5, M. Wallies, ed., 1900, 106.22; ibid., Vol. 6, G. Kroll, ed., 1902, 77.4; ibid., Vol. 17, H. Vitelli, ed., 1888, 521.10,11,14.

4. L. Robin (1908), J. Burnet (1914), E. Frank (1923), J. Stenzel (1959), and J. N. Findlay (1974). On Gaiser and Kraemer see the up-to-date bibliography in Gaiser (1980).

5. H. Cherniss (1945), p. 29.

6. Ibid., p. 71.

7. Ibid., p. 82.

8. Ibid., p. 15.

9. Ibid., p. 58.

10. Ibid., pp. 16, 24, 25, 30, 51, 59.

11. Ibid., pp. 58-59.

12. *Commentaria In Aristotelem Graeca*, Vol. 1, M. Hayduck, ed., 1891, 56.35; ibid., Vol. 9, 151.10, and Vol. 17, 75.34, respectively.

13. Cherniss (1945), p. 10.

14. Aristoxenus (n. 2, above); Simplicius, *Commentaria*, Vol. 9, 453.30, and 454.18.

15. Cherniss (1945), p. 83.

16. Ibid., p. 29.

17. The case for a public lecture is well argued in Gaiser (1980).
18. Cherniss (1945), p. 75; also pp. 47, 59.
19. *Metaphysics* 1090b20-21; 992a33, 1069a26; and 990a35-990b1.
20. *On Generation and Corruption* 329a15.
21. *Posterior Analytics* 83a33. See also *Metaphysics* 1091a6, where the notion of generating number from Unity and the Indefinite Dyad is called absurd (ἄλογα), and 988a1-2 where Plato's theory is called not reasonable (οὐ . . . εὔλογον).
22. An assessment of Cherniss (1945), p. 82, and others, which is not countered by the fact that Aristotle had much to say about mathematics in its simpler forms. For a contrary opinion see Annas (1976), p. 16.
23. For reservations on τοῖς εἴδεσιν, see Ross (1924), Vol. 1, pp. 161-62.
24. Ross (1924), Vol. 1, pp. 171-72, argues that references to εἴδη at lines 10 and 14 are probably spurious, along with that at line 22. If so, the hint derives from some transcriber and not from Aristotle himself.
25. See 991b28-29, 995b15-18, 997a35-b3, 1002b12-26, 1059b3-9, 1076a20, and 1090b31-32.
26. Among the better known loci are *Phaedo* 101C and *Republic* 524E.
27. For this description, see Shorey (1927). See also Milhaud (1934), pp. 271-80; Ross (1924), Vol. 1, pp. 167-68; and Robinson (1953), pp. 2, 3, 181, 192, 197.
28. Cherniss (1945), p. 76.
29. See references n. 27. An exception occurs in the discussion of Ross, who notes the phrase cited below at *Philebus* 56E3-4, but fails to connect it with the further remarks at 61E and 62B.
30. The same conclusion is reached in Wedberg (1955), pp. 113-14, and elsewhere (see Annas [1975], p. 146, n. 1, for other citations). It is true, as Annas points out (1975 and 1976), that these passages do not contain arguments for intermediates that can be neatly identified as bearing the brunt of Aristotle's criticism. My claim is only that the distinction among countable objects, Forms, and intermediates, can be found in the dialogues, not that it is argued for there in any particular fashion. Annas agrees that with all I am claiming in her remark (1975, p. 165) that it "is reasonable to hold that they [Aristotle in the *Metaphysics* and Plato in the *Philebus*] are both talking about intermediates."
31. See n. 24 for the probably spurious character of τὰ εἴδη. Coherent sense can be made of the passage by reading "come the Forms—

i.e., the numbers," stylistically awkward as it may be. As noted above, one of Aristotle's main claims regarding Plato's philosophy is that he made the Forms numbers.

32. Aristotle returns at 988a13-14 to say almost the same about the Forms themselves, but in terms of predication rather than participation.

33. All four causes of Aristotle are discernible in the section of the *Republic* focused around the image of the Divided Line. Before this image we find the description of the ideal philosopher, who is the material cause of knowledge, and the simile of the Sun, which depicts its final cause. The formal cause of knowledge is represented by the Divided Line itself, while the efficient cause is portrayed in the Allegory of the Cave. See also Ross (1924), Vol. 1, pp. 176-77, in this regard.

34. Aristotle's conviction that this principle played the role of matter for Plato may be behind his remark at *Physics* 209b35-210a2 that the Great and (the) Small is the space of the *Timaeus*, which (he says) Plato there called ὕλη. Among several anomalies associated with this remark is that the *Timaeus* does not contain the term ὕλη in the sense of matter at all (compare 69a6). It is of course possible that Aristotle saw an earlier (or later?) version of the *Timaeus* than the one we have which did employ the term in that sense.

35. Cherniss (1957), p. 374.

36. See also 991b9-10, 1073a17-22, 1080b11-12, and 1091b26.

37. Connection with Plato's views as reported at 988a11-14 is established by reference to the Great and (the) Small as unequal (ἄνισον: 1091b32), and to those who call the unequal Evil (κακὸν: at 1091b35, and 988a14).

38. For example, at 1084a12-15 it is reported that "some say" the number of things in themselves goes up only to ten, which limitation is repeated several times in the lines immediately following and at 1088b10. This limitation is attributed to Plato by name at *Physics* 206b27-33. At *Metaphysics* 1073a17-18, however, Aristotle allows that the theory of Ideas has no special discussion of the subject. If Plato indeed held any thesis of this sort, the discussion following this latter admission suggests that Aristotle understood relatively little about it. Another peculiar doctrine attributed to Plato by name at *De Anima* 404b16-26 is that mind is one, knowledge two, opinion the number of the plane (three), and sensation the number of the solid (four). In introducing this particular passage, Aristotle refers to Plato's views in the *Timaeus*. Since nothing of this sort

appears in the *Timaeus*, however, and since other views expressed in this passage probably stem from Aristotle's own discussion "On Philosophy" (see Cherniss [1945], pp. 14-15, for argument), these notions may have originated elsewhere than with Plato himself.

39. E.g., *Metaphysics* 1082a13 and 1091a5.

40. *Commentaria*, Vol. 9, e.g. 151.7,12,14, 453.26, 454.8.

41. *Commentaria*, Vol. 1, 85.17.

42. *Metaphysics*, trans. Ross and Fobes, 6a24-25, 11b2-3. Although the evidential value of Sextus Empiricus' *Against the Mathematicians* in this connection has been questioned by Ackrill (1952) and Vlastos (1963), it may be noted that the expression appears there as well.

43. *Metaphysics* 987b25,26. What Aristotle says here, to be exact, is not that the Great and (the) Small or the Indefinite Dyad *is* the Unlimited, but rather that Plato differed from the Pythagoreans in making his Unlimited a dyad and in making his Unlimited from the Great and (the) Small.

44. *Commentaria*, Vol. 9, 453.24,27, 503.13.

45. Ibid., 453.32, 454.6, 455.10. However, see the following note.

46. Although the expression somewhat more naturally bears the translation 'the nature of the unlimited', it will be argued in the following chapter that in at least one of its occurrences in the *Philebus* the translation 'the Unlimited Nature' is called for. In none of the occurrences in either Simplicius or the *Philebus*, moreover, does 'Unlimited Nature' seem entirely out of place.

47. Or 'the Indefiniteness of the Unlimited'; *Commentaria*, Vol. 9, 453.35, and 455.2.

48. Ibid., 247.35.

49. Commenting on *Physics* 207a29-32, Simplicius (503.13) reports that in his *On the Good* Aristotle said that the Great and (the) Small was matter. The same message is contained in his comment on *Physics* 209b11-17 (542.9-12), with the *Timaeus* named as the place where matter is called the participant and the "unwritten seminars" as the place it is called the Great and (the) Small. The gratuitous identification of the participant and matter in the *Timaeus* made by Aristotle at *Physics* 209b11-13 may have led him to interpret Plato's remarks about the Great and (the) Small in the lecture as veiled claims about his favorite principle, matter. Simplicius naturally would have perpetuated the error. Another Aristotelian characterization of the Great and (the) Small that seems simply mistaken with reference to Plato is that of not-being. A

careful reading of *Physics* 192a6-12, however, seems to leave open the possibility that Aristotle here is distinguishing Plato from some of his followers who in fact were guilty of that characterization. See Cherniss (1945), pp. 18-25, for effective criticism of these peculiar views.

50. Hermodorus may have been influenced by Aristotle's misconception that Plato was trying to anticipate his notion of matter.

51. Cornford (1939), p. 144. This section of the *Parmenides* was discussed at length in Chapter 1.

52. Taylor (1927), p. 22.

53. Ibid., p. 18.

54. Cornford (1939), p. 178. This interpretation is at least as early as Porphyry, via Simplicius *Commentaria*, Vol. 9, 248.6-7), and as recent as Findlay (1974), p. 61.

55. Ross (1924), Vol. 1, p. ix.

56. The derivation under Hypothesis 11 of the *Parmenides* is of the possibility of sensible things, not of sensible things per se. This was argued in Chapter 1.

57. That Cornford entertains so many different conceptions of the Indefinite Dyad appears less strange when we realize that for him (following Robin [1908]) this principle appeared under several guises other than the Great and (the) Small, including "the unequal," "plurality," etc.; see Cornford (1939), p. 155.

58. Cornford (1939), p. 209. Another example of an indefinite qualitative continuum, which Cornford cites from the *Philebus* directly, is the relative pitch of musical tones (p. 157).

59. Ibid., p. 209.

60. Ross (1924), Vol. 1, pp. 170-71. Ross notes that only Porphyry among the commentators connected Plato's Great and Small with the More and Less of the *Philebus*. Ross admits confusion, however, as to the manner in which the indeterminate is subjected to limit in producing quantitative determination, and claims that "there is no hint in the *Philebus* of the elaborate doctrine of which Aristotle tells us, according to which the great and small played a double part, that of uniting with the One to form the Ideas, and that of uniting with the Ideas to form particular things." This claim, we shall see, is incorrect.

61. Stenzel (1959), p. 87.

62. The author of this passage clearly believes that number has something to do with the nature of things. If the author is not Plato, at least he may be taken as speaking in Plato's behalf.

63. The author appears to think that mathematical proportions have something to do with the imposition of Forms and Kinds in nature.

64. Taylor interprets ὅμοιος and ἀνόμοιος in the *Epinomis* passage as "commensurable" and "incommensurable." Not all commentators accept this interpretation.

65. Heath (1921), pp. 91ff.

66. The designation refers to the approximation provided to the ratio of the diagonal to the side of the isosceles right triangle:

side	*diagonal*
1	1
2	3
5	7
12	17
29	41
	etc.

67. The simplest rule for producing this table is to add a side-number to its corresponding diagonal to get the next side, and to add a side to its immediate predecessor to get the corresponding diagonal. This table is equivalent to the unending fraction

$$1 + \cfrac{1}{2 + \cfrac{1}{2 + \cfrac{1}{2 + \ldots}}}$$

in that both yield the series of integral fractions: 1, $1 + 1/2$, $1 + 1/(2 + 1/2)$, etc.; or $1/1$, $3/2$, $7/5$, etc. That this unending fraction equals $\sqrt{2}$ may be seen from the identity $a - b^2 = (\sqrt{a} + b)(\sqrt{a} - b)$, which with the values $a = 2$ and $b = 1$ yields $\sqrt{2} - 1 = 1/(\sqrt{2} + 1)$. By successive substitution we get from $\sqrt{2} = 1 + (\sqrt{2} - 1)$ to the unending fraction in question. The unending series specified by the "table of sides and diagonals" thus provides a numerical equivalent of the irrational quantity $\sqrt{2}$. More notably for Taylor's purposes, it also provides a means of approximating that quantity within any specified margin of inaccuracy. A few simple calculations confirm that the first $(1/1)$, third $(7/5)$, fifth $(41/29)$, etc., members of the series increase in rapidly decreasing increments toward the value of the second $(3/2)$, while the second, fourth $(17/12)$, sixth $(99/70)$, etc., decrease in rapidly decreasing increments toward the value of the first. Thus we have two series of fractions, converging upon $\sqrt{2}$, no member of the first being as large as any member of the second, and no member of the second as small as any member of the first.

68. Taylor (1926), p. 432. Thompson (1929) agrees; p. 47.

69. Taylor (1927), p. 14.

70. In an arithmetical context, ἀριθμός referred to the positive integers for most writers of the classical period; see Knorr (1975), p. 9.

71. In view of thesis (4) that the Forms are numbers, it might be suggested in Taylor's behalf that an intelligible account of (1) carries over to (3) as well. Until we are reasonably sure what thesis (4) means, however, we should resist this move as facile and unhelpful. The explanations of (1) and (3) to be proposed here are in fact sharply divergent.

72. Eudoxus was recognized in antiquity for having developed the theory behind the treatment of proportions in Book v of the *Elements*; see Thomas (1951), pp. 419-21; Struik (1967), p. 45; Knorr (1975), p. 287; and Heath (1947), Vol. 2, p. 121. Kline (1972) maintains that Book v is generally "considered to be the greatest achievement of Euclidean geometry" (p. 68).

73. The translation is Heath's (1947), Vol. 2 (his emphasis).

74. Although the early Pythagoreans identified magnitudes with numbers, this was not accepted by the later geometrical tradition; see Knorr (1975), pp. 26, 91, 95-96. The definition is not applied to numbers in Book v. Hence reference to a numerical interpretation as an analogue.

75. The analogy is due to De Morgan, and is quoted by Heath in his exposition of the fifth definition.

76. Taylor (1927), p. 431, shows that this method applies to all quadratic surds.

77. In Heath's discussion, determination of a particular numerical approximation would depend upon observation of an appropriate construction. The purpose of the theory in its context, however, is not to provide numerical approximations of irrational quantities, but to prove proportionality of ratios, which Heath shows can be done by mathematical reasoning independent of observation (p. 124).

78. Kline (1972), p. 982.

79. Heath (1921), p. 327; see also Heath (1947), Vol. 2, pp. 124, 126.

80. Struik (1967), p. 161.

81. Dedekind (1901), pp. 39-40.

82. For instance, G. Huxley in his essay on Eudoxus in Gillispie (1971), p. 466.

83. Dedekind (1901), pp. 9-10.
84. The complexity of the question whether and in what respects Eudoxus anticipated Dedekind is exemplified in the discussion of Nikolíc (1974), which on successive pages seems both to deny (p. 241) and to affirm (p. 242) that Eudoxus achieved a theory of real numbers isomorphic (p. 240) to Dedekind's. On balance, Nikolíc inclines to the affirmative position on this question (pp. 225, 226, 232, 242).
85. Dedekind (1901), p. 10.
86. Number is defined by Euclid as a multitude composed of units (Book VII, Definition 2). Aristotle identifies numbers as instances of discrete quantities and geometrical magnitudes as instances of continuous quantities in *Categories* 4b20-24.
87. *Definitiones, Geometrica*, Vol. 4, ed. J. L. Heiberg, Leipzig, 1914, p. 84. See Knorr (1975), p. 235, for translation, and p. 248, n. 53, for commentary.
88. *The Commentary of Pappus on Book X of Euclid's Elements*, trans. W. Thompson, Cambridge, Mass., 1930, p. 63 and p. 93, n. 2.
89. Book X, Proposition 9, lemma. A scholium to this proposition states that these unidentified works contained a theorem by Theaetetus, to the effect that if the ratios a/b and m/n are equal, the first and second pair respectively being lines and numbers, then $a^2/b^2 = m^2/n^2$, and conversely (Heath [1947], Vol. 3, p. 30). There is nothing in the context to suggest that the lemma was limited to commensurable quantities; indeed, its apparent similarity in concern to Theaetetus' definitions in his namesake dialogue suggests otherwise. But if the scholium is taken to pertain to incommensurable ratios of lines, it suggests an existing ability to deal with incommensurable numerical ratios as well. We should note that the genuineness of the lemma proper has been contested (ibid., p. 31).
90. Knorr (1975), p. 235.
91. Proclus and Diogenes Laertius. See Heath (1921), p. 291; also ibid., p. 246; Knorr (1975), p. 6; and Heiberg (1922), pp. 34-35.
92. See Knorr (1975), p. 45, in conjunction with *Metaphysics* 1092b8-13. In Knorr's discussion, the "metrical" tradition tracing back to the earlier Pythagoreans is so called because its "principle problem is the measurement of area" (p. 6) in terms of number.
93. See Heath (1947), Vol. 2, p. 280.
94. See Knorr (1975), p. 274, and the discussion following.
95. This reading is supported by an unequivocal use of the same term

to mean 'segmentation' in Simplicius' commentary on the *Physics* (*Commentaria*, Vol. 9, 454.6).
96. Heath (1947), Vol. 2, p. 112.
97. Simplicius (*Commentaria*, Vol. 9, 454.13-14), quotes Porphyry as saying that the Indefinite receives Limit by participating in Unity.

<h2 style="text-align:center">CHAPTER THREE</h2>

1. Initially (11B, 13A), the disagreement seems to be about what things are good—pleasure, enjoyment, etc., on the one hand, or wisdom, intelligence, etc., on the other. By 13B, however, the question has become straightforwardly "What is the Good?"
2. A helpful review of historically available interpretations is provided in Gosling (1975), pp. 153-65.
3. Some recent commentators believe that the Forms do not appear in the *Philebus* at all (e.g., Shiner [1974], p. 41). Others hold that the "ones" mentioned here are Forms, even though they do not fall within the subsequent fourfold categorization of "all that exists in the present universe" at 23C-D (e.g., Gosling [1975], p. 84; Guthrie [1978], pp. 207, 213). Yet others have attempted to locate them under various (see Guthrie [1978], p. 213 n.) or all (e.g., Striker [1970], pp. 78-79) of these four categories. The view developed in the following discussion is that the Forms result from the imposition of Limit, and hence relate to both the second and the third categories. Regardless of the view one adopts on this issue, however, there is no reason on balance to reject the majority opinion that the "ones" listed at 15A3-5 are to be understood as Forms. This does not involve taking a stand on the issue whether Forms in the *Philebus* differ in any ontologically significant way from Forms in earlier dialogues.
4. It is unfortunate that Plato did not put it more directly, since considerable effort has been expended among commentators debating the number of questions actually raised here and what they mean. For recent declarations on these issues, see: Calogero and Klibansky in Taylor (1956), pp. 257-59; Striker (1970), pp. 13-17; Gosling (1975), pp. 143-47, and Guthrie (1978), p. 207. Regarding the issue of number, it may be noted that the second question as formulated in the text above obviously could be broken down into subquestions if for any reason desirable. Regarding the issue of meaning, it may be said that the question as formulated above (1)

291

is what Socrates seems to be driving at, (2) is a question recognizable from earlier contexts (being in fact the old question from the *Parmenides* of how numerous sensible things can participate in a single Form), and (3) is the question answered in the passages following.

5. The questions are raised in connection with "unities" rather than Forms or Ideas explicitly. Indeed, the first explicit mention of Ideas as such in this connection is at 16D1, where their singularity is stressed (μίαν ἰδέαν)—and it has even been questioned whether ἰδέαν here means Idea (Shiner [1974], p. 41). The discussion below will make it clear why I think μονάδας at 15B1 and ἰδέαν at 16D1 both refer to Forms.

6. As Gosling (1975), p. 83, points out, reference must be to the Pythagoreans. This reference is particularly significant in light of the thesis developed in the present chapter that the *Philebus* contains the several doctrines which Aristotle in the first book of the *Metaphysics* said Plato shared with the Pythagoreans.

7. The term ἀεὶ is subject to various translations, including "eternally" (as with Striker [1970], p. 18) and "from time to time" (as with Gosling [1975], p. 83) as well as the "always" above. Since Forms are said to exist eternally, the reference of 16C9 under the first translation is to Forms exclusive of sensible objects. Under the second, in Gosling's reading at least, reference is to sensible objects exclusively. The translation above is intended to provide reference to both Forms and sensible objects. On one hand, as Gosling puts it, "we are often asked to agree that 'there is such a thing as . . .', even in cases where Forms are not in question" (ibid). On the other, as Socrates said at *Phaedo* 100B1, he has always (ἀεὶ) spoken of the Forms as causes.

8. The term σύμφυτον can mean either "natural" or "come about together," or both. "Connatural" seems the best translation in view of the interpretation of this passage developed below.

9. In his commentary on this passage, Alexander says that it refers to the second book of Aristotle's *On the Good* (*Commentaria*, Vol. 1, 262.19; see also 252.20). We know from Simplicius (*In Libros Aristotelis De Anima Commentaria*, M. Hayduck, ed., Berolini, 1882, 18.7-9) that this (now lost) work was supposed to be Aristotle's written report of Plato's lecture "On the Good."

10. Although Aristotle uses πλῆθος here, Alexander's commentary on a parallel passage specifies πλῆθος and πολλά as synonyms in this connection (*Commentaria*, Vol. 1, 250.15). That πλῆθος in this

connection was identical with the Great and (the) Small for Plato, as Aristotle saw it, seems apparent at *Metaphysics* 1087b4-8.

11. After a suggestion of Gosling (1975), p. 85.

12. Literally, one ought not introduce the classification of the indefinite with respect to the multitude.

13. Gosling (1975), p. 154. A helpful review of alternative interpretations available in the literature up to about 1970 is provided on pp. 153-81. In Gosling's estimation, none of these is free from major problems. I hope to show in the discussion following (including Appendix C) how my interpretation avoids these difficulties.

14. At *Statesman* 287C, the Stranger recognizes that definition sometimes requires other than dichotomous division.

15. This is discussed in Chapter 1, sections 3 and 4.

16. Chapter 1, section 4.

17. Notably at *Theaetetus* 202Eff., 207E; *Sophist* 253B; and *Statesman* 277E-278E. Meyerhoff (1958) lists additional uses of alphabetical examples in the dialogues.

18. The parallel with *Phaedrus* 265E is apparent.

19. Gosling (1975) provides a list of points to be accommodated in the interpretation of the "godly method," along with an analysis of how what he takes to be the three main interpretive approaches (the third being his own) fare in this regard (pp. 155ff.). Two problems no less serious than any posed on Gosling's list, for which as far as I can see the three approaches in question have no immediate answers, are (1) how the ontological statement at 16C9-10 relates to the statement of dialectical method following, and (2) how the illustration at 16D is "opposite" (ἐναντίον: 18A9) that provided by the story of Theuth. The interpretation above answers (1) and (2) simultaneously. A summary of how the present interpretation responds to Gosling's points is given in Appendix C.

20. The anticipated project of dividing pleasure and knowledge into Forms (Εἴδη: 19B2; also 20A6 and 20C4), which was supposed to show the relevance of the "godly method" to the question of which of these two is identical with the Good, is postponed when Socrates shows that neither pleasure nor intelligence by itself has that distinction.

21. Gosling (1975), following Striker (1970), translates this passage to read either "everything which is a number in relation to a number or measure in relation to a measure," or "everything which a number in relation to a number or a measure in relation to a measure is" (p. 92). The first is intended to place under Limit everything

that can be characterized by numerical predicates, the second predicates of numbers themselves exclusively. The translation above is aligned with the first, but leaves open more explicitly the possibility that Limit might include measures other than mathematical numbers. Gosling's and Striker's preference of the second is discussed in the text following.

22. The issue here is not whether a place can be found for the traditional Forms in the fourfold classification at 23D (see Striker [1970], Chap. 4, for a discussion). My response to that issue, to be developed in due course, is that the measures established by a (right) combination of Limit and Unlimited come as close as anything to be found in the *Philebus* to the Forms of the middle period.

23. The similarity may appear even closer if Limit is likened to Pattern, Unlimited to Receptacle, and Mixture to Imitation (= Becoming; *Timaeus* 52D3), and it is recalled that in a closely preceding passage (48E) Mind was identified as the creative cause of the world. In view of our conjecture that the Unlimited of the *Philebus* is what Aristotle called the Great and (the) Small, it is relevant that he appears to identify the Receptacle and the Great and (the) Small at *Physics* 209b35-210a1. This may help explain Aristotle's erroneous remark there that Plato called the Receptacle "matter" in the *Timaeus*. It should be noted that neither set of basic principles, that of the *Philebus* or that of the *Timaeus*, bears any significant relationship to Aristotle's categories in the *Organon* (cf. Striker [1970], p. 74).

24. Gosling (1975), p. 156.

25. Ibid., p. 187.

26. Ibid., p. 191.

27. This second characterization of Limit is part of a confusing sequence in which Socrates remarks to Protarchus that they previously had neglected to collect the family of the Limit as they had collected the family of the Unlimited, and then remarks that it might turn out just as well if, with these two rounded up, that one will emerge clearly. For help with "these two" and "that one," see Gosling (1975), pp. 92-93. At any rate, it is clear that 25D11-E2 is a second characterization of the class of the Limit. The first at 25A7-B3 contains no hint of these valuational considerations.

28. Gosling (1975), p. 188.

29. Striker considers problems regarding the valuational character of Limit and the Unlimited particularly devastating against what she calls "the traditional view" (1970), pp. 47-79.

30. Gosling (1975), p. 192.
31. Striker (1970), p. 51.
32. Ibid., p. 53.
33. Gosling mentions 52C (p. 186); 23C and 27A could have been mentioned as well.
34. Striker (1970), p. 58.
35. Crombie (1963), p. 424, author's emphasis. An associated short-coming that Crombie's interpretation shares with Striker's and many others is that it assumes the relation between Forms or Kinds in Plato's method of division is the same as, or similar to, the relation between Aristotle's genus and species. Thus, for example, Gosling characterizes this method as beginning with "the *summum genus* under which" a given object falls, and then "properly dividing the genus so as to be sure we have a proper subgenus or species under which to put our specimen," and so on until "we reach the *infima species* . . ." (p. 156, author's emphasis). The errors of this way of conceiving Plato's method of division are spelled out in Sayre (1969), Chap. 3, sec. 7. We may note that Gosling himself is uncomfortable with it (pp. 174, 175). Since this conception does not seem essential to any of the views under consideration, it is not necessary to address the matter again for present purposes.
36. As Bury explains (1897, p. 43, n. 17) following Badham, ταὐτὰ . . . ταῦτα cannot refer to the two principles πέρας and ἄπειρον, which certainly cannot be said themselves to be in the Unlimited or to express Limit perfectly, but must instead refer to members of the "family of Limit" (e.g., equal and double) at 25D3. A problem besets Bury's translation "instances of limit," however, inasmuch as mere instances presumably cannot be said to express Limit per-fectly. In the interpretation herein proposed, such perfect expression belongs only to the "right combinations" or Forms.
37. Gosling (1975), p. 188.
38. Ibid., p. 159.
39. Striker (1970) explicitly declines to take Aristotle's reports of Plato's later theory into account, on the grounds that the text of the *Phi-lebus* is continuous and coherent, and can be understood in itself, while with Aristotle we find only scattered remarks about assertions of Plato and his school, the understanding of which is in question (pp. 45-46). Gosling, on the other hand, actually refers to Aristotle's comparison of Plato's views with those of the Pythagoreans at *Metaphysics* 987a-b, but only to draw attention to the alleged doc-trine of mathematical intermediaries. His purpose in so doing is to

support his claim that Plato did not "consider mathematical items
... as in any way constituents of objects" (p. 179). Yet among the
points explicitly made in this very passage are that Plato considered
numbers to be causes of the existence of other things (987b24-25)
and that Plato agreed with the Pythagoreans in saying that things
exist by imitation of (although he said 'participation in') numbers
(987b10-13). Since the same is said of Forms (987b9-10), an easy
inference is that Plato considered Forms somehow identical to numbers. And Forms were unquestionably constituents of objects in
Plato's view.

40. All quotations in this paragraph are from Gosling (1975), pp. 165-
66.

41. Notably, the terms used at 25A7-B3 and 25D11-E2.

42. If my analysis in Chapter 1 is correct, the question regarding Eudoxus' interest in the irrationals should be extended to cover *Parmenides II* as well.

43. Gosling (1975), p. 169.

44. Gosling says nothing about Eudoxus' solution to the problem of
irrationals, which according to my account was a crucial step in
the development of the ontology that the "godly method" represents. For this, see Chapter 2, section 3.

45. As Gosling (1975) realizes (p. 178), his interpretation commits Plato
to the belief that a mathematical science of grammar is possible.

46. Ibid., pp. 196-97.

47. Ibid., p. 177.

48. Ibid., p. 176. The assessment of implausibility is due to Gosling
himself.

49. Ibid., p. 200.

50. Ibid., pp. 177, 178, 179.

51. The fact of the matter, of course, is that 15B is not easy to translate,
and that any straightforward reading involves a certain amount of
gloss. Gosling dwells at length on difficulties various commentators
have encountered with the passage, and rejects the interpretation
given in the section above as irrelevant to the illustrations involving
pleasure and knowledge (pp. 143-44). If my account of the "godly
method" is correct, this is simply erroneous. On this account, the
"godly method" is basically the method of collection and division
from the *Sophist* and the *Statesman*, and variety is introduced as
the initial Form is divided into different portions. In the illustrative
definition of the Sophist, for example, the "Sophist of Noble Lineage" is fundamentally opposed (as one who removes the conceit of

false opinion) to the other varieties of sophistry (including those that instill this conceit). Hence Sophistry, although one, is shown to have opposing varieties. By overlooking this connection between the problems of multiform pleasure and the more obvious meaning of 15B—a meaning his own translation makes evident—Gosling has made the task of interpretation needlessly complicated.

52. The fact that ἄπειρον and πέρας are not Forms, and hence do not submit to dialectical division, does not prevent their being subject to collection. A parallel case occurs in the *Sophist*, where examination of the views of "the materialists" and "the Gods and Giants" serves as a collection over forms and Being, which itself (like ἄπειρον and πέρας in the *Philebus*) is not subject to division. See Sayre (1969), Chap. 3, sec. 5.

53. Gosling (1975), p. 203.

54. Ibid., p. 178.

55. Gosling rejects the suggestion, it seems to me rightly, that forms of εἰμί refer only to Forms in the *Philebus* (cf. his commentary on 16C9 and 26D8-9).

56. A secondary meaning, as argued above, is that of "indefinitely numerous," for which we are well prepared by *Parmenides II*.

57. Simplicius was a sixth-century Neoplatonist, whose resources trace back to Plato's immediate associates, not only those (besides Aristotle) who were present at the lecture on the Good (*Commentaria*, Vol. 9, 151.8-10, and 453.29), but also one Hermodorus who wrote some comments on Plato (247.31-33).

58. The expression ἀπείρου φύσιν occurs three times in Simplicius' discussion, and three times in the *Philebus* itself, with variations sometimes suggesting the translation 'the Unlimited Nature' and sometimes 'the nature of the Unlimited'. Either rendition seems acceptable, as long as we remember that what either designates is a principle constitutive of other things and not itself a constituted entity. Regarding the latter rendition, this means that the nature of the Unlimited is not something distinguishable from the Unlimited itself.

59. At *Metaphysics* 1020a13, Aristotle speaks of limited multitude (πλῆθος πεπερασμένον) as number. In a parallel fashion, presumably we may think of limited magnitude as length.

60. The problem is that Porphyry apparently is trying to arrive at some sense in which numerical two is indefinite, thinking thereby to identify the Indefinite Dyad. The sense in question is that two, being even, can be doubled and halved, and thus partakes of excess and

defect, presumably forms of the Great and (the) Small. This approach in the search for the Indefinite Dyad seems completely misdirected. Porphyry appears to have fallen prey to Aristotle's misconception (e.g., *Metaphysics* 1082a13-25, 1083b36) that the role of the Indefinite Dyad was simply to double, a function of the numerical two instead.

61. *Commentaria*, Vol. 9, 55.20, and 56.35. This passage, commenting on *Metaphysics* 987b33, ends with the remark that the observations it contains come from Aristotle's "On the Good," thus linking 987b with Plato's lecture on that topic.

62. I have argued in Chapter 1 that it appears in the *Parmenides* also. In this connection, we may recall that the great controversy between the (mostly German) expositors of the so-called "esoteric teachings," and those of Cherniss's persuasion who argue that nothing is there to expound, is premised on the shared assumption that the contents of Plato's lecture on the Good nowhere appear in his written dialogues. Whether grounds for disagreement between the opposing schools remain after this assumption collapses is a topic for another study.

63. So Crombie (1963) is on the right track in proposing that a variety of the Unlimited "is a . . . quality-range, something like warmth, size, hardness, wetness or anything else which constitutes a respect for comparison" (p. 429).

64. An objection raised above to Gosling's interpretation is that he seems simply to ignore these explicit references to becoming at 25E4 and 26D9, and the supporting references at 27A11 and 27B8, in reaching his conclusion that Limit and the Unlimited have nothing to do with the constitution of particular things. Observing in his commentary on this passage that γένεσις "indicates the condition of physical particulars," he looks past the manifest implications and seizes upon the opportunity instead to take exception with Owen's suggestion that this passage reflects Plato's recanting of his earlier sharp ontological separation between being and becoming. In my view, Owen is right in this suggestion. Equally unaccountable, in light of these passages, is Striker's claim that things resulting from the mixture of Limit and the Unlimited are concepts (1970), pp. 63ff.

65. Jackson (1882), pp. 272-81. All quotations in the text above are from p. 278.

66. In Chapter 1, while examining the architectonic of the second part of the *Parmenides*, we observed that Hypotheses II, III, V, and VII,

appropriately paired as antecedents with their demonstrated consequences, entail conjointly that Unity considered in respect to the others is indistinguishable from the others considered in respect to it, whether it exists or not. In Sayre (1978) I argue that this result can be interpreted as showing that Unity cannot be instantiated independently of other characters nor others from it.

67. Although the *Timaeus* does not figure directly in the argument of this section, supporting evidence that Plato in his later years thought of Forms as serving this role derives from *Timaeus* 53B, viewed against the background of *Philebus* 25A8-B1. In the latter passage, Limit is defined as ratios of numbers or measures. According to *Timaeus* 53A9, the universe before it came into order was without ratio or measure (ἀλόγως καὶ ἀμέτρως). With this to begin with, Divinity formed the sensible world by imposing Form and number (εἴδεσι τε καὶ ἀριθμοῖς: 53B4-5). An intelligible reading of *Timaeus* 53A-B is possible according to which it characterizes the universe apart from intelligence as without proportion of (number or) measure, a condition remedied by the imposition of (measure and) number—i.e., of Form. Since proportion of number and measure is Limit, imposition of Form imparts Limit.

68. Whereas arithmetical numbers comprised only integers, μέτρον could be used (as at *Parmenides* 140B8ff.) to refer to irrationals as well.

69. In the previous section I argued that εἰδοποιοῦν could well be taken literally, as indicating the actual constitution of Forms out of Limit and the Unlimited. In light of our more recent discussion of the sense in which Forms might be constituted from the Great and (the) Small and Unity, Porphyry's use of this surprising term takes on added significance.

70. Findlay (1974) cites a similar claim by Sextus Empiricus, a commentator of less than sterling reputation, to the effect that in the construction of number Unity always sets the limits (p. 429). Cornford (1939) also was prepared to recognize a close relationship between Unity and Limit in a Platonic-Pythagorean context (p. 5).

71. As Annas (1976) puts it, "we know that Porphyry was using Aristotle's version of the lecture, and it is very unlikely that he actually fabricated" (p. 45, n. 55) this part of his report.

72. I have already discussed Gosling's helpful presentation of the main interpretive approaches (including his own), and his comparative analysis of the major weaknesses of each. This analysis is based on two lists of points that he thinks a fully adequate interpretation

would accommodate, one for each of the sections noted above. Discussion of how my own interpretation fares under these criteria is reserved for Appendix C.

73. That the main contents of *Metaphysics* 987b correspond to the ontological claims of the *Philebus* was proposed by Jackson (1882), without reference to the testimony of the early commentators. It is regrettable that the contenders in the controversy over the "esoteric teachings" were not persuaded by Jackson's argument, brief and schematic as it was.

74. Cherniss (1945), p. 10.

75. Simplicius, *Commentaria*, Vol. 9, 151.6-15, 453.25-30; Aristoxenus, ΑΡΜΟΝΙΚΩΝ ΣΤΟΙΧΕΙΩΝ, H. S. Macran, ed., Oxford, 1902, 122.7-14.

76. Aristoxenus, 122.7-14.

77. τὸ πέρας ὅτι ἀγαθόν ἐστιν ἕν (ibid.). Guthrie's translation, "that Limit is the Good, a Unity" (1978), p. 424, lends itself more favorably to the argument below, but seems to me less likely in the context (however, see ibid., n. 2).

78. Extant reports on the contents of this work by ancient commentators are compiled in *Selected Fragments*, being Vol. 12 of *The Works of Aristotle*, translated under the editorship of Ross, Oxford, Clarendon Press, 1952.

79. We should be grateful to one of the main contenders for his bibliography of recent contributions to this topic, in Gaiser (1980).

80. This passage figured in the argument of Chapter 2, section 2, that Plato was aware of a distinction between the so-called "mathematical objects" and changeable sensible objects that can be grouped and counted.

81. Since not all unified mixtures presumably are as good as that of beauty, proportion and truth, the passage makes more sense if we read οἷον for οἷον. My interpretation also suggests this reading, but does not depend upon it.

82. Comparative truth is the primary analogue of the ratio by which the Line is divided.

83. Jackson (1882), p. 284, seems to have anticipated that the Good of the *Republic* may be closely related to the Limit of the *Philebus*.

84. The possibility of different temperature scales does not detract from the fact that all such scales are based on these natural limits. Such scales offer an illustration of one thing that might be meant by "division according to natural joints" at *Phaedrus* 265E1-2.

85. Jackson (1882) would have found only one due measure in the range, his so-called "equable temperature" (p. 278).
86. Ibid., p. 283.
87. As noted, the terms ἰδέαν and εἶδος are used explicitly in this connection at 16D1 and 18C2, respectively. I shall argue that εἶδος at 32B1 might also be rendered 'Form' in this standard sense.
88. Gosling (1975), p. 204.
89. Ibid., p. 205.
90. Taylor translates ἔμψυχον as living organism, and takes this as what is said to be composed from Limit and the Unlimited, ignoring the term εἶδος. Gosling generalizes to "things whose natural combination of indeterminate and determinate makes them alive," taking εἶδος to refer to the form (lowercase *f*) of this combination. Hackforth translates εἶδος as "state" of a living organism, constituted of the Limit and the Unlimited. Jowett translates it as "class" of living beings, made up of the finite and infinite. Dies, on the other hand, translates ἔμψυχον ... εἶδος as "la forme vitale." This latter is the only translation fully consonant with the account of Limit and the Unlimited developed above, inasmuch as neither individual organisms nor classes of such are generated directly from Limit and the Unlimited.
91. The fact that Plato continued through the *Philebus* to hold a doctrine of the Forms as paradigms cannot properly be used as an argument to the effect that his ontology did not change in important respects between the middle and the very late dialogues. Apropos of a remark by Cherniss (in Allen [1965], p. 374) to the contrary, it is worth noting that the sense in which Forms are paradigms in the *Philebus* does not initiate an infinite regress of the type exploited in the *Parmenides*. The only one of the two "third-man" arguments that results directly in an infinite regress, I have argued on textual evidence, is that at 132D-133A. A premise upon which this argument is said explicitly to depend is that the Form and that which resembles it share one and the same character (132D10-E1). But in the theory of the *Philebus* the characters typical of Forms and of sensible things, respectively, are not the same. The characters of Forms are numerically exact proportions or measures that the characters of sensible things only approximate. Furthermore, what imparts characters to Forms is the imposition of Unity, not that of another (or the same) Form as in the case of sensible things.
92. Geach's choice of the standard yard and pound as illustrations of self-predication (1956), p. 267, is fortuitous. There is a sense in

which the standard yard is a yard long (as numerically exact paradigm), but it is not the sense in which another object might be a yard long (by inexact approximation to the paradigm).

Appendix A

1. Other appearances of this paradox in the dialogues are at *Euthydemus* 276D and *Theaetetus* 198E.
2. The (Aristotelian) process of epagoge, sometimes thought to follow elenchus in Socratic methodology, plays no part in recollection. The method of recollection stands alone among the several versions of philosophic method developed in the course of the dialogues as involving a one-way process exclusively. The significance of this will become clear in subsequent comparison with the two-stage method of hypothesis in the *Phaedo*, and the "upward and downward ways" of the *Republic*.
3. Jowett's translation of λόγοις (230B6) as "the dialectic process" is particularly misleading at this point. The practice of this specialist is not dialectic, but sheer refutation.
4. See Sayre (1969), p. 151, n. 13, for citations. To be sure, the method described appears sophistic; but Socrates was a member of the sophistic movement (see Kerferd [1981], pp. 34, passim, in this regard).
5. Consider, as an exception, the mental state of Theaetetus at the beginning of his namesake dialogue.
6. To give up recollection as an epistemological theory, of course, is not to give up the doctrine of immortality. There is no indication of any dissatisfaction with this latter doctrine anywhere in the dialogues.
7. δεύτερον πλοῦν: *Phaedo* 99D1. This method, we may note, is "next best" not to Socratic elenchus but to the impractical ideal of explaining everything according to "what is most excellent and best" (τὸ ἄριστον καὶ τὸ βέλτιστον: 97D2-3). To be called δεύτερος πλοῦς in this respect is no more a slur than identically the same ascription to the "god-given" method of the *Philebus* in comparison with the ideal of omniscience (*Philebus* 19C2-3).
8. See Sayre (1969), Chap. 4, secs. 2 and 3, for explication. A detailed discussion of the method of hypothesis, as developed in the *Phaedo* and the *Republic* may be found in Chapter 1 of that work.

302

9. See the discussions of this term in Robinson (1953), pp. 129-31, and Hackforth (1955), pp. 139-40.

10. The importance of this sequence is stressed at 101E, with the remark that only specialists in disputation (who have no concern for reality) mix the principle and its consequences together. An example of this incaution is provided in the *Meno*, where Socrates, after posing the hypothesis that virtue is knowledge, first purports to establish its truth by syllogistic reasoning (87C-88D), and straightway proceeds to show that its consequences are not compatible with the relevant facts (89D-96C).

11. This is argued in Sayre (1969), Chap. 1, sec. 2.

12. Unless Book VI antedates the *Phaedrus*, with its preview of the method of collection and division.

13. It seems clearly to follow that the square itself is more real than the diagram which represents it. An anomaly inherent in the mathematics of the Divided Line is that the objects of philosophy (D), which are the most real of the four kinds, bear the same ratio to the objects of mathematics (C) and to the objects (B) which are imaged by reflections and shadows (B). That is, if $A:B = C:D = A+B:C+D$, then $B = C$; hence $D:C = D:B$. While many commentators have noticed this anomaly, most are of the opinion that Plato either did not notice it himself or did not acknowledge it. That Plato did notice it is evident through a careful comparison of 511D7-E5 and 533E4-534A5. In the former passage, the states of mind corresponding to the four domains of objects are labeled (d) νόησις, (c) διάνοια, (b) πίστις, and (a) εἰκασία, with proportions among them as above. In the latter, after relabeling (d) ἐπιστήμη, Socrates remarks that as $c+d$ is to $a+b$, so d is to b. At this point, however, he advises dropping the matter, lest it lead to a discussion "many times longer than the preceding." Whether the anomaly had any significance for Plato beyond that merely of an untoward mathematical consequence seems conjectural at best.

14. If the Good were transformed into the Unity of the *Parmenides*, the case might be otherwise.

15. See Bluck (1955), p. 202, for example. Note 7, above, however, argues that reference to this method as "next best" is not to be taken literally.

16. A (barely plausible) countercase might be built on the basis of the puzzling mathematical characteristics of the Divided Line. Two classes of numbers satisfy the conditions: $A:B = C:D = (A+B):(C+D)$, with $B = C$ as consequence. One is the class of

303

integer triplets a,b,d, such that $b^2 = ad$. In this class, the ratio $a{:}b$ may be either rational ($1{:}2 = 2{:}4$, $1{:}3 = 3{:}9$, etc.) or irrational ($1{:}\sqrt{2} = \sqrt{2}{:}2$, etc.). The other is the class of triplets with general form: $\sqrt{n} - \sqrt{m}$, $\sqrt{n} - m$, $\sqrt{n} + \sqrt{m}$, when either n or m is not square. One member of the latter class is the triplet formed by $n = 5$ and $m = 1$, giving the proportion $(\sqrt{5} - 1){:}2 = 2{:}(\sqrt{5} + 1)$. This is the ratio known as the "golden section," which mathematicians and aestheticians from times immemorial have recognized as being particularly pleasing to the eye (for recent testimony and experimental evidence, see Warren McCulloch [1974]). It is (barely) possible that Plato had the golden section (or golden rectangle based upon it) in mind when he constructed the Divided Line, and thought of its unique aesthetic qualities as somehow reflecting the Good as the ideal of beauty. The commentator convinced of this would have the formidable job on his hands of making sense in the context of the extended equality, $A{:}B = C{:}D = (A+B){:}(C+D) = (C+D){:}(A+B+C+D)$, which results from this interpretation.

17. The epistemological counterpart of this theory is the conception of knowledge as some manner of unmediated, and hence nondiscursive, mental perception. At *Meno* 81C6, where the theory of recollection is first introduced, the soul is said to have *seen* (ἑωρακυῖα) all things in this and in the other world (of the Forms). In his first remarks about recollection in the *Phaedo*, for another instance, Socrates speaks of the Equal and other Forms as seen "before our eyes" (προοράω: 74E2,6). Another term frequently used in both dialogues is εἴδω (*Meno* 84A7,8, passim.; *Phaedo* 75D6,7), in the sense of "to see" or "to behold." And the terms 'behold' (θεωρέω, at 247C1) and 'have in view' (καθοράω, at 247D7) are used in the myth of the *Phaedrus*, which contains the third and final reference to the theory of recollection. Although most of these expressions have more abstract applications as well, all suggest access to the Forms by some sort of direct apprehension.

18. Contrary to the speculation attributed to Ryle by Bluck (1956), p. 40, that Forms are considered simple (albeit sublime) objects throughout the dialogues.

19. There is little weight to the conjecture that Plato continued to think of access to the Forms as direct apprehension, as maintained by Cherniss (1936), p. 8, and many others.

20. It is commonly agreed that the arguments in the first part of the *Parmenides* are directed against the theory of Forms in the middle

dialogues. In particular, it is agreed that the two so-called "third man" arguments found therein are directed against the conception of participation involved in that theory. As these two arguments stand, they are brief and incomplete, appearing to involve assumptions that Plato never made explicit. In the debate over what assumptions are necessary for making these arguments valid, commentators have been led to attribute diverse but invariably highly sophisticated theories of participation to Plato's middle dialogues (cf. Vlastos [1954], Geach [1956], Allen [1960]). Although Plato never discussed these theories explicitly, the argument goes, they are needed to make sense of the "third man" arguments, and hence must be implicit in Plato's thought of the middle period. A more realistic reading is that Plato did not have a theory of participation in the middle period at all, and that the arguments in the *Parmenides* relate to an effort in his later years to make the notion of participation intelligible. What is found in the middle dialogues instead is a theory of Forms that relies upon the notion of participation, without any particular concern to make that notion more clear itself. Socrates' expression of uncertainty about the nature of participation at *Phaedo* 100D5-6 (εἴτε ὅπῃ δὴ καὶ ὅπως προσγενομένη; however or in what manner [participation] might possibly come about) speaks for the middle dialogues generally.

21. As Allen points out (1960), p. 49, sensible objects cannot literally resemble Forms.

22. Cherniss is surely right in denying that Forms are themselves properties of particulars (1957), p.373. On the other hand, to suggest in the case of a given Form F-ness that 'F-ness is F' merely states an identity (ibid., apparently; more explicitly, Allen [1960], p. 46) seems too weak, inasmuch as 'F' in that expression presumably designates something about F-ness that leads us to call both it and its particulars by the same name 'F'.

23. According to White (1976), p. 145, Plato's view in the *Cratylus* was "that only Forms can strictly be named." This may bear upon Plato's general disinclination to confine himself to a precise terminology for talking *about* the Forms. Of particular interest in connection with the topic of the present section is that he never seemed to settle upon a fixed vocabulary of participation. Three different verbs were used to refer to the relationship itself, with occurrences in both middle and late dialogues. The most common is μετέχω, which is prominent in the *Phaedo* and the *Republic* as well as the *Parmenides*. Also commonly used in the *Parmenides* is

μεταλαμβάνω, which also occurs in the *Phaedo* and the *Protagoras*. Least common is κοινωνέω, with occurrences at *Phaedo* 100D5 and *Sophist* 264E2 (this latter is problematic, depending upon whether τοῦ σοφιστοῦ there refers to instances or Kinds; most occurrences of this term in the *Sophist* are in connection with relationships among Kinds themselves). A parallel looseness is found in the way Plato refers to the status of sensible things relative to the Forms in which they participate. The sense is always approximately the same: sensible things image, copy, imitate, or resemble, the Forms. However, several terms are used to convey this sense, among them εἰκών, ἔοικα, ἀπεικασία, and ὁμοιότης.

24. Allen's characterization of this aspect as a "fundamental doctrine" (1960), p. 48, for example, may be an overstatement.

25. Cornford (1935), e.g., p. 45. My appreciation of Cornford's discussion of this theory is not diminished by the fact that I do not accept his responses to any of the three questions above. The account that follows is an extension, with different emphases, of the account of the theory in Sayre (1969), which was developed primarily in reaction to Cornford's views.

26. Cornford (1935), p. 38, n. 3, glosses this remark as claiming that no perceptible thing has a perceptual property apart from being perceived, holding on to the notion that such things nonetheless exist apart from being perceived. As argued in Sayre (1969), to the contrary, it is precisely this "commonsense" notion of independently existing perceptible objects that the arguments between 152D and 155C are intended to refute.

27. Cornford (1935), p. 46, n. 5, identifies the active and passive motions as physical objects and sense organs. Similar interpretations are maintained in Runciman (1962), p. 19, and Gully (1962), p. 78.

28. See the useful discussion of McDowell (1973), p. 139, in this regard.

29. The equivalent expressions in Greek do not embody forms of the verb εἰμί.

30. Cornford (1935), p. 48, n. 1; Sayre (1969), p. 78, n. 24; McDowell (1973), p. 143.

31. Runciman (1962), p. 19. Even if this were an accurate reading of the theory in Plato's text, the theory would be different from Berkeley's in fundamental respects. One is that colors, sounds, and sensible things in general for Berkeley are caused (in the only appropriate sense) by mind, whereas in Plato's account they result from motions which are not even remotely mental in nature. Another is

that the occurrence of sensible things admits no distinction in Berkeley's theory corresponding to that between the twin fast motions in the *Theaetetus*.

32. It is not part of Plato's theory that offspring become parents in turn. Whatever continuity physical things may enjoy is not established by genealogy.

33. Again, Cornford's interpretation is too sanguine in allowing that the "eye which sees, or the flesh which feels, is itself a physical object which can be seen or touched" (1935), p. 50.

34. Ibid., p. 49. Jackson is credited with the relevant observation that the theory is never refuted by Plato.

35. In Cornford's own estimation, the argument is "conclusive." Runciman objects to Cornford's conclusion on the grounds that the theory of perception is incompatible with the theory of Forms, which he assumes Plato still held while writing the *Theaetetus*. As Runciman reads the theory of perception, it entails that no object "can be white, or loud, or hot, or hard unless it is being perceived to be so" (Runciman [1962], p. 19). But, he argues, Plato "certainly never thought that, for instance, the whiteness of snow did not exist unless white snow was somewhere being looked at by somebody." This argument is credible only if the expression "the whiteness of snow" is taken to mean the Form Whiteness itself, which certainly is not the same as the color white as it figures in the theory of perception. Runciman's objection thus appears to rest on a basic confusion between Whiteness as a Form and white as a sensible color. Cornford's argument is faulty, but for a quite different reason.

36. For details, see Sayre (1969).

37. The commonly accepted verdict that the *Theaetetus* shows that knowledge cannot be identified with true judgment accompanied by λόγος is simply erroneous. Unlike the first two hypotheses, this third is never submitted to a test for consistency. Failure of 3 or 4 (or dozens) of senses of λόγος to be adequate for the task does not constitute refutation of the hypothesis.

38. Aristotle's comment (*Metaphysics* 1078b15-16) that Plato was concerned with knowledge and its ontological requirements holds good for the later as well as the middle period.

39. The diagrams in Chapter 2, section 7, of Sayre (1969) are intended to make this clear. All five definitions illustrate the procedure of division. The only one of the five divisions that shows any promise of success—that associated with the wax block analogy—is pre-

ceded by a confusing (and probably corrupt) passage clearly meant to provide a collection of typical cases.

40. To the modern fisherman an unfamiliar form of angling, undoubtedly. A quotation from Homer at *Ion* 538D removes the puzzlement of why angling must be performed in daylight.

41. Senses A,X, and B,II, in Liddell and Scott (1883). If the *Theaetetus* had tested these senses, its results would have been different.

42. The term γένος is introduced at 253B9, but not to the exclusion of the more familiar terms εἶδος and ἰδέα, which continued to be used in this context and thereafter.

43. Commentators generally assume that division in the *Sophist* and the *Statesman* proceeds from the more to the less general, and accordingly that Platonic definition in these dialogues anticipates Aristotelian definition by genus and species. This assumption is countered in Sayre (1969), Chap. 3. The hierarchy mentioned in the text has nothing to do with genera and species.

44. The translation "Gods and Giants" favored by some must be due to a prejudice that to be gigantic is to be ignoble. Both the "idealists" and "materialists" in this set-to are greater than life-size.

45. Cornford (1935), p. 243.

46. This characterization "marks off" reality in terms of a coextensive property. To attempt a definition (λόγος) of reality would be wholly misguided, since there is no more inclusive character which could be subdivided into reality and something else.

47. The reason this mark is not explicitly endorsed in the dialogue may be simply that the sense in which the Forms have δύναμιν has not yet been clarified by the time it is proposed.

48. Cornford (1935), p. 249.

49. Kirk and Raven (1962), fr. 347.8-9.

50. Ibid., fr. 352.1.

51. "Socratic irony" in the early and middle dialogues in large part consists in disingenuous self-effacement on the part of Socrates and in blandishment of his respondents. With the departure of Socrates as Plato's main protagonist, a new impersonal "irony of ideas" begins to appear. Three noteworthy examples (all directed against the historical Parmenides) are (1) the correlative extremes of inane Heracliteanism ("everything moves") and Eleaticism ("nothing moves") in the *Theaetetus*, (2) representing the historical Parmenides as unwitting protector of sophistry in the *Sophist*, and (3) turning Parmenides' methodological display in his namesake dialogue into a defense of Pythagoreanism (as shown in Chapter 1).

52. Keyt (1973), pp. 298, 302. The reader is referred to this source for

a survey of alternative interpretations. Although it is not within the scope of the present discussion to attempt evaluation of other interpretations of these difficult and much debated texts, acknowledgment is due an influential account in Lee (1972) developed almost simultaneously with Keyt's. Lee's account is based upon a particularly strong reading of 257C6-7, according to which the Stranger's remark that the nature of Difference (Lee translates 'Otherness') is "cut up" in the same way as knowledge means that the resulting parts of Difference are "directed to" specific Forms—just as parts of knowledge are "directed to" music, grammar, etc. I think it is fair to remark that the resulting intentional interpretation (which as Lee notes on p. 290 leads to an intensional as opposed to extensional construal of Otherness) is not required by the text, inasmuch as parts of knowledge could also be distinguished according to the nonintentional relationship merely of pertaining to music, grammar, etc. Nonetheless, 257C6-7 provides an occasion to impart an intentional interpretation if one so desires, and Lee's reading does not appear to do violence to the relevant texts. Put generally, Lee's understanding of a given part of Otherness, not-X, is that it is Otherness "directed to" X (p. 272); hence to say that a given entity is not X is to say that it "partakes in the specific negative intension, Otherness-than-the-predicate-negated" (p. 293). One possible objection to this account is that it makes Difference (or Otherness) to be a very "busy" Form indeed, inasmuch as each separate entity partakes of it in as many different respects as there are Forms other than those in which it partakes "directly." My main objection to Lee's approach to the passages in question, however, is that it does not lead naturally to the points I think important to make about the logical structure of not-being, which on the other hand emerge clearly and in intelligible sequence with the approach of the text below. This latter approach, I believe, removes the main motivation for adopting Lee's alternative, by showing (contrary to his claims on p. 290) that an intelligible interpretation of not-being can be based on the relationship of incompatibility and that this interpretation provides an account of negative predication. This approach also avoids a consequence of Lee's interpretation which he finds "particularly enigmatic," namely that (in his view) "this carefully constructed doctrine of the Parts of Otherness—its entire apparatus of determinations and antitheses—is left totally unused in Plato's subsequent account of falsity" (p. 299, n. 53).

53. This assumption is not automatic, inasmuch as the expression ἄπειρον πλῆθος is often used in the later dialogues to refer to the

indeterminate character of sensible things. Since it is certainly the case that each Form differs also from all sensible things, the possibility remains at this point that the indeterminate number (ἀπέραντα . . . ἀριθμὸν: 257A6) of other things a given Form is not includes sensible things as well as other Forms. The issue whether this is the case, however, turns out shortly to be immaterial, for a more limited and precise sense of "what is not" begins to emerge in the ensuing discussion. As Lee (1972), pp. 285-88, helps us see, the sense of "what is not" at 256E7 is not the Form Not-Being at 258D6—or the "really what is not" of 258E2-3.

54. The expression is due to Keyt (1973), p. 293.

55. Cornford (1935), p. 295, makes this clear.

56. Cornford draws attention to this passage in the *Statesman* in his attempt to clarify the sense of part in question (1935), p. 293, but focuses on the occurrence of μόριον at 262A9 instead of that of μέρος at 262B1. As a result he reaches the wrong conclusion that the not-Beautiful is not a Form itself. A comparable use of μέρος occurs at *Timaeus* 30C5, which Cornford translates 'species'—apparently in the sense of Form deemed unworthy to serve as model of the visible world (1937), p. 40.

57. In *On Interpretation* 17B3-22., Aristotle contrasts ἐναντίως and ἀντιφατικῶς as contrariety and contradiction. This must be the contrast Plato intended at 257B and 258B. The text below makes clear why I cannot agree with Owen (1971), p. 232, n. 19, that the relationship of incompatibility has no place in Plato's explanation of not-being and of falsehood.

58. Here is a further indication that in speaking of "parts" of the Difference, Plato intended specific Forms and not all "other" Forms indiscriminately. I assume (with Cornford [1935], Frede [1967], Matthews [1972], and others) that 258a11-b1 alludes to the fact that Existence can be parceled out in the same way as Difference (at 257C6-7), although as Owen (1971), p. 239, n. 33, and Lee (1972), p. 283, point out Plato has not explicitly introduced the notion of "a part of Existence."

59. Compare 260B7, where "not-Being" is referred to as "one kind among others" (ἕν τι τῶν ἄλλων γένος).

60. The translation differs slightly from that given in Sayre (1976). Since one problem facing any attempted interpretation of Plato's account of true and false judgment is to make sense of this passage as it stands, I have tried here to provide an entirely literal translation that presupposes no particular interpretation.

61. Keyt (1973) and Moravcsik (1960); see also Sayre (1969).
62. For previous attempts at interpretation on my part, see Sayre (1969, 1970, and 1976). The present interpretation appears preferable to these.
63. This factor seems first to have been emphasized in contemporary literature by Ackrill (1955).
64. Although I agree with Lee (1972), pp. 289-90, that Plato's account of not-Being should be construed so as to support an analysis of negative predication, I disagree with his assertion that all interpretations featuring "relations of incompatibility" (counting the present as one such) suffer the dual defect of lacking "adequate basis in the text" and of not allowing Plato to "account for negative predication statements."
65. This is an important departure from several major interpretations, including Cornford (1935) and Lorenz and Mittelstrass (1966). It is a departure also from my own previous attempts.
66. The conviction that the *Timaeus* embodies Plato's most mature thought continued through the middle ages; see Owen (1953), p. 313.
67. The orthodox view today is probably that represented by Cherniss, who reads the evidence as sufficiently definitive to warrant the conclusion that "the *Timaeus* and *Critias*, whether earlier or later than the *Sophist*, the *Politicus*, or the *Philebus*, . . . *must* have been written after the . . . *Parmenides*," Cherniss (1957), p. 364, my emphasis. For support of the opposing view, see: Owen (1953); Hamlyn (1955), p. 290, n. 3; Runciman (1962), p. 4; and Gosling (1975, p. 157), as well as a list of less recent commentators provided by Cherniss, p. 340, n. 2.
68. Cherniss's singularly lame answer is that Plato considered the objections he raised in the *Parmenides* to the earlier theory of Forms as "either irrelevant or invalid," on the grounds that Plato never refuted them, and that Plato's response to these objections was implied elsewhere in his writings and left for his readers "to discover . . . by themselves," Cherniss (1957), p. 364.
69. Among stylometric evidence bearing explicitly on the chronological ordering of the *Timaeus* and the *Parmenides*, for example, are data concerning the relative frequency of what has been called (e.g., Cornford [1937], p. 12, n. 3) "illegitimate hiatus"—avoidable juxtaposition of vowel sounds that cannot be smoothly articulated together. Although what counts as an instance of avoidable hiatus in many cases is a matter of judgment admitting disagreement among

experts (depending among other things upon the "ear" of the judge), commonly accepted statistics show an average of 40 to 45 instances per page for the *Phaedo*, the *Republic*, and the *Parmenides*, with only about one per page for the *Sophist*, the *Statesman*, and the *Timaeus*, increasing to an average of 4 or 5 in the *Philebus* and the *Laws* (see Cornford [1937] p. 12, n. 3, and Cherniss [1957], pp. 344f.). For one accepting incidence of avoidable hiatus as a definitive criterion of chronological order, as Cherniss does, there is room for debate about the placement of the *Timaeus* relative to the *Sophist*, the *Statesman*, the *Philebus*, and the *Laws*, but none regarding its position in relation to *Parmenides*. Relying upon this criterion, however, involves several assumptions which seem to me dubious. One is that matters of style, such as optional hiatus or end-rhythms (cf. Owen [1953], p. 315), are not freely variable at the author's discretion—i.e., that Plato might not simply have chosen to use different styles in different dialogues for reasons having nothing to do with chronology. Another is that the dialogues were written in discrete temporal sequence, with one finished before another was begun—e.g., that the *Parmenides* might not have been under composition during a period in which parts of the *Republic*, the *Sophist*, and the *Timaeus* also were being worked on. An even more dubious assumption is that the relationship between chronological order and philosophic content the former should be treated exclusively as an independent variable. A firm perception of relevant differences in content within a set of dialogues, to the contrary, can contribute as much to our understanding of their chronological order as vice versa. Other stylometric measures of chronology are discussed in Appendix B.

70. I believe the *Timaeus* antedates the *Parmenides*. A critical assessment of the stylometric evidence to the contrary effect, I believe, will show that the contrary case is not nearly as strong as its supporters urge. At best, the evidence lends weight to the suggestion that *Parmenides I* was written before the *Timaeus*. The doctrinal developments discussed in the present work, on the other hand, suggest strongly that *Parmenides II* was written later. This does not lead automatically to the conclusion that *Parmenides I* and *II* were written at different stages in Plato's career; but the possibility that this is so should not be automatically excluded. Appendix B contains a detailed discussion of stylometric data relevant to this possibility.

71. According to Liddell and Scott (1883), the term μῦθος after Pindar

"assumes the same sense as the Latin *fabula*, and always connotes *fiction*," in contrast with λόγος as "*historic tale*" (compilers' emphases). Later editions drop the comparison with *fabula*, but retain the sense of fiction in opposition to λόγος. Liddell, Scott, and Jones (1968), for example, point out several occurrences in Plato where the term carries this sense, including one (*Republic* 377A5) where the literal falsehood of the fiction is stressed. Both the 1883 and the 1968 editions cite εἰκότα μῦθον at *Timaeus* 29D1 as meaning "likely story," but with no support for the notion that 'likely' here means "likely to be *true*." The sense rather must be close to "plausible narrative."

72. Cornford's caution against attempting to find literal meaning in the *Timaeus*, by somehow "stripping off" its figurative language, is well taken (see Cornford [1937], pp. 31f.). See also Vlastos (1973), pp. 400-401. There appears little merit in the proposal of Skemp (1967), p. 67, based on five alleged occurrences of the expression εἰκώς λόγος, that Plato distinguishes between a true and a false "science" of becoming.

73. Given the proportional equivalence of (images (A)/sensible things (B)) to (mathematical objects (C)/Forms (D)), and to (visible (A + B)/intelligible (C + D)) generally, which implies the equivalence of (B) and (C), the question naturally arises how sensible things and mathematical objects are supposed to be related.

74. Cornford (1937), p. 30, points out the appearance of the key term εἰκώς in both Parmenides (fr. 8, line 60) and in Xenophanes (fr. 35). Plato had precedence for its employment in the *Timaeus*.

75. According to Aetius, as reproduced in Kirk and Raven (1962), p. 284.

76. It is unclear what to make of Cornford's remark that Plato, in the *Timaeus*, "introduced, for the first time in Greek philosophy, the ... scheme of creation by a divine artificer, according to ... a purpose" (1937), p. 31.

77. Possibly relevant also is Aetius, *ibid.*, with the suggestion that justice and necessity are "keys" to creation of which the goddess has charge.

78. This occurrence of ἐκμαγεῖον invites speculation about Aristotle's meaning when he speaks of Plato's alleged belief that the numbers could be produced out of the Indefinite Dyad as "from some waxlike material" (ἔκ τινος ἐκμαγείου: *Metaphysics* 988a1). Despite the temptation of some commentators to identify the Indefinite Dyad with the receptacle of the *Timaeus*, however, there is no sense in

which the latter could assume the remarkable capacities assigned to the former in Aristotle's account.

79. The receptacle presumably cannot be space in the ordinary sense, because space is ordinarily thought to provide for relationships among sensible things. The receptacle is supposed to provide a relationship between Forms and sensible things, which is quite a different matter.

80. One can understand Aristotle's assumption, hasty as it was, that the receptacle of the *Timaeus* was Plato's attempt to provide a principle answering to his prime matter (cf. *Physics* 209b11).

81. The translation of this difficult passage is quoted directly from Cornford (1937), pp. 192-93 (translator's emphasis); the Greek text therefore is not included. Cornford recognized a description of mirror images in this passage.

82. Compare *Republic* 596D9-E3. An added advantage of this image of visual reflection is that it ties in with the closely preceding discussion of reflections from an optical point of view (46A-C). Yet another is that it opens up intriguing possibilities of expanding the images of the Divided Line and the Cave in their ontological dimensions. The ratio of the lower to the adjacent section of the Line may represent not only differences in mental states and in degrees of being, but also a basic similarity in the relationships between reflections and sensible objects on one level and sensible objects and Forms on another.

83. Rivaud's translation.

84. The problem basically is how to account for change at all. One aspect of the problem, of which Aristotle was aware in *On Generation and Corruption* 335b18-21, is how the causal agency of Forms could be intermittent, producing a given character on one occasion and not on another. See also *Metaphysics* 991a8-11 and 1079b12-15. As Skemp (1967), p. xiv, has remarked laconically, the question how offprints of the Forms enter and pass out from the realm of becoming is left vague by Plato.

85. See, for a case in point, Cornford (1937), pp. 196-97.

86. A clear indication that Plato did not consider the reference to a Demiurge to solve this problem is that the (or a) Demiurge is also present in the *Philebus* (27B1), where an entirely new account of the relationship between Forms and sensible things is offered. If the Demiurge solved the problem, an account departing from that of the *Timaeus* in respects other than the presence of the Demiurge would not have been needed.

87. For a graphic illustration, see Cornford (1937), p. 201.

APPENDIX B

1. Guthrie (1978), p. 243. Cherniss (1957), p. 341, agrees.
2. Before Lutoslawski (1905) a substantial number of scholars concerned with such matters located the *Timaeus* before the *Parmenides* and the rest of the so-called "critical group;" see Cherniss (1957), p. 340, n. 2.
3. Notably Raeder, Ritter, and Friedländer; see Cherniss (1957), pp. 341-42 for citations.
4. Owen (1953), p. 338.
5. The pioneering work of Campbell appeared in 1867.
6. By sympathetic (as emphasized by Cherniss [1957], p. 341) as well as unsympathetic critics (see Owen [1953], p. 314, for instances).
7. Two measures that figured prominently in the set-to between Owen and Cherniss are incidence of hiatus and end-rhythms of prose sentences. The former appears as one of the five hundred measures treated by Lutoslawski. Regarding the latter, as Cherniss (1957), p. 342, points out, it must be admitted that available data in this category do not support a later composition data for the *Parmenides*. But no single measure taken individually can settle the matter one way or the other, as Lutoslawski makes clear (p. 184). The force of Lutoslawski's case comes from many measures considered jointly.
8. This question-begging assumption, which was particularly prejudicial against the case for the relative lateness of the *Parmenides*, has been criticized by Owen (1953), p. 314.
9. One result of this stricture, as Owen noted (1953), p. 314, is that "of largely invalidating his own and most earlier and later attempts to order the dialogues by relative affinity of style." In particular, it precludes use of his method to arrive at a reliable chronological ordering between the *Parmenides* (31 pages Didot) and the *Timaeus* (53 pages).
10. In his methodological discussion, Lutoslawski stressed "the insignificance of a single test applied to" complicated problems of dating (p. 184). Presumably he would have had little patience with more recent attempts based on single measures such as incidence of hiatus or end-rhythms of sentences.
11. The fact that Lutoslawski ranked the *Republic* in the middle group and the *Philebus* in the latest, despite their almost identical affinity ratings, calls for explanation.

12. Put simply, the effect was to allow the *Timaeus* (and the other five late dialogues) 50% more opportunities to accumulate points toward its affinity rating than the *Parmenides*. A simple remedy might have been to increase the accumulated total of 243 for the *Parmenides* by 50% to 364, which would yield a relative affinity of 51%—close to the 56% of the *Philebus*. The expedient adopted below instead is to eliminate measures 29 through 181 from consideration.

13. The few cases in which segregation on this basis appeared prohibitively time-consuming (measures 189, 225, and 231) make no appreciable difference in the final results.

14. The following lists specify the peculiarities falling under each of the four classes for *Parmenides I*. Under classes A and B, the number in parentheses indicates the number of occurrences of the associated peculiarity.

A		B	C	D
28(1)	425(1)	24(2)	25	453
203(1)	429(1)	26(1)	239	total 1
331(1)	436(1)	461(1)	317	
332(1)	445(2)	463(1)	453	
340(1)	459(1)	465(1)	479	
349(1)	471(1)	466(1)	480	
352(1)	481(1)	468(2)	total 6	
353(1)	485(1)	total (9)		
371(1)	487(1)			
387(1)	491(1)			
423(2)	496(1)			
	498(1)			
	total (25)			

316

15. The following lists present detailed data for *Parmenides II* (see note 14 for conventions).

A		B	C	D
193(1)	398(1)	26(2)	25	27
198(3)	436(3)	322(1)	202	378
204(2)	445(1)	462(1)	203	448
207(4)	460(2)	463(1)	205	453
213(3)	470(1)	464(2)	206	455
216(1)	474(1)	465(1)	239	458
220(1)	475(2)	467(2)	318	471
221(1)	476(1)	469(2)	326	total 7
224(1)	477(2)	total (12)	332	
228(1)	478(1)		342	
232(1)	481(1)		343	
323(1)	482(1)		349	
338(1)	483(1)		361	
339(1)	484(1)		376	
244(3)	486(1)		385	
352(1)	488(1)		386	
353(2)	489(2)		387	
358(2)	490(1)		452	
370(3)	492(1)		472	
374(1)	493(3)		473	
388(1)	495(3)		494	
392(2)	497(2)		total 21	
394(3)	498(2)			
397(1)	499(4)			
	500(2)			
	total (82)			

16. The following lists present detailed data for the *Timaeus* (see notes 14 and 15 for conventions).

	A		B	C	D
22(2)					
184(1)	329(1)	402(2)	24(7)	199	21
187(1)	334(4)	408(1)	27(3)	203	200
190(2)	335(1)	409(4)	28(1)	228	307
197(2)	336(1)	416(1)	182(3)	231	366
198(5)	344(2)	419(6)	201(1)	232	total 4
205(1)	345(4)	423(2)	208(1)	233	
210(3)	349(1)	426(4)	209(1)	241	
211(1)	351(5)	427(1)	237(2)	309	
213(1)	355(7)	436(3)	268(1)	317	
214(1)	356(3)	439(1)	278(1)	318	
217(1)	358(2)	444(2)	312(2)	341	
219(1)	364(2)	447(3)	313(1)	346	
220(1)	368(4)	455(1)	315(1)	350	
222(2)	369(2)	462(2)	316(3)	367	
226(1)	370(2)	463(1)	319(1)	371	
227(9)	373(3)	464(1)	321(2)	383	
229(3)	374(6)	472(1)	360(2)	390	
230(1)	380(2)	474(1)	379(1)	391	
234(1)	381(1)	475(1)	399(2)	436	
236(3)	382(4)	478(2)	431(3)	469	
238(2)	392(1)	484(1)	432(3)	479	
239(1)	393(1)	490(1)	433(1)	total 22	
310(1)	394(5)	495(2)	434(1)		
323(1)	395(4)	497(1)	460(2)		
324(3)	396(1)	498(4)	461(1)		
	400(2)	499(1)	total (47)		
		500(5)			
	total (177)				

BIBLIOGRAPHY OF WORKS CITED

Ackrill, J. L. (1952). Review of Wilpert's *Zwei aristotellische Früh-schriften, Mind*, Vol. 61, pp. 102-13.

Ackrill, J. L. (1955). "ΣΥΜΠΛΟΚΗ ΕΙΔΩΝ." Reprinted in Allen (1965).

Allan, D. J. (1960). "Aristotle and the *Parmenides*." In *Aristotle and Plato in the Mid-Fourth Century*, I. Düring and G.E.L. Owen, eds., Almquist, Gothenburg.

Allen, R. E. (1960). "Participation and Predication in Plato's Middle Dialogues." Reprinted in Allen (1965).

Allen, R. E. (1970). "The Generation of Numbers in Plato's *Parmenides*." *Classical Philology*, Vol. 65, no. 1, pp. 30-34.

Allen, R. E. (1974). "Unity and Infinity: *Parmenides* 142b-145a." *Review of Metaphysics*, Vol. 27, no. 4, pp. 697-725.

Allen, R. E., ed. (1965). *Studies in Plato's Metaphysics*. Routledge & Kegan Paul, London.

Annas, Julia (1975). "On the Intermediates." *Archiv für Geschichte der Philosophie*, Band 57, Heft 2, pp. 146-66.

Annas, Julia (1976). *Aristotle's Metaphysics, Books M and N*. Clarendon Press, Oxford.

Bluck, R. S. (1955). *Plato's Phaedo*. Routledge & Kegan Paul, London.

Bluck, R. S. (1956). "Logos and Forms in Plato: A Reply to Professor Cross." Reprinted in Allen (1965).

Brown, Malcolm (1972). "The Idea of Equality in the *Phaedo*." *Archiv für Geschichte der Philosophie*, Band 54, Heft 1, pp. 24-36.

Brumbaugh, R. S. (1961). *Plato on the One*. Yale University Press, New Haven.

Burnet, J. (1914). *Greek Philosophy*. Macmillan & Co., London.

Bury, R. G. (1897). *The Philebus of Plato*. University Press, Cambridge.

Campbell, L. (1867). *The Sophistes and Politicus of Plato*. Clarendon Press, Oxford.

Cherniss, H. F. (1936). "The Philosophical Economy of the Theory of Ideas." Reprinted in Allen (1965).

Cherniss, H. F. (1944). *Aristotle's Criticism of Plato and the Academy*. Johns Hopkins Press, Baltimore.

Cherniss, H. F. (1945). *The Riddle of the Early Academy*, University of California Press, Berkeley.

Cherniss, H. F. (1950). Review of Raven (1948), *Philosophical Review*, Vol. 49, no. 3, pp. 375-77.

Cherniss, H. F. (1957). "The Relation of the *Timaeus* to Plato's Later Dialogues." Reprinted in Allen (1965).

Cornford, F. M. (1935). *Plato's Theory of Knowledge*. Routledge & Kegan Paul, London.

Cornford, F. M. (1937). *Plato's Cosmology*. Routledge & Kegan Paul, London.

Cornford, F. M. (1939). *Plato and Parmenides*. Routledge & Kegan Paul, London.

Crombie, I. M. (1963). *An Examination of Plato's Doctrines*. Vol. 2, Humanities Press, New York.

Dedekind, R. (1901). *Essays on the Theory of Numbers*. Trans. W. W. Beman. Open Court Publishing Co., Chicago.

Findlay, J. N. (1974). *Plato: The Written and Unwritten Doctrines*. Humanities Press, New York.

Frank, E. (1923). *Plato und die sogenannten Pythagoreer*. Halle an der Saale.

Frede, M. (1967). *Prädikation und Existenzaussage, Hypomnemata*. Vol. 18, Vandenhoeck & Ruprecht, Göttingen.

Gaiser, K. (1980). "Plato's Enigmatic Lecture 'On the Good'." *Phronesis*, Vol. 25, no. 1, pp. 5-37.

Geach, P. T. (1956). "The Third Man Again." Reprinted in Allen (1965).

Gillispie, C., ed. (1971). *Dictionary of Scientific Biography*. Charles Scribner's Sons, New York.

Gosling, J.C.B. (1975). *Plato: Philebus*. Clarendon Press, Oxford.

Gulley, N. (1962). *Plato's Theory of Knowledge*. Methuen & Co., London.

Guthrie, W.K.C. (1978). *A History of Greek Philosophy*. Vol. 5, University Press, Cambridge.

Hackforth, R. (1955). *Plato's Phaedo*. University Press, Cambridge.

Hamlyn, D. W. (1955). "The Communion of Forms and the Development of Plato's Logic." *Philosophical Quarterly*, Vol. 5, no. 21, pp. 289-302.

Heath, Thomas (1921). *A History of Greek Mathematics*. Clarendon Press, Oxford.

Heath, Thomas, trans. (1947). *Euclid: The Elements*. 3 vols., St. John's College Press, Annapolis.

Heiberg, J. (1922). *Mathematics and Physical Science in Classical Antiquity*. Trans. D. Macgregor. Oxford University Press, London.

Jackson, Henry (1882). "Plato's Later Theory of Ideas." *Journal of Philosophy*, Vol. 10, pp. 251-98.

Kahn, C. H. (1973). *The Verb 'Be' in Ancient Greek*. D. Reidel Publishing Co., Boston.

Kahn, C. H. (1974). "Pythagorean Philosophy before Plato." In Mourelatos, ed. (1974), pp. 161-85.

Kerferd, G. B. (1981). *The Sophistic Movement*. Cambridge University Press, Cambridge.

Keyt, David (1973). "Plato on Falsity: *Sophist* 263B." In Lee, Mourelatos, and Rorty (1973).

Kirk, G. S.; and Raven, J. E., eds. (1962), *The Presocratic Philosophers*. University Press, Cambridge.

Kline, M. (1972). *Mathematical Thought from Ancient to Modern Times*. Oxford University Press, New York.

Knorr, W. R. (1975). *The Evolution of the Euclidean Elements*. D. Reidel Publishing Co., Dordrecht.

Lee, E. N. (1972). "Plato on Negation and Not-Being in the *Sophist*." *Philosophical Review*, Vol. 81, no. 3, pp. 267-304.

Lee, E. N.; Mourelatos, A.P.D.; and Rorty, R. M., eds. (1973). *Exegesis and Argument*. Humanities Press, New York.

Liddel, H. G.; and Scott, R. (1883). *A Greek-English Lexicon*. 2nd ed., Harper & Brothers, New York.

Liddell, H. G.; Scott, R.; and Jones, H. S. (1968). *A Greek-English Lexicon*. Oxford, at the Clarendon Press.

Lorentz, K.; and Mittelstrass, J. (1966), "Theaitetos fliegt. Zur Theorie wahrer und falscher Sätze bei Platon (*Soph.* 251d-263d)," *Archiv für Geschichte der Philosophie*, Band 48, Heft 2, pp. 111-52.

Lutoslawski, W. (1905). *The Origin and Growth of Plato's Logic*. Longmans, Green, and Co., London.

Matthews, G. (1972). *Plato's Epistemology and Related Logical Problems*. Faber & Faber, London.

McCulloch, W. (1974). "Recollections of the Many Sources of Cybernetics." *Forum*, Vol. 6, no. 2, pp. 5-16.

McDowell, J. (1973). *Plato: Theaetetus*. Clarendon Press, Oxford.

Meyerhoff, H. (1958). "Socrates' 'Dream' in the *Theaetetus*." *Classical Quarterly*, N.S. 8, no. 3, pp. 131-38.

Milhaud, G. (1934). *Les Philosophes Géomètres de la Grèce*. Librairie Philosophique J. Vrin, Paris.

Moravcsik, J.M.E. (1960). "ΣΥΜΠΛΟΚΗ ΕΙΔΩΝ and the Genesis of ΛΟΓΟΣ," *Archiv für Geschichte der Philosophie*, Band 42, Heft 2, pp. 117-29.

Mourelatos, A.P.D., ed. (1974). *The Pre-Socratics.* Anchor Books, Garden City.

Nikolíc, M. (1974). "Eudoxus and Dedekind." In *Boston Studies in the Philosophy of Science,* Vol. 15, R. Cohen, J. Stachel, and M. Wartofsky, eds. D. Reidel Publishing Co., Dordrecht.

Owen, G.E.L. (1953). "The Place of the *Timaeus* in Plato's Dialogues." Reprinted in Allen (1965).

Owen, G.E.L. (1971). "Plato on Not-Being." In *Plato,* Vol. 1, G. Vlastos, ed. Anchor Books, Garden City.

Raven, J. E. (1948). *Pythagoreans and Eleatics: An Account of the Interaction between the Two Opposed Schools during the Fifth and Early Fourth Centuries B.C.* Cambridge University Press, Cambridge.

Robin, L. (1908). *La théorie platonicienne des idées et des nombres d'après Aristote.* Presses Universitaires de France, Paris.

Robinson, R. (1942). "Plato's *Parmenides.*" *Classical Philology,* Vol. 37, pp. 51-76, 159-86.

Robinson, R. (1953). *Plato's Earlier Dialectic.* Clarendon Press, Oxford.

Rohr, M. D. (1978). "Empty Forms in Plato." *Archiv für Geschichte der Philosophie,* Band 60, Heft 3, pp. 268-83.

Ross, W. D., ed. (1924). *Aristotle's Metaphysics.* Vols. 1 and 2, Clarendon Press, Oxford.

Ross, W. D. (1951). *Plato's Theory of Ideas.* Clarendon Press, Oxford.

Ross, W. D.; and Fobes, F. H., trans. (1967). *Theophrastus Metaphysics.* Georg Olms Verlagsbuchhandlung, Hildesheim.

Runciman, W. G. (1962). *Plato's Later Epistemology.* University Press, Cambridge.

Ryle, G. (1939). "Plato's *Parmenides.*" Reprinted in Allen (1965).

Sayre, K. M. (1963). "Propositional Logic in Plato's *Protagoras.*" *Notre Dame Journal of Formal Logic,* Vol. 4, no. 4, pp. 306-12.

Sayre, K. M. (1969). *Plato's Analytic Method.* University of Chicago Press, Chicago.

Sayre, K. M. (1970). "Falsehood, Forms and Participation in the *Sophist.*" *Nous,* Vol. 4, no. 1, pp. 81-91.

Sayre, K. M. (1976). "*Sophist* 263B Revisited." *Mind,* Vol. 85, no. 340, pp. 581-86.

Sayre, K. M. (1978). "Plato's *Parmenides*: Why the Eight Hypotheses are not Contradictory." *Phronesis,* Vol. 23, no. 2, pp. 133-50.

Shiner, R. A. (1974). *Knowledge and Reality in Plato's Philebus.* Van Gorcum & Co. B. V., Assen–The Netherlands.

Shorey, P. (1927). "Ideas and Numbers Again." *Classical Philology*, Vol. 22, pp. 213-18.

Skemp, J. B. (1967). *The Theory of Motion in Plato's Later Dialogues*. Adolf M. Hakkert, Amsterdam.

Stenzel, J. (1959). *Zahl und Gestalt bei Platon und Aristoteles*. Hermann Gentner Verlag, Bad Homburg vor der Höhe.

Striker, G. (1970). *Peras und Apeiron: Das Problem der Formen in Platons Philebos*. Vandenhoeck & Ruprecht, Göttingen.

Struik, D. (1967). *A Concise History of Mathematics*. 3rd ed. Dover Publications, New York.

Taylor, A. E. (1926). *Plato: The Man and His Work*. Methuen & Co., London.

Taylor, A. E. (1926). "Forms and Numbers: A Study in Platonic Metaphysics." 1st part, *Mind*, Vol. 35, no. 140, pp. 419-40.

Taylor, A. E. (1927). "Forms and Numbers: A Study in Platonic Metaphysics," 2nd part, *Mind*, Vol. 36, no. 141, pp. 12-33.

Taylor, A. E. (1956). *Plato: Philebus and Epinomis*. R. Klinbansky, G. Calogero, and A. C. Lloyd, eds. Thomas Nelson and Sons, London.

Thomas, I., trans. (1951). *Greek Mathematics*. Vol. 1, Harvard University Press, Cambridge, Mass.

Thompson, D'Arcy W. (1929). "Excess and Defect: Or the Little More and the Little Less." *Mind*, Vol. 38, no. 149, pp. 43-55.

Turnbull, R. G. (1978). "Knowledge and the Forms in the Later Platonic Dialogues." *Proceedings and Addresses of the American Philosophical Association*, Vol. 51, no. 6, pp. 735-58.

Vlastos, G. (1953). "J. E. Raven: Pythagoreans and Eleatics." *Gnomon*, Vol. 25, pp. 29-35.

Vlastos, G. (1954). "The Third Man Argument in the *Parmenides*." Reprinted in Allen (1965).

Vlastos, G. (1963). "On Plato's Oral Doctrine." *Gnomon*, Vol. 41, pp. 641-55.

Vlastos, G. (1969). "Reasons and Causes in the *Phaedo*." *Philosophical Review*, Vol. 78, no. 3, pp. 291-325.

Vlastos, G. (1973). *Platonic Studies*. Princeton University Press, Princeton.

Wedberg, A. (1955). *Plato's Philosophy of Mathematics*. Almquist & Wiksell, Stockholm.

White, N. (1976). *Plato on Knowledge and Reality*. Hackett Publishing Co., Indianapolis.

INDEX OF NAMES AND TOPICS

325

Library of Congress Cataloging in Publication Data

Sayre, Kenneth M., 1928-
Plato's late ontology.
Bibliography: p.   Includes index.
1. Plato—Ontology. 2. Ontology—History. I. Title.
B398.O5S29   1983   111'.092'4   82-61382

ISBN 0-691-07277-9

Kenneth M. Sayre is Professor of Philosophy at
Notre Dame University. He is the author of numerous books on philosophy,
including *Plato's Analytic Method* (Chicago)
and *Cybernetics and the Philosophy of Mind* (Humanities Press).